The Language of Cottonwoods

Essays on the Future of North Dakota

By Clay Jenkinson

Cover painting used with permission by Katrina Case.
Maps and illustrations by Joanna Walitalo.
Photographs by Clay Jenkinson.
Cover design by Skyler Kratofil.

Published by

◄ köehlerbooks ™

3705 Shore Drive
Virginia Beach, VA 23455
800–435–4811
www.koehlerbooks.com

THE LANGUAGE OF COTTONWOODS

ESSAYS ON THE FUTURE OF
North Dakota

CLAY JENKINSON

VIRGINIA BEACH
CAPE CHARLES

Also by Clay Jenkinson

Message on the Wind: A Spiritual Odyssey on the Northern Plains

A Vast and Open Plain: The Writings of the Lewis and Clark Expedition in North Dakota

The Character of Meriwether Lewis: Explorer in the Wilderness

A Free and Hardy Life: Theodore Roosevelt's Sojourn in the American West

For the Love of North Dakota: Sundays with Clay in the Bismarck Tribune

Repairing Jefferson's America: A Guide to Civility and Enlightened Citizenship

Theodore Roosevelt: Naturalist in the Arena (with Char Miller)

Donald Trump and the Death of American Integrity: An Autopsy and a Path Forward

Bring Out Your Dead: The Literature and History of Epidemics

North Dakota

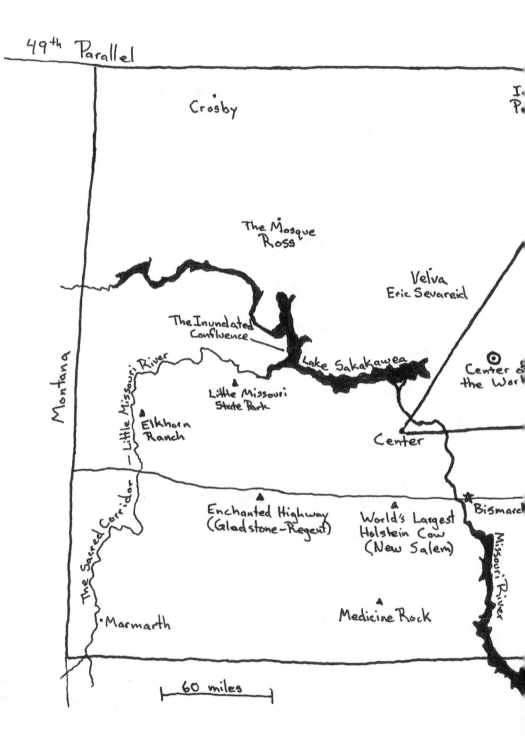

49th Parallel

Crosby

I.
P.

The Mosque
Ross

Velva
Eric Sevareid

The Inundated
Confluence

Lake Sakakawea

Center of
the Wor

Montana

Little Missouri River

Little Missouri
State Park

Elkhorn
Ranch

Center

The Sacred Corridor

Enchanted Highway
(Gladstone-Regent)

World's Largest
Holstein Cow
(New Salem)

Bismar

Missouri River

Marmarth

Medicine Rock

60 miles

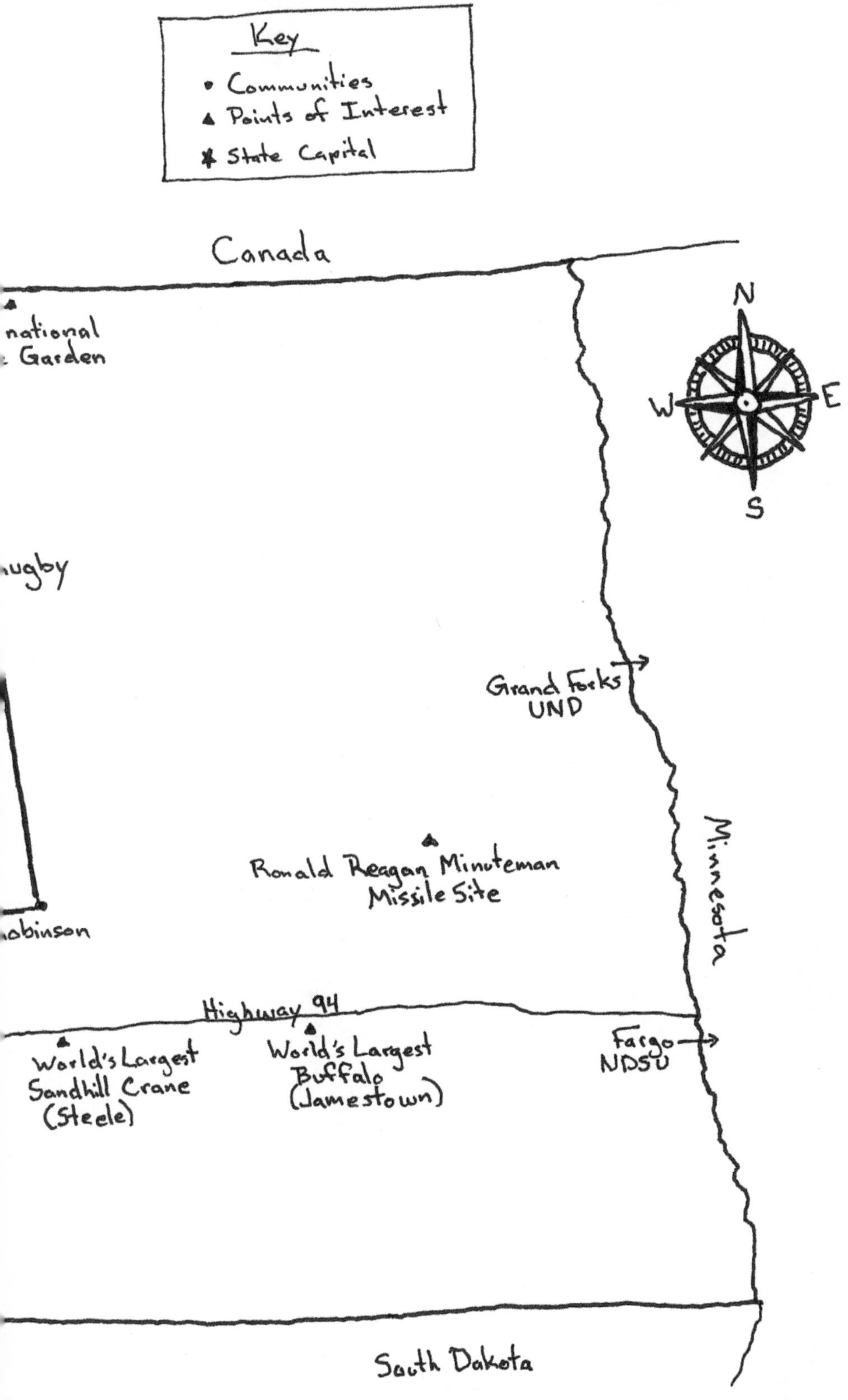

Key

- Communities
▲ Points of Interest
✳ State Capital

Canada

...national
...e Garden

...ugby

N
W   E
S

Grand Forks
UND

▲
Ronald Reagan Minuteman
Missile Site

Minnesota

...obinson

Highway 94

Fargo
NDSU

▲
World's Largest
Sandhill Crane
(Steele)

▲
World's Largest
Buffalo
(Jamestown)

South Dakota

For Catherine Missouri Walker Jenkinson
Who Lived It

TABLE OF CONTENTS

FOREWORD

Clay Jenkinson is a public intellectual. He thinks deeply about issues and shares his conclusions widely. In this book he turns his attention—not for the first time— to North Dakota, the state that nurtured him and to which he returned after study at distinguished universities, including Oxford, and teaching, writing and creative work in other places. The enormous emptiness of North Dakota drew him home, and he began to explore anew the state's grasp on its people, all of its people—lovers of its wilderness, tillers of its soil, drillers for its oil, newcomers, descendants of homesteaders, indigenous people. He turned, too, to the eccentricities of its politics. Nor did he overlook the extremes of the state's climate, the panorama of its landscape, the voice of its cottonwood trees—the species that surely should be the state's arboreal emblem, but which North Dakotans overlooked in favor of a more stately, less rangy, and less well-adapted species, the American elm. The choice is in some ways typical of North

Dakotans. We have never quite gotten things right, although we've been fighting about them for a long time.

The truth about North Dakota is that it attracts attention from outside its borders only in extreme times, like during the extraordinary uprising that produced the Nonpartisan League, the closest any state has ever come to a government of democratic socialists. Democratic Socialists created the nation's only state-owned bank, an institution to which the state's current residents (and especially its politicians) pay daily homage, since it has helped balance the state's budgets, educate its children, expand its farms, build its small towns and mine its resources—in other words, to make the state economically successful, even in the wake of the wreckage of the Great Depression, which struck North Dakota more brutally than almost any other state, causing a dramatic decline in population that took seven decades to overcome. Today, North Dakota gets attention for the stupendous richness of its oil fields and for the rightward lurch of its politics. Less than a decade ago, all members of North Dakota's congressional delegation were Democrats, all three of them. Today not a single Democrat occupies any statewide or federal office. Not one. And the party has been reduced to a remnant in the state legislature. Only one other state gave Donald Trump a larger victory margin than North Dakota.

Jenkinson seeks the soul of his homeland in this book.

It has been a lifelong search for him, and I am extremely proud to have helped set him on this journey. I met young Jenkinson when he was a student at Dickinson High School in one of North Dakota's few real cities, population 7,000, sometimes more, sometimes less, depending on the price of oil mostly, because even then the wide-open, sunbaked and windswept southwestern corner of the state relied on oil for whatever comforts could be created. It was a modest boom and an uncertain one, but it brought open-minded and eager people to the town, including a newspaper editor who'd worked overseas, editing *Stars and Stripes,* and an oil promoter who settled down as circulation director of *The Dickinson Press.* And it brought me, a freshly minted cub reporter. Jenkinson latched on to the *Press*. He was a junior in high school who owned a camera. He got the photographer job at the *Press*, he teases me, because I couldn't take pictures.

Those were great days in a great country. Southwestern North Dakota was under-covered. Reporters from bigger papers showed up once in a while, from Bismarck or far-off Fargo, less often from Billings, Montana, or Minneapolis, Minnesota. Once a reporter from New York City passed through. Unbelievable. Otherwise, we had the territory to ourselves, and we set out to discover all that it had in it, the raw and the cooked.

Jenkinson renewed his search when he returned to the state, and he brought an assortment of entrepreneurial ideas. In effect, he monetized his breadth of knowledge in the humanities, creating *The Thomas Jefferson Hour*, in which he portrayed The Founder addressing fundamental issues of his time and our own. To this he added a kind of travel agency which organized trips to explore all sorts of places: Paris, Rome, Greece, the Panama Canal, California's Central Valley. He became an important scholar of the Lewis and Clark Expedition of Discovery, of Robert Oppenheimer, of John Steinbeck (the California connection). He established the Theodore Roosevelt Center at Dickinson State University in his hometown.

This is his thirteenth book.

Dig in. Enjoy.

It is an important book about an important place, a deep look into the workings of one of the fifty states, at once a look of concern, bewilderment and wonder, a loving look and a critical one that illuminates the quirkiness of the pride that North Dakotans have in the place and in themselves. For an example, read about the competition for bragging rights as the Geographical Center of North America.

Mike Jacobs
Gilby, North Dakota

PREFACE

I f you are not a North Dakotan, please read this book anyway. It is about a very interesting place, and it could just as well have been written about almost anywhere on the Great Plains. At the very least, it has ramifications for the entire region and, to a certain extent, for all of rural America. There are more uncool places in America than cool. Even states like California and Colorado have their "North Dakotas"—think of Fresno and Visalia (California), and of Limon and Lamar (Colorado).

If you *are* a North Dakotan, please read this book through because it is important that we have conversations about our beloved state: its history, its landscape, its identity, its habits of the heart, its future, its spirit of place, its relations with the Native Americans who constitute 6 percent of the population, the fastest growing population in North Dakota. Please don't be offended by the ironies in several of the essays. We have to have a sense of humor about ourselves to live in such an improbable place.

I love North Dakota with all my heart.

There is no posturing in this book of essays. I have written what I think and feel and see. At this writing, I'm sixty-five years old. I have nothing to lose by telling the truth (the whole truth) as I see it. I don't pretend I have greater access to the soul of North Dakota than others. But if my fellow North Dakotans don't recognize themselves in these essays, I will have failed utterly. Nor do I wish to duck issues that are hard for us to talk about. We've had an endless number of feel-good calendars and websites and marketing campaigns that try to present North Dakota as something that it is not or is only very occasionally. I love North Dakota warts (blizzards, windstorms, droughts) and all, and I don't think we can forge a future for this isolated improbable place if we try to convince others and ourselves that this is a kind of rural paradise where meadowlarks sing on every round bale of hay.

Although I have lived elsewhere, I have spent well more than half of my life in North Dakota. When I have lived elsewhere, when people have asked me who I am, I invariably say, "I'm a North Dakotan." This gets everyone's attention. Most people express a little surprise, as if I were saying I am from the Yukon or Outer Mongolia. Aside from being the father of a young woman I love beyond count, my principal allegiance is to North Dakota. There are many places that matter to me greatly that are scattered across America and the globe. But only one speaks to my heart and makes me feel at home. Bury my heart a few miles north of Marmarth, overlooking the sacred Little Missouri River, just below Pretty Butte, and across from the ranch of Linda and Merle Clark.

North Dakota is not an easy place to live. Notice how many older people of means scurry away to Scottsdale, Arizona, or Hemet, California, or Naples, Florida, immediately after Halloween (they stay for the grandchildren) and return only at about Easter. But nobody from Hemet or Palm Springs leaves those places in January to spend a few months in North Dakota.

While I love North Dakota and sing its praises wherever I go, in and out of the state, I find a good deal about my homeland frustrating (I'm sure it's mutual). If you don't feel that love on every page of this book, either you are not reading carefully, or I am a bad writer. Or both.

The working title of this book was *So Who Are We Now?* I knew that would not be the final title, but it encapsulates the purposes of the book. We know who we were—an isolated family farm state that was not glamorous in any way, but we knew our work and our place, and we helped to feed the world. That paradigm has been fraying for the past thirty years as family farms yielded to a kind of unsentimental agribusiness model of food production, as our small towns shrank to the minimal viable cluster of basic services, and as North Dakota became so thoroughly wired to the rest of the world that our distinctive agrarian culture began to blend into the dominant consumer blandness of American life. This book raises the following questions from several different perspectives:

- So who are we now?
- Can we sustain and conserve the extraordinary character of North Dakota (modesty, neighborliness, practical skillfulness, gumption, good sense, integrity, stoicism, resourcefulness) when the agrarian lifeway that nurtured those values has largely disappeared?
- What is our relationship to the land, the rolling hills, the prairie potholes, the bluffs, buttes, and badlands, the swell of the vast and open plains, the endlessness of this lightly populated homeland?
- As we find new ways to extract profit from this place, what landscapes, if any, do we wish to preserve, to protect from economic or industrial development?
- What will the post-agrarian, and (soon enough) post-carbon future of North Dakota look like?

- Who wants to live here and to what purpose?
- What is our post-agrarian identity in a place that is not quite Midwest, not quite true West?
- What sorts of cultural investments might we make to attract visitors and perhaps new North Dakotans?
- How can we make our relationship with Native Americans enrich and improve the lives of all North Dakotans, a source of new creativity, a way forward that blends the best qualities of both cultures to make North Dakota one of the most remarkable places in North America?

I don't pretend to have answers to these questions. As a humanities scholar, I learned long ago that the questions are more important than the answers. I do have one iron conviction that informs every page of this book. If we North Dakotans think we can just continue to amble along in a kind of habitual, reactive way, making the best of whatever comes, and going about the business of life without consciously engaging in a purposeful statewide conversation (or debate) about who we are, what we want from life, and how we can help North Dakota "Be Legendary" in America (not just in our marketing campaigns), we would be making the gravest mistake in our history. The greatest and most consequential North Dakotans—Bill Guy, Bill Langer, A.C. Townley, Sitting Bull, Harold Schafer, Art Link—have all given their best energies to envisioning a thriving rural civilization that embodies something unique to this place at the center of America, tucked up along the Canadian border.

And if we disagree, as my hero Thomas Jefferson put it, let us disagree as rational friends.

NORTH DAKOTA 101

North Dakota is a mid-sized rectangular state snubbed up against the Canadian border at the center of the North American continent. It is the fourth least populous state (after Alaska, Vermont, and Wyoming). It is the most treeless state in America. It is the least and last visited state in America.

From an economic point of view, North Dakota is an exporter of food and fuel for the rest of the world. It also grows decent, talented, and hard-working young people for export.

North Dakota is the second coldest state after Alaska, which doesn't really count. The average annual temperature is forty-two degrees, but *any* North Dakotan would settle for forty-two degrees on *any* day between November and April. It is the fourth windiest state (after Nebraska, Kansas, and South Dakota).

North Dakota is about as far from the capitals of power, money, privilege, entertainment, hipness, and celebrity as it is possible to be. In the larger consciousness of America, it is usually entirely overlooked or forgotten, but to the extent that it is recognized at all, it is synonymous with isolation, flyover country, dullsville, clunkiness, and the middle (even the middle of the middle) of nowhere. For most of the second half of the twentieth century North Dakota was the butt of national jokes.

North Dakota's economy is based on agriculture, energy production, and tourism. There is very little manufacturing. The largest employers in the state are higher education, the K–12 public school system, the energy industry, agriculture and ag-related businesses, and government. Even now, when the family farm paradigm is beginning to implode, one in four North Dakotans is employed in an ag-related enterprise.

North Dakota has the nation's second or third worst drunk driving problem (DUI). It often leads the nation in binge drinking, including by teenagers. Except for its Native American population, North Dakota would be one of the five least diverse states in America. Whites and Native Americans in North Dakota lead essentially parallel lives with little intersection, except in shopping malls and pow wows. There are five federally recognized Indian reservations in North Dakota: Fort Berthold (Mandan, Hidatsa, Arikara), Spirit Lake (Dakota), Turtle Mountain (Ojibwe), Standing Rock (Lakota), and Lake Traverse (Dakota). Native Americans represent 6 percent of the North Dakota population.

Only 3.9 percent of North Dakota is public land, the rest private. Each of the thirteen states farther west has more public land: Montana 29 percent, Wyoming 48 percent, Colorado 36 percent, even California at 45 percent. North Dakotans regard themselves as rugged individualists, self-reliant, and independent. They complain loudly about the federal government, but the truth is that the state routinely receives more money from the federal treasury than it sends in, and the state could never have been settled or survived without federal subsidization of railroads, homesteads, highways, including interstate highways, military installations, missile bases, the alphabet soup of the New Deal, farm price supports, dams, reclamation projects, conservation reserve programs, below-cost grazing leases, and university research facilities.

North Dakota is the home of Lawrence Welk and Eric Sevareid, Angie Dickinson and Roger Maris, Louis L'Amour and Sacagawea. Lewis and Clark spent more time in North Dakota than in any other state: 213 days. The great Lakota leader Sitting Bull surrendered in northwestern North Dakota on July 19, 1881. North Dakota was the last residence of George Armstrong Custer before he rode into Montana to get himself killed in June 1876. More recently, North Dakota was the boyhood home of the actor Josh Duhamel and the NFL quarterback Carson Wentz.

North Dakota has just one National Park, named for Theodore Roosevelt who lived in the badlands of Dakota Territory for about four years (1883-87) before he became the 26th President of the United States. But it has sixty-three National Wildlife Refuges— more than any other state.

Outsiders will tell you that North Dakota is flat, and some of it is, but most of it is contoured and a little of it is rugged. North Dakotans like to speak of rolling hills, coulees and couteaus, bluffs, and buttes. Only the badlands of the western edge of the state are dramatic. One of the world's great rivers, the Missouri, flows through North Dakota on its way to St. Louis and the Gulf of Mexico, and one of the greatest of its tributaries, the Little Missouri, incises its way magnificently through the southwestern quadrant of the state.

The highest point in North Dakota is 3,506 feet above sea level. It's known as White Butte, visited by a few hundred people per year. Most establish a base camp at about 2,200 feet and spend a few days acclimatizing themselves for the final ascent. The lowest point is on the Minnesota border on the Red River near Pembina at 750 feet. There are no mountains in North Dakota, but three slight protuberances call themselves mountains: the Killdeer Mountains (buttes) in the west, the Turtle Mountains (knobs) in the north, and the Pembina Mountains (knobs) in the northeast. All of these are lower than White Butte at 3,506.

North Dakota has a population density of eleven people per square mile, compared to Montana with seven per square mile, South Dakota with twelve, and Minnesota with seventy-one. But most of the population of North Dakota lives along the three main traffic corridors. One in four North Dakotans lives in the Red River Valley within ten miles of the Minnesota border (along I-29). The combined population of the towns and cities along I-94, I-29 and US 2 account for a full 60 percent of the state's population, concentrated in a tiny sliver of the surface area of North Dakota. Most of North Dakota is empty or nearly so, and emptying further, as the rural population gravitates to the cities for the amenities and better access to health care.

As of 2020, North Dakota has 26,100 farms, all "family farms" in some legal sense of the term. The average farm size is 1,506 acres. Fully 90 percent of the surface area of North Dakota is farmed, 39,300,000 acres. This includes pasturage.

North Dakota produces food for the world. The state ranks number one in production of spring wheat, durum wheat (pasta wheat), dry edible peas, dry edible beans, flaxseed, canola, and honey. It also ranks high in production of potatoes, sugar beets, cattle, sunflowers, and soybeans. The North Dakota farm economy has been revolutionized in the past half-century by crop diversity (the era of King Wheat is over), by the development of drought-resistant strains of corn, soybeans, and sunflowers, by new farming methods that don't require frequent plowing (no-till agriculture), and by robotics.

North Dakota produces energy. The western part of the state encompasses some of the largest lignite coal beds in America. As of 2016 North Dakota was ranked number two in oil production in the United States, exporting more than a million and a half barrels per day, second only to Texas. North Dakota has hundreds of years of lignite coal reserves. Opinions vary about how much oil underlies the state, but mid-range estimates put it at around twenty billion recoverable barrels. The state's natural gas reserves are boundless.

North Dakotans have a reputation for being friendly, likeable, law-abiding, decent, hard-working, modest, and above all practical. Physics, not metaphysics. And not just physics, but applied engineering. The people of North Dakota are capable of welding metal, changing oil, weeding a garden, fixing fence, installing drywall, wiring a garage, milking a goat, or butchering a deer. Some of these things are changing pretty fast. They represent the lingering skillset of people who grew up on or have close kin on a family farm.

North Dakota is an acquired taste. Few make the effort. Even many North Dakotans are a little lukewarm about their homeland.

AN ACQUIRED TASTE

North Dakota is not for the faint of heart. A largely homogenous population, very long and often very rough winters, wind that blows like a sonofabitch, a dearth of high-quality amenities, a meat and potatoes diet (nobody would say "cuisine"), a seemingly flat and featureless landscape. It's Applebee's (if you are lucky) and satellite TV. The hordes of young men and some women who came to take jobs in the Bakken Oil Boom formed a kind of tedious chorus; hard to be outside for much of the calendar year, not much to do on a Friday night except drink or bowl, and (this is where it hurts a bit) the people are, well, nice but dull.

Look at it this way. Couples from all over America move to Colorado or Oregon or New Mexico or California or even Montana, but it is hard to imagine many people sitting over the breakfast table saying, "You know what, honey, let's move to North Dakota!" Nobody moves to North Dakota unless it involves a job. Nobody moves to North Dakota for the boutique restaurants, the independent theater, the fly fishing or the mountain hiking. Or for the cultural or ethnic diversity.

So what's the payoff? Why live in North Dakota?

Those who happen to be born in North Dakota might decide to stay because they have kin in the state, because it's the path of least resistance, because they like the pace and comfort of North Dakota and aren't sure they would like the rat race elsewhere. Some stay because they lack the skills and the imagination to leave. But young people, the ones who become National Merit Scholars, who score high on the SATs, often venture off to elite universities in faraway places. They may come back to make their lives in North Dakota—but more often not. Some return after spending several decades elsewhere. And the number one, somewhat defensive, refrain of North Dakota life is, "It's a good place to raise kids." That cannot be enough.

Here's the case for North Dakota.

First of all, the people of North Dakota are not just nice (in the sense of superficial friendliness) but deeply and authentically nice, generous, respectful, decent, kind, helpful, and polite. And outstanding in a crisis. This is a lingering legacy of our rural agricultural past. If dependability and trust matter to you, North Dakota is possibly the best destination in America.

It's easier to find a parking space in North Dakota than almost anywhere else. Traffic and congestion are virtually non-existent. In Bismarck, the state capital, the people joke about a "rush minute" at 5 p.m. It's true that on a Friday afternoon in the summer you will see a loose but long line of pickups hauling boats and fifth-wheel RVs away from the cities towards the handful of recreation lakes in the state, particularly Lake Sakakawea. (In Fargo and Grand Forks, the exodus is always towards Minnesota lake country.)

There are several especially beautiful, even grand, places in North Dakota: Pembina Gorge in the northeast corner of the state; the lovely Sheyenne River Valley, especially the National Grasslands unit southeast of Valley City; the big Karl Bodmer rolling hills country north and west of Williston; and of course the Little Missouri River badlands. These are excellent places to visit. One problem, though, is that these special places are regarded even by lifelong residents as not really representative of North Dakota.

The badlands, for example, are understood as North Dakota's "Montana," a little out of character for a state otherwise perceived as flat and bland.

Not everyone finds the more general landscape of North Dakota beautiful or even pleasing. This includes many of the 760,000 permanent residents of the state. Only a small minority love North Dakota for its physiognomy. When North Dakotans praise their homeland, it is usually for the "culture of decency" rather than the prairie potholes, rolling plains, ridgelines, coteaus, and the alluvial Red River Valley. Almost every defense of North Dakota finds its way to a now-semi-mythical family farm—operated by an uncle, a cousin, a friend of a cousin, or a trusted neighbor. North Dakotans are proud of their agrarian heritage, and almost entirely relieved that they have left those chores behind and migrated for a blue- or white-collar destiny in one of North Dakota's cities.

For those with the patience to see it and willingness to find it, North Dakota is a starkly magnificent place. By Yosemite and Grand Teton standards, there is not much drama in the landscape, but those with eyes to see find a rich palette of tawny pastel colors: rust, charcoal, mauve, golden, brown, yellow, delicate crocus blue, wild prairie rose pink, and the ashen green of yucca. The subtle roll and contouring of the land is an acquired taste. You have to get over the careless habit of tossing it into the conceptual bin of "flatland," but once you have acquired that taste you will find heartbreakingly beautiful (and weirdly addictive) the swells and ridges, the buttes and breaks and bluffs, the endless sea of grass stretching to the far horizon, the disconcertingly agreeable sense that you are a small bipedal creature who does not fully belong in the circle of grass and sky that repeats itself a hundred thousand times on the Great

Plains. Add a distant thunderstorm inching its way from the western horizon, a lightshow of nearly constant heat lightning that dances high in the sky, with occasional skewers of vicious streak lightning, and the first dawning of the slow rumble of thunder from dozens of miles away. Or a ground blizzard in November while you are driving along a black asphalt road with fading yellow stripes, wondering if you are going to reach your destination. You grip the steering wheel and give yourself a little informal internal prayer that your car doesn't break down—*not now, not today.* Or an evening in June when the sun seems reluctant to set at all, lingers in the northwestern sky, and, when it finally slips below the ridge-ragged horizon, illuminates the bottom half of the entire sky all the way around with a subtle pink roseate burnishing, or tangerine, or the color of Bloody Mary mix, all with some streaks of grey and charcoal a few degrees above the horizon. Or that moment when you are out in the middle of nowhere, alone or with a silent friend, and you actually feel the heat of the day drop a full level as if at once, and you become for a moment fully present, alive in every pore, on full alert, and you smile your most natural smile and relax into one of the greatest landscapes on earth. Or that moment on a sandbar in the mighty Missouri River on a ninety-degree afternoon, when you're flat out in yoga style on your back, eyes closed, for twenty minutes, and you realize, as Thoreau once put it, that you have actually begun to cook. Then you open your eyes and what you see—some trick of the ophthalmological nerve structure—is for half a minute or more a photovoltaic X-ray, or a grayscale landscape. As this moment fills you with wild wonder you realize, "This is why we live here . . . it doesn't get any better than this." Hand me a beer.

It's such a mistake to live in North Dakota and not do the training exercises that enable you to fall in love with its improbable windswept aesthetics.

And, of course, there is Fargo, poised like a track star on the Minnesota border, leaning east, the state's largest city, the cultural capital of North Dakota, the one place that does not require some sort of apology as its advocates make the case for its excellence and livability. Fargo would be interesting almost anywhere except in the context of New York, Seattle, San Francisco, and Los Angeles. Whether it is a North Dakota city now—or a kind of city state of the Upper Midwest—is a point of some contention by lovers of Fargo or North Dakota or both.

If I were the tourism czar for North Dakota, each of the welcome signs along the borders of the state would contain these words and nothing more:

North Dakota: Yeah, We Know.

Clay's concept of a highway welcome sign. Don't quit your day job!

SPIRIT OF PLACE ON THE NORTHERN PLAINS

S pirit of place is either something that emanates from the land and into the people who inhabit or visit it, or it is an attitude held by people towards a place. In other words, either the place permeates people with meaning and identity, or people invest a place with meaning because of their historical or personal association with it. When these two types of spirit of place merge, a powerful sense of resonance occurs.

An example of a site on the Great Plains that has spirit of *place* is the Little Bighorn Battlefield National Monument on the plains of south central Montana. I know a dozen people who have visited the site over the years who swear there is something eerie going on there that cannot be explained rationally. They say they can *feel* something—the battle, the ghosts, an energy in the grass, a kind of karma or perhaps lingering historical fallout. My mother (who was not given to the metaphysical) said there is a barely perceptible *"sitz sitz sis sis sitz . . . sitz sitz sis sis sitz"* she literally heard when she was there coming from the wind in the grass, and that this unaccountable sibilance has some sort of historical or spiritual significance. Listen to the grass, I say. If you live on the Great Plains, always listen to the grass. I know a disillusioned history professor who says that anyone who happens upon the site and walks around will inevitably *feel* something heightened there. I know a rational preacher who is skeptical of the Apostles' Creed and the Trinity, but who was visibly moved by the spirit in the grass when he visited the battlefield for the first time. He had been reading about the battle for many years. "Words, words, words," says Hamlet.

Now, whether there is really any intrinsic spirit of place at the Little Bighorn battlefield or just meaning we have invested in it because of the amazing terrible thing that happened there on June 25, 1876, is an interesting question. My mother swore that *anyone* who ventures onto the ridge, someone looking for a Kmart or a place to have a quiet picnic, but with no understanding of what transpired there 145 years ago, would experience some sort of soul's heightening. Others, a little less certainly, are inclined to agree. I'm not so sure. But I have heard some messages on the wind and whether they came from the land or from my psyche on the land, I regard them as authentic.

An example of the second type of spirit of place is a family's home place, particularly a rural family. My family's home place, the site of our *penates* and *lares*, is just south of Fergus Falls, Minnesota. My grandparents Dick and Rhoda Straus lived there for forty years. It was a small rolling hills farm of about eighty-five acres, a third of it pasture, and the rest cropland. They milked cows—just sixteen of them, each with a name like Bess or Whitey or Pal—and at times they raised chickens and pigs, and a half dozen steers for the meat market. We no longer own the farm. That's a long story interesting only to us. But I make the pilgrimage to the home place at least once a year. When I am there, I invariably go into the barn to kick around among the stalls. I can remember which stanchion belonged to which Holstein or Guernsey. I climb up into the hayloft and scramble around a little among what's left of disintegrating hay bales. The smell of dry hay in a barn loft is one of the greatest and most evocative of all smells. Even after forty years, the hayloft is a slightly eroticized place of mystery to me. The ropes and pulleys designed to lift hay from the ground into the loft have never worked. I always walk the entire perimeter of the farm. I make my annual inspection of my grandmother's rhubarb plants out along the lilac bushes west of the house. As I sit in the grass next to my grandmother's big vegetable garden, I loosen my grip on my mind so that the memories and associations can flow. I deplore, mostly on behalf of my mother, the way the new owners have "let the place go," particularly the large brick flower planters that flank the front door. My grandmother was exceptionally proud of her chrysanthemums. Except in the winter those planters were never empty. Grandma lavished gentle attention on her flowers as she would in changing a newborn's diaper. As I walk about on the warm earth of the old family farm, I feel sad and glad and recharged with memory. I feel closer to my roots. I ache for what has been lost: in my life, in my family, in the lifeway of the upper plains and prairie, in rural life, in America. And then I get in my car and drive away.

My mother grew up in that tradition, went away to college and never looked back. She ran away from rural life as if it were a curse, married an urban intellectual who could not really handle a pliers, and scoffed away the idea of baking her own bread or canning her own vegetables. I would probably not be writing this book if she had married a local farmer and slopped hogs. I ache for what she discarded so ruthlessly, and I have hefted my share of hay bales, but I am only fractionally better with a pliers than my father, and I am pretty sure I don't have the right stuff to be a true agrarian. But the agrarian in me—that tendril of rootedness—is what I prize most in my character.[*]

Almost everyone has a home place.

---

[*] We sold the farm to the City of Fergus Falls, MN. The farm buildings were demolished to make room for expansion of the city landfill. The house and barn are gone now, and such rhubarb as now exists grows in my back yard in Bismarck. This makes me sick at heart.

Spirit of place, then, is the *value added* of a site that cannot be measured in economic terms. It is related to the physical landscape, but its significance is metaphysical—or perhaps the physical and metaphysical mated in a kind of irresistible minuet. Ask any person to describe their most important earthly place. For one, it is a terrace on Santorini. For another, it is a coffee shop in Seattle. For a third, it is a calm bay at the base of a calving glacier in the panhandle of Alaska. For most, it is home, or the old home place. Where we go when we have nowhere else to go. Where we go to reconnect. Where nostalgia takes us. The Greeks regarded nostalgia as a disease. νοσταλγία. Perhaps they were right.

We live at a time in human history when place matters less than it ever has before. Almost any American community with a population of more than 5,000 has a Dairy Queen, a Pizza Hut, perhaps a Burger King or McDonald's. Any place with more than 25,000 people has an Applebee's and a Walmart. Small towns yearn for Target, bigger ones for Costco. The American people are fond of national and international chain stores and restaurants. There is some sort of a population trigger algorithm that determines who has access to what plateau of amenities—in shopping, in dining, in lodging. Communities measure themselves—they misuse the term "quality of life"—by how high up the hierarchy of chain store placement they have risen. The difference in the strip of roadside amenities—Honey Baked Ham, NAPA Auto Parts, Barnes and Noble, Panda Express, Toys "R" Us, and Taco Bell—in Aurora, Illinois, a prosperous suburb of Chicago and Aurora, Colorado, a prosperous suburb of Denver—is negligible. It's sometimes called the geography of nowhere. The French observer Alexis de Tocqueville said (1835) Americans are the freest people on earth and they freely rush to homogenous lifestyles and entertainments.

Thanks to satellite and cable television, virtually every American watches the same set of television programs irrespective of state or region of origin. The same sitcoms entertain folks on the Navajo Indian Reservation in Arizona, in Natchitoches, Louisiana, and in Newport, Rhode Island. We drive the same cars and fill them at the same gas stations, which are laid out identically in San Diego and Anchorage. Almost all commercial buildings and cars in America are climate controlled. People walk out of their homes not into nature but into their garages, depart by way of automatic garage door openers, drive to a paved and developed precinct (to shop, dine, work, recreate, worship, or work out), then return home at the end of the day, close the garage doors behind them, and enter their houses, where they spend the great majority of their discretionary time watching the homogenous television programming of America or sitting in front of a computer terminal making and resending memes. American lives are mediated and abstracted and deracinated as never before.

If a century ago our great-grandparents were so deeply rooted in place that their lives were constricted and claustrophobic, we, one hundred years later, live in a manner that is almost entirely detached from place. Americans, de Tocqueville said, are the most restless people on earth. "In the United States a man builds a house in which to spend his old age, and he sells it before the roof is on; he plants a garden and leaves it just as the trees are coming into bearing; he brings a field into tillage and leaves other men to gather the crops; he embraces a profession and gives it up; he settles in a place, which he soon afterwards leaves to carry his changeable longings elsewhere." De Tocqueville wrote these words before the invention of the automobile, the mobile home, and the RV. In the twenty-first century, even when we don't migrate from place to place, we have added rootlessness to restlessness.

That which could be anywhere—Best Buy, Olive Garden, Sam's Club—is also nowhere.

We all acknowledge the general way in which place shapes

character, of course. Put someone who grew up in Mississippi and someone who grew up in New Hampshire on the same debate stage in Chicago and everyone will know the difference, at least the moment these representatives open their mouths. Both are Americans. Both drink soda (though the Mississippian may be more likely to drink Dr. Pepper), both order Domino's Pizza, both watch *The Voice* and *American Idol*. They share lives as consumers, including consumable national cultural commodities. Still, (in descending order) they will almost certainly exhibit differences in accent, to a certain extent in diction, in the way they dress, in body language and style; and they are likely to have quite different political outlooks. Now pluck them out of the artificial environment of Chicago and put them back in their home states, back into their natural habitats, surrounded by their own folk. Back home their state and regional identities are likely to become more pronounced. People regain their default accents and Tocqueville's "habits of the heart" when they go home, and they feel more comfortable there to express their full personality and regional identity without inhibition.

We all acknowledge that there is a Texas type, a California type, a Long Island type, a Minnesota type. The popular cultural caricatures are not far from the truth. But is there a North Dakota type? If a North Dakotan moves to Philadelphia, Dallas, Miami, or Detroit, does anyone say, "There is something about you. Are you by any chance from North Dakota?" It might be possible, from accent and idiosyncrasies of phraseology, for a stranger to place the North Dakotan somewhere in the region between Wisconsin and Idaho, between Manitoba and Kansas, but it would be wrongheaded to argue that the landscape and the social structure of North Dakota stamp an identifiable character on the people who grow up here. It would have been easier fifty or one hundred years ago, but who, outside the borders, cared about the people of North Dakota or gave them a moment's attention?

The Coen Brothers' 1996 film *Fargo* gave the American people a somewhat caricatured notion of how North Dakotans speak, but most North Dakotans don't really talk that way, at least not in so pronounced a manner. The film is actually set in Minnesota's north country, where you occasionally hear echoes of that accent. When the film came out, I indignantly repudiated the caricature, but then I flew from Nevada to Fargo and, at the rental car kiosk, I met a clerk who could have walked right out of the film. My mother had a touch of the *Fargo* accent, as did my sister.

A few weeks ago, without thinking about it, I said *"uffda"* in northern Idaho. The woman I was sitting next to asked, "Did you just say *uffda?*"

"Yes."

"Are you like from Minnesota or the Dakotas?"

"Yes, North Dakota. How did you know?"

"My sister-in-law grew up in Langdon, North Dakota, and she says that sometimes."

State identity is interesting. But my interest is in a spirit of place that is deeper than *uffda,* something more meaningful than a slight variation in diction and what's left of the immigrant accents of North Dakotans whose forbears came from Norway, Germany, Ukraine, or the steppes of Russia. My fascination is with a spirit of place that is available to all North Dakotans, but not inevitable, a spirit of place that is not part of the automatic software that almost every North Dakotan runs by virtue of growing up in this region of the country. I'm talking about a North Dakota identity that people have to make a conscious choice to embrace if they wish to understand it or exemplify it. In other words, spirit of place is a choice, a journey, and a quest, not merely a birthright or the ability to make *Lefse.*

I'm going to make an effort to define some of the elements of a North Dakota spirit of place, knowing that such a definition depends on the eye of the beholder. One of the principal truths of life is that the lens you wear determines what you see. If you wear the lens of economic development as you gaze at North Dakota, you see beneath the surface of the land in X-ray or infrared to the coal, oil, and natural gas fields that beckon from the basement. If you wear the lens of tourism, you see the Lewis and Clark Trail, and Fort Mandan, Fort Union at the confluence of the Yellowstone and the Missouri, Custer's route first to the Black Hills (1874) and then his last journey to the Montana line and on to the Little Bighorn (1876). You see Theodore Roosevelt engaged in comic-hectic self-fashioning in the Dakota badlands (1883-87), or you see water skiing and sport fishing on Lake Sakakawea and Lake Metigoshe. If you wear a Jeffersonian lens, you see family farms diffused across the landscape, co-op grain elevators, virtuous democratic villages. If you come from Vermont or Colorado or Alabama, you see a vast, treeless, empty place you may find disconcerting.

Where you stand depends upon where you sit, and what you see depends entirely on which lens you choose to wear. Spirit of place is mostly a lens we acquire (or earn) because we want not just to occupy land but to inhabit it, to wear it in our bones. Robert Frost had it right at JFK's Inaugural:

> *The land was ours before we were the land's . . .*
> *Something we were withholding made us weak.*
> *Until we found out that it was ourselves*
> *We were withholding from our land of living,*
> *And forthwith found salvation in surrender.*

Anglo-Americans are not good at surrender. Native Americans, on the other hand, were experts at yielding to the universe of life and being all around them (the Wakon, the Medicine, the Great Mystery). Until we White folks learn to surrender a little to their cultural style, we probably cannot really come to terms with the spirit of place of the Great Plains. Native Americans—the Mandan, Hidatsa, Ojibwe,

Dakota, Arikara, Assiniboine, Lakota—invested nearly the whole of North Dakota with sacred energies. There was nothing—except possibly us—that they found fundamentally *Other*.

If North Dakota has a spirit of place, some or all of the following elements must play a role: open space with some sort of statistical minimum of human infrastructure appliquéd on it; a landscape vast and treeless rolling out to the vanishing point in every direction; breeze and blast, to ruin your picnic, shatter your family reunion, and blow out your Memorial Day; flat or gently rolling country suddenly yielding to broken country, coulees, badlands, orgiastic jumble; *Giants in the Earth* skies in which humans are reduced to antlike proportions against impossibly large backdrops in which the land is huge but the sky huger; buttes rising out of the land like shoeboxes, reminders of the dynamics of geology, glimpses of the level of the land a million years ago, grassy remnants plopped down in the middle of nowhere, which the combined erosive forces of wind, water, and ice somehow left behind when they swept everything else into the Gulf of Mexico; the never far from the surface understanding that a very different people lived here and not very long ago, a people who wore very different lenses from ours, whose civilization we did everything in our power to crush and thrust away, but whose spiritual signature on the landscape we still see and feel, and whose lingering presence challenges us right to the core from time to time even now; a sense of the temporariness of human habitations, a kind of joyfully anxious feeling that the wind might just sweep all that we have built away if we don't keep battening it down.

As the Great Plains' greatest novelist Willa Cather put it at the beginning of *O Pioneers!*, "The dwelling-houses were set about haphazard on the tough prairie sod; some of them looked as if they had been moved in overnight, and others as if they were straying off by themselves, headed straight for the open plain. None of them had any appearance of permanence, and the howling wind blew under them as well as over them."

Spirit of place involves a respect for the hard lives of the pioneers who proved up here a hundred plus years ago, laying down crops and crude shelters against the sub-Arctic winters in the most improbable and isolated landscape of America, whose lives are more authentically captured by Rachel Calof than by Laura Ingalls Wilder. Calof:

> Each family was to keep its chickens under its bed and the ends and sides were closed off to form a cage. Also there was a calf which had to be accommodated inside. It occupied the remaining corner opposite Moses's sleeping space. This is how five human beings and twenty-five animals faced the beginning of the savage winter of the plains in a twelve-by-fourteen shack. This is how we lived and suffered. The chickens were generous with their perfumes and we withstood this, but the stench of the calf tethered in the corner was well-nigh intolerable.

Spirit of place on the Northern Plains is the sense that there is nothing whatsoever standing between you and God, the Great Spirit, the Manitou, Allah, or the moons of Jupiter, and that there is no one to wrestle with the Angel of Death but you. An awareness of how few people can or want to live here, and how strange it is to choose to live away from the dense centers of population and the comfort of amenities when, in fact, you could choose to live anywhere. Storms: thunderstorms, windstorms, snowstorms, sleet storms, dust storms, hailstorms, blizzards. A constant looking to the sky for trouble and for answers. If you live in North Dakota, you ignore the western horizon at your peril.

Not everyone will see spirit of place in North Dakota in quite this way. There are cultural elements, too, such as white wooden Lutheran churches out in the middle of nowhere with their steeples pointing up into the middle of nowhere, chocolate chip bars and hot dishes and white cakes in aluminum pans, brilliantly red and brilliantly green combines inching their way across wheat fields, sunflowers lined up in perfect Nuremburg rectilinearity as far as the eye can see. *Fleishkuechle* in one café, *borscht* in another. Ole and Lena jokes at the baby or bridal shower.

I want to draw a distinction between two types of North Dakotans (or Montanans, Oregonians, or Russians). This distinction begins with the understanding that *everyone lives somewhere. Everyone is from somewhere.* If you grow a young person in North Dakota and then transplant her to, say, Seattle or Denver, in what ways does she remain a distinctive North Dakotan? She may like to identify herself as a North Dakotan. She may feel deep loyalty to North Dakota. She may be able to talk about the *Medora Musical* or Theodore Roosevelt National Park, about the state fair or vacations on Lake Sakakawea, but in what meaningful sense is she a North Dakotan? How—on any given day—is she different, if at all, from someone who was grown in Iowa or Florida or New Jersey? What is the North Dakota in a North Dakotan? In what way, if any, does the landscape of North Dakota shape the character of its young people?

I want to make a fundamental distinction that will inform all that I have to say in this book. It came to me in thinking about my father and mother, my sister, and my friends scattered all across North Dakota. I have found in my search for spirit of place that there are two types of North Dakotan: *accidental* North Dakotans and *naturalized* North Dakotans. In the era of Best Buy and seasonal premium sports packages on cable or satellite television, most of us are accidental North Dakotans most of the time. By accidental I mean that we live here, on the near rectangle of North Dakota with its 70,762 square miles, 45,287,680 acres of land, tucked up on the Canadian border, but at any given moment on any given day we are doing something that has nothing to do with place, something we could be doing anywhere or nowhere. At any given moment we dwell in what I'm calling mediated space or by way of mediated experience.

Whenever we eat and shop, work and watch LCD screens, we are not out listening to the wind in the grass or searching the sky for the Northern Lights. Most North Dakotans now spend very little time outside.

Some North Dakotans wish they lived somewhere else, particularly young people. Most North Dakotans are happy enough to be North Dakotans, maybe even proud to be North Dakotans, but there is nothing beyond a kind of pro forma state patriotism and some relatively shallow cultural identity to buttress that pride. In other words, they would have the same pride for another state if they happened to be from that state. Nor is there anything wrong with that.

Many North Dakotans like living where there is no heavy traffic, no commute, no urban labyrinth to negotiate, where life is relatively simple and straightforward, where the population is ethnically unproblematic, where the farther reaches of lifestyle choice do not trouble the general homogeneity and comfort level of the population. In other words, many North Dakotans like living in North Dakota principally because that is the world they know, the world they have always known, while the universe beyond their borders sounds discomforting or menacing or just unfamiliar. These Dakotans might just as well be living somewhere else, but they find no sufficient reason to reject North Dakota, and no compelling reason to choose another place instead. Besides, the family graves are here.

The snowbird phenomenon makes a kind of sense, because North Dakota has brutal long winters, and people with money, like the geese, often prefer to seek a more temperate climate during the severest third of the year. But love of a place, like the love of a woman or a man, requires a holism to be fully authentic. If you love North Dakota only when the winds are still, when the grass is lush and green, when the sun is shining, and when the temperature is above 70 degrees, it may be that you do not really love North Dakota, but rather the *California* or *Colorado* in North Dakota. On any given day in North Dakota, the wind is blowing. It is just as likely to be blowing like a sonofabitch as a mild zephyr. On any given day, it may be uncomfortable to be outside. On any given day, a storm may blow through when you least expect it. On any given day, the temperature may drop thirty degrees in an hour. On any given day, you may need to venture outside with protective gear that would seem like a Mars mission to a Hawaiian.

North Dakotans who make the best of it, who like this place well enough, but would be equally happy in any number of other places, who spend a minimal or at best a modest amount of time out in untrammeled nature, may be said to be *accidental* North Dakotans. My father was such a person, perhaps in part because he was raised in the lake country of Minnesota and he was transferred to western North Dakota by the company that employed him. He would never have come otherwise. How many North Dakotans would never have come here otherwise and, if they could have been born anywhere, would have chosen to be born here? In a sense, it was as if my father was *stationed* in North Dakota by a higher power, by a regional corporation or the military, but if he had ever been given the chance to choose his home place, it would have been somewhere else—bustling Minnesota, at the very least. I believe that most North Dakotans are, as it were, *stationed* in North Dakota. Nor is there anything wrong with this, for people are also stationed in Missouri and in New Mexico and in Delaware. That is the standard paradigm of life for Americans in the twenty-first century. In the digital age, place is an electronic platform rather than a home.

Naturalized North Dakotans are those who have decided to wrestle with the angel of North Dakota and find a way to accept it in all of its moods, and approve it, too—to learn from it, to learn how to live in it, to learn how to be North Dakotans rather than Coloradans or Ohioans. Naturalized North Dakotans know the history of the state, the themes of the historical markers that dot the state's highways. They know how the trails (the Totten Trail, the Bismarck to Deadwood Trail, the Lewis and Clark Trail, the Thieves Road) threaded their way across the plains landscape and to what end. They know something about the way in which Germans, Germans from Russia, Bohemians, Finns, Norwegians, Swedes, Lebanese, and Anglos penetrated west from Ellis Island, the Great Lakes, and the Red River in the course of the Homestead Act migrations, and how to locate on the map the cultural epicenters of those pioneer ethnic groups. They know where to place the Ukrainian Orthodox Crescent and the Sauerkraut Triangle. They know something about cultural footprints of the Mandan, Hidatsa, Arikara, Assiniboine, Lakota, Dakota, and Ojibwe on today's North Dakota, the cultural footprint of Abraham Lincoln, the two Roosevelts, Thomas Jefferson, George Armstrong Custer, the Marquis de Mores and Phillipe Régis de Trobriand. They know such sacred places as Writing Rock (near Crosby), the Medicine Rock (near Elgin), and the Medicine Hole (near Killdeer). They know more or less where the last buffalo hunt occurred in North Dakota in 1883 and they have stood on the hill where Karl Bodmer painted his famous watercolor of Fort Union at the confluence of the Yellowstone and the Missouri Rivers. They know where Sitting Bull surrendered on July 19, 1881, and where he was assassinated on December 15, 1890, in the tragic run-up to the Massacre at Wounded Knee. They have heard of the Ice Caves in the northern badlands, and they would be able to get you there with a good grasslands map.

More importantly, they know where they feel most alive, where they go to refresh their spirits, where they take significant others and special guests to see what North Dakota really is, what it really means.

Hunting is still very important to the adult population of North Dakota, and hunters are very often naturalized, not *accidental*, North Dakotans. Each fall they take the time to get out on the land, in good weather or bad, and though they are ostensibly in quest of deer, duck or pheasant, possibly elk, it is clear that they are more essentially in quest of a living connection with the grass and the landscape of the northern Great Plains. In fact, hunting is now the most significant spirit of place ritual of the North Dakota people. If hunting ceased to be a serious avocation, our slender hold on the soul of the Great Plains might blink out altogether, for the number of hikers, campers, cross country skiers, and wilderness sojourners is negligible compared to the hunting population. Critics of hunting are, for that reason more than any other, misguided. The more people who walk the land, the more people who will fight to protect it from those who would transfer it into cash. Hunters are, paradoxically, some of our best conservationists.

From a spirit of place perspective, North Dakota suffers from the *in-between* problem. Montana has a distinct identity and personality as does Minnesota. South Dakota is very much like North Dakota, but it has edgier Native Americans with a harder, more dramatic history, and it has the Black Hills, which are to the badlands of North Dakota what the badlands of North Dakota are to, say, the Killdeer Mountains. Saskatchewan and Manitoba don't count, because the 310-mile border at the forty-ninth parallel, though invisible from space, may as well be a mile high and equally thick. If you don't think invisible boundaries matter, try taking a handgun into Saskatchewan or seek medical attention first in Grand Forks and then in Winnipeg. Or buy a baguette north or south of the border.

North Dakota is not Midwestern like Minnesota, Iowa, Wisconsin, and Michigan. Nor is it western like Montana and Wyoming. I think it is undeniable that Fargo and Grand Forks identify themselves with the Midwest rather than with the Great Plains. In fact, many people of the Red River Valley regard North Dakota west of, say, Casselton, Cooperstown, and Carrington, much the way the famous *New Yorker* cartoon portrays America west of the Hudson River. Much of North Dakota is flyover country even to North Dakotans. Many citizens of Fargo and Grand Forks are a little embarrassed about North Dakota and they boast that they live in the most livable (most endurable) communities in the state. Fully a quarter of the North Dakota population lives east of Interstate 29, which hugs the Minnesota border. This creates a double problem for North Dakota's spirit of place. Not only is the population congealed on the Minnesota border, leaning east not west, leaning out not in, but it is undeniable that the cultural centers of North Dakota are located in Fargo and Grand Forks, where the idea of North Dakota matters less than it does in Williston, Dickinson, Grassy Butte, Wishek, or even Bismarck or Minot. The wealthier citizens of Fargo and Grand Forks bolt east to the Minnesota lake district on Friday afternoons between May and October, not west to Devils Lake or the Pembina Gorge. If the majority of the thinkers, philosophers, poets, sculptors, painters, musicians, novelists, economists, and sociologists of the state live in the part of North Dakota that essentially identifies itself with Minnesota (which it is not), rather than North Dakota (which technically at least, it is), it cannot be expected that that significant group of cultural leaders is going to do much to help clarify or define or illuminate North Dakota life. Their souls reside elsewhere. They are certainly not rooted in Grassy Butte or Mott, Hazen or Mohall, Crosby or New Leipzig. These urbanites should not be blamed for their detachment from North Dakota. They are, of course, free to pursue their cultural projects in any way that satisfies them. But their allegiances do not do North Dakota spirit of place much good. We pay them to teach our children, to play a key role in their formation as future North Dakota adults. If they know little or nothing about Louis Riel's rebellion in 1885 or the 1864 construction of Fort Dilts out near Rhame, it may be fair to ask how well they are teaching our sons and daughters, and why we pay them to do it. I will address this issue more thoroughly later.

Cultural achievement can occur in scattered places, in the music of Chuck Suchy (who lives south of Mandan) or the ceramic art of Tama Smith (Beach) or Robin Reynolds (Hebron), but historically it has tended to flourish where there is a critical mass of population and prosperity. The Renaissance required Florence, and the Elizabethan miracle required London, not Stratford-on-Avon. The Parthenon gets built in Athens—not Ithaka—and the Guggenheim Museum winds up in New York, not Saratoga or Albany. The only zone in North Dakota where there is any real expectation of a cultural effervescence of the kind that could create a distinctive North Dakota culture is the university and population corridor of Fargo-Grand Forks. And that is the part of North Dakota that is least interested in the North Dakota project. This is a paradox as old as North Dakota history. In spite of the flat-world revolution of the internet, it grows more pronounced every year, whether we like to admit it or not. Imagine if one of the flagship universities were located west of the hundredth meridian. The whole history of North Dakota would be different—and better.

So, add up the following factors: One, the primary cultural population is edgy about North Dakota and it leans out, not in. Two, the cultural exemplars in the rest of the state are so diffused geographically, so isolated, that they do not get sufficient nurturing and cross-fertilization to take on the challenge of creating an authentic North Dakota culture, and they live in communities that are not fully supportive of the eccentricities of artists, humanists, philosophers, poets, and the challenges of art and literature. Three, North Dakota suffers from a fundamental identity problem (in betweenness) that has had a paralytic effect on its attempt (or even its willingness) to create a distinctive state culture. Four, we live at a time when Americans are more culturally homogenized and our common experiences more mediated than at any previous moment in our history. Five, North Dakotans spend less time out of hermetically-sealed environments than ever before in their history. Six, everyone with money flees after the temperate seasons end.

The result is a dearth of serious North Dakota art and literature, in which the remarkable exceptions prove the rule: a weak sense of North Dakota identity in the people, especially the young; a sense that there is nothing here worth preserving, fighting for, staying to protect and enlarge; a yearning to join the deracinated national homogenous culture (as at Maple Grove, Minnesota) that pays attention to North Dakota only to ridicule it; the stifling of the creative impulse in the young people who stay; social discrimination against peoples and lifestyles different from our own; disillusionment; and outmigration, not to mention the most severe teenage binge drinking problem in the nation.

Here, more than in all other places, we need to cultivate spirit of place. If we had it, if we all sought to become *naturalized* North Dakotans, if we fell in love with this place *as place*, we could rock the world. More to the point, the wider world would discover us. Many would come to take a look and some would choose to stay.

So, if my analysis is true, what's the remedy?

1. We need to create a much more serious North Dakota studies curriculum in our schools, K–12 and at the universities. Geography, Native American studies, the varieties of prairie spirituality, and Great Plains literature need to be at the core of that new curriculum.

2. We need far more school field trips—not necessarily to museums and large auditorium presentations, but just out into the middle of nowhere, to the buttes, ridges, coulees, trade and military forts, lonely monuments to David Thompson, and above all to the Indian reservations.

3. We need to use some of our immense energy wealth, our huge and growing budget surplus, to seed young sculptors, painters, essayists, novelists, and poets, not in our cultural

capitals, which have reached a self-sustaining level of cultural activity, but in the less densely populated regions of the state.

4. We need to create several new Centers for North Dakota Studies, to provide them with the same sorts of start-up funds and endowments we have provided for the business entrepreneurial Centers of Excellence across the state.

5. We need to create a range of all-expenses scholarships for young intellectuals who wish to do graduate work in North Dakota, Great Plains, and Upper Missouri studies, and provide special incentives for them to stay in North Dakota for at least a significant period of time following their academic labors.

6. North Dakotans need to write about their experiences, their family stories, their memories, their sense of the history, the identity, and the landscape of North Dakota, their vision of the future and their understanding of what is possible in North Dakota. This includes North Dakotans of all political views, backgrounds, levels of education, professions, and general outlooks. As the Canadian songwriter Ian Tyson put it, we need to "get it all down before it's too late."

7. Above all, all of us need to get out into the open nature of North Dakota, to listen to the wind and the grass, to walk along the ridges, to have picnics in empty places, to visit all the state parks and historical sites of North Dakota, to walk endlessly, to lie on our backs at night looking up at the stars and listening to the coyotes and waiting patiently for the Northern Lights or the Perseid meteor shower.

Will any of these things make the difference? The answer is almost certainly yes. Anything else is the politics of defeatism and decline. In my opinion nothing would be more likely to keep young people in North Dakota than to create a new sense of our identity, a new pride in what North Dakota means—geographically, culturally, historically, ideologically, spatially. Such an enterprise represents a doable and inexpensive investment in our future.

We have nothing to lose but our chain stores.

SO WHO ARE WE NOW?
THE IDENTITY OF NORTH DAKOTA

"After Fargo, the true emptiness of America suddenly opens up, the endlessness of the Great Plains, the desert of brownish grass in the heart of this country. The landscape is gently hilly, and somehow or other everything has a certain orderliness to it, although we rarely see a farm or a settlement. The road is one long strip of concrete leading to nothing and nowhere."
—Geert Mak, *In America: Travels with John Steinbeck*

L et's get right to it. Why would any rational person move to North Dakota?

People move to North Dakota who have fallen in love with one of our sons or daughters. People move to North Dakota because they are transferred there by their employers. People move to North Dakota when they are assigned to one of the two US Air Force bases, when they are sent there by the federal bureaucracy (the FBI, the US Forest Service, the US Fish and Wildlife Service, the Bureau of Indian Affairs), when they take a job at one of our hospitals or when they get a professing job at one of our universities. People move there to seek work in the oil and gas industry. But nobody moves to North Dakota for the fun of it.

A 1930s promotional film declared rightly that Southern California had a "mild, seductive climate." That phrase has never been used of North Dakota. North Dakota has an unmild, and unseductive climate. Winters are long, severe and can be brutal. It doesn't snow much in North Dakota, a semi-arid state, but sudden fierce blizzards sweep through half a dozen times or more per winter. Although the dusks linger endlessly in late June and July, winter is a time of short gray grim days, the temperature usually somewhere between twenty degrees above and twenty degrees below zero Fahrenheit, wind seldom absent, sometimes malevolent. Spring is often postponed so long that, when it finally comes, the weather changes from late winter to early summer in a few days or weeks. It is hot enough for air conditioning for about twenty days in August, though if you manage your windows right you don't really need climate control even then.

North Dakota is one of the windiest places in North America. It can freeze and snow in any month, and does so routinely from October to May, and often in September and June, too. It is not unusual for the state to have a brief starter blizzard in early October. This is usually followed by a few weeks of "Indian summer." Then what Theodore Roosevelt called the season of "iron desolation" settles in for three or four or five adamantine months.

Life is simpler in North Dakota, but it is also narrower in some important respects. I call it the Land of Velveeta. Even in 2019 at a time of historically unprecedented diversity, North Dakota was still 90 percent White. Native Americans constitute 6 percent of the population, Latinos 2 percent, and no other group represents more than 1 percent of the population. Even though satellite television, fiber optic cable, and the internet have connected North Dakota to the rest of the country and the planet—a revolution that makes Great Plains life easier to endure—most North Dakotans feel they are isolated, marginal, out of the loop, as unappreciated as they are unvisited by the rest of the world.

One of North Dakota's greatest sons, Eric Sevareid, called it "a large, rectangular blank spot in the nation's mind." He was born in Velva, North Dakota, on November 26, 1912. He left the state early and didn't return much for the rest of his long and distinguished life as one of the pioneers of broadcast news and America's greatest television commentator. When North Dakotans are asked to name favorite sons and daughters, they invariably name people—Angie Dickinson, Roger Maris, Josh Duhamel—who happened to have been born here but left and seldom, if ever, returned, except to pick up awards for the dubious honor of having North Dakota on their birth certificate.

Not every American even knows that North Dakota exists. Unless you are from the region or know somebody from North Dakota, you probably could name forty states before thinking of North Dakota, if at all. Once, at a Disney World hotel, I checked my family's luggage for the flights home. The young man who handled this transaction asked me where we were headed. "Bismarck," I said. Pause. "Is that in America?"

Just a few days ago I was at a national gathering of Lewis and Clark lovers. A prominent US Senator from Indiana, warming his theme to epic proportions, spoke of the perseverance and stamina of "those great men who spent that hard winter at Fort Mandan in South Dakota." No one in the crowd of 200 even groaned. Even people from states in our region find it hard to say anything interesting about North Dakota. *No trees. Flat. Brutal winters. Theodore Roosevelt National Park. The Medora Musical.* "I got a cousin who goes up every year to do some pheasant hunting."

Checking into a motel in Spearfish, South Dakota a few years ago, I told the young desk clerk, who asked about my day, that I had had a wonderful afternoon driving US 85 from Belfield to the Black Hills. "Oh, yeah," she said, deadpan. "That's like sitting in a room staring at wallpaper all day long." *De gustibus non est disputandum*, I guess. I regard that stretch of highway as one of the five or ten most beautiful drives in America. Ask the next hundred strangers you meet to tell you what they know about North Dakota. What you get is a large, rectangular blank stare.

North Dakotans don't pretend the state is better than it is. They make wry jokes about being the butt of jokes. Their response to the charge of inhabiting a cold, windy, flat, boring, godforsaken place that no cool person would visit except to make fun of visiting a pointless place, is "Yeah, well, we don't want them here anyway." Before the Bakken Oil Rush, the hackneyed answer to all of this derision and abuse was twofold: "Yeah, but it keeps the riffraff out," and "Yeah, but it's a great place to raise children." Since the Bakken Oil Rush, we know that some of the riffraff managed to find western North Dakota after all. In fact, the oil boom brought out some of the riffraff in some of the people of North Dakota.

So who are we now?

We are the great and great-great-grandchildren of the farmers who somehow scratched a living off the land. We value what they did. But we are not as strong as they were, and we know it. We wouldn't go back if we could. We are living, with considerable gratitude and occasional waves of guilt, on the fumes of their gumption and sacrifice. They wanted a better life for their children, and they achieved it. They looked on in wonder and some dismay as their spoiled grandchildren spent recklessly, lived like grasshoppers, and balanced duty with pleasure and self-indulgence. Since 1970, each generation of North Dakotans has had less rootedness, even less groundedness. When I give talks around North Dakota to baby boomers, I ask how many live on a farm. A few. Then I ask how many grew up on a farm. Almost half. Finally, I ask how many have a kinship link to a family farm—a cousin, uncle or aunt, niece or nephew. At this point the great majority of hands go up and there is a murmur of pride and nostalgia that ripples like a brisk breeze over a field of ripe golden wheat. Sometimes there is applause. But ask those questions at a high school graduation speech and the numbers plummet.

My young friends have inherited the goodness and the decency of the North Dakota heritage, but they want to be wired into the amenity grid of urban life far away. The prefer the new hipster coffee house in Bismarck to the cafe at Tower City, not realizing that later in life they will feel the emptiness, even the betrayal of this preference, and they will ache for a slice of the clunky but delicious sour cream raisin pie they enjoyed a few times in Tower City before the zeitgeist swept it all away. Some of my young friends can peaches and even cucumber pickles. Some join scrapbook clubs. But the fact is that my grandmother would cluck disdain at their fancy Cricket cutting machines and their mail order stencils and decals and glue-on objects like 3D suitcases and red wagons and the Eiffel Tower. Long ago, I called my grandmother (a dairy farmer) to ask if she would help me make a quilt. She agreed happily. When I turned up at the farm with several yards of cloth that I had purchased at a Fargo fabric store, and announced my intention to cut up squares of red, blue, tan, yellow, and black and form them into a geometric pattern, she gave me a dark look. "That defeats the purpose altogether. We didn't make patchwork quilts for the fun of it. We made them to use up scraps of cloth left over from other sewing projects. We didn't have the luxury of designing perfect squares. We were determined not to waste anything. We had nothing to waste."

So, we canned cucumber pickles instead.

Who are we now? Can we hang on to the most admirable values of our great-grandparents? Do we wish to? If we sought to, what would that look like and how would we achieve it and sustain it? In an age of wild abundance, does it make any sense to take up the arts and crafts of rural poverty and scarcity? Why not just buy all the blankets you want from department stores? Who sews clothing nowadays? Until you have known poverty you cannot really understand thrift. Thrift was not something our grandparents practiced as an ingenious social experiment like Henry David Thoreau at Walden Pond. It's what they did to survive. We imitate it, but we cannot understand it.

What has made North Dakota different from other places is the combination of the vast and empty plain we lived on and the family farm disciplines, sacrifices, and values that enabled us to survive here. Now that we are awash in prosperity that has nothing to do with lifting a bale or taking a dinner of beef and potatoes and sharp black coffee in a plaid thermos out to the farmer running the combine at dusk, now when we design websites in our leggings and Nikes, and plan our vacations for Prague and Morocco, what really is left of the North Dakota spirit? There are those who will say our state identity and character are not inexorably tied to family agriculture, that we can continue to be a cautious, conserving, preserving, frugal, generous, and self-sufficient people in an age of abundance and Amazon.com. And that we have or can still generate a spirit of place in North Dakota that is not connected to family farming. But we are just fooling ourselves if we think we can maintain a vital connection to the land and to the culture in agri*culture* when family farming is no longer much of what it was between 1889 and 2004.

How many of the twenty-somethings of Fargo or Minot or Bismarck spend any significant amount of time out on the plains per annum? The emerging culture of North Dakota is interiorized, uprooted and detached.

North Dakota has a significant identity problem. It is caught in a limbo of *inbetweenness*. It is neither Midwest nor West, but something indeterminate in between. It is not Minnesota, with its clean and tidy communities, its progressive politics, the Vikings and the Twins and the Minnesota Wild and the Timberwolves, a great and nationally important university, and the metropolis of Minneapolis and St. Paul. Nor is it Montana with Yellowstone National Park, the White Cliffs section of the Missouri River, the Little Bighorn, or the University of Montana writer's program, located in a town that is militantly dedicated to "keep Missoula weird." North Dakota is not quite Midwest (we're too dry and the distances are too great), not quite West (we're the land of John Deere not John Wayne). North Dakota is blah, bland, and—in the minds of others—boring.

And now, as the twenty-first century unfolds, North Dakota is no longer a family farm state exactly, but not yet whatever it is going to become in its post-agrarian era. From statehood in 1889 until about the millennium (in 2000), North Dakota knew what it was and knew what it meant. It was obsessively, almost exclusively, agricultural, a family farm state that produced food for the rest of the country. It was the wheat belt—hard red spring wheat and durum—and cattle country. Young people taking North Dakota history, using the old yellow-tan text *Our State: North Dakota*, took pride in knowing that while we were second in overall wheat production to Kansas (drat that Kansas), we were first in hard red spring wheat. On any given Fourth of July back then, almost a quarter of the entire surface area of North Dakota was carpeted in wheat. That's monoculture. There is something very beautiful in that image, a vast golden carpet of wheat, and that identity—the breadbasket of America, operated by sturdy and independent family farmers who minded their own business and watched the summer skies.

At the height of the agrarian epoch in 1930, there were 70,000 farms in North Dakota, all operated by families, not one owned by a corporation or a consortium of investors. They were "farmy farms" then, with some dairy cattle, hogs, chickens, and big gardens. Now there are fewer than 25,000 farms in all of North Dakota, and only a small number choose to dink around with pigs or chickens or even serious gardens. Those who remain on the land call themselves agri-producers now and they are as likely to be farming the farm program or farming the futures market or farming the insurance industry, or farming the actuarial tables, as putting their hands in the soil.

We knew who we were when we were a clunky farm state. Every hundred family farms supported a town: schools, implement dealers, seed stores and grain elevators, a post office, a couple of banks, a barber shop, a handful of churches, a grocery store, a car dealership, a weekly newspaper, a pharmacy, a café and a steakhouse, a couple of bars, a veterinarian, an insurance office, a doctor and maybe even a dentist. Every few dozen towns supported what we euphemistically called a city—Dickinson, Williston, Minot, Bismarck, Devils Lake, Jamestown, Valley City, Fargo, Wahpeton, Grand Forks—where there were radio and television stations, supermarkets, livestock auction yards, a hospital, and maybe a college. The entire social and economic pyramid rested on those modest family farms.

Back in July 1896 Nebraska's William Jennings Bryan spoke for the pride of North Dakota farmers when he delivered his famous "Cross of Gold" speech at the Democratic National Convention in Chicago: "You come to us and tell us that the great cities are in favor of the gold standard; we reply that the great cities rest upon our broad and fertile prairies. Burn down your cities and leave our farms, and your cities will spring up again as if by magic; but destroy our farms and the grass will grow in the streets of every city in the country."

We North Dakotans were not sophisticated back then, we were not cosmopolitan, we were not flashy or cool or groovy or "with it," but we knew exactly who we were. We knew what we did was important—the most important of all things, we fed the world—and we identified with that wheat (and the oats and potatoes and the flax), and we didn't mind not being sophisticated or any of the rest of it. Today, William Jennings Bryan's great agrarian pronouncement seems merely quaint because it is no longer true. Destroy the farms now and the American people will import their food from elsewhere. But that principle, that sentiment, was the source of identity—and quiet pride—for the people of North Dakota for the first century of our existence.

The golden age of North Dakota agriculture came after the Second World War and it lasted until the 1970s when the Steiger Tractor and other gigantic industrial agricultural equipment arrived on the scene and farmers began to shut down their small dairy operations and get rid of the hogs and chickens. Farms grew dramatically bigger. First the villages and then the towns began to shrink up and die. Schools consolidated—the most agonizing thing that can happen to a rural town short of death—and all that prosperity caused people to drive long distances to do their shopping in the regional market centers, thus endangering the main streets of Crosby and Cando, Harvey and Hettinger, New England and New Leipzig, Leith and Lakota. Attempts to encourage or shame people to shop in their hometowns have all failed. As they drive to the nearest Super Walmart, the rural people of North Dakota know they are pounding nails into the coffin of the small towns they love and call home, but they want abundance, they want uniform quality in their goods and produce, and they want cheaper prices. They also want escape.

Today there are farms in North Dakota of 25,000 acres, some of 70,000 acres, and though they are all technically "family farms," they no longer resemble the farms of our grandparents and great-grandparents. The GPS-driven combine increases yield and efficiency, and its obscene cost—$450,000-$750,000—induces farmers to buy or rent more land to fulfill their business plan—our grandparents never had a business plan—and make the farm operation cash flow. Cash flow back then meant you had money in the fall to pay for repairs and buy new shoes for your oldest children.

Fewer farms, fewer farm children, fewer businesses that depend for their survival on the farm economy, fewer towns that are anything more than retirement camps with minimal services—a couple of churches, a convenience store, a post office, a tanning parlor-cappuccino shop, a café, and a couple of bars. What's still left of the agrarianism that was our reason for being and our source of identity is disappearing all around us. Artificial intelligence, drones, robotic farm equipment, satellite imaging, and intense computer analysis are replacing the farmers who work the fields, the ones Jefferson said "keep alive that sacred fire, which otherwise might escape from the face of the earth." The cybernetic, post-industrial escape is well underway on the northern Great Plains. If you don't have to actually live in North Dakota to operate a successful soybean and sugar beet farm, will you still choose to live there? Or find a home in Oregon or Hawaii and merely study the farm cams? The first fully robotic farm is now being constructed in Cass County, North Dakota. We all know that for the rest it is only a matter of time.

Then who will we be?

Perhaps it would be best to adjust Eric Sevareid's formulation slightly. North Dakota is a large, arbitrary, blank, near-rectangle in the nation's mind.

Sevareid (1912-1992) was the fifth recipient of North Dakota's coveted Rough Rider Award (1964). He was the author of the best book ever written by a North Dakotan, *Not So Wild a Dream*, published right after the war in 1946. Although it has a superb chapter about growing up in Velva (population 1,267), Sevareid wrote the book in Carmel, California, overlooking the Pacific Ocean. North Dakota is always easier to love in absentia than on that late January day when the sun don't shine, the temperature is −17, and the wind chill takes it down to 57 below. Sevareid was maybe the last American journalist to get out of France when it fell to the Nazis on June 14, 1940. With Edward R. Murrow and William L. Shirer, he helped to invent broadcast news as we know it in the wake of Hitler's annexation of Austria in the spring of 1939. He covered the end of the war in Italy and France. He was, in fact, traumatized by what he witnessed—the fierceness of the fighting, bad American generalship,

the atrocities perpetrated by the retreating Nazis, and the retribution atrocities against Nazi collaborators committed by the French freedom fighters as the Germans cleared out. By 1963, Sevareid was the principal television news commentator in the United States. Two or three evenings per week Walter Cronkite would turn to Sevareid to ask for some perspective. Then, for two and a half minutes, Sevareid would deliver thoughtful, historically rich, gently witty, and moderately liberal commentary. He had Olympian confidence, a beautiful voice, and yet an oddly nervous bedside manner. During the broadcast, he sometimes had to clutch his hands together to keep them from shaking. There was no background footage, B-roll. We saw only the melancholy beauty of Sevareid's Nordic face. From 1963-1977, at a time when there were only three national media outlets (two, really), Sevareid functioned as the Greek chorus of American life: his commentaries on Vietnam, Malcolm X, Watergate, LBJ, the space program, the assassinations, women's liberation, the Civil Rights Movement, the youth movement, and campus unrest were a central prompt in the national conversation during one of the most momentous and tumultuous decades in American history. He once said he had an easy job. All he had to do was serve as America's Oracle of Delphi for three minutes every weekday afternoon.

How much any of this had to do with the fact that Sevareid happened to have been born in North Dakota is unknowable. In his memoir, *Not So Wild a Dream*, he declared, though not in quite these terms, that you could take the boy out of Velva, but you cannot fully take Velva out of the man. Everyone is from somewhere. Brian Williams is from Ridgewood, New Jersey, Nora O'Donnell is from San Antonia, Texas, Michael Smerconish is from Doylestown, Pennsylvania, Lester Holt is from California. Generally speaking, the viewer doesn't care. Nobody watching CBS in those years would have said, "Hey, that guy seems (or sounds) like a North Dakotan." Sevareid hailed from Mount Olympus, not some pointless village on the northern Great Plains.

Although Sevareid was one of the greatest of all North Dakotans, and maybe the best writer the state has ever produced, he is largely forgotten today. People who qualify for Medicare remember him, often fondly. People whose first big media figure was Ted Turner (or perhaps Connie Chung) have no idea who Sevareid was and, when told, respond with variations of ho-hum. He is not even remembered among young North Dakotans for his post-high-school canoe trip from St. Paul all the way to Hudson Bay with classmate Walter Port, an adventure so reckless that he said he could not in later life think about it without shuddering. It's one thing for young and middle-aged North Dakotans to dismiss a stuffy old White news commentator from the era of radio and black and white television, but it takes some willful ignorance to be unaware of a heroic rite of passage canoe trip that might have cost young Sevareid his life and would be hard for any pair of adventurers to complete successfully today. Sevareid wrote about that dangerous adventure in his first book, *Canoeing with the Cree* (1935).

But now add insult to injury. The great journalist and writer has been displaced even in Velva, his hometown, by a pretzel maven named Dot. Dot Heinke (1955-) invented Dot's Homestyle Pretzels™ in 2011. She wants the world to know that she still lives in a modest Houston home (probably to be on hand to greet the Chinese pretzel tankers at the harbor) and makes frequent visits to her beloved North Dakota, but for all we know she owns a private island in the Bahamas, collects live tigers and jaguars, and serves her "Reserve" Homestyle Pretzels in solid gold bowls.

As with so many of the greatest inventions and discoveries of human history—Archimedes shouting *eureka* in the bathtub, Newton observing the fall of an apple during an epidemic, penicillin, the microwave, Velcro, Teflon, the Veg-O-Matic—Dot discovered her path to greatness more or less by accident. Here's my semi-apocryphal version of the Dot origin story. There were people in the family room in Arizona and the NFL was on the big screen.

Dot was in the kitchen preparing snacks. That's what North Dakota women do. On a whim, she decided to "spice up" the bowl of pretzels by sprinkling them with a few "secret spices and herbs," now under national and international trademark review. She served her concoction to universal applause and *voila*—she became a snack-food billionaire. The company has been astonishingly successful. For a couple of years Dot's Homestyle Pretzels were available in the Dakotas and part of Minnesota. Then, suddenly, they were all over the northern Great Plains and the Midwest. And now there are Dot's pretzels all over America, far from the Houston Super Bowl Vortex, and here come new products—a tart Southwestern variation, a candy bar, and a fish and chicken crumble of bits and pieces no doubt left over from the packaging process. Shore Lunch Fish Breading, gird your loins.

One recent fawning newspaper article included the following sentence: "Dot Heinke is a disrupter." Yes, Dorothy Heinke invented broadcast news while Hitler's Germany was crushing all of Europe. Yes, she reported one of the most significant stories of twentieth-century history. Yes, her plane went down over Burma and she managed to keep a group of survivors alive for more than a week while surrounded by a tribe of headhunters. Yes, she wrote one of the finest autobiographies of the twentieth century. Yes, she helped America heal from the catastrophe of John F. Kennedy's assassination in Dallas on November 22, 1963. Yes, her memoir, *The Princess and the Pretzel*, gets to the heart of the North Dakota identity. Meanwhile, poor Eric Sevareid is in sad eclipse. I don't resent Dot's ingenuity or her business acumen. Sure, I wish I had had the genius to sprinkle a little mustard compound on some pretzels and serve them to my family during the Super Bowl, but a man has to know his limitations. I know with certainty that I don't have the right stuff.

When I entertain guests from elsewhere—many of whom come just for the absurdity of visiting North Dakota—I invariably take them to Velva (on our way to other attractions). I make one of them go to the counter of the huge Cenex convenience store, which is a gas station, grocery store, fast food kiosk, limited auto parts store, and bait shop rolled into what in my childhood would have been known as a "gas station." My guest buys some gum or a bag of chips and then asks, innocently, at the till, "Who's the most famous person ever to come from Velva?" There is not a moment's hesitation. "Dot Heinke of Dot's Pretzels." If my guests follow up with a question about Eric Sevareid they get puzzled looks. Did he play for the Vikings? Dot's pretzels proliferate on special displays in every direction throughout the store. "I mean she didn't exactly invent them here—it was at their winter home in Phoenix—but she's from here. She still comes here sometimes." Right.

God bless North Dakota's pretzel Dot Vinci.* But if you are a backwater state without a lot of bragging rights, and Eric Sevareid came from among you, you want to make a big deal about that every opportunity you ever get. Roger Maris and Eric Sevareid. Roger Maris, Angie Dickinson, and Eric Sevareid. These are serious cultural icons. Not to mention Theodore Roosevelt.

Not only does our ignorance of this colossus of American journalism say something pretty ironic about how a self-conscious wannabe state makes the case for itself in the national arena, but it also signifies the shallowing of American culture, and radical presentism. Presentism is often defined as judging previous eras by *our* standards of enlightenment, but it also means *living completely in the present with open indifference to the traditions of the past.* If Sevareid were alive, he would put together a great and ironic commentary about losing his fame to Dot Heinke—and Kim Kardashian, and Tucker Carlson. He'd quote from Herodotus and Cicero, say wonderfully wry and self-effacing things about the tribe of journalists in general and himself in particular, and reflect on the mustard-spiced pretzel

---

*   Note: I actually love Dot's pretzels and I have deep admiration for Dot, too. I don't know why I am snarking at her. Somebody had to stick up for poor Eric Sevareid!

as an American phenomenon. I would love to hear him finish up by turning and saying, "Walter?"

North Dakotans are conservatives with a small *c*—and also increasingly outspoken Conservatives with a capital *C*. They are suspicious and often derisive of things that slip in from the east and west coasts of America. They take pride in their devotion to common sense, the basic rhythms of life, and all that is practical. They are uncomfortable with metaphysics, theory, and abstraction. If you quote Archimedes, "Give me a lever and a place to stand and I will move the earth," North Dakotans don't read that as a metaphor; they want to figure out precisely where you would have to place the lever.

North Dakotans believe in education, including higher education, but they want it to be about skill-building and workforce training, not the philosophy of Kierkegaard or the epic similes of *Paradise Lost*. If his biographer Henry Randall said Thomas Jefferson "could calculate an eclipse, survey an estate, tie an artery, plan an edifice, try a cause, break a horse, dance a minuet, and play a violin," North Dakotans, particularly those who grew up on farms, can weld a bead, strip an engine, wire a kitchen, plumb a sewer line, throw up drywall, install a carpet, change the oil, the tires, and the engine rings, kill a varmint, organize a church supper, apply for a grant, teach Sunday school, and pour a concrete slab. And that's just the women! The practical competence of the average North Dakotan is still breathtaking. They can pull a calf as readily as pull an all-nighter. When something goes wrong, they don't spend any time wringing their hands. They just put on their overalls and galoshes and get to work.

Like other rural Americans, North Dakotans love the internal combustion engine. Although kayaking, canoeing, cross country skiing, and bicycling have grown in popularity in the past thirty years, North Dakotans overwhelmingly prefer the jet ski, the snowmobile, the ATV, the motorcycle, the power boat, the riding mower, and the pontoon. They like to roar around, and they are not overly fastidious about mufflers. I have a neighbor who has one of everything, and special bays in his four-car garage to store it all. The house is an appendage of the garage, almost an afterthought.

On election night, when they show the map of blue and red America, the nation's vast redneck crescent embraces the Deep South, the Great Plains, and some of the northern Mountain West. Within the state of North Dakota, the only blue counties are in Indian Country. Fargo may be heading towards blue but for the moment it is still reliably red. North Dakota has almost always been conservative but at some point following the arrival of recently deceased Rush Limbaugh on the national stage (1988), and with the advent of silo'd cable news channels (Fox vs. MSNBC), North Dakota became a deep red state. In 2016 Donald Trump won 63 percent of the vote in North Dakota, which tied with Kentucky, and was just behind Trump's best states of Oklahoma, West Virginia and Wyoming. In his 2020 bid for re-election, the now twice impeached Trump's standing among North Dakotans deepened, garnering 65 percent of the vote.

In the past twenty years, what had before been North Dakota's skepticism of the national government assumed virulent form. The words "liberal" and "progressive" became so loaded with contempt that they reminded one of the snarly lip of former Alabama governor and presidential candidate George Wallace. Cheered on by Limbaugh, Sean Hannity, Laura Ingraham, Mark Levin, Michael Savage, Bill O'Reilly, and more recently Tucker Carlson, the majority of North Dakotans have embraced the politics of outrage, grievance, and resentment.

As the brand of rural Republicanism took on this tone and edge all over America, the people who live in North Dakota simply joined the parade. They adopted the talking points of the conservative pundits, but I believe it has more to do with what North Dakotans regard as "the bankruptcy of liberalism" and the "failure of the welfare state" than with the hard-right policies of the Conservative Movement.

Take firearms, for example. North Dakotans are comfortable with guns. The majority of North Dakota men, and quite a percentage of women, have been around guns all of their lives, have learned how to use them, have taken gun safety courses, and tens of thousands, perhaps hundreds of thousands, have hunted for birds or deer. Therefore, all discourse about gun restriction annoys North Dakotans, indeed offends them, in part because it seems to question their basic competence. And above all else, North Dakotans are competent. Even though more North Dakotans are on food stamps, WIC health programs, Medicaid, and other federal assistance programs than they like to admit, the longstanding mythology that "I'd work at McDonald's before I ever got on food stamps," remains deeply rooted in the North Dakota character.

The hypocrisy of the farmers and ranchers who sneer at the welfare state and yet cheerfully cash their farm program checks is palpable, but it does not cause the recipients to lose any sleep. The massive common sense of the North Dakota people makes them openly contemptuous of what they style "political correctness," a term which in rural America covers a great deal of ground. Even being told that Asians prefer to be called *Asians* rather than *Orientals* and that we should probably say *Romani* rather than *Gypsies* makes most North Dakotans snort and paw the ground. Like all others, North Dakotans don't wish to be told what they should do or think or speak, what their political attitudes should be, and they particularly resent the implication that they are backward, bigoted, unenlightened, or racist. Most North Dakotans are none of these things.

Such statements as, "It's not surprising then that they get bitter, they cling to guns or religion or antipathy to people who aren't like them," or "You could put half of Trump's supporters into what I call the basket of deplorables," serve only to harden North Dakotans against "the liberal agenda," and no amount of argument will convince them that these statements should not be permitted to sum up all you need to know about important national figures like Barack Obama and Hillary Clinton.

Thus, when the NCAA insists that the UND sports teams change their name from "Fighting Sioux," North Dakotan are more angry about being preached at and patronized by outside elites than they are really devoted to the nickname and the mascot. Although that endless and divisive controversy ended in 2012, you still see *Fighting Sioux Forever* bumper stickers, sweatshirts, and other regalia on a regular basis. When Blue America decried the treatment of the Lakota at Standing Rock during the calamitous DAPL pipeline crisis of 2016-17, the condemnation by outsiders hardened the attitudes of far more North Dakotans than it convinced. In fact, the pipeline crisis probably represents a significant setback in White-Indian relations in North Dakota. North Dakotans are on the whole skeptical (at varying levels) about campus assault, date rape, sexual harassment, bullying, and hostile workplace claims, and if the victim was wearing a low-cut blouse or had five drinks before returning to the young man's dorm room or apartment, most North Dakotans are going to question her judgment more often than take her side.

As North Dakota got rich with the Bakken Oil Rush, all of these attitudes hardened. In bars and coffee houses during the oil boom, I heard North Dakotans sneer at the way other states are governed, especially Minnesota, a significantly more liberal state with a strong conservation ethic, sometimes referred to in North Dakota as "the People's Republic of Minnesota." At some point North Dakotans forgot that it was God who put shale oil under our prairies (rather than under Minnesota or South Dakota), and that we were reaping the benefit of technologies that were not developed in state and could never have been funded using North Dakota monies alone.

One has to acknowledge these attitudes if you want to understand North Dakota. North Dakotans are a proud, independent people who live in one of the most difficult and unglamorous states in the union. Since we have all pulled ourselves up by the bootstraps (we think), or are descended from those who did, our attitude is, "Hey, if I can pay my bills on time, so can you. If I can work three jobs, why should I subsidize your food stamps? I milk 75 cows twice a day and you expect me to guarantee your health care?"

North Dakotans are famous for their work ethic. They always show up. They always work hard. They are uncomplaining. They usually do more than whatever is required. Companies all over America like to hire North Dakotans because they are polite, respectful, and they have an exemplary work ethic. High schools still routinely give awards to students who have never missed a day of class in twelve years. Because North Dakotans possess and cherish these habits, they are disdainful of anyone who appears to be taking advantage of the American welfare system. This is one reason why White North Dakotans have a hard time showing much sympathy for Native Americans who don't seem to be able to get their lives together. White North Dakotans generally swear they don't have a racist bone in their bodies, and they have no prejudice against American Indians, but they cannot understand why so many of them have problems with alcohol, drugs, domestic violence, suicide, and the law. Most North Dakotans not only reject the charge that America perpetuates structural or systemic racism, but most refuse to believe such a thing even exists.

During the pipeline crisis, one of my professional colleagues said she will be able to take the Lakota Indians more seriously when they stop living in squalor and molesting their children. Nothing that I could say, nothing her preacher could say, nothing the Pope could say, would convince her that this is an inadequate, incomplete, insufficiently generous, and indeed racist way to look at the social problems on the Standing Rock Indian Reservation—or any other.

North Dakotans don't much like to be reminded that the state has always been heavily subsidized by the federal government, from the gargantuan land grants that enabled the transcontinental railroads, the military occupation of North Dakota as we were wresting it from its aboriginal sovereigns, the largess of the Homestead Act and its cousins the Timber Act and the Desert Lands Act, the massive federal relief programs that almost alone made it possible for North Dakotans to survive the Dust Bowl and Great Depression, federally funded rural electrification, the Jones-Bankhead Act that permitted bankrupt badlands ranchers to remain on the land they had lost to the banks and keep the home place in fee simple (no such safety net for ND insurance companies, car dealerships, restaurants, or janitors), the massive subsidies of the US Farm Program, the federal highway assistance programs, including the Interstate Highway System (1955-1975), federal disaster relief for floods, drought, hail, and the occasional tornado, the construction of Garrison and Oahe Dams, the subsidization of the coal industry, particularly the nation's only Coal Gasification Plant at Beulah, the ongoing US military presence in North Dakota, federal aid to North Dakota's universities and colleges, and even to K–12 public school education.

In fact, North Dakota has consistently taken in more dollars from the federal treasury than it has sent there in taxes. The myth of the self-reliant rugged individualist is not nonsense, but there is something pretty hollow at its core not just in North Dakota, but throughout the American West. And yet, not one in a hundred North Dakotans will admit the truth, perhaps not one in ten thousand.

Almost all North Dakotans have been on a gravel road. Most North Dakotans have driven across the state in one direction or the other. A solid majority of North Dakotans have been to the badlands, by which many actually mean the tourist town of Medora, which is *in* the badlands but is not really *of* the badlands. Dramatically fewer North Dakotans have been to Grassy Butte or Rhame or even Stanley. Many North Dakotans of the Red River Valley look down on the rest of the state. They believe their cultural superiority is all that keeps North Dakota from becoming a haven for White nationalists and the posse comitatus. When they venture west of Valley City, they joke about it with their friends as if they were visiting the Australian outback. For many legislators and bureaucrats, the worst thing about serving in government is having to live in Bismarck. But for the people of Hettinger and Halliday, Bismarck is Mecca.

If you are from Minnesota, you can make the case that you are from a cool and remarkable state, even though the larger world may not entirely agree. Most Americans have heard of Lake Wobegon, Garrison Keillor's gently satirical fictitious town ("that time forgot") out on the Minnesota prairie. Everyone knows about the Minnesota Vikings. Most people know of Minnesota's two vice presidents, Hubert Humphrey (1964-68) and Walter Mondale (1976-80). And Al Franken, the smartass *Saturday Night Live* comedian who for a time was a US Senator from Minnesota. Those with literary sophistication know that Sinclair Lewis (1885-1951) started his life in Sauk Center, Minnesota, and recast it as the burg of humbug and philistinism in his 1920 novel *Main Street*. Bob Dylan (née Robert Zimmerman) started his life up in Hibbing on the iron range in northern Minnesota and Prince (née Prince Rogers Nelson) grew up in Minneapolis. F. Scott Fitzgerald was born in St. Paul. Two Minnesotans have been awarded the Nobel Prize for Literature, first Sinclair Lewis (1930), most recently Bob Dylan in 2016.

North Dakota has never produced a president or vice president. Theodore Roosevelt spent a few years romancing the badlands of Dakota Territory (1883-87) before he became the undisputed heavyweight champion of our national politics. We cling to his fame and though he spent less than one full year of elapsed time out in the Little Missouri River Valley, we cherish his declaration that he would never have become President of the United States had it not been for his time in North Dakota (1910). None of our US senators since William L. Langer has achieved national fame. Some prominence, no fame. Our celebrities (like actors Angie Dickinson and Josh Duhamel) grew up in North Dakota and then hurtled away to where the action is. Not that national celebrity is much of a criterion of state affiliation or affection. We know the Kardashians are from California, but from where does Meryl Streep hail? Or Jimmy Kimmel?

So how do you write about a bland place that has low state self-esteem and an ice chip on its shoulder? It is possible. Kent Haruf's *Plainsong* is a powerful novel about the eastern plains of Colorado and except for a few geographic details it might just as well have been written about North Dakota. Larry Watson had intended to give his 1993 novel *Montana 1948* a North Dakota title, but his publisher advised him not to doom the book to the remainder bin. Almost any of Ivan Doig's seventeen books could have been written about western North Dakota. Linda Hasselstrom's outstanding prose and poetry, including *Windbreak: A Woman Rancher on the Northern Plains*, could have been written in western North Dakota, but they were not. This list could go on at some length. O.E. Rølvaag's *Giants in the Earth* (1927) is arguably the greatest work of fiction about the North Dakota pioneer experience, but its fictional homestead was set in South Dakota. If it has any competition for best Great Plains novel, the crown may belong to Willa Cather's *My Antonia*, which the eminent British critic John Carey regards as perhaps the greatest work of American fiction—period. Like many of Cather's other novels, *My Antonia* is set in south central Nebraska, but it speaks powerfully to our ethnic pioneer experience. Name the greatest work of North Dakota fiction, or for that matter the greatest North Dakota book?

So what is it about North Dakota? Why is our state literature so weak? North Dakotans are just as smart as their neighbors, and maybe better educated. Creative talent is presumably a rain that falls evenly over the landscape of the heartland. Name five active North Dakota novelists, poets, or essayists. Well, Tom Isern, Louise Erdrich, Debra Marquart, Melanie Hoffert . . . only Isern actually lives in the state. Montana has a richer state literature than North Dakota. Think of James Welch, Annick Smith, Bill Kittredge, cowboy poet Paul Zarzyski, Ivan Doig, Rick Bass, Daniel Kemmis, Thomas McGuane, Stephenie Ambrose Tubbs. . . Minnesota has a richer state literature than North Dakota. Even South Dakota (!) has a richer literature than North Dakota: O.E. Rolvaag, Elizabeth Cook-Lynn, Paul Goble, Linda Hasselstrom, Frederick Manfred, Kathleen Norris, Dan O'Brien, Sally Roesch Wagner. Why should this be? To be sure, North Dakota has produced great writers. Larry Woiwode's *Beyond the Bedroom Wall* is arguably the greatest novel by a living North Dakotan, and Louise Erdrich's many novels, beginning with *Love Medicine*, represent major North Dakota literature, if you wish to confine them to that category. There are other serious writers in North Dakota, too, and more coming. I do not in any way mean to diminish their achievement. But the point is undeniable, that North Dakota is surrounded by states with a richer *state* culture than we have.

Why should this be so?

To create literature about a place, you have to have something to write about. You have to find your homeland interesting. You have to believe that there are stories here worth telling. You have to have cultural confidence. And you have to graduate from the Laura Ingalls Wilder school of prairie storytelling, where many of our novelists are still stuck, because that era is over forever. It was something of a cliché even when it was closer to the actual experience of Dakotans than it is now. North Dakota is not a family farm state anymore, and yet most North Dakota writers want to sing the song of the lost agrarianism, not whatever it is that North Dakota has become or is becoming. Since we have not yet developed a post-agrarian narrative about who we are, why we live here, what matters to us, and how we relate to this place, the stories we tell are stories that could be told anywhere.

It is often said as a kind of wry joke that when basic institutions were being handed around at statehood, the founding fathers of Bismarck had the choice of securing either a university or the state prison and, as the character Grail Knight says in *Indiana Jones and*

the Last Crusade, "They chose poorly." But it is not a joke at all. If Bismarck had insisted upon a university and let the prison be located somewhere else, the story of North Dakota would be quite different. The fact that the state's two flagship universities are located on the Minnesota border is little short of a cultural catastrophe for North Dakota.

The University of North Dakota had 14,648 students in 2019, North Dakota State University 14,432. Together that constitutes 53 percent of the college and university students of North Dakota. Both of those large institutions are within five miles of Minnesota. UND has a faculty of 823, NDSU of 858. By the third decade of the twenty-first century only a small minority of those professors had a research interest that focused on North Dakota. If you are a historian but your field is medieval gender construction in Poland, you are not advancing North Dakota studies. If you profess literature and your field is the poetry of Samuel Taylor Coleridge, you are not paying any significant attention to North Dakota culture.

There is also the paradox of excellence. Because of the glut of PhDs in the United States, and too few academic jobs to absorb the annual crop, applicants swarm toward every available university job in the country no matter how obscure or uninviting the zip code. It is not unusual for a university in the heartland to receive several hundred applicants for a single starting faculty position, at a salary that makes for a somewhat pinched economic life. This is good news for North Dakota's institutions of higher learning. It is a buyer's market. The days when rural universities had to take what they could get are long over. The vast majority of today's applicants were not raised in North Dakota or on the Great Plains. They come to Grand Forks or Fargo not because their life goal was to live and work on the prairie, but because that's where they were offered a job. They often find it difficult to adjust to the climate (including the social climate) of North Dakota, the flatness of the Red River Valley, the low population density of the state, the instrumental pragmatism of the students, the dearth of amenities they came to take for granted at the prestigious institutions where they studied, and the lack of ethnic and cultural diversity. They decry the provincialism and the naïveté of many of their students. Usually but not always privately, they make fun of students' backgrounds and their accents, their conservative politics, and their immunity to urban culture.

And, frankly, these faculty members are not very interested in North Dakota. They regard their university as a kind of city-state within a host community that is acceptable to them but not exciting. The major associations and loyalties of their lives remain elsewhere. They lean out, not in. Their families and closest friends live elsewhere. Most of them have research interests that have nothing to do with North Dakota. Most of them venture seldom, if at all, into the North Dakota heartland. If they go anywhere within the boundaries of North Dakota, it is usually to another university, to the state capital in Bismarck, or possibly to Medora, North Dakota's premier tourist destination (and then usually for a conference). Most of these scholars eventually warm up to their host communities, and they learn to appreciate the warmth, good sense, and integrity of North Dakotans. They tell good-humored jokes about their plight. They say they pine for a proper bagel. Most of their time is spent with students, other faculty members, and in the lonely world of reading, grading, and academic research. No matter where they come from, however, they tend not to take their vacations in North Dakota—that would actually seem absurd to them, because they are not convinced there is anything much to see in North Dakota besides empty land, grain silos, windmills, bland small towns, and people for whom the life of the mind is not a priority, including, of course, the students whose parents and grandparents pay their academic salaries. Grateful though they are to have jobs in the profession for which they trained so hard, many, perhaps most, are ready to be plucked out for a better gig elsewhere if such opportunity should come.

The purpose of higher education is not merely to prepare young people to be accountants, schoolteachers, pharmacists, bankers, farmers, nurses, lawyers, and doctors. It is also to help them become complete human beings, responsible adults, good citizens, critical thinkers, and well-informed Americans. Higher education within our boundaries should also help to complete their formation as North Dakotans. Otherwise, why not send them to university in Iowa or Massachusetts or California? If the professoriate has no particular interest in the history, tradition, culture, geography, demographics, biology, or identity of North Dakota, does not know that North Dakota has a socialist state bank and a socialist state elevator created during a brief era of intense agrarian discontentment, does not know about the Pick-Sloan Plan that tamed the Missouri River at the expense of the sovereignty and lifeways of the Mandan, Hidatsa, Arikara, and Lakota Indians, does not know of the late-frontier cattle boom in the Little Missouri River Valley, a miniature surge of cowboy and ranch life that brought Theodore Roosevelt to Dakota Territory, does not know about Lawrence Welk or Lewis and Clark or Roger Maris, does not read the novels of Larry Woiwode or Louise Erdrich or the poetry of Thomas McGrath, has no understanding of the immigrant waves of Germans from Russia, Norwegians, Fins, Swedes, Germans from Germany, and Ukrainians who came to the northern prairies under the terms of the 1862 Homestead Act, has no understanding of the significance of the battles of Whitestone Hill or Killdeer Mountain, then how can they understand the students they teach, and how can they help those students understand who they are, where they come from, and whereunto they are headed, as one Renaissance humanist put it? Why would we let university faculty take our hard-earned tax dollars but deliberately ignore who we are?

As a taxpayer, I don't particularly mind paying professors who are not doing North Dakota studies, but I do resent paying individuals who are indifferent to North Dakota or even derisive of North Dakota. I believe every new hire at the universities across the state should include two requirements. First, every new professor should be required to write a memo on the subject, *What does my research have to do with North Dakota, and how might I incorporate North Dakota's history, geography, economy, and culture into my classroom teaching?* It is not that everyone could make such a determination, particularly during the first year or two or residency in the state, but it would encourage new hires to think about these questions in a creative way. It might plant a seed. Second, I believe every new hire should be required to take a North Dakota Naturalization Course, including several field trips, and not merely to Medora to sit in the Burning Hills Amphitheater to watch the *Medora Musical* and make an obligatory loop around the South Unit of Theodore Roosevelt National Park. The naturalization course would feature lectures by North Dakota historians and cultural leaders, require a three-day retreat during which these new faculty members would read a significant North Dakota book together (e.g., Louise Erdrich's *Love Medicine* or Tom McGrath's *Letters to an Imaginary Friend*; Custer's *My Life on the Plains* or *The Rachel Calof Story* or Ann Marie Low's *Dust Bowl Diary*). Some of the graduates of this orientation course will perhaps become naturalized and not merely accidental North Dakotans. All of them will be better professors and student advisers thanks to this orientation.

On October 12, 1960, Pulitzer Prize-winning novelist John Steinbeck crossed the Missouri River on the great old Memorial Bridge on US 10 between Bismarck and Mandan. It took his breath away. "Here is where the map should fold," he wrote. "Here is the boundary between east and west. On the Bismarck side it is eastern landscape, eastern grass, with the look and smell of eastern America. Across the Missouri on the Mandan side it is pure west, with brown grass and water scorings and small outcrops. The two sides of the river might well be a thousand miles apart."

Steinbeck's insight was more telling in 1960 than it is today. The lands west of Bismarck-Mandan are less distinct from the rest of the state today than they were then. Drought resistant grains, including corn, can now be planted west of the Missouri River with success. In Steinbeck's time only the most optimistic farmers dared grow corn in western North Dakota and then not very often. Even wheat was only planted every other year, the rest of the land left in summer fallow. Today's western North Dakota is also more manicured than it was then. If you want to fold the map where East and West meet, you'd need to put the fold at Glen Ullin or Hebron now. Traveling East to West on I-94, you see your first real butte at Crown Butte, twenty miles west of Bismarck. You see your first oil derricks a few miles west of Dickinson. There is some broken country between Bismarck and Dickinson, especially on old US 10 south of the interstate highway, but you don't really see broken country until you have driven west of Dickinson.

Steinbeck's startling experience as he drove his truck camper across the Missouri River bridge is one of the best reminders that North Dakota is really two states, or sub-states: one quasi-Midwestern, one quasi-Western; one abundant in Jeffersonian till agriculture, the other best suited to grazing livestock. Thomas Jefferson's America and Theodore Roosevelt's America meet somewhere west of the Missouri River. You could legitimately create a state decal with two men shaking hands in the middle of that bridge, one wearing cowboy boots and a Stetson hat, the other work boots and a grain cap. The cowboy half of North Dakota has a more romantic mythology—a gentle introduction to the Old West—but the eastern half of the state is where the power and money and population reside. Only two of North Dakota's colleges and universities are located west of the Missouri—Dickinson State University and Williston State College—both with limited enrollments. Nine colleges and universities are situated east of the Missouri River. As with most Midwestern places, eastern North Dakota has no romantic mythology, no easy to define identity. The West has cowboy poetry gatherings, rodeo, colorful costuming, what's left of a set of courtly manners borrowed from the pages of Owen Wister's *The Virginian*, even a distinctive lingo ("my knee's all stove up"). No such culture in the east, no farmer poetry gatherings, no distinctive garb, no horse for Desperado to ride off on into the sunset. And the sunset, by the way, is located in the West, not Duluth or St. Cloud.

If North Dakota were one of these two basic cultures or the other, but not both, the state's identity would be stronger. My point is that North Dakota suffers in its identity and its cultural confidence because we are neither West (lots of space, not so many people) nor Midwest, but stuck in between.

If you had to nominate quintessential North Dakotans, who would make the short list? In the minds of the 125,000 residents of Fargo (with 40,000 more next door in Moorhead), there is Fargo, and then there is . . . the rest of North Dakota, with Grand Forks given a kind of honorable mention with an asterisk. So now we have three North Dakotas: West Dakota (with the badlands), East Dakota (farms), and Fargo the city-state. In my opinion, Fargo deserves its pride and its outsized sense of itself, and though it wears that identity in a somewhat condescending and off-putting way, there is no denying that it has reached a cultural takeoff point which permits it to do all sorts of things, to encourage all sorts of things, to tolerate all sorts of things, and to aspire to all sorts of things that would be unthinkable anywhere else in North Dakota, with the possible exception of Grand Forks (thus the asterisk). Whether the things that Fargo can now create, support, or permit have anything much to do with North Dakota is a very interesting (and sobering) question. The national cultural commentators who visit Fargo to observe its vibrancy and who decide to rent a car to go see some of the rest of North Dakota, will be warned, superciliously, to lower their expectations as they cross the diversion channel of the Sheyenne River. You're heading to the outback, just so you know. You like Applebee's?

The North Dakota identity problem has still another famous

marker, located within shouting range of Steinbeck's Missouri River. The 100th Meridian bisects the state. It runs north to south from Dunseith to Harvey to Tuttle to Steele, and then on into South Dakota (Pierre), Nebraska (North Platte) and beyond. It's not important from a Greenwich, base meridian, point of view, but the hundredth divides the United States into two near halves, and it serves as the line of demarcation between American lands that get enough rain to produce crops eight or nine years out of ten, and the other half of the country (the West), the land "beyond the hundredth meridian," as historian and novelist Wallace Stegner put it, where irrigation is necessary (or certainly desirable) to enable stable till agriculture. The hundredth meridian was designated as the frontier between East and West by the one-armed Civil War veteran, water czar, and visionary John Wesley Powell (1834-1902), who determined in the 1870s that traditional Jeffersonian agricultural practices would break down west of that line of longitude. In his stunning—and systematically ignored—government monograph, the *Arid Lands Report* of 1878, Powell recommended that Mr. Jefferson's rectangular survey grid system be replaced in the arid and semi-arid West by a sensual long lot system so that no homestead parcel could ever be deeded out that did not have direct access to a watercourse. Powell suggested that we abandon Jefferson's blockish template for new states in favor of what he called "watershed commonwealths," holistic basin resource republics (i.e., irregularly shaped states) that could manage and distribute their scarce water resources under the aegis of a single overarching jurisdiction, and not engage in endless interstate water conflicts (think of the Colorado River wars between Arizona and California) that make it harder to formulate reasonable resource decisions. Powell actually ventured to the four new states of 1889, to their constitutional conventions, to warn North Dakota, South Dakota, Montana, and Washington, that they should plan for water-scarce development and not fall into the one-size-fits-all development pattern that dated back to Jefferson's *Plan for the Government of the Western Territories* of 1784. Powell addressed the North Dakota Constitutional Convention on August 5, 1889. He said, "All other wealth falls into insignificance compared with that which is to come from these lands from the pouring on them of the running streams of this country. Don't let these streams get out of the possession of the people. If you fail in making a constitution in any other respect, fail not in this. Take lessons from California and Colorado. Fix it in your constitution that no corporation—no body of men—no capital can get possession and right to your waters. Hold the waters in the hands of the people." All four new states listened politely and then politely ignored Powell's passionate recommendations.

Major Powell was right about watershed commonwealths. The fact that the Red River basin is shared by two countries and five *states* creates a significant amount of jurisdictional tension. North Dakota and Minnesota sometimes dispute how to handle the periodic floods on the Red River. They disagree about how to facilitate the freshening of the Red River with imported waters from the Missouri-Mississippi basin. It's much more tense up at the forty-ninth parallel. The United States and Canada, particularly the province of Manitoba, disagree significantly about the wisdom of trans-basin diversions—i.e., the lifting of water from the Missouri River (one basin), and sending it over the low continental divide (1490 feet, just east of Jamestown) to the Red or Sheyenne River (a second basin). Powell opposed these transfers because they tend to leave one jurisdiction high and dry in order to deliver water to the other (think of Owens Valley and voracious Los Angeles, ca. 1905). If it had not been for Canadian objections, the ill-fated Garrison Diversion Project (also trans-basin) would probably have been completed in the last three decades of the twentieth century. The North Dakotans who live along the Souris River (a tributary of a tributary of the Red) sometimes question the manner in which Saskatchewan handles flows during high-water years. If the entire Red River basin had been fashioned into one of Powell's watershed commonwealths, basin management would have been much easier.

In Powell's ideal world, North Dakota would not have been a nearly rectangular state. The Missouri-Mississippi portion (south and west) would have been one state, or part of one bigger state, and the Souris-Red portion (north and east) would have been all or part of a separate state. Something like that nearly happened. The Louisiana Purchase of 1803 gave the United States the entire Missouri watershed, but it did not include the three-fifths of the state that drain north and east toward Lake Winnipeg and Hudson Bay. It wasn't until 1818 that Secretary of State John Quincy Adams negotiated the treaty that gave North Dakota the land that now props up Minot, Wahpeton, Devils Lake, Grand Forks, Fargo, and even Eric Sevareid's Velva.

It has always been fashionable to declare that it would have been wiser to create East Dakota and West Dakota, more or less along Powell's hundredth meridian, rather than North Dakota and South Dakota. It is certainly true that western North and South Dakota have more in common with each other than with the rest of the states to which they are attached, but that configuration would have made East Dakota rich and West Dakota relatively poor. The identity problem of North Dakota would be solved, however. East Dakota (farm country with two great cities, Fargo and Sioux Falls) would be a Midwestern powerhouse. West Dakota (ranch country studded with buttes, with two sets of badlands and the Black Hills) would be a sparsely populated recreational paradise.

In my opinion, it would have been wiser to just leave it at Dakota (no North, no South). There is something romantic about one humongous northern Great Plains state, a kind of US answer to Saskatchewan. Geometric borders are what the Lakota called Medicine Lines—important to White people, impossible for antelope, grizzly bears, pronghorn antelope, buffalo, or Native Americans to discern from clues in the landscape. Only the North Dakota-Minnesota border makes any sense. But the Minnesota-North Dakota border would make no sense to John Wesley Powell, who would wonder why any rational leaders would design states that must share and co-manage a resource as precious and divisive as a flood-prone river with a limited flow 95 percent of the time.

You might sense you were crossing a continental divide up at the roof of the continent in western Montana, Wyoming, and Colorado, but unless you were an expert in hydrology you could never know you were crossing one in North Dakota. Some travelers assume that the green "Continental Divide Elev. 1490" sign between Valley City and Jamestown is some kind of North Dakota joke. It is not. It marks the low, almost imperceptible divide between the waters of the Sheyenne-Red-Hudson Bay watershed and the James-Missouri-Gulf of Mexico watershed. Near Harvey, North Dakota, the headwaters of the James (Gulf of Mexico) and the Sheyenne (Hudson Bay) nearly interlock. It is a fascinating landscape, seldom visited, because North Dakota does a poor job of teaching its young people what extraordinary stories lie within our borders.

Some maps divide North Dakota into three unequal parts: the narrow Red River Valley in the east, the Drift Prairie (essentially the rest of the Red-Souris basin), and the Missouri Plateau. This map could be simplified into two districts: the portion of North Dakota that was scoured by the last glacial episode, the Wisconsin Glacier of approximately 14,000 years ago, and the portion south and west of the Missouri River drainage, which escaped the Wisconsin Ice Sheet.

So who are we now, anyway? Our identity has been the family farm and the nearby village where you go for parts. Our identity has been thrift, caution, and endurance capped at death by prosperity to be enjoyed by our children or theirs, unless they, too, sacrifice their lives to the land. Our identity has been an inferiority complex that has been paradoxically coupled with pride and even a touch of smugness in our knowledge that we live in a difficult, unforgiving place. Our identity has been a quiet, strong, and not outspoken patriotism that has oversubscribed war bonds and recruitment quotas even when we have had serious doubts about the justness of the war (e.g., 1917). Our identity has been a sense of being exploited by out-of-state interests—banks, railroads, milling and mining companies, oil corporations, and the federal government. Our identity has been a satisfaction that we are jacks of all trades and masters of none. Our identity has been that we help to feed the world, that we are not manufacturing the Pocket Fisherman or Ginsu Knives, but growing wheat and soybeans, sunflowers and corn and potatoes, and beef cattle. I remember a wonderful Farmers Union bumper sticker from my childhood: *Farming is Everybody's Bread and Butter.* We have been—for more than a hundred years—what the poet English Thomas Gray might call mute inglorious Jeffersonians, quietly certain, as Jefferson put it, that we who labor in the earth are the chosen people of God. We knew who we were.

But who are we now? Can we hang on to the most admirable values of our great-grandparents? Do we wish to? If we sought to, what would that look like and how would we achieve it? What has made North Dakota different from other places is the combination of the vast empty plain we lived on and the family farm disciplines, sacrifices, and values that enabled us to survive here. Now that we are awash in prosperity that has nothing to do with lifting a bale or milking a cow with a name, what really is left of the North Dakota spirit? There are those who will say our state identity and character are not inexorably tied to hyper-industrial agriculture, that we can be a decent, lawful, neighborly, hard-working, friendly, and modest people who live and work in cities, who have no vital connection to the land, who travel elsewhere when we travel, and who want the amenities of life that have traditionally not been available in North Dakota. I very much doubt that we can maintain our traditional North Dakota character—it's virtually all we had—as we remove ourselves more and more from the agrarian culture that shaped those values. I get the opportunity to discuss this problem with all of the best minds of North Dakota, a few of them credentialed, most of them just smart citizens from all across the state. When I ask them how we will maintain the North Dakota character in the post-agrarian centuries, they look off and finally stammer out anecdotage about young people who have taken up canning and quilting.

How many of the twenty-somethings of Fargo or Minot or Bismarck spend any significant amount of time out on the raw plains? The emerging North Dakota culture is interiorized, mediated, climate controlled, and uprooted. Can we hang on to the most admirable values of our great-grandparents: thrift, perseverance, the postponement of gratitude, neighborliness, stoicism, and a punishing work ethic? How? Now that we are comparatively rich and exceedingly comfortable, what is the incentive to save scraps of cloth and darn socks? If Amazon Prime will deliver anything you wish free anywhere in rural America, what value is there in cooperating with your neighbors or even communicating with them? When I got married, after all the wedding gifts had been inventoried, my wife and I simply ordered the rest of our china to fill out twelve full place settings. My grandmother looked at us across the dinner table and said, "Your grandfather and I did not complete our china until we had been married for seventeen years."

The long-term problems of rural America probably cannot be solved. Fewer and fewer people are needed to produce our food supply. As the number of farms declines and the birth rate among farmers plummets, the number of towns and villages needed to service the farm population begins to collapse. In previous generations farmers had larger families partly because all Americans had larger families then, but more specifically because it took a significant number of children to do all the chores (a euphemism for hard physical labor) a diversified farm required to succeed, even in a minimal sense. A higher birth rate is not coming back to rural America. The logical conclusion of artificial intelligence (AI) and the hyper-mechanization of agriculture means that eventually North

Dakota's farms will be no more visited than today's oil derricks—occasionally, by roving managers with advanced technical skills but no interest in mounting a combine. With the triumph of robotics, AI, field cams, GPS-driven machinery, drones, and advanced satellite surveillance, the North Dakota farmer will be able to sit on Waikiki Beach and bring in the crop. Such limited on-site labor as is required will be handled by relatively inexpensive contract personnel. O' brave new world. North Dakota farmers will come back to the state to hunt just as out of state hunters do now. Not all of this will happen overnight, but it will happen faster than you think.

The people who remain in North Dakota will mostly live in the cities. The people who remain in Mott, Harvey, Crosby, Langdon, and Napoleon will stay because they prefer rural life, perhaps because they are fearful of urban life, because they need to take care of aging family members, some of whom remained in rural North Dakota to take care of *their* parents and grandparents. Some few will remain because they are too unimaginative to seek happiness elsewhere. Nobody likes to talk about this because it seems harsh and judgmental, but in some instances there is a cultural Darwinism at work. It's a paradox.

The rural people I know are some of the finest individuals I have ever met. But there are fewer and fewer of them and they are being asked to shoulder burdens that are no longer sustainable. We all know the small-town woman who drives a school bus, heads up a dozen civic committees, writes grants for new EMT equipment, organizes the July 4 parade, supervises a scout troop, belongs to a book club, a quilting club, a scrapbooking club, and sings in the Lutheran church choir. That's when she is not performing her day job handling the phones at the First State Bank. Where will we grow her replacements?

I have witnessed the social disintegration of a small rural county elsewhere on the Great Plains, where I have some distant family ties. In the past twenty-five years, I have observed a general collapse of civility, manners, deportment, dress, and compliance with the little, seemingly minor, laws and habits of the heart that hold a community together. Social restraints and social decorum have measurably diminished. Grandmothers talk with a vulgarity they would have washed out of the mouths of their children twenty years ago. Guns have been transformed from a constitutional right to an angry fetish, the only item in the Bill of Rights that seems to have absolute authority. The mainline churches have declined because the local congregations are almost always passionately opposed to the policies of their national synod. Grim, literalist, super-patriotic, and xenophobic churches have sprung up at the edge of town to replace them. People wear their sweats to church on Sundays. Dollar General has moved in. The grocery store is likely to close.

Local culture wars are fought with a viciousness that leaves permanent scars in the community. Whereas thirty years ago these towns were pert and tidy, filled with purposeful people who believed their social decorum set them apart and made it possible to live well in so isolated and windswept a place, now the towns have a certain Appalachian feel. Opioids circulate as freely as Tylenol. Binge drinking is out of control. The local sheriff is powerless to clean up the town. The public schools have abandoned the arts. Almost no solid literature is taught in the classroom because it is felt the students are no longer able to read Orwell or William Golding or even Harper Lee. The wall of separation between church and state is sneered at when it is not openly ignored. It is not poverty that has wrought these changes, but the politics of resentment that has come to dominate rural life. A kind of militant individualism has replaced community feeling. The mottos seem to be, "Don't Tread on Me," and "I Am What I Am: Take it or Frickin' Leave It."

If this portrait of rural America is valid, the small towns of North Dakota are unlikely to attract the kind of vibrant, quirky, socially liberal young people who would be needed for any sort of renaissance. Meanwhile, they are very likely to continue to empty out. Because of this pattern of inexorable rural decline, North Dakota has no choice but to accept whatever economic development comes its way. The tepid resistance to the worst excesses of the Bakken Oil Boom was fueled by fear—that if we looked at it cross-eyed, the industry might pack up and go away. We needed the economic infusion, no matter what the disruptions and negative consequences. At least it wasn't a national nuclear waste dump, though a few of the rogue companies did their best to make it so. The myth that oil development is somehow clean industry silenced any expression of anxiety. Almost nobody wanted the goose that was laying the thick black eggs to go away. To oppose the oil boom was seen as foolishness and perhaps unpatriotic. The downside was a mere feather in the scale of all the obvious benefits accruing to the state of North Dakota.

And so we find ourselves in a serious identity crisis as we move into the middle decades of the twenty-first century. We know who we were, but we are no longer sure of who we are, and we have not really begun to try to formulate who we intend to be at the time of North Dakota's bicentennial in 2089. We are more prosperous (and more populated) than at any previous moment of our history. It would never be wise to discount prosperity and full employment as the baseline of success. But the great question is a variation on William Jennings Bryan's Cross of Gold speech in 1896. If the people who live here prosper but mostly live in the four largest cities, or the ten large-enough cities, and the small-town culture of the state continues to disintegrate and the countryside empties out, will we still be North Dakota? If whatever is left of family farming slips away in the face of robotics and new bonanza megafarms, and we continue to produce the same quantity of food, perhaps more, will we still be North Dakota? If we become more like Maple Grove,

Minnesota, or Aurora, Colorado, but spend less and less time out on the windsweep of the northern plains, will we still be North Dakota?

I feel mostly loss when I contemplate a North Dakota in which the agrarian character has slipped out of our hands and hearts.

ON CERTAIN EFFIGIES:
WITH APOLOGIES TO MONTAIGNE

"These giant effigies were metaphors for the passing away of the American frontier: art preserved in pallid likeness what progress had destroyed."
—Karol Ann Marling, *The Colossus of Roads: Myth and Symbol Along the American Highway*

Remember, there is kitsch even at Troy, the site in northwest Turkey of the great conflict of the ancient Mediterranean world, the Trojan War, the subject of Homer's magnificent epic poem *The Iliad*. Even at Troy there is a cheesy wooden replica of the Trojan Horse, the one the Greeks left on the beach when they pretended to abandon their ten-year siege, and from which—in the middle of the night—the Greek Seal Team Six, led by many-minded Odysseus, emerged to sack Troy and murder most of its men, and such women and children as they did not carry away as slaves. Even there, I have taken a photograph of my mother photo-smiling from one of the upstairs windows in the wooden effigy.

America's roadside effigies really belong to the era of narrow blacktop roads rather than interstate highways and turnpikes. It's much easier to stop to gaze at the World's Largest Pelican in Pelican Rapids, Minnesota, on US 59, than at the World's Largest Prairie Chicken at Rothsay, on I-94, even though it takes much more time to drive through Pelican Rapids than to do the easy-on, easy-off visit to the Prairie Chicken. It was easier to stop at the World's Largest Buffalo in 1957 when you traveled North Dakota along US 10, than ten years later when you had to exit I-94, and thread your way back to the WLB on frontage roads. When children beg their parents to stop at the World's Largest Sandhill Crane at Steele, North Dakota, the request is less frequently granted than it would have been in the US 10 era, when drivers expected to have to gear down through the towns and villages and when stopping did not involve rapid deceleration and the patriarch's grumpiness over loss of time.

What is Mount Rushmore in the Black Hills of South Dakota but another roadside attraction? Or Stone Mountain, Georgia? Or the Big Texas Steak Ranch at Amarillo? Or the world-renowned Wall Drug in South Dakota? Or the World's Largest Chicken Wing in Madeira Beach, Florida, often flanked by live (world's largest?) Hooters Girls? In each case, some local person had an idea—a visionary, an eccentric, a loner, an entrepreneur, a marketing guru, an underappreciated artist. In every instance, at some point somebody convinced the local establishment, often the local boosters, either to get on board or at least get out of the way, and up went the World's Largest Pelican or Prairie Chicken or Jackalope, sponsored by the Lions Club, the Jaycees, the Chamber, the CVB, the Optimists, the Rotarians. They are put up to promote economic development. They are put up to promote tourism. They are put up to "put our town on the map." They are put up to show pride in a local heritage or a local industry. They are put up because someone woke up one morning with a notion. They are put up to separate our hometown from the herd of other nondescript towns in the region. They are put up because a community down the road put something else up and that wounds the pride of our town. They are put up to give writers like Sinclair Lewis something to denounce as boosterism, Babbittry, philistinism, schlock, tastelessness, kitsch, and vulgarity.

Take Mount Rushmore, for example. It did not originate in teary-eyed patriotism. South Dakota historian Doane Robinson (1856-1946) was scrounging around (ca. 1924) for a gimmick to lure tourists to the then-under-visited Black Hills. His original thought was to carve up the tops of the spindly granite Needles in Custer State Park with legendary busts: Annie Oakley, Buffalo Bill Cody, Lewis and Clark, Jim Bridger, Red Cloud, Sitting Bull, Sacajawea, etc. Fortunately, he couldn't raise public support for that reckless, even insane project, which would have resulted in one of the worst viewshed travesties in American history. We owe a great debt to a writer and editor named Cora Johnson of the *Hot Springs Star*, who opposed the plan and convinced her fellow South Dakotans that Robinson's "pop goes the weasel" Hall of Fame scheme would be a desecration of the Black Hills.

Robinson, undeterred, shifted his attention to a place called Mount Rushmore, named for a New York title attorney who had no authentic connection to the Black Hills, and well, you know the rest. "Scenery alone," Robinson wrote, "will not sell the Black Hills to the world." Mount Rushmore now attracts up to three million visitors per year. You can argue that Mount Rushmore is itself a travesty and a desecration, particularly to the Lakota and the Cheyenne, but nobody can deny that it has been a successful investment in South Dakota tourism. The economic impact has been incalculable. The National Park Service alone estimates that Mount Rushmore brings $182.4 million of economic benefit to western South Dakota per annum. Nearby they are still blasting away at the much more ambitious and massive Crazy Horse monument. I have only one question—If you asked Crazy Horse (ca. 1840-September 5, 1877) if he would want millions of tons of a mountain in the Black Hills blown away by White people to memorialize his resistance to the theft of Paha Sapa, what might he say?

The Founding Father John Adams said that the essential human impulse was "the passion for distinction." Each person wants to be the most *something*—the most beautiful, the richest, the most powerful, the best sprinter, the finest ceramicist, the best cake decorator, the smartest person in the room, the best writer, the one with the longest dreadlocks. Understand this, Adams said, and you will be able to marshal the energies (and impulses) of a civilization.

I had better start by declaring my credentials. My parents and I once visited, over a four-day period, ten World's Largest effigies in neighboring Minnesota (Loon, Prairie Chicken, Otter, Walleye, Pelican, Black Duck, and two Paul Bunyans and two of his Blue Ox Babes). I'm ashamed (and delighted) to admit that I have close to a hundred photographs of my father sticking his head into the open mouth of the World's Largest Walleye and fake-sucker-punching, using Renaissance tricks of perspective, the World's Largest Pelican (at Pelican Rapids). We wept to learn that the World's Largest Loon (at Vergas, Minnesota) had in fact been stolen during a Vergas all-class reunion. Local law enforcement officers were unable to solve the crime, but, using cutting-edge forensic procedures, they did announce, as a suspicion only, that the perpetrators might have been intoxicated reunion attendees. The World's Largest Loon was subsequently returned to its plinth on the shores of Vergas Lake. All was forgiven.

It has been a lively and sometimes acrimonious debate in my parents' household whether that was the most pointless vacation we ever took or the greatest, or the greatest because the most pointless. I can only report that we returned to western North Dakota fulfilled but spiritually exhausted. In fact, we were so overwhelmed by the sublimity of what we had seen, what we had together experienced, that we did not have the strength to stop at the World's Largest Buffalo at Jamestown on the way home, which invites an even deeper examination of effigies.

The towns of North Dakota sprang up mostly along railroad lines, more or less arbitrarily situated on the largely undifferentiated landscape of the Great Plains like pins abstractly stuck on a map every ten miles. A few communities are located in inevitable places, especially those sited along rivers: Minot, Williston, Bismarck, Fargo, Grand Forks, Valley City, Jamestown. But most towns were just plopped down on the treeless prairie to service and be served by the emerging transportation infrastructure. If you take North Dakota's main corridor, I-94, running 352 miles east to west, west to east, along the lower third of the state, how do you differentiate Casselton from Tower City, Medina from Steele, Richardton from Taylor? When they were sited between 1870 and 1885, nobody could know that Jamestown would do well but Cleveland and Tappen would never flourish, that Dickinson would become the seventh most populated North Dakota city, but South Heart, Belfield, and Gladstone would never quite reach a launch point. So how do you give your lackluster, arbitrarily located hometown a little edge or a little pride or a little surge of recognition? A touch of competitive advantage? How do you stand out on the vast steppes of America? You give your town a nickname, perhaps. Dickinson called itself the Queen City of the Prairie. Minot called itself The Magic City. Hebron chose Brick City. Or you attract a significant institution: Jamestown got the state mental hospital, Bismarck the state prison (and the capitol), Dickinson and Valley City small public colleges (now universities). Or you throw up the World's Largest Sandhill Crane.

At the moment, the six-hour, 352-mile drive across I-94 in North Dakota (east to west) is broken up by four unmistakable roadside attractions: the World's Largest Buffalo at Jamestown; the World's Largest Sandhill Crane at Steele; two hours later, the World's Largest Holstein Cow in New Salem, and a metallic mesh of ten Geese in Flight at Gladstone, the portal to the Enchanted Highway between Gladstone and Regent. In addition to that, the cross-state motorist has the opportunity to gaze at the deep trough carved by the Sheyenne River at Valley City; at what Meriwether Lewis called "the mighty and

heretofore deemed endless Missouri River" that separates Bismarck
and Mandan and eastern from western North Dakota; at the beginning
of butte and breaks country west of Mandan; and then at Painted
Canyon Scenic Overlook (the badlands) west of Belfield. As you drive
west from Bismarck to the Montana line, you find the landscape more
and more dramatic and compelling. North Dakota is not unique among
Western states in featuring grass mesas known as buttes, but I-94 has
the distinction of passing through one of the finest butte corridors in
America. From the highway (east to west) you have the opportunity to
gaze at Little Heart Butte (south of Mandan), Crown Butte just north of
the freeway (milepost 44), a pair of similar conical buttes (MP 113, the
subject of much adolescent boys' humor), Custer Lookout at Antelope
(MP 91), Young Man's Butte just east of Richardton (MP 88), the Radar
Base buttes just east of Dickinson (MP 64), and then—west of Belfield—
Square Butte (MP 18), Bullion Butte (20 miles to the south), Camels
Hump Butte (MP 11), and Sentinel Butte (MP 10). These buttes may
not be the world's largest, but they are very imposing, and a lover of
Western landscape might be forgiven for regarding them as inherently
and infinitely more beautiful than a fiberglass or metal effigy.

It would have been possible, I suppose, to erect the World's Largest
Cowboy or the World's Largest Theodore Roosevelt at the portal of
the Little Missouri badlands, perhaps even bestriding the freeway in
his "authentic buckskin tunic," but the fact is that where the landscape
is something better than drab (to the uninitiated motorist), such
effigies are not required. It's where the landscape is perceived to be
dull, monotonous, featureless, bland, endless, and flat (all vicious and
oft-repeated slurs against the beauty of the North Dakota prairie and
plains), that giant roadside effigies are erected as a makeweight. A
giant "Teddy" Roosevelt would desecrate the very badlands that altered
the trajectory of his life, but the World's Largest Sandhill Crane does
not do appreciable damage to the landscape around Steele, North
Dakota. In fact, the sculptor of effigies should be advised to craft
something fictional or based on pop culture, and perhaps especially

an outsized fictional critter, rather than a historical figure, because (as we are learning) one man's hero is another's unwoke demon, and public perceptions of figures from our past are changeable. At the time of my writing this chapter, the James Earle Fraser statue of Roosevelt is being plucked down in front of the American Museum of Natural History in New York, and the Proctor equestrian statue of TR has been removed from Roosevelt Park in Portland.

Lest you think the Canadians are somehow more sensible or civilized than Americans (which, of course, they are), remember that Canada displays the World's Largest Chuck the Channel Cat (thirty feet) at Selkirk, Manitoba, on the lower Red River; Mac the Moose at Moose Jaw, Saskatchewan; Ernie the Turtle at Turtleford, Saskatchewan; the World's Largest Mosquito at Komarno, Manitoba; and Wally the Woolly Mammoth at Kyle, Saskatchewan.

North Dakota's neighbors to the east and to the south, Minnesota and South Dakota, have many more roadside attractions. Minnesota may well be the motherlode of World's Largests, and South Dakota has some right to regard itself (amid heavy competition) as the tourist trappiest place in America. Fair enough. But South Dakota also has the Mitchell Corn Palace—truly unique in the world—Wall Drug, and one of America's top ten national icons, Mount Rushmore. Some of the lesser attractions in the Black Hills—Trout Haven, the Cosmos Mystery Area, Reptile Gardens, and Bear Country USA— are both popular and schlocky. So, if you don't care about the sanctity of the Black Hills, have any notion of cultural modesty, subscribe to the idea of unmediated nature, or feel solidarity with the Native Americans whose homeland it was and—according to treaty—still is, you have to see Black Hills tourism as an astounding success story. Cora Johnson may have preferred her Black Hills untrammeled, but for most tourists, the more you trammel America the better they like it. They want a variety of options for miniature golf, Ripley's

Believe It or Nots, haunted houses, go-cart rides, taffy shops, wax museums, and patriotic pageants. If you stripped away everything that a purist might find objectionable in the Black Hills, and erased Mount Rushmore and Crazy Horse Mountain, too, visitation would plummet. The Black Hills-area amenities infrastructure would collapse. From the perspective of the Chamber of Commerce, a visitor is a visitor (within limits). If it takes the national Cabbage Patch Doll Museum or a miniature golf course with a Star Trek theme, bring it. Or the insane Sturgis Bike Rally for that matter.

North Dakota may be said to have a modest array of World's Largests and other roadside attractions. But North Dakota is a modest state.

The World's Largest Earl Bunyon stands vigil on ND 23 just east of New Town, North Dakota. He's about twenty feet tall and about two feet wide. He has seen better days. He was erected by a rancher and cowboy named Fred LaRocque with the help of some first-boom oil field welders in 1958 to protest the impact of Garrison Dam and Lake Sakakawea on the farms and ranches of the Missouri River valley in North Dakota.

Earl was the younger, ectomorphic brother of the more famous Paul Bunyan (of Minnesota and Wisconsin). Why they spelled their last names differently is not clear. If your name is LaRocque you would think you would be fastidious about spelling other people's names correctly.

The original signage at the Earl Bunyon site was written to inform passersby that it was not only Native Americans who were displaced by the rising waters of Lake Sakakawea. In one of the several facelifts the statue has undergone in the last couple of decades, the White man's lament was removed, perhaps because of the whopping disparity between Garrison Dam's impact on White and Native American communities. Garrison Dam indeed disrupted

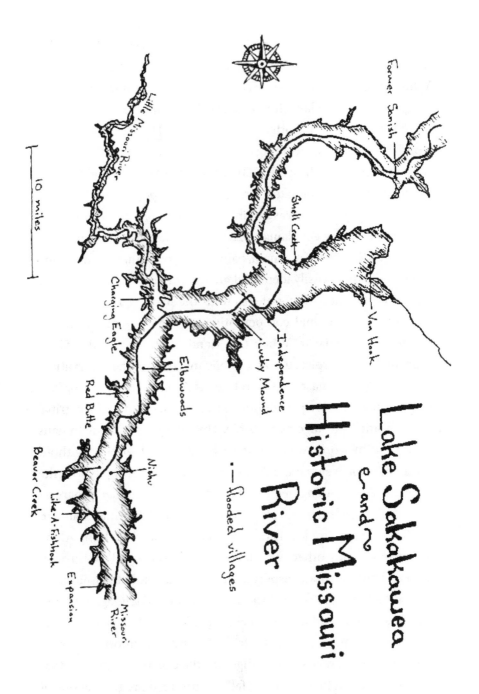

Lake Sakakawea
~and~
Historic Missouri
River

— flooded villages

Garrison Dam was a flood-control project that inundated
the heart of the Mandan, Hidatsa, Arikara world.

some White ranchers, the majority of whom lived on Dawes Act ranches that were carved out of Native American lands and sold to Whites as surplus after Native Americans were *permitted* a window of opportunity to claim homesteads for themselves *on their own land*. Garrison Dam shattered the Mandan, Hidatsa, and Arikara world. Nine villages, including the tribal headquarters at Elbowoods, were drowned. The best 152,360 acres of the Fort Berthold Indian Reservation were inundated forever. A full 80 percent of the 1950s reservation population was forcibly relocated from the bottomlands up onto the windswept plains—325 families. Native American sacred sites were identified in a "wham, bam, thank you ma'am" manner, and some of the more easily identified graves were relocated. The tribes were not informed of any of this until the plans were set in, well, concrete. The eventual compensation package was pitiful, racist, indifferent, colonialist. When the Mandan, Hidatsa, and Arikara expressed their displeasure at a public meeting on the reservation, the dam's White master, General Lewis A. Pick (1890-1956), flew into a rage and vowed to eliminate as many elements of the tribal compensation package as possible. How dare a bunch of Indians whose entire world was about to be shattered forever without consultation or even minimally just compensation get uppity with the US Army Corps of Engineers and the dynamics of human progress?

Earl Bunyan had better pipe down about the White man's lament.

Not long ago I took a visiting friend to tour Garrison Dam. Along with about twenty others we gathered in the lobby, walked through the dam's turbine room, inspected the penstocks and the surge tanks, and peered into the control room, where one middle-aged man in shorts, a T-shirt and a John Deere cap ran the whole system. Our guide was a smart, articulate, friendly, and well-informed young woman who was serving as a ranger for the Corps of Engineers that summer before returning in the fall to a pre-med program at one of our best universities. She knew her kilowatt hours and her acre feet. People asked questions about fish, about how the North American power grid works, about how many homes are powered by Garrison Dam, etc. During the seventy minutes we were there, our competent and gracious docent did not volunteer a single word about American Indians. It was, in fact, the military industrial complex in a confident, relaxed mood. (If a dam designed to conquer the Missouri River, built by the engineering arm of the US Army, led by the general who had just built the Burma Road, is not the military industrial complex, I know not what is.) So, when at the end of the tour our guide asked for the third time if there were *any more questions*, I asked, as innocuously as possible, "Can you tell us anything about the dam's impact on the Indians of North Dakota?" She looked at me for a couple of seconds, averted her eyes, stammered out the beginning of a couple of sentences that didn't go anywhere, paused for a considerable amount of time and then said, "Well, I don't really know anything about that. I think there were some relocations. But I do know that I've heard that the Indians were well compensated." She then made it clear that she had said everything she knew or thought she knew.

As my friend and I drove away to look at the spillway, he said, "How can it be in the year 2019 that this dam tour doesn't proactively have a few careful and sympathetic sentences to say about the Mandan, Hidatsa, and Arikara's displacement and suffering in the aftermath of the construction of Garrison Dam? It's just plain appalling that this is not a commonly understood story in North Dakota history. It's not that she would need to wring her hands and say this never should have happened, but how about a simple acknowledgement that the dam was built on sovereign land belonging to the Three Affiliated Tribes and that while there may have been many winners in the taming of the Missouri River, the Mandan, Hidatsa, and Arikara were perhaps the principal losers?"

I defended the bright young tour leader. She grew up in North Dakota. You could say that the White people of the state are in denial about the colossal devastation of Garrison Dam on Native peoples, but it is much more likely that they are merely indifferent. It's not part of their narrative of North Dakota history. It's unlikely that most White North Dakotans can be made to understand the complexity of American frontier history, of White-Indian relations, of the ongoing confusions of the "domestic-dependent-nation" legal status of sovereign Indian tribes, and of the cost of empire. For most North Dakotans, that was then and those of us alive now bear no responsibility of any sort for what happened between the advent of Lewis and Clark in 1804 and the closing of Garrison Dam in 1953.

Earl Bunyon had better hold his chicken wire and fiberglass tongue.

I have a special affection for Earl Bunyon, who is three times human size, lean as a beanpole, dressed in now pale blue jeans with the cuffs turned up, a white collarless shirt, a raffish blue jean jacket, and a white hat pulled pretty far down over his eyes. He is holding a brand and leaning on a cane. According to LaRocque himself, Earl was fashioned from old wagon wheels (torso), drill stems (arms), chicken wire, and cement. Earl's eyes are so big, open, and blue that he looks a little like an anorexic uncle of Woody the Cowboy from *Toy Story*. The signage says that the model for this Earl was another Earl—Earl Forman. I guess I would have liked to have seen him, the leanest cowpoke in the lower forty-eight.

The World's Largest Sandhill Crane at Steele is without question my favorite roadside effigy in North Dakota. I cannot help loving the crane more than all the rest, even though I love some of them, too. For one thing, like the seven monuments on the Enchanted Highway, the crane was fashioned by a North Dakotan, within the state of North Dakota. Effigies fabricated somewhere else by a fulfillment company, however excellent the workmanship, have less appeal to me than those conceived and executed by actual North Dakotans. "Sandy," the forty-foot-tall, 4.5-ton sandhill crane was built by James

Miller of Arena, North Dakota, in 1998-99. According to the sign erected on the site, "James was a self-taught ironworker and farmer and used his talents to build many farm signs with themes like fishing, hunting, and farm animals."

There is a lovely innocence in the prose of the interpretive sign at the site. It is worth quoting in full but in gulps:

"Sandy" the World's Largest Sandhill Crane was built in 1998-99 by James Miller of Arena, ND in his farm shop.

There's your provenance. Arena is a town of, well, zero people, located thirty miles north of Steele. Whether *Sandy* is the best possible name for the World's Largest Sandhill Crane is open to debate, but we can be reasonably sure it was not suggested by the artist James Miller.

When contacted about building this tall statue, James said he was up *for the task.*

No hesitation. Mr. Miller didn't just agree to do it. He was *up* for it. Nowhere in the Sistine Chapel is there signage letting us know whether Michelangelo volunteered to execute the frescoes or was drafted by Pope Julius II, whether he was *up* for the task or reluctant.

He (Miller) proceeded with drawings, which were then transferred to a steel inner framework. Rolled sheet metal was welded into place and finally the crane was painted. The body was built in one section, the neck and head in another, and the legs were made of pipe. It was fully assembled at his shop, then transferred to the site location on a lo-boy.

What can one say? Of course, he started with drawings! So did Raphael at the Vatican. North Dakotans are a very practical people. We like to know how things were built. We want to know what materials went into Sandy the crane, in what order, and just how and where the finished product was assembled. It might have been easier to transport Sandy in sections and bolt or weld her together on the site. But that is not how the artist James Miller proceeded. We also want to know just how Sandy made the journey of thirty miles from shop to freeway roadside. It was a lo-boy [more often, low-boy]. For those not trained in the macrobiotic mechanical arts, a lo-boy is a strong metal trailer, built on two levels, one not very far above the ground, designed to carry heavy loads, including vehicles. North Dakotans are very much interested in trailers, loads, hitches, and transportation generally.

But what about the many farm signs with themes like fishing, hunting, and farm animals that Miller crafted before he took on the big sandhill crane project? Where is the museum or gallery where we could see some of these works, and have the joy of watching the increasing artistry and mastery of James Miller's career? I would very much like to see some of his other (smaller) art objects. On a second interpretive sign at the site, we learn that Miller was *called upon by others* to create the World's Largest Sandhill Crane. It was not his idea. He merely responded to the artistic summons. In this iteration, we learn more details about the creation.

Rolled sheet metal was welded into place and finally the crane was painted.

It seems very important to the interpreters to assure the visitor that Sandy was complete, fully assembled, and ready to erect, before it ever left James Miller's shop. We know, by contrast, that the World's Largest Holstein Cow in New Salem was not the work of one man; it was not even built in North Dakota; it arrived in New Salem in 1974 from far away, in three sections, which had to be fastened together on site. The second crane sign has a photo of Miller smiling happily wearing glasses and a baseball cap.

But there is more. The committee that commissioned and erected the World's Largest Sandhill Crane thought a good deal about what might be called the *user experience.* Even before the invention of the cell phone selfie, they knew that people who came to the site would want their picture taken with Sandy in the background. The problem is that Sandy is very tall and very thin. If you get far enough back to include all forty feet in the photograph, the crane is too thin to be impressive in the photograph. So how to prevent selfie frustration? The answer was some clever excavation and another sign. The landscape artists scooped out a hollow not far from the base of the effigy, on the north side, and then thoughtfully informed the untrained traveler how to take advantage of this clever bit of landscaping. A small metal sign declares, *For Best Photo Opportunity Photographer Stands in Hole Subject Stands on Hill Crane Will Be in the Background.* Take that, World's Largest Pelican or World's Largest Prairie Chicken! A hollow was made, a text written, and a sign fabricated and installed. Nobody can ever leave the World's Largest Sandhill Crane with a rotten photograph, because its creators have provided explicit directions. I can confirm their wisdom. I have taken photographs of friends at the World's Largest Sandhill Crane from a number of different angles, but from any perspective other than the recommended hollow, the result is disappointing. No other World's Largest can compete with the work of the people of Steele for user accommodation.

I would not trade the signage at Steele for the most sophisticated interpretive paragraphs in the world, written by internationally acclaimed sandhill crane experts or popular culture professors. Do not tell me that for more information I should visit the website of the North Dakota Game and Fish Department. Do not explain that sandhill cranes are among the great birds who use the Central Flyway of North America as their road to and from the Arctic. Do not issue some jargon-dense postmodern screed on the nature of kitsch. I love the signage just as it is. In fact, take the signage away from the site at Steele and you are left with just an impressively large metal sandhill crane. The folks who did this thing humanized it, paid proper respect to the artist, explained how a small committee and a talented local iron worker turned an idea on paper into a significant and extremely charming roadside effigy. This is the North Dakota I love most. It is folksy and a little clunky and not very sophisticated, and above all it is still innocent. This is the North Dakota we must not let altogether slip away. This is what North Dakota means, what gives it its remaining claim to distinction. North Dakota's guilelessness rouses derision among the upper tiers of America's intelligentsia, and it even makes twenty-first century North Dakotans blush a little. But in a world of posture and disingenuousness, it is profoundly authentic, so small town, so sweet, so life affirming.

The World's Largest Holstein Cow (Salem Sue) was erected in New Salem, North Dakota, in 1974. It is thirty-eight feet high, made of fiberglass and weighs plenty. But it is hollow, and it is secured on four sides by strong guy wires. It was the first effigy erected in North Dakota after the World's Largest Buffalo in Jamestown in 1959. The total cost was $40,000. The project was spearheaded by the New Salem Lions Club, which continues to maintain the site.

At one time North Dakota had more than 1,500 dairy farms. As of this writing, there are sixty-six dairy farms left in the state, thirteen of which are located in Morton County. That makes Morton County the dairy capital of North Dakota, thus vindicating Salem Sue. The next densest dairy counties are Stark with seven, Emmons with six, Stutsman with five, Hettinger with four. Those numbers will continue to drop. Once a routine feature on a family farm, a dozen or a score of milk cows in a classical arched barn, dairy herds today have to number in the hundreds to cash flow, and North Dakota is too isolated, with too few people, to be able to compete on a national scale. A few of the remaining dairies in North Dakota are now robotic.

Citizens of New Salem and Morton County take pride in the agrarian tradition in North Dakota. Most of the people who take Exit 31 off of I-94 to visit Salem Sue probably do not make the connection to the history of dairy farming in North Dakota, but they know a good roadside attraction when they see one. The New Salem Lions

Club reckons that between five and ten thousand people make the pilgrimage to Salem Sue per annum. At the entrance station the Lions have installed a cream can with a donation slot, suggested contribution—one dollar. Is that enough to maintain the World's Largest Holstein properly? Yes, says local Lion Allan Tellman, and in some years there is even enough surplus to help fund other Lions Club projects. Lions Club International specializes in funding optical projects, including providing eyeglasses to those in need.

I'm sorry to have to report that the World's Largest Holstein may have been conceived on the plains of North Dakota, but it was fabricated by Sculpture Manufacturing Company in La Crosse, Wisconsin. It was brought to North Dakota in three parts (on low boys?) and assembled on site on a hill north of town.

So far as I know, Salem Sue is the only North Dakota World's Largest that has inspired a ballad. The "Ballad of the Holstein," sung to the tune of "Joy to the World," contains this verse, among others:

We've got the world's largest Holstein cow,
That looks across our fields,
Her presence shows that New Salem grows,
With milk-producer's yields.
With milk-producer's yields,
With milk-producer's yields.

As World's Largest effigies go, the Holstein of New Salem is superbly fabricated. It does not have the slightly lumpy and misshapen feel of many such roadside monuments, which often look as if they were someone's grade school paper-maché project blown up by a gigantic 3-D printer. This one is finely articulated. The all-important milk bag with pinkish white udders is not only anatomically correct, but tasteful in its Brobdingnagian, larger-than-life way. Talk about verisimilitude. The milk veins on the sides of Salem Sue's udder are delicately highlighted with blue paint.

The World's Largest Holstein and the World's Largest Buffalo in Jamestown rise to the level of public art. They were both professionally fabricated to be as realistic as giant fiberglass and cement effigies can be. The World's Largest Sandhill Crane and the monuments along the Enchanted Highway represent a high level of folk art, which is a separate genre.

The two biggest concerns of the civic leaders who gave us Salem Sue are the shelf life of a fiberglass effigy and the prospect of a cow-tipping storm. "When we had this built," Allen Tellman explained, "the cost was forty thousand dollars. With inflation, that might come to one hundred thousand today. But we have done some checking. To replace the cow would cost upwards of a million dollars. Well, we just couldn't ever do that." It might be worth getting a second estimate— that seems a little steep. Fiberglass, meanwhile, deteriorates over time, and no matter how much epoxy repair work you have done, at some point the fibers are going to disintegrate and unravel. The World's Largest Holstein is looking pretty good after twenty-five years of North Dakota wind and snowgrit, but if you inspect it closely you can see where the wear is beginning to bite.

"We are just one tornado from disaster," Tellman said.

I had the opportunity to spend some time with the four members of the Lions Club who led the community effort to fund and erect the World's Largest Holstein in the early 1970s. Aside from Tellman, who is the youngest of the four *by several decades*, the others are all in their eighties, at least. One of them still operates a large traditional dairy farm north of New Salem. They were funny and self-effacing, easily amused, exceptionally modest, and full of stories and anecdotes, some of which had to do with "Salem Sue." In a previous interview, I had asked Tellman, who runs New Salem's only grocery store, and a fine one, to assess the economic impact of the World's Largest Holstein. Like every other maker or manager of North Dakota's roadside effigies, he was flummoxed by my question.

"Well, I suppose some people who go up there also buy gas and snacks here at the gas stations out by the interstate. I get a few people in the store. Probably not too many people venture downtown [a mile or so to the south]. It amounts to *something*, I suppose." But the elderly dairy farmers I met were unimpressed by my interest in econometrics, even a little indignant. "We did this," they said, "because we are proud to be farmers, proud to be dairy farmers. That was the whole purpose of the project."

I love that.

From 1889 (statehood) until somewhere just into the twenty-first century, North Dakota was not just one of the nation's leading farm states, but a self-consciously *family farm* state. North Dakota was then, in some respects, the most Jeffersonian place in America—highly independent farmer citizens living on the land they tilled, raising stock, growing crops, gardening, gathering eggs, and butchering their own critters. "Those who labor in the earth are the chosen people of God if ever he had a chosen people."

My grandparents were proud dairy farmers in western Minnesota. Each cow had a name like Daisy or Blossom or Whitey. When they sold the herd at auction (on the farm) in the late 1970s, my grandfather Dick Straus was so upset at the diaspora of his life's work that he had to go in the house during the bidding, because he did not want his friends and neighbors to see him weep.

Once North Dakota was the proud home of the **World's Tallest Structure, the KVLY-TV communications mast** near the village of Blanchard, in Traill County. It was built in 1963. It towers 2,063 feet over the essentially flat surrounding countryside. Its status lasted just eleven glorious years. By 1974 it had yielded its world's tallest status to a radio tower in Warsaw, Poland, but that tower apparently felt so guilty about its one-upmanship that it collapsed onto the shoulders of Karl Marx. Then in 2008 Dubai threw up a fabulous skyscraper named the Burj Khalifa. At 2,722 feet, the Burj Khalifa rises more than 650 feet higher than the KVLY tower in North Dakota. It currently ranks as the world's tallest structure. Two other structures in the Far East, the Tokyo Skytree (a communications tower topped with a restaurant) and the Shanghai Tower (a skyscraper), now dwarf poor KVLY. Perhaps more to the point, all those rivals permit human access all the way up, while only a handful of intrepid engineers have ever been to the top of the KVLY mast in North Dakota. You drive as close as you can, get out of the car, and gape upwards. That's it. That's the experience. If you really wanted to climb it you could, but you'd have to bring a couple of stepladders to reach the welded metal ladder that is positioned too high for casual ascent, and then do a remarkably dangerous thing, with no chance of a celebratory shot of Jagermeister at the top or the glass of champagne you can buy at the top of the Eiffel Tower. The KVLY tower is now merely the fourth tallest structure on earth, which, among other things, forced it off the state map of North Dakota. I've been to it several times. It's, well, tall, and it's, well, dull. If there were a jackalope at its summit or a Christmas tree star or the world's largest potato effigy, it would instantly become one of the most visited places in North Dakota. But its purposes are purely functional. And it couldn't keep up.

The David Thompson Memorial was named for a British-Canadian explorer (1779-1857), a cartographer, and a master of celestial navigation. In fact, he spent so much time gazing at the moons of Jupiter or our Moon in its proximity to a number of easily identifiable fixed stars that he earned the name *Koo-Koo-Sint*, The Stargazer, among the Native Americans of the Rocky Mountain region. Who would not want such a moniker? Thompson worked for both the Hudson's Bay Company and the Northwest Company. He is said to have traveled more than 56,000 miles in his thirteen years in the North American West, much of it on foot, and he mapped 1.9 million acres of ground. He has been called the greatest land geographer of all time. Thompson was exploring the American and Canadian West at the same time that Lewis and Clark were tracing the Missouri, Snake, and Columbia Rivers (1804-06). Thompson was the first person to explore the entire length of the Columbia River, which Lewis and Clark picked up only at its confluence with the Snake.

Thompson was one of the great celestial navigators of his era. When he reached the Mandan and Hidatsa earthlodge villages in today's North Dakota, he determined their latitude to be 47.17.22 N. and the longitude to be 101.14.24 W. Seven years later, Meriwether Lewis, who was aware of Thompson's previous visit to the Mandan world, *corrected* Thompson's celestial work. With considerable haughtiness and American pride, Lewis declared that the actual longitude of the villages was 99.26.45 W. Mr. Jefferson's young friend was messing with the wrong geographer, however. Thompson's findings were nearly correct; (the actual longitude is 101.27.00 W). Lewis' were off by a full two degrees.

Thompson's monument can be found on the east bank of the Souris (Mouse) River about eight miles northeast of Velva, North Dakota. If it gets one hundred visitors per year, I'd be surprised. It may be the least well known roadside attraction in North Dakota. The road, by the way, is gravel. The monument, which is remote and not always easy to find, consists of a concrete globe with rudimentary latitudinal and longitudinal lines, resting on a pedestal. The incised words are difficult to read against the mottled marble of the base, so I reproduce them here:

1770 DAVID THOMPSON 1857
Geographer and Astronomer
Passed near here in 1797 and 1798 on a
scientific and trading expedition.
He made the first map of the country which
is now North Dakota and achieved
many noteworthy discoveries in the Northwest.

There is a wonderful simplicity and lonely nobility to the Thompson monument. It was commissioned by the Great Northern Railroad and dedicated on July 17, 1925. The placement of the monument was not as arbitrary as it may seem. Thompson was sent from today's Winnipeg to the Mandan and Hidatsa villages in 1797-98 to map the route, and to clarify, if possible, the border between the United States and British North America (Canada) in the aftermath of the Jay Treaty of 1795, which required the Brits to relinquish trading establishments in territory belonging to the United States. He passed the bend of the Souris River not far from the site of the monument.

Nobody could claim that the David Thompson monument was erected as a tourist attraction or to raise the profile of Velva or Verendrye or Karlsruhe, which are its nearest inhabited neighbors. It is a paean to the Enlightenment, a tribute to an adventurer who deserves to be ranked with Lewis and Clark, James Cook, and Alexander von Humboldt as one of the great explorers of the Second Great Age of Discovery. Anyone can stumble onto the World's Largest Pelican or the World's Largest Buffalo, but you have to make a concentrated pilgrimage to the David Thompson monument. In other words, you have to be willing to explore, even to get lost. Unless you care about the history of ideas, you may find it underwhelming.

The Enchanted Highway is without question the densest cluster of World's Largests anywhere, any one of which would have established their creator Gary Greff as an inspired, highly-talented, homegrown folk artist. These seven giant sculptures have been classified as the World's Largest Scrap Metal Sculptures, which, thanks to "Scrap," seems a bit dismissive. Begun in 1989, the Enchanted Highway is spectacular in its own way, monumental in its scale and complexity, impressive for all the legwork its creator had to do to get farmers to cooperate in leasing small roadside acreage to the project. North to south the sculptures depict:

- **Geese in Flight** (2001)—ten geese flying in an oval webwork of metal
- **Deer Crossing** (2002)—two metal deer, a male and a female, jumping over a fence
- **Grasshoppers in the Field** (1999)—the World's Largest Grasshoppers
- **Fisherman's Dream** (2006)—the World's Largest fishing medley
- **Pheasants on the Prairie** (1996)—the World's Largest cluster of pheasants
- **The Tin Family** (1991)—the World's Largest robotic nuclear farm family
- **Teddy Rides Again** (1993)—the World's Largest depiction of Theodore Roosevelt riding away on a bucking horse

They are all—in their entirety—the work of Greff, a Regent farmer, former school teacher and school administrator. Greff is voluble, upbeat, modest, and untouched by artistic arrogance in any form. He makes no attempt to call attention to himself, but he will talk to the end of time about his art. He insists that he wants no fame, no credit, no special treatment for thirty years of time-consuming, expensive, and exhausting artisanship. His only chagrin is that entities, including the state of North Dakota, have been mostly indifferent and sometimes ungenerous both in attitude and in the provision of funds.

Everyone has their favorites on the Enchanted Highway and there is a wide variety to choose from. I'm comparatively lukewarm about Teddy Rides Again, which is based on J.N. "Ding" Darling's farewell cartoon tribute to TR in 1919. Ding depicted Roosevelt as a cowboy even in death, though it was more than thirty years since he left behind his life as a rancher, cowboy, and big game hunter in western North Dakota. I'm lukewarm, too, about Deer Crossing and even Pheasants on the Prairie. They all have their advocates. But I am wild about Fisherman's Dream, which is the most whimsical and droll of Greff's sculptures. He told me in an interview that the array depicts all of the common North Dakota fish species—northern pike, walleye, rainbow trout, bluebill, catfish, and bass. The viewer observes fish and fishermen both above and below the water line, wonderfully depicted far overhead by an elongated blue lake surface that resembles a giant serrated bread knife. On top of the waves a fisherman in a boat has cast his line. Below is the sunken wreckage of another fishing boat. Greff 's humor is fully on display here. The trout, breaching the surface and big enough to eat the hapless fisherman whole, is about to devour a beautifully crafted dragonfly, which hovers just outside the trout's lips. The other fish are floating underwater through metal seaweed, which enabled Greff to raise each of the fish high above the surface of the prairie. Fisherman's Dream is the most complex of the sculptures and the one most dependent on annual maintenance.

The Grasshoppers in the Field array is spectacularly impressive, depicting one of the historic scourges of Great Plains agriculture in a compelling and delightfully grotesque manner. Greff's family of grasshoppers guard the surrounding prairie like survivors of a 1950s atomic disaster movie, like creatures from the book of Exodus or an O.E. Rolvaag novel, ready to devour the crops of North Dakota. Some North Dakotans dislike the grasshoppers because they remind them of hard times.

Greff's Tin Family is high-quality folk art *and* just great fun. The array is a whimsical parody of Grant Wood's *American Gothic* (1930), but with the addition of *junior,* who bears some resemblance to Bart Simpson from the subversive television cartoon series. Topped with a beanie, licking a big red sucker, and wearing a No. 14 team jersey, *junior* does not inspire a lot of confidence about the future of North Dakota agriculture. He's unlikely to be inducted into the FFA (Future Farmers of America). But his mother represents all the farm women in North Dakota history beautifully, and with considerable dignity.

Wearing a church lady hat over her wiry hair (made of scattered wire, like an elderly woman who has had one too many chemical perms), in a yellow button-down smock, she carries a basket of prairie flowers. Pa, well, he is holding a pitchfork like Grant Wood's original. Whatever burdens you carry with you as you turn south to explore the Enchanted Highway, you cannot see the Tin Family without cheering up. It is pure delight, wonderfully and whimsically wrought by a self-trained Dakota metal artist.

The Enchanted Highway has been both very successful and not particularly. It has not made Regent, North Dakota, a significant destination and, aside from Greff's souvenir shop on Main Street, it would be hard to make the case that the community has received any measurable economic benefit from the sculpture series. If saving Regent really was Greff's purpose, all that can be said is that the Enchanted Highway has helped perhaps a little. When I interviewed him, he provided the usual refrain—perhaps some gas sales, souvenirs, chips and candy. If he was seeking personal fame and fortune, both have proved elusive. Greff still lives very modestly in Regent, in a house once owned by his parents. He pours everything he has or can raise into maintaining all that spread out, windblown metal sculpture. He dreams of doing still more for Regent, including an ambitious shrine dedicated to The Immaculate Heart of Mary and the Sacred Heart of Jesus. This huge undertaking would completely transform St. Henry's Catholic Church, whose current Sunday attendance is miniscule. It would include a metallic copse of trees, the stations of the cross, and metal paintings on all the interior walls of the church. This grand capstone to Greff's career will require funds that have not been forthcoming. He reckons he needs three to five million dollars to do it justice, and he is determined not to abandon his vision. He is seventy-one years old.

In 2012, to raise funds for the church project, he transformed Regent's empty public school into the Enchanted Castle Hotel, complete with restaurant and bar and Arthurian theme rooms.

On any given day you are much more likely to encounter full-body armor in the hallways than live human beings. Greff undertook this additional, expensive investment in the hope that people would be drawn to North Dakota's only medieval-themed hotel, which would bring more traffic off I-94 down the Enchanted Highway, and possibly serve as a funding source for the maintenance of the sculptures. So far that gamble has not paid off. Occupancy by hunters has stalled.

Emily Dickinson wrote, "Fame is a fickle food upon a shifting plate." Greff insists that personal fame means *nothing* to him, though that is very hard to believe about someone who has devoted thirty years to creating monumental public art in a remote landscape. Still, you don't need to spend much time with him to be convinced that he is telling the whole truth, at least as his surface consciousness understands it. Most North Dakotans know that the Enchanted Highway exists even if they have never seen it. Only a few would be able to name Gary Greff. To the extent that he is known outside Regent and the immediate region, Greff has the reputation of being a lone-wolf artist, talkative, quirky, inspired, and very talented. But a lone wolf.

The most significant problem with the Enchanted Highway is that it is off the beaten path. The simple fact is that there is really not any *other* reason to turn south on County Road 100½ Avenue SW. The Enchanted Highway is to North Dakota what North Dakota is to America—so remote as possibly not to exist at all. To see all of it, you must drive all thirty-two miles down (with multiple stops to gawk, read the interpretive signs, and take photographs) and then all the way back. The experience, if you give it anything like the attention it deserves, takes at least two and a half hours, more if you stop in the souvenir and sandwich shop or examine the Greff's in-town sculptures in Regent.

If Greff made any mistake in his conception of the Enchanted Highway, it was installing Geese in Flight at the north end of the sculpture array along North Dakota's principal highway, I-94, rather than one of the more colorful, outlandish sculptures, such as the giant grasshoppers, the ambitious fishing tableau, or the robotic farm family. As Eric Peterson, the author of *Roadside Americana: Landmark Tourist Attractions*, writes, "the fact of the matter is that the more over-the-top and exaggerated a totem at highway's edge, the stronger its magnetism." Geese in Flight is beautiful, tasteful, delicate, and—if this is not a contradiction of terms for a gigantic metal sculpture— understated. It is actual art, not roadside kitsch. People driving by the Gladstone Exit on I-94 would be much more likely to turn off to see the rest of the sculptures if something more over-the-top had been installed at the point of maximum visibility. Cultural historian Karol Ann Marling has written, "The publicity value of roadside curiosities, it would seem, increases in direct proportion to their curiousness." If it were the World's Largest Lipstick-Wearing Hog, with an invitation to see still more down the blacktop highway, Regent would be sitting pretty. If shlock and kitsch are the keys to visitation, Geese in Flight fails because it is tasteful and elegant. Someone driving by who did not know about the six sculptures between Gladstone and Regent might think they would be witnessing more of the same. But the mass of humans would rather be delighted than impressed.

Still, the Enchanted Highway certainly has been a success in the world of Americana. It receives a great deal of attention throughout the Midwest—and beyond. North Dakota Tourism routinely features the sculptures in its literature and on its website. Lovers of roadside kitsch from all over the nation, and world, invariably include the Enchanted Highway in their articles and blogs. Unfortunately, so far, Greff's sculpture array is better known than it is visited. He deserves more credit, more support, and better funding than he has so far received.

Rutland, North Dakota, is the proud home of an annual Uff Dah Festival in October. Rutland (population 53) is (was) also the home of the **World's Largest Flipped Hamburger.** I will state candidly, though with no joy and indeed considerable sorrow, that as one of America's foremost aficionados of the World's Largest phenomena, I do not regard a temporary, organic, and indeed perishable, World's Largest meat substance as fully legitimate. The World's Largest (flippable) Hamburger was no sooner cooked, and flipped, than it was consumed. This would seem to defeat the purpose of creating the World's Largest anything.

Is it inappropriate to ask, too, for some clarification on the adjective *flipped*? Is it possible that there is a larger hamburger somewhere in America that was never flipped, or never successfully flipped? And what, might one ask, is the glory of flipping the patty? Perhaps to make sure it was evenly cooked. In the name of permanence, I would have hoped that the citizens of Rutland would have shellacked the hamburger (once properly flipped), or covered it with epoxy, or for that matter bronzed it. But to dream it up (to use the term of choice in the World's Largest lexicon), go to all the trouble to truck in 3,020 pounds of ground beef, cook it, then perform the almost impossible feat of flipping it intact—and after all that to gobble up the evidence in plain sight, seems problematic, and possibly insane. All that now remains to memorialize the World's Largest Flippable Hamburger is the sixteen-foot grill, which stands on Sargent County Road 10 just north of Rutland.

It is clear from the available evidence that Rutland feels some anxiety about that flipped burger. They have attempted to draw public scrutiny away from the alleged burger by staging an annual Wife Carrying Contest at the Uff Dah Festival. It is even more disturbing to learn that, according to the official rules of the Rutland Wife Carrying Contest, the wife in question need not be your own. Without blushing, Rutland declares that, "She . . . could be your neighbor's or search further afield." Oh, my. She must be at least 107 pounds (that should not be an insuperable challenge in North Dakota), and Rutland authorities have declared that you may carry her in any way you wish. I shudder to speculate.

In the name of the Greek goddess Hygiea and all that is just and humane in the world, I can only hope that the giant hamburger flipping apparatus, a "crane with chains attached," was first scoured with the World's Largest Beaker of Lysol using the World's Largest Brillo Pad. I assume the Sargent County Health Department was on hand with inspectors wearing clown-sized white gloves.

It is also upsetting to see one North Dakota community enter the culture wars against another. The Rutland website has the temerity to admit that the previous World's Largest Hamburger was the achievement of Tower City, North Dakota, a community merely seventy-nine miles from Rutland. Alas, poor Tower City. It would be dispiriting enough to lose the hamburger title to some upstart town in Montana or Wisconsin, but to be shouldered off the bun (as it were) by a fellow town of southeastern North Dakota is a serious betrayal of the North Dakota spirit.

One wonders what might come next in Rutland—the World's Largest Slim Jim, the World's Largest Fleishkuechle, the World's Largest Cheese-Infused Bratwurst? Let World's Largest perishables rot and mold. No, I know not what others might say, but I say, give me fiberglass or give me death.

And finally, the granddaddy of them all, **the World's Largest Buffalo** at Jamestown.

It was sculpted in 1959 by Jamestown College artist and faculty member Elmer P. Peterson (1928-2020). The effigy was not his idea, however. He was hired by Harold Newman, a prominent local billboard promoter who said he wanted "to create something so big and magnificent that passersby would have to stop in the city." Peterson was not a fabricator of roadside kitsch. He was a serious artist, trained at the University of Wisconsin, and he would go on to have a serious career as a sculptor. When he was interviewed at the age of eighty and asked what he would still like to create, Peterson said he wanted to sculpt the Lakota visionary Black Elk (who lived on the Pine Ridge Indian Reservation) and the great writer of westerns, Louis L'Amour, who grew up in North Dakota. It would have been altogether fitting and proper had Jamestown commissioned Peterson to sculpt a tribute to L'Amour, the author of more than one hundred novels and 250 short stories (320 million copies in ten languages), to grace the grounds of the National Buffalo Museum at Jamestown, built in 1993 to increase the attraction of the World's Largest Buffalo. Unfortunately, in 2010 marketing mandarins named the World's Largest Buffalo "Dakota Thunder," which feels more like a bad rockabilly band or a beer sold at the annual Sturgis Bike Rally than a worthy tribute to North America's most majestic quadruped.

I had the opportunity to interview Mr. Peterson in early July 2019. He was just under ninety years old, living alone in Galesberg, Wisconsin. He was lucid, witty, full of information about the creation of the World's Largest Buffalo, and still creating art. Peterson is best known for his La Crosse Players in La Crosse, Wisconsin, and his Martin Luther at Texas Christian University. At the start of his distinguished career, Peterson molded concrete onto a steel frame to create the World's Largest Buffalo, twenty-six feet tall, forty-six feet long, and a full sixty tons. That's a lot of concrete. Not even the worst North Dakota winds are likely to tip that bovine. The tornado would lose.

For a very long time, the World's Largest Buffalo was the only giant effigy in North Dakota. It was so readily visible from US 10 and (later) I-94 that probably no North Dakotan was unaware of its existence, and most families made at least one pilgrimage to the site. It remains not just the granddaddy of North Dakota's World's Largests, but one of the finest World's Largests in America. If you ask a thousand North Dakotans what they know about Jamestown, some will mention the North Dakota State Hospital (for the mentally disturbed), or the Anne Carlsen Center (for individuals with developmental disabilities), but virtually everyone will say that it is the home of the World's Largest Buffalo. Peterson's superb sculpture is the standard against which every other effigy in North Dakota (and beyond) must be judged. When the sculptures that make up the Enchanted Highway have rusted into oblivion, when the fiberglass of the World's Largest Holstein has disintegrated, when the World's Largest Sandhill Crane has flown away to a winter-feeding ground in Mexico, the World's Largest Buffalo will continue to stand silent sentinel on a hill just south of Jamestown. In fact, if North Dakota ever receives a series of nuclear strikes (as was quite possible between 1962 and 1989), the last thing standing on the prairie will be Peterson's early masterpiece.

It must be clear by now that my attitude towards North Dakota's World's Largest culture, though a little wry at times, is overwhelmingly positive. But one truly unsettling thing about these effigies is that they express a kind of insecurity about our homeland on the northern Great Plains. Even the Enchanted Highway's lovely array of metal sculptures seems to say that the land on either side of the blacktop road is not in itself enchanted. But if you stop your vehicle somewhere between Greff's displays and just gaze at the western plains of Dakota, you have the opportunity to embrace a subtle beauty that is, for those who have eyes to see, much more beautiful than any welded thing, however artful. One reason that North Dakota has had such a hard time committing itself to the protection of its landscapes, particularly out in the oil zone, is that we have never really learned to love the vast and open plain on which we are fortunate enough to live. There is a sense of inferiority in the way North Dakotans think about their homeland. It is not Lake Tahoe. It is not Glacier. It is not the Ozarks. But it is magnificent in its own subtle, understated way, for those with the will and the eyes to see. And until we collectively realize that, we are, I'm afraid, going to sell our birthright for a bushel of genetically-modified corn and a mess of carbon.

It's satisfying to have fun with the Midwestern World's Largest phenomena, but these effigies raise some serious questions about our history and what we choose to commemorate as we look at the primordial Great Plains in the rearview mirror. Why is it that we seem to lavish loving attention (and expense) on things we chose to eradicate in the conquest of the North American continent? Viewed through this more critical lens, a giant tribute to the bison is troubling and problematic, particularly when we stop to consider the centrality of the buffalo to the economic and spiritual lives of Native Americans, whose cultures and sovereignty we have done our best to eradicate in the past two centuries.

At the time of Lewis and Clark (1804-06) there were perhaps as many as fifty million buffalo in North America, at the very least tens of millions. Some significant percentage (5 percent? 10 percent?) grazed in today's North Dakota, a treeless grass plain ideally suited to feed the great American quadruped which shared the plains with a range of other mammals (elk, bighorn sheep, deer, antelope). The historian and essayist Dan Flores calls that lost world the American Serengeti. If ever there was an American Garden of Eden, this surely was it. When I try to imagine it, I ache for all that we have lost, for all that has been erased to get us to . . . well, just what? Fishing derbies on Lake Sakakawea for species not indigenous to the Missouri River? The Fargo Film Festival? A sea of flaring oil pads? The Dickens Festival in Garrison? What does Charles Dickens have to do with the American outback?

Lewis and Clark ate their first buffalo on August 23, 1804, at the bottom of today's South Dakota. From that moment until they began to cross the Bitterroot Mountains on September 9, 1805, they were never really out of sight of bison. Meriwether Lewis reported that he observed more than 3,000 at one point in northwestern North

Dakota, and perhaps as many as 10,000 in a single broad valley in north central Montana in July 1806. On April 22, 1805, Lewis wrote, "I asscended [sic, throughout] to the top of the cutt bluff this morning, from whence I had a most delightfull view of the country, the whole of which except the vally formed by the Missouri is void of timber or underbrush, exposing to the first glance of the spectator immence herds of Buffaloe, Elk, deer, Antelopes feeding in one common and boundless pasture." He was a few miles from today's Williston, North Dakota, the industrial hub of the Bakken Oil Boom. On August 29, 1806, on the return journey, Lewis wrote: "I assended to the high Country and from an eminance I had a view of the plains for a great distance. From this eminance I had a view of a greater number of buffalow than I had ever Seen before at one time. I must have Seen near 20,000 of those animals feeding on this plain."

Lewis was in south central South Dakota at the time. You get the idea. Essentially infinite numbers.

William Clark, who was floating down the Yellowstone River in the summer of 1806, reported seeing untold numbers of buffalo *day after day* until he ran out of adjectives and patience. On July 24, 1806, he finally just gave up. "[F]or me to mention or give an estimate of the different Spcies [sic, throughout] of wild anbimals on this river particularly Buffalow . . . would be incred012able. I shall therefore be silent on the Subject further." That was then.

Just seventy-seven years later, three quarters of a single century of the history of North America, young Theodore Roosevelt traveled by train to western North Dakota to kill a buffalo. It was September 1883. He wanted to bag one of the great quadrupeds before it was too late. The Smithsonian biologist William Hornaday (1854-1937) attempted to determine the number of buffalo that remained in North America at the turn of the twentieth century. To the best of his knowledge, he reckoned that there were a few hundred left, maybe a thousand. That represents a 99.99 percent species collapse in less than a century. Hornaday reckoned the species would go extinct. So did Theodore Roosevelt, George Bird Grinnell, and virtually all others who examined the numbers and tried to assess the inexorable march (and cost) of American civilization. Roosevelt, like several others who loved buffalo, even allowed himself to think it might be okay if the buffalo went extinct. "While the slaughter of the buffalo has been in places needless and brutal," he wrote, "and while it is to be greatly regretted that the species is likely to become extinct, and while, moreover, from a purely selfish standpoint many, including myself, would rather see it continue to exist as the chief feature in the unchanged life of the Western wilderness; yet, on the other hand, it must be remembered that its continued existence in any numbers was absolutely incompatible with any thing but a very sparse settlement of the country, and that its destruction was the condition precedent upon the advance of white civilization in the West, and was a positive boon to the more thrifty and industrious frontiersmen." Those were the words of the greatest presidential conservationist in American history.

Nobody can report the exact number of buffalo in North Dakota today, but the North Dakota Buffalo Association estimates that there are approximately 12,000 scattered across 70,762 squares miles (45,287,000 acres), mostly in commercial herds. That comes to one buffalo for every six square miles. That's one for every 40,000 acres. There are perhaps as many as 500 buffalo in the two larger units of Theodore Roosevelt National Park. The Mandan, Hidatsa, and Arikara have a herd on the Fort Berthold Indian Reservation and the Lakota have a larger one at Standing Rock. If these numbers are accurate, the North Dakota herds represent just over 2 percent of the buffalo in America today. A purist would argue that none of these buffalo are *wild* in the fullest sense of the term, since each of the ranges is relatively small and at some point every buffalo now alive in North Dakota finds its mobility terminated by a fence. The best buffalo ranges now in existence in America are at Yellowstone National Park, where much of the puny remnant herd found sanctuary at the turn of the twentieth century, and the new American Prairie Reserve in east central Montana, on its way to providing a 3.5-million-acre fenceless buffalo reservation in lands either managed by the US government or slowly being discontinued as cattle ranches, while their attendant service towns shrink away in one of the most isolated landscapes in the United States.

Let's take a modest number and estimate that there were a million buffalo in North Dakota before White people, railroads, and gunpowder entered the picture. If so, it would have been impossible to travel more than a few dozen miles in any direction at any time without seeing gangs of buffalo. Today you can, if you work at it, see a live buffalo in North Dakota on any given day, but it would also be possible to live an entire life in the state without ever seeing one. If you find the Great Plains beautiful today, just imagine what this landscape looked like when the American Serengeti was intact— buffalo, pronghorn antelope, two species of deer, elk, bighorn sheep, mountain lions, wolves, coyotes, grizzly bears, foxes, and prairie dogs. It makes you ache merely to think about it. And of course, the Native peoples who lived in that Serengeti in a steady-state economy that had been refined over many centuries.

I'm interested in the logic of White people. Perhaps I mean the psychology of settler communities, colonizers, occupiers, *conquistadors*. They essentially extirpate the bison in the course of a mere seventy-five years, mostly without making use of more than a small percentage of the carcasses, and often none at all. Then when the buffalo are all gone, White people erect monuments to an animal they casually decided was incompatible with their brand of civilization. There is something fascinating in this, and perverse. It's not much different from sticking plastic deer on the Kentucky bluegrass of a suburban lawn far from Kentucky. What exactly is being signified? Not sympathy. There would be no buffalo in North Dakota today were it not for Theodore Roosevelt National Park, White Horse Hill National Game Preserve (formerly Sullys Hill

NGP), Indian reservations, and a few commercial herds, which do not exist to celebrate the buffalo but to turn them into meat products. In 2020 nationwide, 69,000 buffalo were commercially slaughtered.

What does this signify? It seems to me that the message is *loss*.

It wasn't until Native Americans were vanquished and most of their homelands stripped away that their dignity and nobility seeped into the consciousness of the American people. Until then they were seen at best as an unfortunate impediment to White domination of the continent, at worst as savages, barbarians, terrorists, and vermin. You don't have to spend more than an hour with the newspapers of Yankton and Bismarck in the 1870s to see actual calls for extermination. In one of its nicer moods, the *Bismarck Tribune* wrote, "The American people need the country the Indians now occupy... An Indian war would do no harm, for it must come sooner or later... Custer's expedition [the 1774 Black Hills Expedition] may be the pebble which dropped in at an opportune moment will set the mighty sea of American thought in Motion." They have it, we want it, and we'll do whatever it takes to get them out of the way. Dehumanization is always the first step.

James Earle Fraser's iconic sculpture "End of the Trail" was first fashioned in 1894, just four years after the US Army, including veterans of the Seventh Cavalry, massacred between 250 and 300 almost entirely unarmed men, women, and children of the Lakota nation at Wounded Knee, South Dakota. When the incident occurred, on December 29, 1890, South Dakota had been a state for just one year. Fraser's sculpture of "the vanishing Indian" is one of the most iconic images of the American West. You see it everywhere, reproduced in bronze, plaster, on stained glass, on beaded belts and medallions, on posters, decals, mugs, bumper stickers, commemorative plates, and much more. The twin messages of "End of the Trail" are *nobility* and *farewell*. Fraser would not have created "End of the Trail" in

1876 or 1883, the year Roosevelt came west to kill his buffalo, and Buffalo Bill Cody's Wild West premiered at North Platte, Nebraska. The Native Americans of the American West had to be conquered before they could become ennoblized and worthy of sympathy. The buffalo of the Great Plains had to be erased from the Great Plains before a community like Jamestown would try to tell the world this effigy somehow represents North Dakota. How is it that a state like North Dakota borrows nobility and romance from a creature it killed off to possess the landscape, and then replaced an ideally evolved plains ungulate with a similar but less hardy grass-eating creature trucked in from somewhere else in the world? What is a Hereford but a puny and less troublesome grass-eating quadruped? North Dakota was utterly ruthless with respect to its Native Americans during the homestead era, but etched the outline of a Native American in full headdress on its state highway signs once conquest was complete. What, exactly, does that signify? "This is Indian Country"? Well, not really. We had to thrust these sovereign people aside before we could create a civilization that includes the road you are driving on? We've pauperized these people, but we want to borrow a bit of romantic luster from them even so? Meet Red Tomahawk, one of the Indians who assassinated Sitting Bull!

The charade continues today. In a recent state tourism campaign (2019) featuring North Dakota's most recent gift to Hollywood, Josh Duhamel, the preternaturally handsome actor is photographed on the cover, grinning at a shirtless Native American in full ceremonial regalia kneeling on a buffalo robe, with metal arm bands above the elbow, a headdress (though not of feathers), an eagle-bone vest, a sharp lance with an elongated metal tip, and a range of feathered accoutrements. They have made a connection, the Native American from the past and the actor in T-shirt and jeans from the present. It's a beautiful photograph in its way, and if you are from North Dakota you realize that this is a re-enactor at Fort Lincoln State Park, but to someone from Jupiter (or Indiana for that matter), what the magazine cover seems to signify is that if you come to North Dakota you can find an Indian *just like this*. But where would you look? Aside from a re-enactment or a pow wow, you would never see a Native American dressed like that. This is not how they walk through a grocery store or the mall, not how they renew their driver's license at the NDDOT, not how they enter a restaurant or show up for work at the bank. The Native American in the cover photograph represents an idealized portrait of a past that is, well, past, and sadly misleading in some important ways. The Native American, whose name is Alan Demaray, is locked in the past like a museum piece, and a famous North Dakota-born actor who no longer lives in the state is digging him across time. It would be more appropriate, if less dramatic, if Duhamel were meeting one of the professors of UTTC (United Tribes Technical Center) or a Native American oil executive or a Native American beef producer or Scott Davis, the former director of North Dakota's Indian Affairs Commission, who was seldom seen on the first floor of the judicial wing of the state capitol carrying a lance and dressed in a bone vest. It needs to be stated again, without varnish: Euro-Americans could not abide Native Americans living in their traditional way on lands that Whites coveted. The US government's Religious Crimes Code of 1883 actually banned traditional Indian religious ceremonies and observances, including the Sun Dance and the Mandan's sacred Okipa Ceremony. The Religious Crimes Code was used as justification for putting down the Ghost Dance phenomenon at the end of the same decade. The Native American represented on the cover of the North Dakota Travel Guide had to be vanquished and displaced in order that Minot High School could eventually produce Josh Duhamel. If you want to suggest that North Dakota has a new attitude toward Native Americans, the image you want to present is not of a past that never was but a present in which White people and Native Americans work side by side, wear more or less the same clothing, drive more or less the same vehicles, eat some of the same food, get the same health care, and shop at the same stores. If you want to picture Indians in Native dress, get your photographs at a pow wow.

When newly-elected North Dakota state representative Ruth Buffalo was sworn in at the North Dakota Capitol on December 3, 2018, she chose to wear traditional Mandan, Hidatsa, and Arikara regalia, including a shawl and an eagle feather fan. She looked stunning. Her educational credentials are stronger than most members of the North Dakota legislature. She has a BA, MA, MBA, and MPH (Masters in Public Health). She runs a successful consulting business. Some members of the legislature (and others) rolled their eyes (or were actually offended) that Ms. Buffalo was sworn in wearing traditional regalia, just as some bigots were offended back in 2007 when Minnesota congressman Keith Ellison, a Muslim, took the oath of office with his hand on a copy of the *Koran.* It happened to be Thomas Jefferson's copy of the *Koran* (how cool is that!), on loan from the Library of Congress, which exists to serve members of Congress in any way it can. If you believe that swearing an oath on a sacred text makes you more likely to keep that vow, then it would make sense to put your hand on *your own religion's* sacred text, not pro forma on a copy of the Judeo-Christian Bible. If I, as a Christian protestant, swore an oath on a copy of the Hindu *Bhagavad Gita,* it would not bind me as thoroughly as when I took that oath on my own tribe's sacred text.

There is a delicious but sad irony in the Ruth Buffalo story. If the North Dakota legislature had invited her (as a private citizen) to come provide an invocation at the beginning of the session or to come representing the Mandan, Hidatsa, and Arikara, some of them at least would have said, "Oh, and can you wear your costume?" In other words, if she came as a tribal rep, as a legislative guest, they would have wanted her to wear traditional regalia ("your costume"), but if she came before them as a member of the state House of Representatives, then she should wear the dominant culture's legislative costume, the pantsuit! White people like to lock Native

Americans into the past. We would rather not deal with them as contemporary Native Americans, in or out of regalia, but we are quite happy to display them as traditional "Indians," so long as we get to make that choice and they do not threaten our hegemony. When they choose to dress in a traditional way away from a pow wow or a reservation ceremony, White people get edgy. But when Native Americans dress in jeans and a T-shirt, some White people think, "Hmmph. Some Indian!" The Native American novelist Tommy Orange commented on this recently, in a discussion of his most recent book, *There There*. "White people always want us to dress in the same way. I know of no other culture that is expected to dress in just one way."

Very few White North Dakotans will decline to express a generalized sympathy for Native Americans ("what we did to them"), and lament that Indians cannot quite seem to recover their cultural confidence. But the overwhelming majority of the White people of North Dakota feel, tepidly or passionately, that it is time for Native Americans "get over it." In some this reads as "get over it, already," and in others it is a genuine if racist hope (we are all complicit) that Native Americans will experience a cultural renaissance that will keep them Indian in ways that please us, but assimilate so fully that we will no longer have to think of them as a paupers or a nagging social problem. There are plenty of open racists in North Dakota; I have listened to dark drunken late-night fantasies of running down Native Americans who are walking on the shoulders of ND roads. I'd say that there may be 50,000 or more open racists in North Dakota. But most White North Dakotans think of themselves as enlightened and tolerant on the *Indian question*. They know that American Indians have had a rough go. They try not to be too put off by the sorry Third World state of a few of North Dakota's Indian towns today. They read the reports of suicide, meth, opioids, domestic violence, alcoholism, huffing, fetal alcohol syndrome, and obesity and they quietly, perhaps even secretly, wonder "if Indians will ever get it together." They don't want to judge Native Americans—but they do—and they justify their righteousness by telling themselves and each other that since they wouldn't tolerate that sort of self-destructiveness among their own White community, then why should they suspend their normal set of values just because Indians are a historically-oppressed people? You can find plenty of North Dakotans who believe that the reservation system is failed socialism, that the experiment (whatever exactly it was) has been a colossal failure, and the best thing we could do now is terminate every reservation in America. This signifies that these North Dakotans wish Indians would disappear, at least as Indians. It's just a polished-up twenty-first century version of Colonel Richard Pratt's nineteenth-century mantra, "kill the Indian, save the man." Outrageous though it sounds, I have heard North Dakotans say, particularly during the recent DAPL pipeline crisis, that if they could snap their fingers and make Indians simply but peacefully disappear, they would not hesitate to start snapping. That is the part of the story effigies don't convey.

The North Dakota Travel Guide paragraph, "About the Cover," on page three reads in its entirety: "Photographer Tyler Stableford captured North Dakota native and actor Josh Duhamel enjoying On-a-Slant Indian Village at Fort Abraham Lincoln State Park near Mandan. It's one of many attractions where you can experience the rich culture of our state." "North Dakota native"—there's a bit of irony. At no point in the 2019 Travel Guide is the actual Native American on the cover identified. He's just an "Indian," but Josh Duhamel, who needs no caption, is identified twice on the cover alone and also in the "About the Cover" paragraph inside.

MEDICINE ROCK:
SEEKING THE SACRED IN THE MIDDLE OF NOWHERE

"The sacred is like rain. It falls everywhere but pools in certain places."
—Lakota elder

T he official state map of North Dakota highlights two places with red ink in Grant County, a larger-than-average, irregularly shaped county south and west of the state capital in Bismarck. One of the designated highlights, at the top of the county, is Heart Butte Dam, a modest dam on a still more modest stream that creates a modest but important summer recreational area in a state that has few lakes. The other highlight, at the bottom of the county, is the Cannonball Stage Station SHS (State Historic Site). Grant County has a population of 2,300 or so, most of whom live along the east-west ribbon of ND state Highway 21. In the villages of Lark, Carson, Leith, Heil, Elgin, and New Leipzig. Heil and New Leipzig give you a good sense of the demographics—White folks whose forebears were Germans and Germans from Russia. According to the most recent census, there are thirty-four Native Americans and two African Americans living in Grant County, which encompasses

1,666 square miles, more territory than the sovereign state of Rhode Island with its 1,212 square miles and a population of 1.6 million. The term we like to use out here is "sparsely settled." If this abandoned piece of America sounds like it might be chosen as a rural haven for White supremacists, stay tuned.

The official state highway map of North Dakota does not mark Medicine Rock SHS. Although the State Historical Society of North Dakota (SHSND) owns, maintains, and interprets the eleven-acre sacred site, it prefers not to advertise its existence, not wishing to encourage merely casual tourists to venture for this purpose into the heart of the empty quarter in south central North Dakota. Partly this is a way of protecting the unsupervised site from vandals. Partly it is a way of limiting the number of people who cross the fields and pasture of the private property owner who ranches at the base of the butte that serves as the pedestal beneath the Medicine Rock. Mention of Medicine Rock SHS is probably also omitted from state maps to prevent visitors from disappointment.

Aside from a historical marker at the top of the butte, a chain link fence that tightly envelops the Medicine Rock itself, and the residuum of petroglyphs once incised by man or God on the sandstone outcropping, there is nothing there. Even in an empty state it is about as isolated a place as you could imagine. If only the ranch headquarters were not nestled on the south end of the butte, you could really enjoy some agoraphobia there.

If Medicine Rock weren't marked on county maps and more detailed North Dakota atlases, you would never find it. You might not find it even with those maps, because Medicine Rock is more or less identical to half a dozen other nondescript sandstone outcroppings in the vicinity, any one of which might be the home of the sacred oracle. A tiny, hand-painted white sign (Medicine Rock→) attached to a fencepost at the end of the east-west gravel road (78ᵗʰ St. SW) points toward the bluff. Medicine Rock is surrounded by private ranch and farmland in every direction. A man named Delbert Rosin lives on the farm at the base of the bluff. His son Andrew lives in a new home nearby. The Rosins plant their crops right up to the crotch of the hill until the incline makes it impossible to maneuver a tractor safely. They turn their cows loose on the corn stubble in the fall. The result is a dark excremental simulacrum of a polka dot grassland. Welcome to North Dakota sacred ground.

Blue late-model Subaru full of gas. A pristine unopened bag of red Twizzlers "licorice" at my side. Camera. Smartphone (camera). The DeLorme *North Dakota Atlas and Gazetteer*, featuring back roads, recreation sites, and GPS grids. Light coat. Heavy coat. Gloves and stocking cap. Serious boots just in case. Winter emergency kit. The indispensable 1938 *WPA Guide to North Dakota*. A fresh pouch of Sir Walter Raleigh tobacco, string, a cotton bandanna handkerchief, and a pocketknife. And a perfect Saturday-in-late-March companion, a friend who would never deface a monument, almost never trespass, and could never be disappointed in visiting a lightly interpreted, largely insubstantial historical site in the middle of nowhere.

To get to the Medicine Rock you leave Bismarck in an internal combustion vehicle. There's compromise number one, for no true pilgrim in the pre-Euro-American era got there except on foot or, only at the very end of the period, on horseback. If you had to walk to Medicine Rock from the Missouri River, up the serpentine Cannonball River, you'd have a couple of days to think about your spiritual questions before you reached the site. Not much else to do on that journey except keep an eye out for clear pools of water, watch for potential enemies, kill a deer or a buffalo if you happened upon one at a hungry moment, and gaze at the endless broken countryside. And pray. From high above the land the countryside looks mottled and dimpled in every direction forever, like an LP phonograph record that has baked all summer in the sun, with the thin brown ribbon of the Cannonball winding in oxbows and s-curves through the viewshed, in no great hurry to reach the buxom Missouri. If it weren't for the Homestead Act (1862), the Dawes Act (1887), and the plow, you'd be in the heart of America's central grasslands, a vast region environmental historian Dan Flores calls American Serengeti.

You drive from Bismarck to Mandan across the Missouri River, and then south of Mandan on ND 6 to Flasher and then to Carson on ND 21. These are wee vestigial villages so abandoned that they scarcely register as human gathering places. Carson is, however (ahem), the *county seat* of Grant County, population: 284. Probably one in ten residents is employed by the county. Which presents something of a paradox. At birthhood, states were divided into a plethora of counties (3,142 nationwide) so that everyone in every jurisdiction could drive a buggy or a horse to the local seat of government and back again in a single day. That's why North Dakota has fifty-three counties, one for every 14,000 people. The county officers (the registrar of deeds, the local judge, the state's attorney, the county treasurer) were meant to serve the larger population in a frugal, efficient, and localized way. Now, ironically, it is the surrounding population that props up the county government, not the other way around, in part because in North Dakota's twenty-some most marginal counties a significant percentage of the local population now works directly for county government. Whenever some outside consultant suggests that North Dakota consolidate its counties (from fifty-three to say twenty or fifteen or even five) to save money, avoid duplication of services, and to acknowledge that conditions of transportation are not in the twenty-first century what they were in the late nineteenth, the rural people of North Dakota cry out in anguish. No matter what they say publicly about the beauty of "local government" and "knowing your county commissioner," their chief concern is where local folks would work if no longer for the county.

In towns like these, the gas station and convenience store is out on the highway. One, two or three saloons. Maybe a post office. Perhaps a senior citizens' center in an empty downtown store. Possibly a joint tanning booth/latte facility. It's at least possible that one of the old bank buildings is now an Airbnb. I might be describing Carson, but it could equally be Robinson or Wing or Sykeston or Leonard or any number of other ghostly towns on the plains. On any given day you are most likely to find folks in the bar or the post office. I love these towns, though I would not live in one of them.

There are four churches in Carson: one Presbyterian, two Lutheran, one Catholic. Are they sacred places? They represent a Judeo-Christian heritage that began more than 2,000 years ago in a place far, far away across the globe. No matter what the "author" of the *Book of Mormon* Joseph Smith might say, the origins of Christianity had absolutely nothing to do with the Western Hemisphere or the New World, unless God annexes continents the way Dallas does suburbs. Christianity was not shaped by the landscape of the Great Plains, or by the climate, the quality of sky, the wildlife, the grass, the wind (John 3:8), the watercourses, or the spirit of place of North Dakota. It was alien to the spiritually intense indigenous people who had lived here for thousands of years and had learned not only to live very lightly on the land (a violation of Genesis 1:28), but also to harmonize their cultures quite beautifully into the larger circles of life available here, in *this* place, 6,399 miles from Bethlehem. Jesus never saw a pronghorn antelope or a prairie dog. Or Wall Drug. But if the Catholics of Grant County, ND, have gathered at St. Theresa Catholic Church for ninety-two years, surely that place is sacred in its own, somewhat more contingent, way.

You drive from Carson almost to Elgin, to the eastern suburbs of Elgin (population 642). The town website says it all. "Elgin is nestled in the rolling hills of southwestern North Dakota. Elgin has a strong business sector, with Jacobson Memorial Hospital Care Center at the hub. Our community has a wide range of churches [five], available housing [more by the month], and a great school system." I'd say south *central* North Dakota. "Nestled" is the kind of word you pay your young webmaster/marketer to craft, fresh from her communications degree at NDSU. The headline of the Elgin website declares, *"Not in the fast lane. Life in the best lane."* All communities make the most of whatever they have and make the best of what they lack. Still, if this is the best lane, I'll eat my head. I suppose there are people in the greater Elgin metroplex who regard life there as close to ideal, but if you need more than gas or a loaf of bread and orange juice, you will be driving either to New Salem (36.8 miles) or Mandan (58.2) for basic Maslovian amenities. Home entertainment systems are nearly the only remaining entertainment.

But wait! Grant County High School won the State Class B Girls basketball championship in 2018—Grant County 53, Killdeer 44. Small communities remember these moments for decades. Often enough a fading billboard on the edge of town announces the heroic achievement to anyone who passes through. If you have never seen a whole rural community go gaga over a successful sports team (parades, receptions, ecumenical religious services, "Coyote Days" sponsored by the Main Street merchants, many heedless breachings of the wall of separation between church and state) you have not experienced one of the most delightful and life-affirming rites still left in America. To observe an entire town make the pilgrimage en masse to the state Class B tournament in Bismarck or Minot (after four pep rallies and a prayer service), in a tight purposeful caravan, to eat together at Applebee's and then go on together to the game, every person as excited as if it were their wedding day, is to make you fall in love with America all over again—the astounding innocence of the American people at their best. It's not like being a Packers fan and drinking beer while wearing a foam cheese hat at Lambeau Field in Green Bay. It has a purity that professional or even college sports have long since left behind.

Small heartland towns often seem to emerge straight out of central casting from Sinclair Lewis' savage *Main Street* (1920), even if they think of themselves as no worse than Garrison Keillor's more genial Lake Wobegon. A small town can come apart over whether the Harry Potter books, given their encouragement of witchcraft, can be permitted to sully the public library, open Tuesdays and Thursdays 2-4:30 p.m. But these hapless towns can also be places where the magic of our former neighborliness, decency, faith, family, patriotism, and agrarian rootedness linger. They are the home of the goat tie contest and the bake sale so the high school seniors can go to the Black Hills on Senior Skip Day. Just let a not-particularly-liked farmer have heart bypass surgery on the eve of wheat harvest, and you will see the combines of four, five, ten neighbors converge on his fields to bring in the crop in a single afternoon. And enough red-frosted flat cake and cheesy potatoes to finish off a senior citizens' center.

From Elgin you drive south six or seven miles on a good gravel road. Then you turn east (left) on Grant CR 78 (gravel). As you approach Medicine Rock you drive past one possibly sacred sandstone hill after another—and no matter how many times you have been there you wonder if you have made a wrong turn—before you finally wind up at the right place at the end of the road. You've been driving through the endless broken plains until the last quarter mile, when you pass a new ranch house with windows looking out on the bluff and then an old ranch yard not far from where you park your vehicle. In most seasons you can turn left now and drive partway up the hill on a two-track trail. I have done so, but it feels like cheating, so it's best to park near the bottom, just off the road, and walk the half mile to the top. That way you worry less about trespassing and you feel, in some limited sense, that you have earned the experience.

The Medicine Rock may have been sacred for hundreds or even thousands of years—or forever for that matter—but for the Euro-American White people who would wrest 97 percent of North Dakota from its Native sovereigns in the course of the next four score and six years, and erase virtually the entire Mandan, Hidatsa,

Arikara, Dakota, Lakota, Ojibwe, and Assiniboine cultural footprint, it all began with an Arikara leader named Piaheto or Too Né, who was traveling through the bottom half of today's North Dakota with Lewis and Clark as the Missouri River cottonwoods shed their leaves in the autumn of 1804. The expedition had reached the Grand River Arikara earthlodge villages on October 8, a couple of weeks after a harrowing encounter with the Lakota, who had attempted to exact a significant toll for permitting the flotilla of three boats safe passage through the sovereign Lakota nation. Lewis and Clark determined not to be intimidated and after a tense four-day standoff near today's Pierre, South Dakota, they managed to bluster their way through Lakota territory for the price of a wad of tobacco. Word traveled fast on the Missouri River. Two weeks later, the Arikara's "Grand Cheif in Councel [sic]" assured the expedition leadership that "the road was open & no one dare Shut it, & we might Departe at pleasure." The geopolitical dynamics have been essentially the same ever since.

Piaheto was traveling on the expedition's keelboat on a diplomatic mission to the Mandan Indians, who lived one hundred miles upriver at the mouth of a tributary called the Knife. The Arikara and the Mandan had lately been engaged in a low-level war, better understood as skirmish and counter-skirmish. In their paternalistic way, Lewis and Clark were insisting to anyone who would listen or pretend to that the Native Americans of the Louisiana Territory must now live in peace with each other under a broad security umbrella provided by the United States government. This was President Jefferson's *Pax Americana*. All tribes agreed to this demand under the immediate pressures of the expedition's council awning, assuming that the expedition's interpreters managed to make their message understood, and a few tribes actually tried to abide by what Lewis and Clark insisted upon once the flotilla had gone around the next bend of the Missouri River. Having nothing better to do between October 12-26 on board the expedition's keelboat, Piaheto (whose other name, Arketarnarshar, translates as "chief of the town" or "mayor of the Arikara") provided a running commentary on the countryside through which the great river flowed. He proved to be a voluble and valuable informant. He provided the names of creeks and streams along the way, identified abandoned Mandan villages, and explained some of the cultural traditions of the Arikara. It was he who informed Clark about the Medicine Rock, and Clark was the first Alphabetical Man to write an account of the phenomenon. On October 17, 1804, Clark wrote, "This Chief tells me of a number of their Treditions about Turtles, Snakes, &. and the power of a perticiler rock or Cave on the next river which informs of everr thing none of those I think worth while mentioning."

There's the Enlightenment's ethnographic spirit!

The *next river* was the Cannonball, which today marks the northern boundary of the Standing Rock Indian Reservation and, in Jefferson's time, more or less represented the southern boundary of the Mandan nation. The sacred site Piaheto described is seventy-one miles west of the banks of the Missouri River. William Clark would not have taken the time to visit the site even if he had found the Arikara and Mandan *treditions* more interesting. (At no point did the Lewis and Clark Expedition deviate more than two dozen miles from whatever river they were traveling.) Winter was coming. The captains knew the river road was soon going to close. The expedition was in a hurry. With so much else to think about that winter, including the myriad preparations in advance of the expedition's arduous 1805 journey from Fort Mandan to the Pacific Ocean, Clark would probably have forgotten all about the Medicine Rock, but two of the Corps of Discovery's principal informants among the Mandan, Sheheke-shote (Big White) and Oh-he-nar (Big Man) brought the subject up again when they visited Fort Mandan on February 21, 1805. Clark's journal account is fascinating:

a Delightfull Day put out our Clothes to Sun— Visited by the big white & Big man they informed me that Several men of their nation was gorn to Consult their Medison Stone about 3 day march to the South West to know What was to be the result of the insuing year—They have great confidence in this Stone and Say that it informs them of every thing which is to happen, & visit it every Spring & Sometimes in the Summer—"They haveing arrived at the Stone give it Smoke and proceed to the wood at Some distance to Sleep the next morning return to the Stone, and find marks white & raised on the Stone representing the piece* or war which they are to meet with, and other changes, which they are to meet"** "This Stone has a leavel Surface of about 20 feet in Surcumfrance, thick and pores***," and no doubt has Some mineral qualtites effected by the Sun.

The Big Bellies**** have a Stone to which they ascribe nearly the Same Virtues.

Clark's informants were excellent. The Medicine Rock *is* three very hard days of walking from the mouth of the Knife River. The sandstone outcropping *is* approximately twenty-five feet in diameter, and it *is* porous. But it is Clark, not Sheheke-shote, who attempts an alternative scientific explanation for the oracle, "... no doubt has Some mineral qualtites effected by the Sun."

The Enlightenment meets the sacred.

Major Stephen H. Long (1784-1864) visited the Upper Missouri in 1820. He was almost certainly taking his cues from the 1814 paraphrase edition of the journals of Lewis and Clark prepared by Philadelphia man of letters Nicholas Biddle. Long gave the Hidatsa name for Medicine Rock as *Me-ma-ho-pa.* He wrote, "The Minnetarees [Hidatsa] resort to it, for the purpose of propitiating their Manho-pa or Great Spirit,

---

*   Peace
**   Clark uses quotation marks here because he is trying to record the actual statements of his informants, as translated from Mandan to French by a local trader Rene Jusseaume, and then from French to English by expedition member Francois Labiche. Clark is listening carefully.
***   Porous
****   Hidatsa

by presents, by fasting, and lamentation, during the space from three to five days." Long said the presents might include guns, horses, or "strouding," a coarse fabric useful in making blankets and blanket coats.

On his arrival, he deposits the presents there, and after smoking to the rock, he washes a portion of the face of it clean, and retires with his fellow devotees to a specified distance. During the principal part of his stay, he cries aloud to his god to have pity on him; to grant him success in war and in hunting, to favour his endeavours to take prisoners, horses, and scalps from the enemy. When the appointed time for lamentation and prayer has elapsed, he returns to the rock, his presents are no longer there, and he believes them to have been accepted and carried off by the Manhopa himself. Upon the part of the rock, which he had washed, he finds certain hieroglyphics traced with white clay, of which he can generally interpret the meaning, particularly when assisted by some of the magi [medicine men], who were no doubt privy to the whole transaction. These representations are supposed to relate to his future fortune, or to that of his family or nation; he copies them off with pious care and scrupulous exactness upon the skin which he brought for the purpose, and returns to his home, to read from them to the people, the destiny of himself or of them.

Aside from Long's snarky conviction that the whole thing was a fraud perpetrated by spiritual charlatans "who were no doubt privy to the whole transaction," his description of the workings of the Medicine Rock is quite useful, and more detailed than any other historical account. It seems strange that the writer of the North Dakota Historical Society's 1963 interpretive sign at the site (see below) seems either not to have been aware of Major Long's account, or he discounted it. Long is certain that the Medicine Rock had more uses than merely improving the buffalo hunt.

When Prince Maximilian of Wied-Neuwied (1782-1867) made his way up the Missouri River in 1833, he too carried with him Nicholas Biddle's edition of the journals of Lewis and Clark (1814), plus maps that Clark himself, now a venerable old Missouri River patriarch in St. Louis, permitted Maximilian to copy from the archives of the 1804-06 transcontinental expedition. Maximilian's journal (now splendidly published in three volumes by the University of Oklahoma Press) was in some respects a running commentary on the maps and journals of Lewis and Clark. One explorer blazes the trail for the next, and the next.

Maximilian must have asked about the Medicine Rock during the winter he spent at the American Fur Company's Fort Clark (near the Mandan and Hidatsa villages) in 1833-34. A young man named Red Feather informed Maximilian that "one may get there on foot from the Mandan villages in a fast two-day march; if one walks slowly, in three days." That would be very fast walking either way. The distance is 96 miles. To the extent that he could render it accurately, Maximilian noted that the Mandan word for Medicine Rock was *Mih-Chóppenisch*, the Hidatsa word *WíhdäKatachí*. According to Red Feather, the Mandan and Hidatsa "go there when their war parties move out."

> They do not go to the rock during the first evening but camp before and sacrifice a few items, like small pieces of cloth and such, to the rock. The next morning they walk up to it . . . the partisan* interprets the impressions and figures on the rock and predicts the outcome of their venture. Then they smoke.

That description was written during the upriver ascent in 1833. But Maximilian returned to the subject of the Medicine Rock in the course of the long, dreary winter at Fort Clark.

---

*   Lead pilgrim.

The stone is described as being marked with the impressions of the footsteps of men, and animals of various descriptions, also of sledges with dogs. The Indians use this stone as an oracle, and make offerings of value to it, such as kettles, blankets, cloth, guns, knives, hatchets, medicine pipes, &c., which are found deposited close to it. The war parties of both nations,* when they take the field, generally go to this place, and consult the oracle as to the issue of their enterprise. Lamenting and howling,** they approach the hill, smoke their medicine pipes, and pass the night near the spot. On the following morning they copy the figures on the stone upon a piece of parchment or skin, which they take to the village, where the old men give the interpretations.

These three accounts, by Clark, Long, and Maximilian, written over twenty-nine years, are the best documents we have about Medicine Rock. The men who wrote these words, particularly Prince Maximilian, were making a concerted effort to record as much of Native American cultural traditions as they could given the transitory nature of their encounters, the press of their other responsibilities, and the difficulties of verbal and cultural translation. Maximilian perhaps deserves special praise, because despite his use of the word "howling," his sympathies were clearly with the indigenous peoples he encountered as against their Yankee tormentors. Maximilian's mission, and the reason he brought with him a painter (Karl Bodmer) who was instructed to depict Native American dress, lodges, weapons, domestic items, adornment, and accoutrements with *photographic* fidelity, was to record the Missouri River's indigenous lifeways before it was too late. Thus, German Prince Maximilian was one of the first Euro-Americans to promulgate the Myth of the Vanishing Indian. The myth has legs well into the twenty-first century.

Important though they are, these written accounts of the sacred

---

*   He means Mandan and Hidatsa, not the Mandan and their enemies.

**   This is certainly a Eurocentric choice of words.

dynamics of the Medicine Rock cannot be accepted at face value. None of the three White men made the pilgrimage to the site. They were all sufficiently steeped in the history of Western civilization to see Medicine Rock through the lens of the ancient historians Plutarch and Herodotus. They could only try to make sense of Medicine Rock by comparing it in their minds to the Oracle at Delphi in Greece. They were naturally skeptical (derisive might be a more accurate word) about the possibility that Medicine Rock actually delivered sacred wisdom to those who approached it in the right spirit and after proper preparation. Such was the Enlightenment. When the Lewis and Clark Expedition's Patrick Gass later observed a Mandan gratitude ritual involving buffalo skulls, he wrote, "Their superstitious credulity is so great, that they believe by using the head well the living buffaloe will come and that they will get a supply of meat." Fellow Corps member Joseph Whitehouse was somewhat more generous. "Some of them & indeed the most of them have Strange & uncommon Ideas, but verry Ignorant of our forms & customs, but quick & Sensible in their own way & in their own conceit, &c &c."

My fellow pilgrim, the perfect companion and friend, and I reached the parking spot at Medicine Rock in late morning. It was a gray late-winter day, eighteen degrees above zero, wind out of the northwest at fifteen miles per hour. Some snow across the fields but not much. The pasture we had to walk through was firm, though it was so full of cow pies that avoiding them was like avoiding the cracks in an urban sidewalk. She had never been there before, but she was willing, curious, open-minded, eager. Her politics were center-left, but she was never doctrinaire, and she had more friends on the right than on the left. She felt a serious respect and sympathy for Native Americans, including their increasing outspokenness and assertion of their sovereignty and treaty rights. This, by the way, distinguishes her from approximately 80 percent of the rest of the White people of North Dakota.

It took us approximately twenty minutes to reach the crest of the butte. While we climbed, I explained that we would certainly see prayer bundles tied to the chain link fence that wraps pretty tightly around the Medicine Rock itself to protect it from vandalism. As we summited, she said, "WTF? Boy, you weren't kidding about the chain link fence. That pretty much destroys the vibe, don't you think?" True, it's impossible not to sneer at the chain link fence. For starters, how can you wall off the sacred? That alone seems wholly (and holy) wrong. It's sacrilege. If the state feels the need to protect the Medicine Rock from desecration, why a chain link fence? Is that the best we can do? The sacred rock seems imprisoned now, confined, constrained, off limits. Caged. Chain link fencing is unescapably contemptuous. It's used to wall off dog walking parks, construction and demolition sites, urban parking lots, and childcare facilities on the Mexican border. If Medicine Rock is sacred, surely it deserves better than chain link, the least reverent and expensive of fence options. Worse, the *old* chain link fence was in bad shape, so a couple of years ago the State Historical Society of North Dakota installed *new* shiny chain link fencing precisely where the old fencing had stood. Was there no talk of an upgrade? We are a pragmatic people, but this is pretty soulless pragmatism.

If there has to be a fence, even a chain link fence, why does it have to be so tightly wound around the rock? Why couldn't there be a ten- or twenty-foot perimeter between the rock and the fence? If the State of North Dakota lists Medicine Rock among its curatorial sites, then surely it intends for people to visit the site from time to time. People who visit historic sites want to take pictures—to prove they were there, to share with their friends, to remember their adventures. The fence at Medicine Rock grips the central feature of the site so tightly that it is impossible to take a photograph worth having. It looks as if Medicine Rock is in lockup, as if the authorities are afraid that it might just wander off in the night if it weren't fenced in or that someone might find spiritual clarity there even now. Given the appalling history of White treatment of Native Americans on the Great Plains, chain link fencing cannot help but evoke a kind of spiritual incarceration.

Here's another paradox. There are different types of sacred sites, but this one is sacred, if we understand it correctly, for being a message deliverer, an oracle. By throwing up a chain link fence, the people who now control the site have walled out anyone who actually wants to visit the sacred place as a sacred place, not just a somewhat interesting historic site in the middle of nowhere. Remember, the Native American aspirant washed a section of the sandstone with water, carefully positioned offerings, placed a bit of rawhide on the surface of the Medicine Rock, camped nearby overnight, and then came back to see what had developed. I use that metaphor purposefully. The Medicine Rock would either "write" its answer on the surface of the sandstone rock or on the leather medium, the "film." If you lock that sign generator up, not only do you possibly offend it (I am serious) and perhaps cause it to stop delivering the sacred (I am serious), but you have pre-determined that it is sacred no more (if it ever was), or perhaps should be sacred no more. To fence it is to declare that it no longer delivers meaning.

Mr. Governor, Tear Down This Wall!

It is, of course, clear that the prime purpose of the perimeter fence is to protect the Medicine Rock from defacement and graffiti. The problem of vandalism is a serious one. There are soul-dead morons who will despoil any monument, any significant outcropping, any sandstone pillar, almost any tree, from ancient Troy to the battlefield at Shiloh, from the Eiffel Tower to Echo Canyon in Dinosaur National Monument. A few years ago, I took a group of highly-educated people through the White Cliffs section of the Missouri River on the Lewis and Clark Trail in Montana. A Colorado woman brought her two early-adulthood children with her on the ten-day canoeing and hiking adventure. Her son, who was studying to be a ballet dancer, climbed up to the famous Hole in the Wall with the rest of us, performing "entrechats and sleight of foot tricks" (Ferlinghetti) for our amusement and admiration, all the way up and all the way down. At the top, when everyone else found a spot to sit and gaze out on the silent endlessness of the Missouri River corridor, he took a jackknife out of his pocket and began to carve his name into the sandstone cliff. In the gentlest possible way I said, "Ryan, please don't do that." He persisted. I said, "*Ryan! Please* don't do that." He did not turn to reply. "Why not? I want to. Everyone does it." I took a few steps toward him. "This is one of the most beautiful places in the American West. It's beautiful in part because it is still a wild place largely untouched by human intrusions. It's really important that you don't vandalize this place. As the tour leader, I have to ask you firmly to desist." He shrugged and said he didn't care what I thought, and went back to his desecration. Then I said, "Ryan, if you continue, I am going to tackle you and take away your knife. And then I'm going to ask you and your family to leave the trip." He jammed one more vicious gouge into the sandstone wall just to mess with me, and then waltzed sullenly off the hill. I did not rat him out to his mother, but he, of course, was sullen for the rest of the day.

The State Historical Society of North Dakota put up its cairn and historical sign at the Medicine Rock in 1963. William L. Guy was governor, John F. Kennedy was president. It was thus erected on the other side of the 1960-2000 multicultural revolution in America, but as these things go, it is pretty good. Nothing embarrassing or egregious. But without question it was written by a non-Indian. Note: the Italics are mine.

> *For many years* Indians *assembled* here to hold *their pow wows* and invoke the support of the Great Spirit that there might be *success on the buffalo hunts* that followed. The dance circle to the west of this marker is mute evidence of the thousands who

spent hours in the dance ceremonial, while *feasts* were held nearby. In the great cleft in the rock to the east of this marker, offerings of *trinkets beads and tobacco* were cast to *propitiate ATE*, their god. This site was used by the Indians *for many years* and few comparable areas are to be *found*. The carvings on THE MEDICINE ROCK attest to the hours spent *recording the types of wildlife* then so plentiful in this region.

Where to start? *For many years.* Ten or ten thousand? You would think it could be made a little more specific than this. *Assembled?* That suggests a parade or a school assembly or the Elgin Rotary Club. *Pow wows.* Whatever else was going on here, it wasn't a pow wow. It feels as if the writer asked himself, "What do Indians do when they get together? Well, pow wow, of course." *Success on the buffalo hunts.* Yes, certainly, but I don't think the Medicine Rock's powers were limited to the hunt. *Feasts.* Unlikely. The people who visited this site were almost certainly traveling light and eating little. It was not a place to feast, but a place to pray. Individuals and groups were more likely to have been fasting. *Trinkets beads and tobacco.* Aside from the breakdown of punctuation, the correct inventory would be tobacco certainly, beads maybe, trinkets, no. *Trinkets* is generally the word for what White men gave to Natives for things like Manhattan Island or the Black Hills. Lewis and Clark carried trinkets as tokens—fishhooks, beads, curtain rings, miniature mirrors, ribbons—signifying the industrial superiority of their home civilization. I don't know what the Mandan word for trinket is, but I'm guessing there is no such word. *Propitiate ATE, their god.* Propitiate just feels wrong. While it was not unknown for Native Americans to seek to propitiate being(s) beyond themselves, this seems like a White man's term for *seek guidance of.* Hard to know what to make of *ATE*, but it has the feel of "destiny," "fate," or "Great Spirit." *Their god* tells you who wrote the sign: god with a lower case g, the god of pagan people who have not yet known the One True God. It almost feels like air quotes: "their," as it were, "god," as it were. *Recording the types of wildlife.* This wasn't an eighth-grade science project for the Mandan-Hidatsa Encyclopedia Americana.

I mean no disrespect. This is a pretty sensitive historical sign, for that period, all things considered. Still, it is helplessly Eurocentric. Frankly, it's how a well-meaning White person who had no real idea how Native American spirituality worked would write such a sign. And yet there were Native Americans nearby in 1963 who could have shed light on this site and there were Native Americans all over the Great Plains, including the Mandan, Lakota, Hidatsa, and Arikara, who, if called upon, could have written or helped write the interpretation. Markers aspire to permanence. A historical marker is not a draft that can be erased and rewritten from time to time. It's important to try to get it right.

If a Native American rewrote the signage today, what would s/he say about this place? I would very much like to know. The good news is that the State Historical Society of North Dakota is currently working (2021) to rewrite the interpretive panel, with full participation of Native American elders and experts. The new signage will undoubtedly bring greater insight and sensitivity to this extraordinary place on the northern Great Plains.

My friend and I sat at the top of the bluff, but not actually on Medicine Rock, and gazed off into the distance in every direction. The best adjective is for our viewshed is *endless*, though someone else might say empty, dull, or godforsaken. That's what I love about Medicine Rock. To the untrained eye, it appears to be a nothingburger in the middle of the middle of the middle of nowhere. There is undifferentiated grazing land in every direction, punctuated by low buttes, hills, ridges, and bluffs, with a few tilled fields here and there on land that should never have been plowed. The wind blows more or less incessantly. It is often a stiff wind. You could sit here all day and maybe not see a single vehicle on the gravel roads five or ten miles away to the west and south. You could linger all day and never see any wildlife either, though Henry David Thoreau's advice is worth considering. "You only need sit still long enough in some attractive spot in the woods that all its inhabitants may exhibit themselves to you by turns."

You cannot help feeling swallowed up by the sheer vastness of the land, and its economic uselessness. Without wishing to depreciate the term, that makes it sacred to me.

We sat on top of the bluff gazing, half-dozing, daydreaming, listening for the message on the wind. If you had a heart attack and died here, how long would it take for someone to find you? Not long if you left your car at the base of the hill, but if you were dropped off by someone else and died here, it might be months before you were found, and by then much of you would have been eaten by coyotes, badgers, foxes, insects, and who knows what else. The feeling you get in such places is not helplessness and not even insignificance, though surely that is the best takeaway. The feeling I get is a kind of strange empowerment. And silence. I can spend hours just listening to the silence—the occasional whistle of the wind across your ears or rasping through the brittle grass; the liquid perfection of the meadowlark; mournful doves; now and then a brief (not quite sure you heard it) drone of a plane crossing the empty quarter at 38,500 feet. An owl at dusk.

It's so silent that you can hear yourself think. Thank God I live in America, where there are still places like this. Thank God the state historical society's claim on this place gives me a legitimate reason to come here, because I would not dare just climb someone's privately owned bluff to look around the Great Plains in this way. Thank goodness this is a seldom-visited place. If 5,000 people per year came here, it would be ruined by familiarity and the inevitable weekend waffle truck. Thank goodness North Dakota is so sparsely populated. I'm a plainsman; I like some breathing and stretching room in my life. Thank goodness there is so much land on the northern plains that is too marginal to turn to soybeans or even wheat. Give us a few things that are not fungible, please, O *Mih-Chóppenisch.* Thank goodness the internal combustion engine exists to bring me to such a place, because there is no way I would seek it out on horseback or on foot. But thank goodness you cannot drive right up to the chain link fence. You have to stretch your legs a little to get to the site.

Up on the edge of Medicine Rock I feel a little smug. I live in a flyover state, and in that negligible, unglamorous state I am drawn to even more negligible places. I don't regard this as *my* place and I don't seek to protect it in order to keep others out. I'm glad there is enough payoff to draw me here, equally glad there is not enough payoff to draw thousands here. Montana, the Dakotas, Nebraska, and Wyoming are full of such places, but they are mostly privately owned and the owners are on the whole pretty edgy about what they claim as theirs. I suppose I am with Jean Jacques Rousseau at heart: "The first person who, having enclosed a plot of land, took it into his head to say this is mine and found people simple enough to believe him was the true founder of civil society." The illusion that humans can own land is to my mind preposterous. Native Americans found it bewildering and preposterous, too. Therefore, when Euro-Americans really determined to break Native cultures, we forced them to adopt our conventions of private property.

While my friend walked around the butte and prayed in her own way, I spent half an hour trying to think about what this place must have been before the Industrial Revolution. I wondered what it would be like to be here during a thunderstorm. That would be spectacular, but I wondered if it might be too powerful an experience, perhaps even overwhelming. I'm planning to drive out some late afternoon this summer when my local Doppler Radar™ predicts a serious thunderstorm in Slope, Hettinger, and Grant counties. I wondered what it would be like to watch the Perseid meteor showers from here on a blanket in mid-August. I have never heard a coyote here, but I don't suppose you could avoid that if you spent the night. I wondered what it would be like to hear a Lakota or Mandan drum group here. You'd have to be invited. Unlikely.

I wondered how many people live within ten miles of the site? Twenty or thirty? Not more than that, perhaps fewer. I wonder how many people who live within fifty miles have ever climbed up here. How many more than once? The local rancher told me (spring 2019) that only a few dozen people visit the site each year. I would have thought they numbered in the medium hundreds. He said Native Americans used to come in greater frequency, but they are returning less often now. I asked if there had been any spike in visitation during the DAPL pipeline crisis of 2017, when people from all over the country and indeed all over the world came to the Standing Rock Indian Reservation to show solidarity and protest yet another assault on Indian dignity and Indian sovereignty. "No," said he. Does he mind people visiting the site, which is only accessible by driving or walking over his private property? "No, everyone's welcome." Did he ever feel any concern when Native Americans came to the site? "None at all." Once in a while, he stopped his work to watch them dancing up on the ridge. Did Native Americans ever stop at the house to ask directions, seek permission, or ask for help with their vehicles on the sometimes-muddy road? "No."

I had not known what to expect when I walked into his farmyard—house, shop, detached garage, collection of round hay bales, the usual strew of vehicles, a yard light. A friendly dog ran over working s-curves in his excitement. The farmer might have told me he did not appreciate me disturbing his Saturday work. He was hauling manure to a corn field—four, five, eight loads. There was a certain Sisyphean feel to his haulings as seen from several hundred feet above the ranch trail. He might have told me he didn't really appreciate people invading his private property to get access to a site he was technically obligated to make accessible. He might have said I was okay, but he was not that eager to see any of *your Native Americans* drive onto his farm. But he was none of these things. He was perfectly friendly, welcoming, hospitable, curious. Agreeable. Eager. Well informed. Maybe a little rural lonely for human contact. Nothing he said could be construed as critical of Native Americans at any level.

Come one, come all.

Who gets to decide what is sacred? If back in 1960 the state historical society had determined, after careful study, that the site had no sacred significance, and refused to spend any of its limited resources protecting a place it found insufficiently interesting for its imprimatur, and had the Mandan and Lakota people persisted in visiting the site, they would almost certainly have been shooed off any ranch owner's private property, quite possibly at the end of a gun. But who on the staff of the state historical society gets to make that choice? Who made the assessment then? That that individual or team was non-Native is virtually certain. It was 1963 in a different North Dakota and in a different America. Whom did they consult among Native people? It seems likely that this transaction, this transfer of private to public land, this official stamp of historical approval, was conducted entirely by White ranchers, working with White county commissioners, White archaeologists, White agency administrators, White historians, White lawyers, a White construction crew, and White writers. A document in the files of the State Historical Society of North Dakota indicates that on September 7, 1960, Gotlieb Zeller, Sr., and Harold and Esther Rosin, sold 11.88 acres to the state of North Dakota for a payment of $1. (President Jefferson bought the Louisiana territory for three cents per acre). If cultural leaders of the Mandan had come to the State Historical Society in 1960 seeking state protection for the site, would they have been taken seriously? What if on that basis an agency archaeologist visited the site and concluded, *marginal, I suggest we pass*? Then what?

So, how did the Medicine Rock come to be sacred? Assuming White folks don't frack it or strip mine it or level it for corn production, will it always remain sacred? Or is it spent? What are the possibilities?

I'm not really sure. Maybe it was always sacred, a kind of spirit vortex on the surface of the earth, and Native peoples had the antennae to sense the energy at some time long, long ago. A Lakota seer wrote, "The sacred is like rain. It falls everywhere but pools in certain places." Anthropologist Deward Walker reminds us that "sacred sites are places of communication with the spirits, portals where people enter the sacred . . . where spiritual power can be accessed and even attained." Or perhaps something remarkable happened here—a revelation, a vision quest, an inexplicable celestial phenomenon, a strange encounter with wildlife, an impossible victory in combat, an instantaneous certitude, love at first sight, a powerful dream—and it became sacred from that time forward. Perhaps Native individuals 200 years ago or 2,000 years ago happened on the site and felt strange energies present, and then had those energies confirmed by others.

I visited the site not long ago with a friend who has spent the last forty years cheerfully extracting carbon from underneath the surface of North Dakota and shipping it to the highest bidder—not an individual I would most expect to know much about the sacred. But when he stood on top of Medicine Rock and I asked him why it is sacred, he looked around for a minute or two and said, "It's the lichens."

It is true that the top of the Medicine Rock is almost entirely varnished with lichens in a wide variety of pastel colors: orange, three or four shades of green, yellow, black, brown, charcoal, gray, white, reddish, dark red, and even sky blue. Blue. I had never seen blue lichens before. And when I knelt to study them, to slow down long enough to notice them for the first time, I found that they were astonishingly beautiful. Possibly this is a clue to the sacredness of the place. As William Blake put it, you have to train yourself "To see a World in a Grain of Sand and Heaven in a Wild Flower, Hold Infinity in the palm of your hand and Eternity in an hour." My extractor friend, who has a serious love of western North Dakota, said, "The other outcroppings around here don't have lichens. That's the difference. The Natives recognized that immediately. And who knows what they thought about how such colorful lichens wind up on rock surfaces?" I knew from my study of Lewis and Clark that virtually all the Native Americans they met (1804-06) preferred gifts of blue beads to those of any other color. The understanding I had was that it was difficult if not impossible for Native Americans to manufacture blue pigmentation themselves. So, if the Great Mystery chose to carpet this rock with a Rorschach array of colorful lichens, including blue, maybe that signified something that helped confirm that this was a sacred place. Maybe the oracle *wrote* in lichens.

Several of the early accounts of Medicine Rock mention that there is a fissure in the rock formation that was regarded as important by Indian visitors. Often enough, it is fissures in the earth that wind up as Delphic shrines. Where the earth emits fumes from somewhere in the interior, through some fracture or fissure in the broader continuity of the land, humans pay special attention. Think of Yellowstone National Park, for example. When a quarter section somewhere in America suddenly subsides for no good reason, curious people flock to the site. And the owners throw up a chain link fence to ward off liability lawsuits. A good fissure forces us to wonder what's really going on down there, what's beneath the surface, what kind of energies are swirling underneath the lands we walk so complacently and take so completely for granted. In places like Yellowstone, and Kilauea Volcano in Hawaii, those subterranean energies percolate up through the surface. Surely there are lesser, more subtle fissures everywhere.

I've been to Delphi in Greece five or six times in my life. I've studied ancient Greek culture more thoroughly than I have studied Great Plains Indian culture, and I don't feel I really understand the nature of the sacred in either of those worlds. Neither Delphi nor the Medicine Rock has ever spoken to me. It is sometimes thought that the priestess at Delphi (known as Pythia) sat astride a sulfurous fissure and that the vapors intoxicated her in some creative way, threw her out of her left-brained paradigm and enabled her to see something beyond the usual reach of the conscious mind. According to the ancient historian Herodotus, Pythia answered questions in dactylic hexameter, a complicated meter. What could be better than vatic mastery delivered up in ancient Greek prosody? The priestess' answers were often wry and sometimes puzzling.

Nobody knows just how Delphi became sacred. Apparently, Zeus regarded it as the center of the world. It was also a sanctuary for the Greek god Apollo. That couldn't have hurt, but the sanctuary may have come *after* the site was recognized as sacred. One account says that shepherds noticed that their goats, grazing on the side of the mountain of Parnassus, suddenly began dancing in an orgiastic way when they ventured near the fissure. Drunk goats. When the shepherds approached to investigate, *they* began to gyrate too. If this is true, Delphi was sacred because it was sacred (or toxic). I have asked questions at Dephi twice—both in great reverent sincerity. Perhaps my gifts have been inadequate. I am pretty sure my antenna is bent. Next time I am hiking up to the site from the sea and taking a gift.

North Dakota has a Medicine Hole in the Killdeer Mountains. On top of the southern butte (elevation 3,314 feet) there is a chalky fissure that some believe is the vent of a significant underground system of caverns and crevices. Some Mandan, Hidatsa, and Lakota regard the Medicine Hole as the vaginal fissure through which buffalo were born into the world. Thus its name. Even if from a scientific perspective we regard this as implausible, it's a beautiful origin myth. We also now understand, as our forebears did not, that there are truths that have validity beyond their scientific verifiability. The Mandan believe(d) that the Earth is a living being capable of birthing creatures like the buffalo—and humans, too. The Mandan believe(d) they found their way up onto the land from a subterranean lake (though not necessarily at the Medicine Hole).

The Mandan tell the story of their subterranean origins with their characteristic sense of humor. The people had a good enough existence in the underworld, but when a vine grew up so high that it found its way through a fissure to the surface, the first great culture hero of the Mandan decided to climb the vine and see what he would find at the top. The world into which he emerged was a Garden of Eden compared to the life below. He climbed down to report his great discovery. Soon all the Mandan people began climbing up to the surface of Mother Earth. Unfortunately, an old fat Mandan woman decided to make the ascent, against the pleadings of her friends and family. She was only part way up when her weight broke the vine and she fell back to the subterranean world. Thereafter, all those who remained below were destined to live there forever, including the woman of great girth. To that subterranean world the Mandan return after they die.

Like many other Native cultures, the Mandan believed that the Earth birthed everything that is, that grasses were her hair, hillocks her breasts, and that to plow the earth or to dig for minerals was to do violence to the Great Mother, who provided all good things for humankind. It's not that the Mandan didn't grow corn and beans and sunflowers using hoes made of bison shoulder bones, mine flint for arrow points, and harvest medicinal plants, not to mention kill deer, bison, and antelope for food. But they did so with a strong conviction that they could not do these things wantonly or with spiritual indifference. They were aware that in the great circle of life they might of necessity kill a bison, but at the same time they cheerfully acknowledged that they themselves would eventually die and molder into loam, and that loam would spring forth in prairie grasses, which the buffalo would eat to thrive, and they in turn. . . .

If you stop to think about how the buffalo (*bison bison*) came to be, you wind up exploring the world of North American megafauna—the paleo-bison, taurine cattle, etc. It isn't long before your eyes glaze over and you nearly lose interest in trying to figure it all out. We get that the modern bison evolved from something else and that the buffalo has not been locked in this form from time immemorial. Fair enough, but the science takes the romance out of the story and leads one to conclude that probably somewhere far back some rat or badger-like thing was the progenitor of North America's most magnificent quadruped. The Mandan story is just better in every way.

Earth birthed this great creature as it now is, and the Earth made it clear that humankind would benefit greatly from the gift. Don't tell me there was once a giraffe with a shorter neck. In the eyes of any child who has not yet studied evolution, the buffalo clearly arrived in the universe fully formed in precisely the shape and size it now occupies. It had to come from somewhere, just as you and I came from somewhere. For some Mandan and the Hidatsa the Medicine Hole is that somewhere. Given the utter dependence of plains tribes on the buffalo—food, shelter, clothing, implements, armaments, cooking vessels, sacred masks, game pieces, glue—it is hardly surprising that the Mandan would want to know how the buffalo came to be, and from what fissure in the earth it came up onto the land. The buffalo was central to plains Indian lifeway in a way that nothing is sacred to the lifeway of White denizens of the plains. You'd have to bundle the car, the grocery store, the house, gardening tools, and winter clothing in one entity to get close.

If anything is sacred, the buffalo is sacred. And once upon a time, there were 60 million of them, thousands surely in the vicinity of the Medicine Rock at any given moment of time. Then White men came. Now there are perhaps 500,000* left in the world. Unfortunately, the Medicine Hole site is privately owned, not maintained by the State Historical Society of North Dakota, and though the ranch family has been generous towards Native Americans who seek to make pilgrimages to the site, recent land-use controversies have led them to close access to the merely curious. Thus a North Dakota medicine

---

*   362,406 according to the National Bison Association.

rock equally important as *The* Medicine Rock, and in a much more impressive landscape, is now off limits to those trying to make sense of sacred places on the Great Plains.

We had been outside the perimeter for about half an hour and now it was time to go in. The fence is designed to keep people out, but since the nearest park ranger is a hundred miles away, and the nearest person who cares whether you jump the fence is at least an hour away by car, we didn't spend much time looking over our shoulders. I had done this three or four previous times, but back then the old fence had been beaten down by visitors to facilitate access. The new fence was more formidable. I was mansplaining all of this to my companion when she said, "So if it is fenced how do we get in?" I said we would have to climb over, that I had done it before, not to worry, nobody was watching, no real crime, and besides how dare they fence in the sacred? We were both wearing winter parkas. So, I grabbed the fence at about ear level and lurched up and over the top, not without tearing a bit of the bright REI blue fabric. She climbed over the top more gracefully and suddenly we were catching our breath on the lowest slab of sandstone.

We examined petroglyphs of turtles, hoof prints, and other uncertain figures etched into the lower slabs of sandstone. There were no space aliens of the sort you see in the American Southwest. I had read that one piece of sandstone bearing petroglyphs had been broken off the Medicine Rock and formerly put on display in the Heritage Center (the State Historical Society museum) in Bismarck. I regard this as a serious blasphemy. Like the Elgin Marbles, it should be returned, if possible, to the site from which it was rudely looted long ago. I would think that NAGPRA (the Native American Graves Protection and Repatriation Act of 1990) should require that. The glyphs that now adorn Medicine Rock are presumably authentic and historical, but it is quite possible that they have been *enhanced and improved* by more recent visitors. Some people find this sort of thing irresistible.

What is the Native American concept of Medicine with a capital *M*? It's not triple bypass surgery or chemotherapy. But it is not purely spiritual, either. It is a kind of mind-body wholeness that does not end at the outer rim of the body. It is a sense of presence (presentness) among energies that cannot be measured or boxed or bought. It is an awareness that the world is awash in spiritual energies, that *the spiritual* radiates through everything and from everything. It's there all the time, like X-rays and gamma rays and FM, but it doesn't do you any good unless you develop the receiver to be able to tune it in. This requires spiritual discipline. For Native Americans this often involved an interruption of normal rhythms: fasting, walking, sweating, chanting, aloneness, self-mutilation, incessant dancing or prayer, consultation with elders and spiritual leaders. If you could get out from under your own ego attachment, you could see beyond the range of Newton and hear beyond the range of Edison.

The Lakota spiritual leader Lame Deer (1903-1976) argued that the words *medicine* and *medicine man* are inherently reductive, misleading, Eurocentric, even racist. What we call Medicine Rock would not be given that name today, any more than Lake Tahoe's Squaw Valley would be given such a name today. The Medicine Rock would probably merely be called—in English—a sacred place. Lame Deer said, "'Medicine man'—that's a White man's word like squaw, papoose, Sioux, tomahawk—words that don't exist in the Indian language." He cautioned that these hidden powers and perceptions are not to be approached lightly, that medicine energies can bite if they are not treated with proper respect and humility. The word *medicine* has no adequate, no non-reductive meaning in English, but it means something like a person, a place, an event, a phenomenon that is imbued with spiritual energies, which—properly approached or interpreted—confer understanding or advantage or mind-body integration to those who have access to it. It does not so much mean physical or spiritual wellness as a heightened presentness and an awareness of the metaphysical significance of seemingly normal things, events, and transactions. Sitting Bull had essential conversations with meadowlarks in the years that led up to the Little Bighorn. More to the point, he listened with reverence and respect.

Perhaps the closest thing we have to Medicine in Judeo-Christian culture is the Catholic mass. The mass is a sacrament beyond reason. No merely rational person would believe that a priest can call Jesus into a wafer and that when you eat the wafer you are ingesting God. That's a wild idea, but Catholics (and some other Christians) believe it is truth. Unless you grew up in the Catholic Church and you simply accept the truth of the Mass because you accept the truth of the Mass, you can only come to terms with it if you are willing to acknowledge that there is mystery at the heart of who we are and how we relate to the divine.

I have been at the Medicine Rock many times. When I first visited the site, there were dozens, perhaps even scores of tobacco bundles (tobacco tied round into a piece of cloth) on the fence, strewn among the sandstone outcrop, and in the bushes. More recently the number of prayer bundles has diminished significantly. The local rancher believes the family or community that made pilgrimages to the site may have turned elsewhere or lost belief. Perhaps these things work in cycles. If the site is no longer delivering something worth the voyage, perhaps it is the chain link fence, perhaps it is the confiscated slab "on loan" to the Heritage Center, perhaps it is the tillage right up to the fence line. Perhaps it is the intrusion of people—like me, perhaps?—who have no legitimate reason to be there.

Once, many years ago, I took friends from out of town and my mother to see Medicine Rock. I don't know what they were expecting but I am pretty sure they were all disappointed. I had to talk hard to convince them that the site was interesting or important—I would have settled for either. It was a bitterly cold day just before or just after Thanksgiving. My mother—for whom there is no sacred place—climbed up without hesitation and had me take a picture of her gesturing like Rocky Balboa on top of the sacred rock. And we wonder why it doesn't speak to us! Then she used the photo for her Christmas card. Those who received the photo card were not informed that we were at a place regarded as sacred by Native Americans. We could have been on any old bluff in North Dakota (or elsewhere for that matter). I don't know much about the sacred, but I am guessing that you have to attenuate your ego more than Mother did to get a signal.

Non-native though I am, I find my way to the Medicine Rock when I have something I want to pray my way through. I also have a replica in my bedroom of the San Damiano Cross of St. Francis of Assisi (ca. 1182-1226). Young Francis was praying beneath the cross in the chapel of San Damiano just outside of Assisi when the Lord spoke directly to him. "Francis, Francis, go and repair My house which, as you can see, is falling into ruins." At first Francis misunderstood the sacred instruction, as we are all apt to do. He thought God wanted him to repair the San Damiano chapel, so he began to collect coins for that purpose. Only later did he realize that the church he was to repair was the whole enchilada. I have been waiting for God to speak to me directly from the moment I visited Assisi ten years ago and purchased a beautiful 18-inch replica of the cross, because I would rather just take the call, no matter how onerous the commandment, than earn it by fasting, or sweating, or following those who, as Thoreau puts it, have been "chained for life, at the foot of a tree; or measuring with their bodies, like caterpillars, the breadth of vast empires." Like most impatient wasichus (purblind White folks) I want to take my spiritual nourishment like Valium or Ritalin or Viagra (consult your doctor if your spiritual experience lasts more than four hours).

When I am really troubled or perplexed, I get in the car and drive either to the badlands along the Little Missouri River north of Marmarth, North Dakota, or I climb the nearest accessible butte. If I am in serious need of help, I drive to Medicine Rock. And if I am in profound spiritual disarray, I go all the way to Bear Butte in South Dakota, the most sacred place I know. But that is a long journey.

In the course of a long life of deep and genuine respect for the Native American cultures of the Great Plains, I have prayed and smoked and fasted and sweated, lain in what I regard as sacred places, chanted praise and perplexity, prayed out loud and prayed silently, done deep breathing exercises, even engaged in very low level and bourgeois sacrifices of the flesh. I have attempted to listen to the grass and listen to the wind. At times I have almost "heard the mermaids singing," but in the end, like T.S. Eliot, "I do not think that they will sing for me."

I go to Medicine Rock not to pretend, for a couple of hours, to be a "White Indian," which I believe is a serious breach of cultural respect. I go because I want to pray on a crested butte in the vast and open plain of western Dakota, and I know that it is a prayer site, that many others have prayed there, some of them non-Native, and that if my heart is true, I cannot do any harm to myself, to others, or to the place by making a humble pilgrimage there. I do not ever enter the "Indians Only" trails at Bear Butte or anywhere else. I try to do what I do with intentionality and respect, and my prayers at such places are ecumenical—and thus probably inert. I go there to be alone. I go there because I know I will not be disturbed. I go there because I believe there is a message to be discerned there, if you stop long enough to listen with more than just your ears. I go there because I want to cast my limited spiritual lot, at least to a certain extent, with the people who figured out how to live in this place long before Columbus stumbled onto the shores of the Western Hemisphere and Europeans began to plop their Palestinian paradigm onto the landscape. I go there because to go there is a time-consuming, deliberate act, and during the eighty-minute drive, I ask myself what

I want to learn. On the return journey, if I am not craving a Big Mac or a pizza, I try to reflect on what I heard myself say.

After a couple of hours at the wee summit of Medicine Rock, I am suddenly conscious that it is late afternoon and we had better start heading back. Truth told, I feel a little ridiculous. There are at least ninety churches in Bismarck, North Dakota, many of them with their doors unlocked. God is either going to hear me in any of those dozens of churches or on my knees in my bedroom or not, and I don't have any right (or perhaps any reason) to try to connect with the "Great Spirit," if that's what this is somehow about. Why did we come here at all? What, if anything, have we accomplished? Or learned? Who do I think I am? (There's a seemingly simple question). We decided to walk around the rock one more time before climbing back up over the fence. My friend began to laugh.

"You idiot, there's a gate here, and it's unlocked. Wow. Next time, save the heroics and the mansplaining, *s'il vous plait.*" We jumped the fence to get into the site, feeling like spiritual anarchists, and we walked out through the open gate. The Medicine Rock had humbled us after all.

The mosque at Ross, North Dakota.

The death of a cottonwood tree. The earth, the earth alone abides.

Pretty Butte not far from where Theodore Roosevelt
killed his first buffalo.

Medicine Rock, all chained up and nowhere to go.

Mythologizing both the past and present in North Dakota. Alan Demaray with a Hollywood actor.

The most remote ICBM missile site in North Dakota, with a bit of protest signage.

Earl Bunyon, the wire-thin cousin of Minnesota's Paul Bunyan.

Burn, baby, burn.

Where temporary oilfield housing goes to die.

The merry prankster Bill Bender at the center of something.

The new center of North America at Center.

Contempt. Low water crossing south of Marmarth on the sacred Little
Missouri River, plus an oil truck.

The author at the grave of Governor Arthur A. Link
at Alexander, North Dakota.

Swords into Ploughshares: Monsignor James Shea
celebrates mass at a missile site.

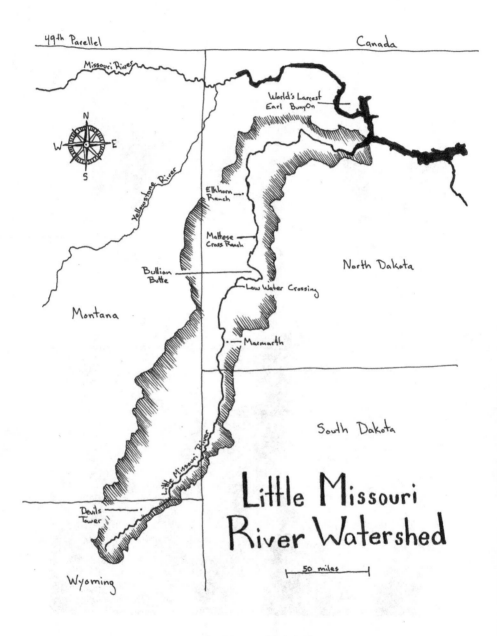

The sacred corridor: the valley of the Little Missouri River. Can we agree to protect this much of North Dakota?

"WHERE ALPH THE SACRED RIVER RAN:"
THE THREAT TO THE LITTLE MISSOURI RIVER

"A man is rich in proportion to the number of things which he can afford to let alone."
—Henry David Thoreau

"A live deer in the woods will attract to the neighborhood ten times the money that could be obtained for the deer's dead carcass."
—Theodore Roosevelt

I'm camped along the edge of the Little Missouri River north of the village of Marmarth in a lean cluster of cottonwood trees. The temperature is about sixty-eight degrees, subsiding about two degrees per hour. It will not freeze tonight, but as Hamlet says, it will be "a nipping and an eager air" come midnight, when I venture out on tender pampered white feet and wince-foot it just far enough from my tent for respectability's sake to pee. The cottonwoods are thin and wispy here, with some bare and shattered limbs and a few fallen branches to serve as camp pews. I'm maybe thirty feet from the riverbank, but the Little Missouri itself is a dozen yards farther away.

The river is low. I walked across it three times in the last two hours. The highest it got was just below my knees. If I had the car keys and a cell phone in my pants pocket, I would not have gotten them wet.

I'm the only person here, the only person for miles in any direction. My modest blue and white REI tent is set up facing west in the hope of a thunderstorm. I can see a few white-faced Herefords off in the distance. Occasionally, one of them bawls for no apparent reason. I am waiting for the first yip and croon of the coyotes. The sun is going to set within the next half hour. The sky is mostly cloudless, serenely autumnal, and the river is a magical reflected blue against the tawny and russet grasses and the golden yellow of the cottonwood leaves, in this little corner of the Great Plains. Down on the western horizon there are some charcoal gray clouds. That should enhance the sunset. The cottonwood leaves are not yet at their maximum beauty, but that day will come within the next week. At that point, if you catch it, the Little Missouri River valley is as beautiful a place as exists on earth—a lazy pointless western river threading its way around graceful s-curves and cutting the badlands steadily badder.

I'm boiling water (not from the Little Missouri!) on a marvelously efficient little stove no bigger than a grapefruit. My freeze-dried dinner tonight will be kung pao chicken. These camp meals have come a long way in the last thirty years. Some of them are positively delicious. If my calculations are correct, the moon will rise about 9:30 p.m., more full than not. There is nothing I am afraid of here but man. It is exceedingly unlikely that anyone would spot me here or know I have set up camp in this little copse on a grass bench of a remote river that is mostly just left alone. I am happy.

I've been a proud North Dakotan all of my life and I know the state about as well as anyone. I love North Dakota passionately, but not unconditionally. I would not camp along the Red River over on the eastern lip of the state (certainly not), or the Souris or the James or the Cannonball or the Heart. Maybe I might camp along the Missouri north of Bismarck where there are a few remote sandbars and sand beaches, but you cannot really cavort in the Missouri anymore, not since the 1950s and '60s when the great dams turned one of the world's great rivers into a series of colder, deeper, inhospitable slack water reservoirs. I might camp along the Sheyenne River south of I-94 down near Fort Ransom, but only at an approved National Grasslands site. When I spend the night in the Little Missouri River Valley, I always make sure that I camp on the American Commons, on US Forest Service National Grasslands sections, easily recognized on the maps because they are shaded in forest service green. I do not camp on private land unless the owner and I are friends. Even camping on the commons is a modest risk because every acre of grassland lies within the perimeter of someone's cattle ranch. Even though they lease that public land from the US Forest Service, and I am one of the 340 million owners of the property, some of the ranchers get a little edgy about people hanging out on land they fundamentally regard as their own, no matter who holds the actual title.

Thanks to the existence of Theodore Roosevelt National Park in three units (70,446 acres) and the 1.2 million acres of the Little Missouri National Grasslands, I feel at home in the Little Missouri River valley. I don't light fires when I am alone out there. I don't leave fence gates open. I don't mar the landscape or leave any trash. What I'm here to extract is spiritual.

After eating my fill, I sealed up the aluminum ziplock bag. I'll eat the rest cold for breakfast before I hoist my pack over my shoulders a little after first light. The sun has set, but the afterglow is perfect. You can see pink roseate light all the way around the circle of land and sky that is the American West. I'm sitting with my back to a large bare fallen cottonwood log. It's too dark to read, and I'm too lazy to scrounge for my headlamp. There are so few moments like this in a summer. Well, actually, so few in a lifetime. The temperature has continued to drop; I feel a little chilled. If someone handed me a jacket I'd put it on, but I actually like the feeling. It makes me feel alive, in the moment. Present. I'm sitting somewhere in the vast lonely outback of America just glad to be alive. If I understand the concept of the sacred, this place is undoubtedly sacred, at least to me. The only thing that will get me into that tent is sheer fatigue when I cannot keep my eyes open to the stars any longer. Then I will insert myself into my ultra-light sleeping bag and drift off.

The Little Missouri River originates among the Flatiron Hills and Missouri Buttes of northeastern Wyoming, near the town of Oshoto (population ca. 5) and not far from Devils Tower, to which the Missouri Buttes are geologic cousins. It is a pretty miserable little plains river in Wyoming and through southeastern Montana and all the way to about the North Dakota-South Dakota border south of Marmarth. Only then does it begin to etch the landscape and, soon enough, to carve it. If you happened upon the river anywhere south of Marmarth, and did not already know what river it was, you would never guess that it was the Little Missouri, because we associate the Little Missouri with breaks, buttes, coulees, striations, badlands, and even canyons—not open plains country. Until it slips by Pretty Butte north of Marmarth, none of those characteristic features really appears. After that the river starts to get more dramatic every few miles as it flows north from Marmarth to the base of Bullion Butte, which is so massive that it forces the river to loop all the way around it to the east and north. Theodore Roosevelt used to take the cutoff on the west side of Bullion Butte, thus saving more than forty miles of river riding. On one occasion, because he was Roosevelt, he rode the entire oxbow, just to enjoy that experience. Later he wrote, "There were all kinds of things I was afraid of at first, ranging from grizzly bears to 'mean' horses and gun-fighters; but by acting as if I was not afraid I gradually ceased to be afraid."

The Little Missouri first feels like the Little Missouri a few miles south of Medora. Most people experience only the stretch of the river in Medora and the south unit of Theodore Roosevelt National Park, where it cuts badlands of a yellow and gray sort, with some blackish lignite coal veins thrown in, supporting light vegetation, particularly on the north face of buttes and cliffs. But you have not really experienced the badlands until you drive off pavement and get the smell of dust in your nostrils.

The badlands of North Dakota seem to come straight out of central casting, the kind of landscape you'd set a Roy Rogers or John Wayne or Clint Eastwood movie in. It's the Old West on a modest scale—broken country in every direction, rugged hills, cliffs, ridges, and buttes, with a broad (though miniature) valley at its center and a lazy serpentine shallow plains river running through it. The badlands of North Dakota have a kind of droll, whimsical, slightly improbable feel about them, perhaps because they appear so suddenly as you approach from the east. Then, as you drive along undifferentiated plains country, the bottom of the land just drops out. Roosevelt said the badlands reminded him somehow of the poetry of Edgar Allan Poe. It's hard to believe this shallow, sluggish river carved so dramatic and breathtaking a landscape. You have to change your watch to geologic time to make sense of it. There are occasions in the southern part of the Little Missouri River in North Dakota south of Interstate 94 when you think you might be on the Moon or Mars and there are times when the river valley north of the Elkhorn Ranch unit feels like a mild version of the Grand Canyon. The river bites deeper into the land as it flows north.

In his landmark 1945 book about the Missouri River, the historian Stanley Vestal devoted a chapter to the Little Missouri corridor. "The Badlands of the Little Missouri cover hundreds of square miles with one of the most fantastic landscapes in North America, a welter of strange ridges and bare hillocks, pyramids, domes, and buttes, barred with horizontal stripes of varicolored strata, red, yellow, brown, and gray, which contrast beautifully with the silver sage below and the dark cedars on the eroded slopes. They form a labyrinth of waterless dead hills and dry coulees—an unearthly country, fantastic and tumultuous—at once serene and incredible. . . . It was tough country for soldiers and cavalry horses, but for the man with an eye for beauty and a taste for solitude it seems a genuine garden of God." There are other places like it in the American West, but none quite like it.

Famous rodeo champions have emerged from the Little Missouri Country: Elmer Clark of Marmarth, Jim Tescher of Medora, and Grassy Butte's Alvin Nelson, the 1957 World Saddle Bronc Champion who married Kaye Nelson who was Miss Rodeo North Dakota. She still lives out there on the ranch, far from even the Grassy Butte post office.

The first known White person on the river was a solo adventurer and fur trapper named Baptiste Lepage who traveled from the greater Black Hills country to the mouth of the Knife River along the Little Missouri in the fall of 1804. There, at what became Fort Mandan, he happened upon a huge camp of almost fifty White people, the Lewis and Clark Expedition just beginning to bed down for the long plains winter at a crude log compound. The expedition's leaders hired Lepage on the spot to fill the position previously occupied by private John Newman, who was court martialed, pummeled, and drummed out of the expedition earlier that fall for uttering mutinous expressions near the mouth of the Grand River at what would become the North Dakota-South Dakota border eighty-five years later. In his final report to Secretary of War Henry Dearborn, dated January 15, 1807, Lewis spoke highly of almost every member of the Corps of Discovery, but about Lepage, who had not been recruited back east to be a member of the exploring party, Lewis was less generous. "Entitled to no peculiar merit," he wrote. Unfortunately, no-merit Lepage kept no journal on his solo trek, wrote no subsequent memoir. We don't know if he floated the Little Missouri (probably) or hiked along its banks (less likely). He was surely the first White man to descend the Little Missouri from near its source to its mouth. The first of two. It's eerie enough to be out there alone today. Imagine 1804.

The Hunkpapa leader Sitting Bull (1831-90) liked to locate his winter camps on the upper Little Missouri, probably closer to today's Alzada, Montana, or Camp Crook, South Dakota, than to Marmarth, North Dakota. George Armstrong Custer followed the Little Missouri upstream (south) to get to the Black Hills in 1874, thus inspiring the Cheyenne and the Lakota to call his route the "Thieves Road." Custer also spent some time dinking around in the badlands south of Medora on his way to his death at the Little Bighorn two years later. The mastermind of that wipeout was Sitting Bull. When Crazy Horse was finally promised a secure reservation sanctuary, he wanted to locate it in the Powder River Country, the next great watershed to the west. Some of the great Texas cattle outfits established satellite ranches in the Little Missouri valley in the early 1880s—The 777, the Reynolds Brothers, the Berry-Boice, the OX, the Continental Land and Cattle Company, and others.

And then came TR. Young Roosevelt traveled to the badlands of Dakota Territory in September 1883 to kill a buffalo. He was twenty-four years old, as bold as he was physically fragile. He had a difficult hunt, partly because the weather was lousy for the entire two weeks he was there, but mostly because by the time he shot his stately bull, a straggler, on September 20, 1883, there were not more than 500 buffalo left in all of America. Kid Roosevelt killed his first buffalo on the upper reaches of Little Cannonball Creek, on the Dakota-Montana line (probably just inside Montana), not five miles from the Little Missouri. The late Merle Clark of Marmarth knew where the kill occurred, just west of his ranch, but he never got around to taking me to the spot. He said he had been there with a US Forest Service Ranger in the '70s, and that at one point there had been a metal stake at the presumed site. It was never a good idea to doubt Merle Clark, but he was a busy man with a very wide range of historical, industrial, and paleontological interests, and we were never able to arrange the trek.

I have pitched my tent at the source of Little Cannonball Creek, presumably within a mile (at most, two) of the kill site. But I have found no stake. Roosevelt's two Dakota Territory ranches were on the Little Missouri River, forty miles apart, one headquartered on the east bank (the Maltese Cross), one on the west bank (the Elkhorn). When he brought his agreeable but civilized wife, Edith, to the badlands in 1890, along with his sister Corinne and several others, the wagon on which they were conveyed from Medora to the Elkhorn rumbled through the river twenty-three times, sometimes at breakneck speed. Edith Roosevelt never crossed any river in the world more often in less elapsed time. And she was not nearly so DEE-lighted in the adventure as her husband of four years. She never returned. He seldom did either because his destiny was now back in the national arena.

It was in the Little Missouri country that Theodore Roosevelt transformed himself—and was transformed—into that larger-than-life, mock-heroic exemplar of the strenuous life that rattled the world after he returned to civilization around 1890. Roosevelt regarded his badlands sojourn as the most important formative experience of his life. He told a US Senator from New Mexico that he would be willing to lose the memory of every other adventure of his life if he could only keep one. "I would take the memory of my life on the ranch, with its experiences close to Nature and among the men who lived nearest her." In important respects, he *became* Theodore Roosevelt on the banks of the Little Missouri River. For the rest of his life, he exaggerated the amount of time he actually spent in the North Dakota badlands and embellished his adventures in the direction of John Hay's *Pike County Ballads* and the dime novel. I have a close friend, a badlands bookseller and a historian, who enjoys puncturing the balloons of TR's badlands stories. But what is the point of that? The West has always been the home of the tall tale. Just read Mark Twain's *Roughing It*.

It was thanks to his time in North Dakota that Roosevelt became the nation's first cowboy president. It was in the badlands of Dakota that Roosevelt began to formulate his conservation ethic and natural resource policies. It was from among the gentlemen and desperadoes of Dakota Territory that TR recruited the core of his Rough Riders in 1898. Stopping in Medora in 1900 while campaigning for President McKinley's re-election, gazing from the back of his campaign train at the grangers, hunters, cowboys, children, and ranch women he had known in the most impressionable period of his young manhood, Roosevelt uttered one of the most important sentences of his life. "It was here that the romance of my life began." Not in Wyoming on the Powder. Not in Montana along the Yellowstone or Musselshell. Not in South Dakota along the Belle Fourche or the Cheyenne. Not in Colorado's fabulous western slope. But on the banks of the Little Missouri River. Listen to his outstanding prose:

This, like most other plains rivers, has a broad, shallow bed, through which in times of freshets runs a muddy current, that neither man nor beast can pass; at other seasons of the year it is very shallow, spreading out into pools, between which the trickling water may be but a few inches deep. Even then, however, it is not always easy to cross, for the bottom is filled with quicksands and mud-holes. The river flows in long sigmoid curves through an alluvial valley of no great width. The amount of this alluvial land enclosed by a single bed is called a bottom, which may be either covered with cotton-wood trees or else be simply a great grass meadow. From the edges of the valley the land rises abruptly in steep high buttes whose crests are sharp and jagged.

He exaggerated the quicksand.

If the Little Missouri River valley transformed TR from a sickly New York punkin lily to one of the most strenuous, adventurous, and remarkable men in American history, that alone should make us want to preserve the landscape that worked that consequential metamorphosis. The St. Paul *Pioneer Press* caught up with Roosevelt as he passed through the Minnesota on his way back to New York in June 1885, two years into his adventures. The former Albany dandy now appeared "rugged, bronzed and in the prime of health. . . . There was very little of the whilom dude in his rough and easy costume, with a large handkerchief tied loosely about his neck; but the eye glasses and the flashing eyes behind them, the pleasant smile and the hearty grasp of the hand remained. . . . The slow exasperating drawl and the unique accent the New Yorker feels he must use when visiting a less blessed portion of civilization have disappeared, and in their place is a nervous [the word is being used in a positive sense] energetic manner of talking with the flat accent of the West."

Roosevelt loved the press, but not as much as the press loved Roosevelt.

Later, in 1903 John Burroughs wrote, "His ranch life had been the making of him. It had built him up and hardened him physically, and it had opened his eyes to the wealth of manly character among the plainsmen and cattlemen. Had he not gone West, he said, he never would have raised the Rough Riders regiment; and had he not raised that regiment and gone to the Cuban War, he would not have been made governor of New York; and had not this happened, the politicians would not unwittingly have made his rise to the Presidency so inevitable."

There are a couple of other really attractive plains rivers in North Dakota—the Cannonball, the Heart, the Grand among them—but I don't hike or camp along them because they are almost entirely privately owned. The idea of public domain has a reassuring effect on the soul. I thank God I live in a country that still has large fragments of public land. America would be a sad place if the privatization advocates got their way and private property obsessives got all of it. They are trying.

My point is simple. The Little Missouri is North Dakota's only truly public river. It is the most beautiful river in North Dakota. It is also the river with the most colorful story tradition, though the Red was once important as Minnesota spilled over onto the prairie, and the great Missouri can boast Lewis and Clark, Prince Maximilian, the American Fur Company, Forts Union and Clark, Custer at Fort Lincoln, the steamboat era, and the monuments of the of the gigantic dam building era of the mid-twentieth century. Partly because it is not tied to such a heritage, the Little Missouri is better known for its aesthetic and spiritual value than its history. It has the enormous advantage of having been for the most part left alone. The Little Missouri is North Dakota's greatest single natural wonder—believe it or not there are others. It has a unique heritage. In a state that is 95 percent privately owned, with virtually every inch of its surface paved, tilled, occupied, overbuilt, and manicured, we can afford to carve out one sliver of magnificent landscape to leave in its natural state, or more precisely *as near as possible* to its natural state. We could, but we do not need to, develop the Little Missouri River valley and turn its resources (water, oil, incredible beauty, and unusualness) into cash. Only a spiritually bankrupt people would do so.

The Little Missouri River is not an abundant water resource. Official flow statistics show it varying from 110,000 cubic feet per second (cfs) to zero [sic] and averaging only 534 cfs. The Missouri River proper, by contrast, averages 87,520 cfs. That means that the Missouri, on average, carries 163 times more volume than its diminutive eponymous tributary. North Dakota stores 22 million acre feet of water behind Garrison Dam, and even with the Bakken's heavy water demands for fracking, the state now uses only 1.6 percent of the Missouri's annual flow of 17 million acre feet. So, why would the oil industry draw water from the hapless Little Mo when you have an infinite water source nearby? Because they can. Because nobody protests, because there are too few environmental watchdogs, and because the intake structures are so far from the main traveled roads of North Dakota that they are almost never visited, but also because the 1975 Little Missouri Scenic River Act is both toothless and ignored, because the North Dakota state government, including the three-member Industrial Commission, seems to be more comfortable working on behalf of the oil and gas industrial complex than for the sanctity of the Little Missouri River, or the preservation of the North Dakota badlands.

Put it another way. The Little Missouri River may not be an abundant water resource, but it is a magnificent aesthetic resource, while its gigantic nearby cousin, the Missouri River, aesthetically compromised for the last seventy years thanks to the US Army Corps of Engineers, is an essentially limitless source of water for industrial use. To tap one is a drop in the bucket. To tap the other is to destroy its sanctitude.

I claim a special relationship with the Little Missouri River. I believe I can securely declare that I am the only living person who has walked the entire length of the river, from Oshoto, Wyoming, to Halliday, North Dakota (much of it twice). One journey took six weeks when I was thirty-five, the other seventeen days when I was fifty. I was married on top of Pretty Butte near Marmarth in 1986 overlooking one of the most beautiful stretches of the Little Missouri. I have ridden horse along five segments of the 150-mile Maah Daah Hey Trail. I have driven the entire length of the river five or six times, source to mouth and back again, and I have photographed virtually every vista with successive generations of camera equipment. I have flown over the entire course of the river several times and photographed much of it from the air. My daughter, Catherine, was baptized in the Little Missouri River, a source of considerable alarm to her mother.

I have taken fifty groups to the Elkhorn Ranch and nearly every time we have waded into or across the river in every season. Back in 1985, on my first (full) sojourn along the Little Missouri I had my only out-of-body mystical experience on a ridge near the river, a few miles north of Camp Crook, South Dakota. If there is more under heaven and earth than is met with in your philosophy, Horatio, I encountered it that night. The next morning, I felt as if I had wrestled with the angel Gabriel and survived. But I kept my name—the old Adam dies hard. I'm not quite sure what brought it on—fatigue, the mystic rhythm of walking, mind-body-soul integration, the ghost of Crazy Horse, the moon in the clouds, spirit of place.

I have canoed long sections of the river, once on the windiest day I have ever experienced in the badlands. My mother's ashes are scattered in the river just north of Marmarth, and mine will be too, in a blink of a geologist's eye.

Rivers are many things. They supply municipal water. With the help of the US Army Corps of Engineers they become navigation channels. They float pleasure craft. They carry away sewage. They create hydropower. They provide irrigation water for farmlands in their corridor. They serve as boundaries, often (perhaps always) tense boundaries, between state and sometimes national jurisdictions— the Rio Grande, the Colorado, even the Red River of the North.

From the standpoint of what a river can do for a civilization, the Little Missouri is worthless. It irrigates a puny number of acres. It provides no municipal water. If you want to float the Little Missouri in a canoe or kayak you have to be on call between the months of April and July in hopes of catching the two brief annual rises in the river, because in August you can only navigate the Little Missouri if you drag the boat behind you. It's a more acute version of the old joke about the big Missouri: "The only problem with a boat trip on the Missouri River is you have to take the boat." The French seignior the Marquis de Mores built a dam at Medora in the 1880s to enable his workers to cut ice out of the river in winter to supply his slaughterhouse, his abattoir, his shambles. But the river carried it off the moment his workers stopped shoring it up. No trace of it remains and the best historians cannot even determine where it was located.

The Little Missouri River corridor is very lightly populated. That is good and bad news. Good news because it lowers the human impact on a fragile and precious natural resource. Bad news because it means that the Little Missouri has comparatively few protectors and advocates. Depending on how you count, there are four, maybe as many as six, towns on the Little Missouri, none of them very big. Alzada, Montana, population 152; Camp Crook, South Dakota, population sixty-four; Marmarth, North Dakota, population 143; Medora, North Dakota, population 132. If you throw Grassy Butte (population 255) and Twin Buttes (population twenty-three) into the hopper, you get to 769 people. Those are the Little Missouri's *urban* dwellers. The entire ranch population of the river must be well below 1,000, perhaps now fewer than 500. Add all that together and the river *serves* maybe as many as 1,500 people.

Thanks to its isolation, its low population density, and its pitiful volume, the Little Missouri has mostly been left alone by those who wish to extract wealth from the plains of North Dakota. There is no dam on the Little Missouri, but there are dams on the Cannonball, the Heart, the Missouri, the James, the Sheyenne, and even the Yellowstone, though those Yellowstone River structures are so modest that they are not really counted against the river's reputation for being the longest undammed river in the country.

Several attempts have been made to protect the Little Missouri River corridor. In 1975 the North Dakota legislature passed the North Dakota Little Missouri State Scenic River Act. The legislation was one of North Dakota's responses to the first national energy crisis (1973-79). At the height of the crisis there was a plan to build up to twenty-two coal gasification plants in North Dakota. To forestall one proposal to build such a plant in the Little Missouri corridor, the legislature passed the scenic river bill, which was partly inspired by the passage of the National Wild and Scenic Rivers Act in 1968. The legislation declared, "The commission may advise local or other units of government to afford the protection adequate to maintain the scenic, historic, and recreational qualities of the Little Missouri River and its tributary streams. The commission shall also have the power and duties of promulgating management policies to coordinate all activities within the confines of the Little Missouri River when such action is deemed necessary." Because this would seem to have granted the new commission the authority to restrain all sorts of irresponsible development along the Little Missouri, legal clarification was sought from North Dakota's then-Attorney General Nicholas Spaeth (a Rhodes Scholar). His legal opinion so greatly limited the scope and jurisdiction of the legislation as to render it merely advisory, even merely rhetorical. Nick Spaeth may have been the attorney general, but he never understood the spirit of North Dakota, particularly western North Dakota. No significant stricture has ever emerged from the commission, and for many years it simply ceased to meet. Under the leadership of Governor Doug Burgum (elected 2016), an attempt was made to revive the commission, but the revival was mostly characterized by rancher frustration and a nearly universal feeling of futility. It would be possible to seek an updated AG's interpretation of the 1977 enabling legislation, which remains in effect. Or the North Dakota legislature could pass a supplemental bill to give greater teeth to the commission, particularly in light of the intense carbon extraction that came to North Dakota in the second decade of the twenty-first century. Such legislation is, to put it mildly, exceedingly unlikely.

On several occasions since the passage of the National Wild and Scenic Rivers Act in 1968, the US Forest Service has studied the possibility of designating several segments of the Little Missouri River under one or more of its three protection categories. The last study was conducted in 1997. It concluded, "Residents who attended scoping meetings in North Dakota were opposed to federal designation . . . . These residents indicated they were opposed because of the impacts that designation might have on their use of private land within the river corridor. Most expressed support for the current management of the river." Without federal protection, North Dakota's most remarkable and fragile river is vulnerable to industrial development. The state scenic river designation does nothing to protect the Little Missouri. It merely provides the *illusion* that someone is looking out for the river.

At the height of the Bakken Oil Boom, North Dakota Attorney General Wayne Stenehjem, one of three members of the North Dakota Industrial Commission, which oversees oil, coal, gas, and water development, brought together a range of stakeholders to consider what he called an Extraordinary Places initiative. The idea was to designate a handful of places in North Dakota that deserved special protection from routine industrial development. Under Stenehjem's leadership, the process was thoughtful, inclusive, and cautious (even timid). Representatives of the oil and gas industry, county and state government, the conservation community, a humanities scholar, and members of the public were at the table. The deliberations continued for several months, and the stakeholders were able to agree that while no oil or gas development would be prohibited under a Special Places designation, a "red flag system" would be adopted, by which industry would be encouraged to show heightened sensitivity in drilling and other oil-related activity near the perimeter of the three units of Theodore Roosevelt National Park, near Bullion Butte, along the shores of Lake Sakakawea, at the confluence of the Yellowstone and the Missouri Rivers, and at a few other places that the informal committee regarded as specially deserving. The Extraordinary Places stakeholders went out of their way to reassure everyone that the initiative, if adopted, would not prevent a single barrel of oil from being extracted in western North Dakota and that nothing in the initiative was intended to limit or discourage the freedom of private property owners who sought to develop their minerals. In the end, an ad hoc landowners group sprang up overnight to join forces with the North Dakota Petroleum Council and the oil industry to derail the proposal. After all that throwing about of brains, a much-watered-down alert system was adopted for a few sites. And so the beat goes on. Most of the land that might have been protected by the initiative lies within the corridor of the Little Missouri River.

The windfall of oil and gas revenues has been so satisfying to the vast majority of North Dakotans that their attitude, even if they might have quibbled with the phrase, can be summed up in Sarah Palin's three words: "Drill, Baby, Drill." It turns out that no landscape was particularly *special* to the great majority of the people of North Dakota. For most Dakotans, the view was not only "out of sight, out of mind," but "what can there be worth protecting out there, anyway?" Most North Dakotans have never been to the badlands, to the confluence of the Missouri and the Yellowstone, to the butte quadrant south and west of Interstate 94 between Belfield and Belle Fourche, South Dakota. Most of those who have been to North Dakota's badlands have stayed on paved roads. Roosevelt's Elkhorn Ranch is seldom visited. Most North Dakotans could not locate Bullion or West Rainy Butte on a map within a hundred miles. You can't love what you don't know. The great majority of North Dakotans live far to the east of the badlands country, far to the east of the landscape of carbon extraction. They were the great beneficiaries of the Bakken Oil Boom because it filled state coffers and lowered taxes, and all of it occurred somewhere over the rainbow out in that empty quarter. Drill, baby.

The question we need to ask ourselves is: Is nothing sacred? Is everything instrumental, commodifiable, fungible? Is everything for sale? Is there nothing in North Dakota that we can collectively agree to protect?

Most of the ranches along the Little Missouri River are what can be called *heritage ranches*. They are owned and lived on by genuine stock producers, many of whom have deep family roots in the badlands. They may derive a little extra income from oil leasing and development, or perhaps someone in the family works in town (for the health insurance), but for the most part these are ranches needing cash flow to survive. The quality of ranch management varies somewhat of course, but for the most part the rangelands of North Dakota are well-managed. But there is a paradox here. Many of these ranchers have a special appreciation of the Little Missouri River. It is no mere resource to them. They take pride in living in this narrow zone of great beauty and history, the stomping grounds of legendary figures. They would like to protect the Little Missouri corridor from the wrong kinds of development, if possible. But many of them benefit handsomely from energy development in the corridor and, even if they sought to slow down industrial development, their inveterate hostility to outside interference in their lives and ranch operations, particularly *federal* interference, has left them without the tools they would need to restrain unbridled oil and gas development. They have, in fact, overtly rejected the very tools they would need to preserve what they most value: their lives as the last free and independent cattlemen on the western ranges of America.

It might be useful to make a brief survey of the ways in which the Little Missouri River has already been affected, and in some cases degraded, by what is called progress. I know that not everyone is going to agree with me in what follows. In some moods, I don't always agree with myself on some of these questions. I am always particularly unhappy when my views upset anyone in the grazing community, because I deeply respect the ranchers of North Dakota, trust their judgment and their (sometimes ornery) commitment to stewardship, and I believe, without question, that heritage ranching is the highest and best use of the grasslands of western North

Dakota. Nevertheless, I will plunge ahead for two reasons. First, my purpose in writing this book is to encourage a statewide, even regional, conversation about the history, identity, status, and future of North Dakota. I believe that conversation needs some bold new thinking, some useful conversation prompts, whether you agree with them or not. Second, we need more badlands and Little Missouri River purists, even absolutists. God knows there are enough who regard the badlands and the river as useful only insofar as they can be made to produce wealth and profits. We need a few individuals who are willing to make the case for conserving the Little Missouri unapologetically, if only to provide some counterweight in the badlands debate.

When Theodore Roosevelt and the Marquis de Mores were in the badlands country in the 1880s it was still mostly open range, though de Mores upset virtually everyone by trying to fence off the property he actually owned, as opposed to all the land that he and everyone else were merely squatting on until such time as nesters filed legal homestead claims in the Little Missouri country. That's one reason they opposed the formation of Billings County—squatting is easier to get away with in no-man's-land, much harder when you start checking squatters' claims against various state and federal land tenure laws. They all knew that barbed wire fence in the badlands spelled the end of a romantic era of open range, which required a couple of collective regional roundups per year to sort the cattle to everyone's satisfaction. That era has long since slipped away. Fences and cattle guards are ubiquitous now, and though neighbors help each other out at branding and shipping time, everyone tries to keep his or her cattle within their own ranch perimeter. In the last couple of decades, ranchers have increasingly strung barbed wire even across the Little Missouri River itself to prevent their cattle from wandering onto neighboring ranches. This is technically illegal, but nevertheless not uncommon. In my hikes and canoe trips down the river, I have come upon these cross-river fencings on a number of occasions. I get the point, of course, but I find them upsetting and I am always tempted (though I would never actually do it) to cut the fences in the name of the sovereignty and freedom of the Little Missouri River. These loosely slung fences are in fact quite dangerous because they are seldom, if ever, marked with red flags or slow-moving vehicle signs, and it would be quite possible for canoeists to get hurt if they did not spot the nearly invisible wire in time. A friend of mine who lives in the southern badlands reports that at least nine of these fences were strung across the river in one recent summer.

Within North Dakota there are (so far) two low-water crossings (bridge-like structures) on the Little Missouri, both south of Medora, and six bona fide bridges: one at Marmarth, three at Medora (if you count the railroad bridge), one on US 85 on the east end of the north unit of Theodore Roosevelt National Park, one on ND 22 northeast of Killdeer, and one unauthorized bridge thrown up by a lawless desperado by the name of Wylie Byce. Billings County has been trying to erect a bridge somewhere near the Elkhorn Ranch for many years. It seems likely that they will succeed one of these days.

The two low-water crossings were built south of Medora between 1990 and 2005. The one fifteen or so miles south of Marmarth is so remote and unobtrusive that almost nobody knows it is there. The more emphatic low-water crossing at the Three V Ranch just south of Bullion Butte gets more traffic. These crossings are essentially just ugly concrete slabs slopped down in the river, with steep gravel approaches on either bank. The river, constricted, passes through a couple of squarish culverts around which the concrete was poured. During the brief periods of high water, the Little Missouri rises above the grooved surface of the structure and traffic comes to a halt for a number of days.

These low-water crossings serve their purpose, which is to move traffic across otherwise remote stretches of the Little Missouri River at the lowest possible cost and with the least inconvenience to the ranch community. I respect the ranchers who use them, but I find the low- water crossings deeply offensive. They make it impossible for canoes and kayaks to float under or through them, but—far more importantly—they are just butt-ugly and grossly utilitarian. Anyone floating the river has to get out and haul the canoe around the blockage. Although this is a fairly small inconvenience, it signifies utter contempt for recreationists and—what is much worse—for the Little Missouri River itself. If a crossing is necessary, then build a proper bridge, preferably something aesthetically handsome, something that resonates with the heritage of the badlands of North Dakota or the ethos of the American West. If there must be bridges, then let them contribute something valuable to the landscape. Instead, these soulless slabs merely degrade the landscape—as if some concrete company had an unused load in the hopper and just dumped it into the river to get rid of it. The Little Missouri deserves better. The badlands deserve better. North Dakota deserves better. They should be removed and replaced by bridges that contribute something to the romance of the badlands.

The low-water crossings signify the failure of North Dakota to develop a genuine conservation ethic. A people who understood the magic of the badlands and the Little Missouri River would insist that any public structures built in the corridor show respect, even reverence for the spirit of place. Anyone who thinks I am making too much of this should go visit the crossings, which can be found on Google and on detailed maps of the Little Missouri country. Try to imagine such slabs being tossed into the upper reaches of the Colorado River or the Arkansas, the Gunnison or the Snake or the Yellowstone. Imagine such travesties in Oregon, Colorado, California, or even Montana.

The Bully Pulpit Golf Course just south of Medora is starkly beautiful. It is widely admired and has won awards. For thousands of people, it is the deepest they ever really get into the North Dakota badlands. From a purist's point of view, however, it is a violation of the integrity of the badlands, because it overlays a patina of highly manicured Kentucky bluegrass that could not survive without irrigation (i.e., sprinklers) on a place that is *already* stunningly beautiful without any help from landscape architects, thank you very much! It is a way of putting the *not-there* over the top of the *there* in the heart of the badlands, and keeping it alive with constant transfusions of water and fertilizer. No cattle or buffalo graze on the fairways. The people who use the Bully Pulpit Golf Course rave about its beauty, but they do not stray off of the manicured fairways and greens. They are comfortable on Kentucky bluegrass, not on buffalo grass or among the sagebrush. Still, if you think about it, how is it really much different from a campground in the national park that supports RVs that are more luxurious than the houses of most of the people who live on earth and in each of which, on any given summer night, you can see the blue glow of a widescreen television set piping in reruns of *Mannix* or *Three's Company*? If national park campgrounds were off limits to everyone who would not sleep on the ground in a tent, they would be very lightly occupied. In North Dakota, as in much of the American West, the fifth wheel camper trailer is regarded as *roughing it*. Mark Twain would be savagely amused.

There is a certain irony in naming the golf course the Bully Pulpit. Theodore Roosevelt called golf as a "sissy sport," and advised his hand-picked successor, William Howard Taft, never to be photographed golfing, lest he be regarded as a snob or a swell. But that was then. Golf is now the preferred participatory sport of a certain class of Americans, particularly those of wealth, power, and privilege. Bankers and lawyers don't usually join slo-pitch softball teams. They golf, and what they love about golf is its refinement, its insistence on strict rules of etiquette, and the fact that you can play eighteen holes without ever breaking a sweat or being out of breath. It makes perfect sense that the Theodore Roosevelt Medora Foundation would regard the Bully Pulpit Golf Course as essential to its economic success. I respect the work of the foundation and the passion of the nation's golfers. But the Bully Pulpit imposes a Scottish ball and stick game on the heart of Roosevelt's old stomping grounds. Just ask yourself what his reaction would be to this transformation of the badlands.

As usual, Roosevelt has something important to say about such developments. When he saw the Grand Canyon for the first time, on May 6, 1903, President Roosevelt congratulated the people of Arizona (and the Santa Fe Railroad) for not throwing up a hotel at the end of a special railroad spur on the south rim. Roosevelt's words should be adopted as the Mission Statement of America's National Parks, and they certainly should have special potency in the badlands which became one foundation of his greatness:

> Leave it as it is. Man cannot improve on it; not a bit. The ages have been at work on it and man can only mar it. What you can do is to keep it for your children and your children's children and for all who come after you, as one of the great sights which every American, if he can travel at all, should see.

Most visitors to Medora regard the Bully Pulpit Golf Course not as a mar or a scar, but a welcome improvement on the natural landscape, or at least a lovely complement to the badlands.

For the past fifteen years, Billings County has been attempting to get all the permits in place to build a bridge across the Little Missouri River somewhere in the northern reach of the county. The project heats up every few years and seems likely to break ground, then falls back for one of several reasons. For one thing, Billings County made a strategic error by seeking US Department of Transportation funds to defray some of the costs. This set in motion the cumbersome and exacting wheels of the federal Environmental Impact Study (EIS) permitting process, giving opponents of the bridge the opportunity to make their concerns known and at least to slow down the rush to pour concrete. The irony is that Billings County has enough money to build any number of bridges without the help of the federal government, the perennial favorite whipping boy of the Sagebrush Rebels of the American West, including North Dakota's west. The conservation community, along with a significant percentage of the ranch community, feels that the Elkhorn bridge is unnecessary, that it would magnify the negative impact of oil and gas development in the heart of the badlands, and that Billings County has not been fully candid about the purposes of the bridge. In fact, a significant number of conservationists argue that the Billings County commissioners, or at least a couple of them, have been bent on building the bridge chiefly to offend and defy the conservation community and—perhaps more important—to shatter any notion that the heart of the badlands can be preserved in something like its pristine condition. They want to get a foot in the door so that every subsequent attempt to argue for the sanctity of the badlands becomes harder.

Several of the heritage ranchers who live where the bridge is likely to be built do not want it on or near their property. They have vowed to fight it with all of their very considerable wealth and credibility. Perhaps the greatest challenge to the bridge is the Elkhorn Ranch Site, an official unit of Theodore Roosevelt National Park, which, from an engineer's point of view, is unfortunately situated right where it makes most sense to build a bridge between Medora and the US 85 bridge adjacent to the north unit of the park forty miles to the north. National parks have enormous political weight and authority in these situations, thanks to their 1916 mandate "to conserve the scenery and the natural and historic objects and the wild life therein . . . as will leave them unimpaired for the enjoyment of future generations." The NPS mandate has particular potency in this case because the location in question would bring dust, noise, traffic, and industrial development to Roosevelt's remote sanctuary in the North Dakota badlands, where he grieved the death of his first wife, wrote parts of several of his books, found his adult character and his mature voice, and formulated a number of the conservation principles and policies that later made him the most serious conservationist among all presidents of the United States. The patron saint of this place is not Calvin Coolidge, but Theodore Roosevelt. Because it is the only national park devoted to the memory of a single man, the nation's foremost conservationist, it would seem indisputable that Theodore Roosevelt National Park should be afforded even more than usual protection in the vicinity of his home ranch in the badlands, the Elkhorn. Almost everyone who has studied this question with anything like an open mind has concluded that the Elkhorn Ranch should be preserved inviolate as one of the shrines of American conservation, and that to build a bridge in its vicinity would be like throwing up a shopping mall at Thoreau's cabin site on Walden Pond, or cutting down the last redwood tree to build an interpretive center in honor of John Muir.

Even so, the bridge project moves perhaps inexorably towards a construction start in the next decade despite a lack of federal funding and court challenges. Billings County argues that the bridge is essential for emergency police, fire, medical, and ambulance services, but virtually every rational person knows that its real purpose is to facilitate the oil extraction industry. We should continue to resist the Elkhorn bridge by all legitimate means of non-violent protest. If we found a rich vein of gold at the heart of Devils Tower in Wyoming, we would not tear it down to get at the gold. The 843 acres of Central Park in New York would be worth hundreds of billions of dollars to developers, perhaps trillions, but New York has not, even during its periods of bankruptcy, ever seriously considered selling off Central Park, which attracts 53 million visitors per year and helps to make one of the world's most frenetic cities more livable. If it were determined that the shortest and most efficient subway route through Rome would have to burrow through St. Peter's Basilica, nobody would advocate plucking down Bernini's magnificent

Baldacchino di San Pietro to ease congestion in the city. There are some things that are too precious to sacrifice to progress and the profit motive. The Little Missouri River is one of those things.

The question I face now that my beloved daughter is grown and my career is finally invulnerable to political attack is, What would you fight for? What would shake you out of your Barcalounger and into the streets? What, if anything, would you get arrested to protect? What would you chain yourself to a Bulldozer to prevent? Are you prepared to go to jail or prison to prevent an unnecessary and disruptive bridge from being erected near Roosevelt's Elkhorn Ranch? How much do you fancy being a pariah in your home community, perhaps even among your friends? In the last ten years I have in fact thought long and hard about these questions. One must not be glib about matters of this gravity, and I have to factor in that I am not by temperament a radical, a protester, or even an activist. It's easy to talk about chaining oneself to a Bulldozer, but when the moment actually comes, who is really prepared to click shut that padlock and say, "Here I stand. I can do no other"? So much easier to write a letter to the editor and wring one's hands at dinner parties.

Moreover, if you add up the number of things that have happened in my lifetime while I sat around wringing my hands, you wind up with a watered down application of Martin Niemöller's famous formulation, "First they came for the communists, and I didn't speak out because I wasn't a communist... ." When they desecrated the front range of the Killdeer Mountains in the last decade, thus transforming one of North Dakota's most beautiful and historically important viewsheds into a scattershot metallic inferno of storage tanks, pumpjacks, and flaring, I did nothing. When the Industrial Commission voted down the Extraordinary Places initiative so as not to offend the oil industry and concerned landowners, I did nothing. When industry put a saltwater disposal plant right on the lip of the breathtaking canyon of the Little Missouri River northeast of Killdeer, I did nothing. Well, actually, I wrote a newspaper column about it that brought down the wrath of the Drill Baby Drill crowd on my head. When the US Forest Service and Billings County permitted a gravel mine in plain sight on the eastern viewshed of the Elkhorn Ranch, the view Roosevelt had from the verandah of his Elkhorn cabin, I merely wrung my hands. The bridge builders are counting on my cowardice, on your cowardice, on public indifference, on the fact that so few people have ever bothered to get themselves out to the Elkhorn Ranch—or anywhere deep into the badlands for that matter. I have brooded about these questions endlessly. I'm old enough now to believe that if I am ever going to grow a pair of genuine principles for which I am willing to put everything on the line, that time has surely come. Nor do I have much left to lose. There is not much I would fight for—long training in the humanities has taught me to see both (indeed, more) sides of almost every issue. But I would fight to stop this bridge, just as I would fight to prevent North Dakota's most charming and improbable highway, ND 16 north of Marmarth, from ever being paved. Easy to say, of course. If they tore down the state capitol I would lament its loss, but I would not carry placards to the site.

It's a slippery and a dangerous slope. Every time we permit the Little Missouri River to be compromised by profit-seeking industrial capitalism, we weaken its integrity and make it easier the next time to make further inroads, including new roads, bridges, diversions, gravel mines, field leveling, irrigation structures, industrial water intakes, holding ponds, subdivisions, and pleasure parks. At some point the Little Missouri country would cease to be the holiest landscape of North Dakota and become just another damaged place in the American West.

The argument for drawing fracking water from the lower Little Missouri west and north of the Killdeer Mountains is that by now it is close to its confluence with the Missouri River proper and therefore the water won't be missed; that from a purely rational point of view taking water from the Little Missouri is wiser than trucking it from water depots or Lake Sakakawea, because they would involve more truck traffic, more dust and congestion, greater transport costs, greater damage to the state's transportation infrastructure; that hardly anyone lives or goes there so nothing in the most popular corridors of recreation or scenic appreciation is being impaired.

To which I say, bullshit. We have already done irreparable damage to the Missouri River in damming it at Fort Peck, Garrison, and Oahe. Lake Sakakawea contains an essentially unlimited amount of water, and the North Dakota State Legislature has subsidized public works projects that move a modicum of that water to the heart of the oil fields. The abundance of Lake Sakakawea water is essentially infinite from the perspective of North Dakota oil development. At this point, having done just about all the damage we could possibly do to the Missouri River basin, we have earned the right in the upper basin to use some of our fair share of its storage capacity, and not merely run the water down to the pointless navigation channel below Sioux City or the conurbations beginning with Omaha, Kansas City, and St. Louis. There is no saving the Missouri River in North Dakota and there is no use in trying to preserve all the water that is stored behind Garrison Dam. Nor will even unbridled oil development reduce the level of the lake by an inch. On the other hand, the Little Missouri River is so valuable as a wild thing, as perhaps *the last wild thing* in North Dakota, that we can afford to work around it in our quest to suck Bakken oil out of the earth and ship it off to faraway refineries. A drop in the bucket of the Missouri equals the whole flow of the Little Missouri.

Meanwhile, plans have been moving quietly forward to drill hundreds of oil wells in the Little Missouri River corridor in the next decade, many of them not merely near but directly adjacent to the river. If this ambitious project goes forward we can expect a dense array of access roads, scoria pads, storage facilities, pumpjacks, pipelines, water diversions, holding ponds, electrical power lines, and salt water disposal facilities that will transform North Dakota's single most important (and vulnerable) scenic landscape into an industrial sacrifice zone. The scheme, if implemented, would effectively destroy the North Dakota badlands for at least the next hundred years. As usual in North Dakota, the project inches forward with virtually no public awareness or comment.

Every assault on the integrity of the Little Missouri is a wound to that which is beyond economic metrics. Each wound makes the next one easier. Each wound weakens the argument for protection. Each wound in fact invites the next. Which brings us to Wylie Bice's rogue bridge across the Little Missouri in Dunn County, just west of the Killdeer Mountains. He threw it up in 2013 without bothering to get the proper permits. Some of it trespasses on federal lands managed by the Bureau of Land Management (BLM). It wasn't until a citizen looking around with Google Earth noticed it and sent word to the outstanding environmental watchdog Jim Fuglie that the bridge came to the attention of the media, the people of North Dakota, the North Dakota government, the US Forest Service, and the BLM. That alone indicates the impoverished status of the conservation community in North Dakota, not to mention a weak media. A man built an unauthorized bridge across an officially scenic river in the oil zone without attracting notice? A stealth bridge in the badlands? Billings County has been waiting for more than a decade to build its bridge across the Little Missouri River using legitimate means. Bice just did it. It was a ballsy thing to do, not to mention arrogant and illegal. The BLM, once notified (by a mere citizen!), became suitably embarrassed. It huffed and puffed and pondered what an appropriate federal government response would be to Bice's act of anarchy and defiance. And of course, in the end, in August 2019, the federal agencies stopped wringing their hands just long enough to slap Bice's. There will be an unspecified fine. There may be a land swap.

In my opinion, Bice should be required to dismantle the bridge, slab by slab. He should be required to pay a fine for every load of water or any other commodity he has hauled over that bridge. He should lose any federal grazing rights he now holds on the seventy-five BLM acres in question or any other federal parcel he has leased.

The confluence of the Little Missouri and the Missouri proper has been damaged, even destroyed, by Garrison Dam. It must have been absolutely stunning, because even now the landscape at the confluence is some of the best on the entire Missouri River. It's Karl Bodmer Country. Lewis and Clark reached the confluence on April 12, 1805, just five days after departing from Fort Mandan en route to the Pacific. Meriwether Lewis wrote, "It is 134 yards wide at it's [sic, throughout] mouth, and sets in with a bould current but it's greatest debth is not more than 2½ feet. it's navigation is extreemly difficult, owing to it's rapidity, shoals and sand bars. . . . the country through which it passes is generally broken and the highlands possess but little timber."

When I make lists of things I would like to turn back the clock to see in what is now North Dakota, the confluence of the Little Missouri and the Missouri is always near the top, along with the Mandan, Hidatsa, Arikara, and Lakota in their pre-contact lifeway, the entire state carpeted with nothing but native grasses and other flora, buffalo, elk, bighorn sheep, deer, mountain lions, coyotes, wolves, grizzly bears, and prairie dogs in their uneasy equilibrium on what must have been the American Serengeti, and the Missouri River when you could actually wade across it in the autumn of a dry year. Today, it is impossible to see the Little Missouri disembogue (to use Lewis' word) into the Missouri near Twin Buttes, even if you could get close enough, which is nearly impossible. Without a single defender or advocate, without a Thoreau, a Muir, a Brower, an Edward Abbey, or a Rachel Carson to raise the alarm, one of the greatest places on the northern Great Plains was flooded out forever—at least in human historical terms—by the engineering arm of the United States Army still hepped up on the testosterone that helped us help win World War II. I would give all that I have to spend a late July afternoon standing in the two-and-a-half-foot shallow just before the Little Missouri passes its load to what Lewis called "the mighty and heretofore deemed endless Missouri River." I have done just that with my friend Steve Beckham where the Yampa joins the Green in Dinosaur National Monument. To stand upright where a shallow stream meets a much bigger and more powerful river on a hot summer day is heaven on earth.

Since approximately 1957, Lake Sakakawea has covered the confluence of the Missouri and Little Missouri with 100 feet of artificially clean water. In fact, the reservoir backs the Little Missouri up at least forty miles, all the way to Lost Bridge on ND 22. I have flown over the area in small planes on a number of occasions in hopes of experiencing what was one of the Missouri basin's finest confluences, but the scene looks bloated, forbidding, and even dangerous now. Who would not have wanted to wade across the river there, surrounded by the big Missouri River badlands? In all of the files of the US Army Corps of Engineers, there is not a single lament for what Garrison Dam did to this spectacular confluence. If industry wants to tap the flow of the Little Missouri, they can have all they want from Lost Bridge on down to Garrison Dam as far as I am concerned, but not a drop above. They have damaged North Dakota enough without the need to take more from what's still alive of the Little Missouri River.

Lost Bridge was once truly lost.
Now its replacement is purely instrumental.

I canoed that lonely stretch back in 1978, when the great drowned trees that once lined the banks of the Little Missouri represented a kind of shattered cottonwood Golgotha, every bald bleached white branch covered to eeriness with cormorants. The trees were dead but they had not yet collapsed into the lake. It was a scene out of the novel *Deliverance*. We floated past tens of thousands of black cormorants in the last dozens of miles of a dead river. They kept up an unearthly concert of sheer howling. Because of the great permanent industrial Corps of Engineers flood and because Little Missouri Bay is on the Fort Berthold Indian Reservation, it is now one of the most remote and least visited places in North Dakota. My friend Steve and I canoed along in silence, our eyes fixed on what must have been several hundred thousand raven-feathered birds. We were floating through Dante's *Inferno*. We camped on the south shore and then looked out on the swollen waters of what had once been the last stretch of the Little Missouri River. I have never been back. If Thoreau had visited the scene, he would have said that each of those dead cottonwood trees represented a single member of the Mandan, Hidatsa, or Arikara nation whose homes had been drowned by *progress*, sovereign Indians who had been pressure-relocated up on the windswept bluffs of the *utopian* new community of New Town, and whose river bottom lifeway was destroyed forever by White occupiers who could not be bothered to consult those who would lose most to the dam before they began moving earth and pouring concrete. And then, to add insult to injury, they named the industrial reservoir Sakakawea, after a Shoshone woman who had been assimilated into the Hidatsa culture by the time Lewis and Clark arrived in 1804. Would she have been in favor of Garrison Dam? Would she have wanted an artificial reservoir to be named in her honor?

Where can you get access to the Little Missouri River? In all three units of Theodore Roosevelt National Park, of course. If you drive the gravel road ND 16 north or south of Marmarth you occasionally encounter the river suddenly, without warning, in a way that can be thrilling, no matter how often you have driven the road. You can drive East River Road from the Logging Camp Ranch all the way to the Elkhorn Ranch, and West River Road from Bullion Butte to Medora. The two best views of the Little Missouri in North Dakota are from the hilltop at Wind Canyon in the south unit of TRNP, a hike of no more than fifteen minutes from the parking lot of the asphalt loop road, and from Oxbow or River Bend Overlook in the north unit of the park. The view from either plateau on ND 22 (north or south, one on the Fort Berthold Indian Reservation, one near Little Missouri State Park) is magnificent and breathtaking, but much of the beauty has been damaged—and for some, destroyed—by unrestrained oil development on both sides of the river. It used to be that the view from ND 22 as the road dropped precipitously into the Little Missouri River valley was perhaps the single most beautiful sight in North Dakota. But first the forces of progress widened ND 22 (during the '70s-'80s oil boom). Then they tore down Lost Bridge (1994), one of the most romantic structures in North Dakota, and replaced it with a dumb low "modern" concrete bridge. More recently—an act of aesthetic insanity—Dunn County permitted industry to build a salt water disposal facility right at the entrance of Little Missouri State Park and right on the southern lip of the once-breathtaking canyon, the most sublime place in North Dakota.

Lost Bridge was one of the modest wonders of North Dakota life. It was built during the '30s when there was only a two-track trail to connect it with anything. That's when it got the name Lost Bridge. You could not come upon it on ND 22 without smiling and appreciating the isolation and primitivism of North Dakota before World War II and the progressive years of the 1960s. From the south plateau you looked down into the immense stark valley of the Little Missouri as it approaches its confluence with the Missouri, nature jumbled in every possible chaotic form, and there down at the center of the viewshed—almost like an HO-scale model—was a gleaming little silver arch bridge. It was droll. It was still droll and improbable even when ND 22 was paved. It felt like a lonely scene from the Old West or something thousands of miles out in the Australian outback. And then, for safety's sake, i.e., to facilitate oil traffic, they plucked it down and threw up something that has never taken anyone's breath away, never caused a single traveler to smile. At the time of demolition, a pitiful little span of Lost Bridge was saved and erected as a monument on the side of the road. At one point there was a large explanatory metal sign affixed to the span, but it has since disappeared or been dismantled.

I can hear the cheerleaders for industrial progress scoff and groan as they read these paragraphs. "This guy is some sort of elitist who is opposed to progress and prosperity . . . He's a nostalgist who just wants North Dakota to remain the marginal backwater of his childhood. . . He'd rather see congestion and horrific vehicular accidents on funky and dangerous blacktop roads than improve traffic safety in the oil zone . . . He's an enemy to oil development . . . He'd like to keep us poor rather than one of the few economic hot spots of the nation . . . This is what too much education will get you . . . Apparently he opposes American energy independence . . ." You know what? There is some truth to those charges. Like all North Dakotans who lament where things have been heading in the past couple of decades, I wrestle with these paradoxes, and I fight my susceptibility to nostalgia for a lost golden age. Still, as former North Dakota governor Arthur A. Link put it back in 1973, "We do not want to halt progress. We do not plan to be selfish and say North Dakota will not share its energy resources. We simply want to ensure the most efficient and environmentally sound method of utilizing our precious coal and water resources for the benefit of the broadest number of people possible." You have to be an emphatically pro-development state for that statement to be regarded—as it is—as a conservation manifesto.

I live by one simple iron conviction: It would be possible to engage in serious oil and gas development in North Dakota without degrading the most sensitive, spectacular, sacred, and magnificent landscapes of the state. It would require a bit of tiptoeing near those few places, and it might even cost a bit more to bring up the oil and gas, but we are awash in oil revenues and some of them, surely, should be spent to protect the places we love most. Unit development, sensitive facilities placement, horizontal drilling, noiseless pumpjacks, and camouflaging paint would reduce industrial impacts in these few places dramatically. We have no excuse for not insisting on special development protocols for special places. If we North Dakotans don't cherish our magnificent landscapes enough to insist upon cautious, thoughtful, deferential development, we certainly cannot expect the oil and gas industry to protect us from ourselves. All the evidence points to the same conclusion: if we tell industry what we value, and provide incentives for compliance and disincentives for indifference, we can extract all the energy from under our landscape without destroying our homes and homeland and our character and value system in the name of prosperity.

It is dusk now. The coyotes seem to be closing in, but I know enough from a lifetime of camping out here that they never actually venture into someone's camp and they always seem closer than they really are. The stars are beginning to blink on. If I could snap my fingers and make this evening last for eternity I would do so, even if that meant I could never hike back to my Subaru. I have never in my lifetime felt more complete or more truly at home than on the bench lands of the Little Missouri. I spent the honeymoon of my engagement in a weeklong hike from Marmarth to Medora. One of the handful of the greatest moments of my life played out at the Logging Camp Ranch near Amidon, ND, the last time I hiked the length of the river. It was the hottest summer in modern North Dakota history. It was the seventh day of my hike. It was 104 degrees by noon every day. At 9 a.m., three hours into the day's trek, I crawled up the banks of the Little Missouri and staggered under my sixty-pound pack to a modest white ranch house owned by Robert Hanson, a man so courteous, thoughtful, and gentlemanly that he seems to have walked off the page of Owen Wister's *The Virginian*. I've known Robert Hanson for much of my adult life. He's one of the most respected ranchers in North Dakota, and he has the reputation of being the philosopher of the Little Missouri corridor. He knew I was coming, unless I had to give up trying to hike the river in such oven-like circumstances. Dehydration was a serious risk on that seventeen-day journey, but I was too stubborn to quit and I didn't know when I would have another chance. When I tumbled into the ranch yard at the Logging Camp that morning, I threw down my pack and turned on the hose and just doused myself for ten minutes, drinking as much as my gullet could hold, then showering my head to continue to cool off, and drinking again. Bob Hanson was working over in the corral about fifty yards away. I knew he had seen me stagger up to the house. With his characteristic courtesy he let me drink my fill and lie comatose on his lawn for a while. Finally, after about twenty minutes, he walked slowly out of the corral and over to where I was sitting in my stupor. He stood over me for a minute or so in his stately way, amused by the spectacle of the bedraggled pilgrim who had washed up on his lawn like a flushed prairie dog. Then he simply said, "Would it damage your philosophy if I invited you in for lemonade?"

It would not. And as Robert Frost says in a poem about two men sharing an evening under a telescope, that morning we had some of the best conversation I ever had.

The Sierra Club's David Brower went to his grave in November 2000 convinced that not opposing Glen Canyon Dam in Arizona had been his greatest mistake. A book published when it was too late was entitled *The Place No One Knew: Glen Canyon on the Colorado.* When passionate citizens oppose industrial progress in magnificent places, they are vilified in the short term and almost invariably vindicated in the long run. In fact, they often wind up winning friends from among the very folks who once sought to tap the resource.

If we find the moral courage to save the Little Missouri River valley today, we will congratulate ourselves one hundred years from now, just as we congratulate Theodore Roosevelt for bucking the industrial zeitgeist a century ago to set aside 230 million acres of America's public lands as National Park, National Monument, National Wildlife Refuge, National Game Preserve, and National Forest. He took a lot of heat at the time. Nobody can regret Roosevelt's work to save the Grand Canyon from commercialization, and yet at the time his bold and decisive executive action made fierce enemies of very powerful people. Almost every one of his National Forest designations was denounced as un-American government overreach. Nobody can wish we had not established Yellowstone National Park in 1872, Glacier National Park in 1910 or Theodore Roosevelt National Memorial Park in 1947.

I have sealed up what's left of my kung pao chicken. The breeze in the cottonwoods is heavenly and hypnotic. I could not be happier if Eve walked barefoot into camp with a Granny Smith apple. Venus is quivering above the western horizon. Was that a low rumble of thunder? Time will tell. I feel sleep pulling me out of the moment. But I know, as Thoreau put it in the last sentence of *Walden*, that the sun is but a morning star.

THE HEART OF EVERYTHING THAT IS

I f you open an atlas to a map of North America, it is immediately clear that North Dakota is at the center of the continent. It may be tucked up in the forgotten attic of the United States, but it is at the center of North America. North Dakota is a more or less rectangular state just below the forty-ninth parallel, equidistant from the Atlantic and Pacific Oceans. From a geometric perspective, it would be better if the eastern boundary of the state were a straight line instead of following the sinuosity of the Red River of the North, but that is water under the bridge now. Even so, nobody gazing at the outline of the state for the first time doubts its essential rectilinearity. From a Native American or center of the continent point of view, it would have been more appropriate if the state were a perfect circle of 70,762 square miles and all the states and provinces on its perimeter had to bend around it. Make it a circle, call it Dakota (it's only "North" in the lower 48), and let the state motto be *"The Heart of Everything That Is.*

Most Americans have a dim view of North Dakota, to the extent that they think about it at all. Most don't. It's the least visited state and it is the last visited state. I once called Raven Maps (headquartered in Medford, Oregon) to ask when they would be releasing their map of North Dakota. Their large, highly detailed, handsomely tinted landscape maps of the world, the United States, and individual states are the most beautiful I have ever seen, distinguished as much for their artistry as their cartography. They wrote a one-word reply, "Last." And when the big laminated map finally arrived in its magical cardboard tube, I had to admit it was pretty dull. Mostly green lowlands, with a few score of miserable looking prairie lakes—potholes really, and the pale blue scar of Lake Sakakawea across the northwestern sector of the state. If you want to see a great Raven Map, try Utah or Colorado or California or Montana. If you want to see relatively dull Raven Maps, go to Iowa and North Dakota. Ain't enough contour, ain't enough sublimity, ain't enough American West to make the North Dakota Raven Map interesting. Farm country.

So how does a dull, mostly flat state that produces wheat and sunflowers and cattle and potatoes differentiate itself from 49 others, most of which are more immediately interesting to the untrained eye? If you are California, you can point to world class beaches, Hollywood, San Francisco Bay, Big Sur, Muir Woods, Berkeley, Mount Whitney, the Santa Monica Pier. If you are Colorado you can point to the Royal Gorge on the Arkansas River, Great Sand Dunes National Park, Boulder's Pearl Street, Vail and Aspen, the breathtaking road between Montrose and Durango (US 550), and Dinosaur National Monument. And if you're North Dakota? Well, there is Medora, and Theodore Roosevelt National Park and, well, maybe the confluence of the Yellowstone and the Missouri, though that once-pivotal center of North American commerce at Fort Union has been terribly compromised by oil development.

If you are a low-attraction state searching for some mark of distinction, something that makes you unique, it doesn't hurt to be the home of the Geographic Center of North America. People are drawn to such oddities: Four Corners (where Colorado-Arizona-New Mexico-Utah come together), the signs at the various continental divides, the Hundredth Meridian, the northernmost point in Maine, the southernmost point in Florida, the source of this and the geographical center of that. I have a good friend who belongs to the Extra Miler Club, a loose coalition of eccentrics who are determined to step foot in every one of the 3,143 counties (or county equivalents) in the United States. They hold conventions and talk about, well, visiting counties, especially the dozen or so that you can't just drive to on a Saturday afternoon. I suppose it is not fundamentally different from stamp collecting, though the carbon footprint is a little problematic.

There was a time in American history when these sorts of distinctions mattered more than they do now. When the national paved highway system was relatively new and touring by jalopy was a greater (and more risky) adventure than it has since become, Chambers of Commerce and other booster organizations scrounged around for anything that would "put their town on the map" and lure in some travelers. It was then (1918) that Lebanon, Kansas, declared that it was the geographic center of the United States and Rugby, North Dakota, insisted (1931) that it was the geographic center of North America. It was the era of Route 66, after all, when motels came in the shape of Indian teepees and spaceships and cacti and barrels of root beer. It was the era of the World's Largest Ball of Twine and S.P. Dinsmoor's grotesque but somehow alluring sculpture, Garden of Eden, at Lucas, Kansas. The geographic centers at Rugby, North Dakota, and Lebanon, Kansas, combined the lure of roadside attractions with the irresistible magnetism of cartographical oddities. There was a time when thousands, even tens of thousands, of mostly American tourists made the pilgrimage to these sites. Even now, thousands of people stop to get their photos taken on continental divides, hopping instantly from one state to another (and sometimes peeing into both oceans at once!), sprawl over Four Corners to rest for a moment simultaneously in Arizona, Utah, California, and New Mexico, or bestride the feeder rivulet of the Missouri at Lemhi Pass to imitate Lewis and Clark Expedition member Hugh McNeal, who on August 12, 1805, "exultingly stood with a foot on each side of this little rivulet and thanked *his god* that he had lived to bestride the mighty & heretofore deemed endless Missouri." I have bestridden the endless Missouri there many times. I stop at the cairn in Rugby, North Dakota, every time I pass through the town, no matter where I am going and how busy I am. There is something irresistible about standing in two states or two time zones at the same moment, or climbing a tower in eastern Colorado to see fives states simultaneously.

I admit to being susceptible to centers, continental divides, prime meridians, sources, confluences, tallest peaks, World's Largests and World's Onlys. My mother, daughter, and I have lined up with one foot on either side of the Prime Meridian at Greenwich, England. I have stood (well, doubled over coughing up a lung) at the summit of Mt. Whitney, the highest point in the lower 48 states. I have drunk from the source of the Mississippi, the Missouri, and the Little Missouri Rivers. I have, in a life vest, floated the confluence of the Missouri and the Judith in east central Montana. I have walked the entire course of the Little Missouri River from Devils Tower to Twin Buttes, North Dakota (twice). I attended the last performance—inevitably *Hamlet*—at the old Guthrie Theater in Minneapolis (March 5, 2006), the last performance of the Grand Ole Opry at Ryman Auditorium in Nashville (March 9, 1974), and the last performance of the Black Hills Passion Play at Spearfish, South Dakota (August 28, 2008). I call my home in Bismarck, North Dakota, *Meridian House* because it lies on the western verge of the Hundredth Meridian, the longitudinal number John Wesley Powell regarded as the true line of demarcation between the East and the American West. I gravitate to heights of land, sources of rivers, mountain passes, interlocking streams, border cairns, and every sort of continental divide. In fact, I never cross one without a rush of geographic satisfaction, partly for the fact of the divide, but also for our scientific capacity to determine how they snake across the broad landscape separating the waters of the Atlantic from the waters of the Pacific.

It gives people a deep sense of Clark Griswold satisfaction to stand at Four Corners in the American southwest, but if the pilgrims who journey to Four Corners learned six weeks later that the monument had been deliberately plunked down ten miles from the actual meeting point of the four states, they would be disappointed, perhaps even outraged. When Fort Clatsop out near the mouth of the Columbia River was rebuilt during the Bicentennial of the Lewis and Clark Expedition and it became clear that it was not being reconstructed on the actual site of the expedition's historical winter compound, I lost considerable interest in the site. The you-are- there factor in historic places accounts for much of the satisfaction. I don't want to visit some arbitrary place near Hardin, Montana, that is more or less the same as the site of the Battle of the Little Bighorn: I want to try to stand on the exact spot where Custer went down for the last time on June 25, 1876. Don't fob me off with plausible proximity. I remember climbing up the pulpit in the chapel of Lincoln's Inn in London and positioning myself exactly where my favorite poet John Donne (1572-1631) delivered the first of his famous metaphysical sermons. The hair stood up on my arms. I felt something mystical. I was a true pilgrim. I have walked in the footsteps of Lewis and Clark and camped *in* Karl Bodmer's famous painting of the Stone Gates of the Missouri.

In 2018, my daughter and I rented a skiff and rowed out on Ullswater Lake in the English Lake District to find the exact spot where young William Wordsworth was overcome with guilt after stealing a boat at the same shore where we found a modern marina. We were not going to turn back until we located the precise spot in the lake where, as you pull away, the taller mountain behind the closer mountain looms up like a dark angel of moral retribution. It's all Pythagorean. When we found the spot where Wordsworth learned one of life's most important lessons, from Nature not the Bible or the social order, we faux high-fived, not wishing to overturn the boat on a nerd quest of that magnitude. It was one of the happiest days of our travels together. A year earlier in Greece we had walked hand in hand through the cyclopean Lion's Gate and up to the castle (megaron) of Homeric commander Agamemnon at Mycenae. I recited Heinrich Schliemann's famous telegram, "Today I have looked upon the face of Agamemnon," and she—my glorious young classicist—recited the first dozen hexameters of the *Iliad* in ancient Greek. We live for this sort of thing. On another occasion, we wept together at the tomb of Virgil at Naples.

The Earth is a pear-shaped globe on which almost nothing natural is a straight line. Think of Manhattan Island between the Hudson and East Rivers, with Long Island stretching far out to the East, and a jumble of oddly shaped boroughs in every direction. Or the coasts of Norway with tens of thousands of fjords and inlets. Those represent the natural patterns of the planet. But then, to paraphrase Rousseau, some rationalist drew a line from the North Pole to the South Pole through Greenwich, England, called it the Prime Meridian, and convinced the world to accept that as the baseline for all other longitudinal gridlines. It wasn't a slam dunk. Paris wanted that distinction (Prime Meridian) along with a number of other places in Europe. In the 1880s the rising adolescent United States made an attempt to wrest the Prime Meridian from Britain, whose sun was just begging to set, and very nearly succeeded. The Prime Meridian had to be located *somewhere* and once you accept the claims of Greenwich, the rest of the lines follow logically all the way around the globe. Latitude is even more rational because the east-west lines all parallel each other. The result is a wonderful latticework grid.

Thomas Jefferson's prime directive to Meriwether Lewis was to get the latitude and longitude of every site on the Missouri and Columbia Rivers that would easily be recognized by later travelers. Poor Lewis dutifully tried to fulfill Jefferson's *desideratum* (to use a very Jeffersonian word) all the way from St. Louis to Astoria and back again. He failed. Jefferson was disappointed. In 1816, seven years after Lewis killed himself at a squalid frontier inn on the Natchez Trace, former president Jefferson wrote William Clark a semi-snarky letter saying that his otherwise masterful map of the American West was inadequate because it did not include latitude and longitude to mark Lewis' discoveries.

For reasons that are not entirely clear, humans find it meaningful to get their bodies to some of these arbitrary gridlines and features on the Earth. The urge also exists in the temporal arena. I spent the night of the Millennium on top of Bullion Butte in southwestern North Dakota, because I wanted to mark that moment in the place I love most on the Great Plains. It was minus 22 degrees Fahrenheit with a forty mile an hour wind—life-threatening cold—but I popped open a bottle of champagne at midnight to mark the pivot between the twentieth century and the twenty-first, between the second millennium and the third, in that lonely, windswept spot on the Great Plains. My mother asked only that I mark the spot on a map before leaving so she could recover her car if I perished on the butte top.

Back in 1918, when the United States Geological Survey determined that Lebanon, Kansas, was the geographical center of the United States, up went a cairn. Then in 1959 the United States admitted the forty-ninth and fiftieth states, Alaska and Hawaii. That shattered the claims of Lebanon. The new Center of the Nation was determined to be a site near Belle Fourche, South Dakota (439 miles away). Assuming we do not admit Puerto Rico or Guam as new states and that the United States does not soon break up into Blue and Red confederacies, Calexit and Texit, that designation is unlikely to change, even if the District of Columbia is admitted as the fifty-first state.

The method by which Rugby was declared the Geographic Center of North America in 1931 may have satisfied the people of that simpler and pre-cybernetic era, but the best word to describe it now is *lame*. I had all of my life assumed that back in 1931 the experts at the US Geological Survey used what were then approved and definitive methods to determine the center of the continent. I wasn't exactly sure what those methods had been, but I reckoned they were mathematical, scientific, systematic, professional. But then I learned that the experts who designated Rugby ascertained the center of the continent by balancing a map of North America on the tip of a pencil or a pin. This pathetic exercise, which would barely deserve honorable mention in an eighth-grade science fair, laid the foundation of Rugby's greatness? The only response to this has to be, "Are you kidding me?" Who isn't both flabbergasted and appalled to learn this? How can the pencil test be regarded as scientific? Did these eminent geographers just pull a map sheet out of an atlas after closing the bar one night and mess around with the pencil tip until they found the balancing point in the map? Or did they cut out the outline of North America from a map with a scissors and *then* find the pivot point? That would be the first thing we'd have to ascertain. And which map? We know that all two-dimensional depictions of North America are serious misrepresentations. There is no perfect way to turn a three-dimensional globe into a two-dimensional map sheet without ruinous distortion. Mercator? Peirce Quincuncial? Robinson? Dymaxion? Choose your distortion.

Although Lebanon, Kansas, was put into eclipse with the admission of Hawaii and Alaska in 1959, it still has several important advantages over its rivals. It designates the center of the lower 48 states—of America. Do we really care about Canada and Mexico? We naturally feel patriotism towards the United States and perhaps even to our home states, but almost nobody feels a sense of pride in being from North America. Moreover, if you take the time to explain to someone the importance of the Geographic Center of North America, they will agree in the abstract, but any glance at a map of the United States reminds them and you that Kansas is actually at the center of the nation and North Dakota is a thing tucked up against the Canadian border. Optics matter more than GIS data points. You have to strain to regard North Dakota as central—to anything—and in your heart you understand that any claim it makes to centrality is illusory, provincial, possibly pitiable. In the perception of the citizens of the United States, North Dakota is not central geographically, not central economically, and certainly not central culturally. The state is a mere cypher in America's imagination. What is North Dakota's analogue to the Dorothy of Oz story? More people know the sentence, "Toto, I have a feeling we're not in Kansas anymore," than know the last sentence of the Gettysburg Address or the actual language of the First Amendment. Ask a thousand strangers from elsewhere to name a North Dakota cultural fact of any sort. The best you can hope for is some recognition that Lawrence Welk was born there. "Didn't Fergie have a connection to North Dakota at some point?"

The claims of Lebanon, Belle Fourche, and Rugby were mostly uncontested from 1960 to 2016. In truth, however, these geographic designations have never been as stable and final as they seemed to chambers of commerce and trusting tourists. Historians of cartography and mathematicians at the United States Geological Survey, with vast arrays of computers in their arsenal, confirm that the scissors-and-pin trick was a standard practice for much of the twentieth century and they assert—with some bemusement—that "it really is just about as good a method as any other," according to Jeffrey Stone, an expert on the Lebanon, Kansas, story and a professor at Hill College at Fort Worth, Texas. Stone is not saying that the balancing pin method is unassailable from a scientific perspective, but that among the range of imperfect methodologies for determining the center of the continent, it is not that bad, really. "There is no definitive way to determine the geographic center of any entity with an irregular coastline," Stone said in a recent interview. "No methodology can ever pinpoint an indisputable geographic center. All you can ask for are more precise and less precise determinations. There are just too many variables."

Officially, the United States Geological Survey (USGS) began to edge away from geographic center designations almost as soon as it established them. One of its publications, entitled *Geographic Centers of North America,* weasels out of the controversy by saying, "There is no generally accepted definition of geographic center, and no completely satisfactory method for determining it. Because of this, there may be as many geographic centers of a State or country as there are definitions of the term." I'm sure Rugby suppressed that little Government Printing Office publication back in 1964. The National Oceanic and Atmospheric Administration is equally maddening. NOAA's chief mathematician Oscar S. Adams weighed in on the problem in an official 1960s publication. Adams began by declaring, "Determining the geographic center of an irregular area on the earth's surface is a precarious business at best. There is no unique solution and none of any scientific significance." After explaining some of the problems and making a survey of several possible methodologies, Adams wrote, "It would seem then, in view of these uncertainties, that it is not an advisable thing to do to make any definitive statement regarding the matter. . . As things are constituted, the resulting point would not only depend upon the definition adopted but would also depend upon the investigator and upon the tools employed in the investigation." Who knew there would be a Heisenberg Uncertainty Principle behind the business of throwing up commemorative cairns on the Great Plains?

Then, as if he were the spiritual great uncle of some future man of mischief, Adams wrote, "If there were some rational definition so that all computations would necessarily lead to the same result, then some meaning might be attached to such a result. However, in most cases it is nothing but idle curiosity that leads to an interest in such a point, or some man may want it definitely located in his front yard."

Enter Bill Bender, the former mayor of Robinson, North Dakota (population 37), and the owner of Hanson's Bar, which claims to be the oldest bar in North Dakota. As Mr. Bender gleefully tells the story, he and a couple of his buddies stayed late after closing the bar one night talking about the future of Robinson. Rational answer: no future. When a Google search informed them that Rugby's big claim to fame pivoted on a dumb map balancing trick, they decided to pull the #2 lead pencil out from under the famous fifteen-foot cairn up on US highway 2. Knowing that there is no mathematically certain way to confirm that Rugby is the actual geographic center of the continent, and that that center might just as well be somewhere else—Robinson, for example—they determined to stake their own claim. Bender has called his method "barstool science." Things got even more interesting when Bender and his merrymakers discovered that poor over-confident Rugby had somehow allowed its Geographic Center of North America trademark to lapse. That kind of complacency and gross negligence should not be rewarded, they reckoned. So, they began the paperwork to capture the trademark from its legal limbo: Geographical Center of North America. At Robinson™.

When Rugby pushed back and made a stink, including a legal stink, about the trademark, which under American intellectual property law can apparently be found to maintain some lingering legal validity even *after* it has been allowed to lapse, Bender considered spending the money to litigate the matter, but in the end he cheerfully surrendered, took down the sign he had erected out on the highway (ND 36), stuck it in a corner of the bar, and shrugged off the whole enterprise. Anyone with access to the internet can easily read the saga, which now left the whole designation business in limbo—Rugby's claims were thin and fragile, Robinson's whimsical and happily irresponsible, and nobody was any longer quite sure on what spot North America pivots.

So far so good. But how theoretically do you determine the Geographic Center of North America? As I see it, there are two fundamental problems here. First, what is North America? Are the westernmost Aleutian Islands part of North America? Is Puerto Rico part of the continent, a piece of the main? What about Greenland? Second, how do you determine the geographic center of a curved space? If the world were flat, and you could determine what North America embraces, all you would have to do is draw a perimeter-to-perimeter rectangle that linked the continent's northernmost, easternmost, southernmost, and westernmost tips, then fold the map twice to determine the center.

It gets worse. Once you look into the history and politics of geographic centers for an hour or so, you realize that the *actual* scissors-and-pin pivot point was not in Rugby at all, but sixteen miles away near Balta, ND (population 275). You feel a little cheated when you learn this. I suppose it makes sense that Rugby, a metropolis of 1,502 citizens, located on a major east-west national highway, US 2, was in a better position than Balta to capitalize on "center" status. Fair enough, but here's the critical thing about a geographic designation: It has to be the exact spot or it's meaningless. It cannot be "somewhere conveniently near the geographic center of North America," or "the nearest significant market town to the actual geographic center." The minute you start playing this game, you defeat the whole purpose of the enterprise.

As soon as I learned the truth, I ventured on gravel roads to the nameless slough northwest of Balta where the famous pin stuck back in 1931. There is no signage, no marker, no cairn. Apparently, a few local folks put a sign out in the slough a few years ago to mark the spot, but it has disappeared. The Chamber of Commerce of Rugby has no solid alibi. At Balta you have to know what you are looking for, and even then you are likely to miss it. As you gaze into the muddy slough and try to take an Instagram-worthy selfie, you have only one grim thought: Rugby is humbug. Death to Rugby! A cairn at a place that is approximately the center of the continent is like collapsing five feet from the finish line of the Boston Marathon and later claiming that you were, well, approximately there.

It's just the same at Belle Fourche at the northern extremity of the Black Hills. It proclaimed itself the true Geographic Center of the Nation after Alaska and Hawaii joined the union in 1959. This had the effect of displacing and eclipsing Lebanon, Kansas, which proudly held that honor for forty years. Thereafter, Lebanon was forced to settle for the anemic title of being the Geographic Center of the *Contiguous* United States. That's a serious asterisk. I've been to the Lebanon site on a number of occasions and I can report that these days it is a pretty thin and forlorn cultural magnet.

But the winner, Belle Fourche, is no more the Geographical Center of the Nation than Rugby is the Geographical Center of North America, *even before* you bring in GIS experts to rethink the data and the methodology. The South Dakota city (population 5,602) has erected a handsome plaza on the north edge of town, with an elaborate stone compass and appropriate signage and a visitor's center. The planners were clearly riffing on the success of Four Corners in the American southwest. Belle Fourche freely admits that the *actual* center of the nation is a couple of dozen miles north and west of the town, presuming, I suppose, that most tourists will prefer the well-crafted urban monument to some technically accurate pinpoint out on the endless prairie. The Chamber of Commerce monument is so polished and professional that you almost let yourself believe Belle Fourche's claim, but as with Rugby, it is nothing more than the nearest convenient market community to the actual site—a spot so out of the way and off pavement that most tourists would decline to turn off US 85 to seek it out.

I have been several times to the *actual* certified center of the nation. It is, in fact, way cooler than the expensive and polished sculpture in Belle Fourche, *because it is authentic!* It's where it's supposed to be. The power and authenticity of being on the precise spot and not fudging the iron laws of geography are way more fascinating than all that fancy marble in Belle Fourche. The rancher who owns the property has installed a gate in the cattle fence along the gravel road that passes just to the south of the G-spot. Out in the field, where the small round USGS disk indicates the exact location, there is a short flagpole with a seen-better-days American flag snapping in the wind. Next to the road there is a hand-painted sign proclaiming, *The True Center of the Nation* and a somewhat misshapen and unstable cairn, hastily erected, not altogether unlike the professional monument at Rugby, but wonderfully informal, lazy, and haphazard. The work of an afternoon, no cement truck required. It's about as wild and lonely a place as you could ever visit, absolutely nothing to see but undifferentiated Great Plains grassland in any direction forever. It is precisely what you would want a geographic center to be. If it were situated in downtown Cincinnati or Butte, Montana, it would be only mildly interesting. But when it's marooned out there in the true middle of nowhere, and you have to make the pilgrimage on unpaved, uncertain gravel roads with entirely inadequate directional signage, suddenly the center of the US has absurdity value, which greatly deepens the joy of arrival. It's like the World's Largest Ball of Twine on steroids. You look around at that site and drink in the immensity of the North American Continent. If you are subject to agoraphobia, you are going to be popping back in your car sooner rather than later. It's a stark place, a true (unadorned) Great Plains destination—godforsaken, windswept, a little eerie, alone out there. *"I wouldn't want to have my car break down here,"* you find yourself thinking, or even saying.

Alas for all the lies, and the lying liars who lie. From a tourism and chamber of commerce perspective, I suppose these fudgings make a good deal of sense. But from a geographic perspective, they are pretty troubling to the geo-nerd who takes these designations seriously. No 5-pt. disclaimer at the bottom of the sign or brochure that says, "Note, the actual geographic center is located not far from here." I cannot claim I married Charlize Theron because I stood next to her at her wedding.

The question of what constitutes North America turns out to have a somewhat arbitrary answer. As with so many things, it depends on whom you ask. The United Nations defines North America as Northern America, Central America, and The Caribbean. The USGS definition is nearly identical. All I can suggest is that you buy a map of North America and start cutting it out with your best scissors. You will soon throw up your hands in despair trying to determine what to do about Puerto Rico and Cuba, how to include islands and not distort the paper cutting, how to handle the Aleutians, and whether to include the polar icecap.

It's so much easier and more satisfying to think simply about these things, make the pilgrimage to Rugby, get your selfie, and post it on social media. For at the heart of this business is a fundamental and, in many respects, insoluble problem.

I drove out to Robinson not so long ago to see the new rival Geographical Center of North America at Hanson's Bar. For reasons I cannot quite explain, I regard myself as a fierce Rugbyite. I assumed that the Robinson claim was nothing more than a sick publicity stunt, a pointless and cheap assault on poor Rugby, and that the guy who did this, some sort of smug and disreputable Alpha-male local bar owner, must be what we locally like to call a pukehead. I was prepared to defend Rugby from a barstool across from the big mahogany-framed mirror featuring bumper stickers with sayings like, *Unaccompanied children will be given espresso and a free kitten. It must be five o'clock somewhere. You can't drink all day if you don't start in the morning.* I was prepared to utter ironic, and even sarcastic things to this Bill Bender and maybe get into a scuffle with him at (or near) the center of North America.* I am serious. The lout.

---

*   Note: I have in fact never been in a scuffle.

To my great surprise, he turned out to be a decent and thoughtful man. A man with an excellent sense of humor. He was certainly not a jerk. We have become good friends. I'm still a staunch Rugbyite (I'm not sure why), but Bill Bender finds that amusing, not threatening.

Bender's clever whimsies got him national attention. Enter Professor Peter A. Rogerson of the University of Buffalo. Dr. Rogerson, a SUNY Distinguished Professor in the Department of Geography, had recently written an academic article about geographic centers of states and counties (though not of the continent). When he read about Bender's stunt in the *Wall Street Journal,* Rogerson decided to try to solve the problem once and for all. Using the accepted USGS definition of North America, he traced the perimeter of the continent with 30,000 electronic waypoints (think of a connect-the-dots kids' activity book). Thanks to GIS software, each of those waypoints provided him accurate latitude and longitude for that tiny bit of the North American shore. Then, using azimuth equidistance mapping programs, he calculated the center point from which all lines radiated to the edge of North America. He had no idea going in where that center would be, an attitude which distinguishes him from Rugby, which wants to retain its center status irrespective of science, and Robinson, where Bender and his disreputable pals simply declared themselves the center of everything without even locating a slide rule. "Here, hold my beer!" When Dr. Rogerson's computers finished grinding out the data, the *exact center of the North American continent* turned out to be neither Rugby nor Robinson, but—wait for it—the town of Center, North Dakota, the county seat of Oliver County, 143 miles southwest of Rugby, and 88 miles from Robinson. Professor Rogerson confidently ruled out both Rugby and Robinson for the title of Center of North America.

So, the most scientifically sophisticated experiment ever undertaken to determine the Geographical Center of North America, conducted by a man of sterling credentials, gave us the town of Center. Really? The center at Center? What could be more anti-climactic than that? You cannot absorb this fact without a sense of deflation. You want your geographic center to have a more impressive, more romantic, more exotic name than well . . . Center. How about Ouagadougou or Katmandu?

So, let's review. Geographic Center claimants include Lebanon (Kansas), Belle Fourche (South Dakota), Rugby (North Dakota), Balta (North Dakota), Robinson (North Dakota), and now Center (North Dakota). It's all pretty confusing. The proliferation of these designations and the controversies that have lately sprung up have the effect of diminishing the importance of each and all of them, until the well-meaning geographic pilgrim just throws up her hands and starts collecting county seats or highest points in all fifty states instead. If there were one and only one mathematically and cartographically certain GEOGRAPHICAL CENTER and no rivals, nothing slipshod or screwy about the designation, that site would be worth visiting. But if I have to factor in proximity, access, availability of amenities, conventions and visitors' bureaus, rival claims and dueling scientific methodologies, and a postmodern assertion that there is not even a theoretical pinpoint to mark and celebrate, then the whole thing is nothing but a source of frustration and disillusionment. I'd rather visit the World's Largest Cob of Corn than search for something that doesn't exist. Or just flip a coin to decide where to spend my summer vacation.

I had the pleasure of interviewing Dr. Rogerson not long ago about his role in the controversy. He is a wonderful resource, serious but playful, curious but never doctrinaire. He explained his method to me. I had many questions. Among my biggest was, if we asked two or three other geographers to work this problem without telling them how you (Dr. Rogerson) went about it, would they possibly come to different conclusions? In other words, how do we know that you solved the problem? Dr. Rogerson said he could not be sure others would come to the same results, that of course he would be interested in conducting that blind experiment, and though he is pretty sure he has it right, he would not bet his life or career on it. "Any scientifically-sound methodology is going to produce approximately the same results, depending of course on how you define North America." Well, there's some wiggle room!

Jeffrey Stone of Hill College at Fort Worth was less confident. Dr. Stone said no two researchers would be likely to produce the same results unless they used the exact same number and location of waypoints, and precisely the same definition of North America. "You might get dozens of 'answers' if you let everyone choose their own methodology."

Alas.

So, where does that leave us? Surely Dr. Rogerson's mathematical, computer-crunched model is more accurate than fiddling around with a two-dimensional map and a pencil tip. Bye, bye, Rugby—and Balta. And Robinson? No credible claim. If Bender and his churls of Nottingham Forest had not fastened upon their satanic publicity stunt after closing hour, the *Wall Street Journal* would not have published a front page feature on the issue, which means that Dr. Peter Rogerson of Buffalo would not have sprung into action with an algorithm in either hand, which means that the quiet town of Center (minding its own agrarian business) would not now be confirmed as the Scientific Center of North America, which means that the good people of Rugby would be able to sleep at night, and the world would seem orderly and stable.

To paraphrase Shakespeare, some towns are born great, some achieve greatness, and some, like Center, have greatness thrust upon them.

In a learned paper, Dr. Rogerson wrote of "the rather strong level of attachment that individuals and communities can sometimes have with these locations. On the one hand, it might be argued that the locations are somewhat gimmicky—for individuals and families they represent quirky places to stumble on and stop along the way in the midst of vacation trips, and for communities they create opportunities to erect monuments, to locate plaques, and hopefully, to attract tourists. The associated attachments often run surprisingly deep—deep enough for communities to do (usually good natured) battle with each other, and for journalists to run feel-good, public interest stories on what lies at the core of their region."

I do honestly feel sad for the chagrin in Rugby. The citizens of Rugby do have "the rather strong level of attachment" Dr. Rogerson describes. Even Bender feels a twinge. When the whole thing was getting national attention, he offered to take part in a celebrity boxing match with Rugby's mayor, winner take sign. After a brief period of negotiation, nothing came of it. Bender desisted when Rugby got stern about the disputed trademark. So far, they haven't changed their signing to "Former Geographical Center of North America," or "Not So Very Far From the True Geographical Center of North America." They are simply sad and perplexed, as they have a right to be.

We can be as whimsical about all of this as we please, but there are some serious consequences. The chaotic events of the past five years have damaged every one of the Geographic Center claimants, even Center, the ostensible winner. Although a few intrepid tourists will visit all the claimant sites, I predict that most people will just lose interest in the idea of a Geographic Center of North America, because there really isn't one, or only one, and turn away to more satisfying pursuits. North Dakota will be diminished.

When Rogerson had completed his study, the public relations folks at the University of Buffalo realized that this could generate some good publicity for the school. Soon the story of his GIS experiment (and its surprise solution) was rattling around the internet. Behind the beautiful forty-five-foot-long wooden bar in Robinson, Bill Bender merely shrugs at his loss. Always a skeptic, but still intrigued by the idea of geographic oddities, Bill and his friends Jeff Whitman and Victor Backman created (at another late-night brainstorm session) the ICDC, the International Center for Determining Centers, the world headquarters of which, as you might expect, is at Hanson's Bar in Robinson, North Dakota. The ICDC has vague aspirations to become a 501(c)(3) nonprofit foundation and think tank—on call to help to determine the center of, well, anything anywhere. Bender is more than half serious about this. In the interests of full disclosure, I must reveal that I am now a proud board member of the ICDC. I have decals to prove it. "They can take our geographic status away from us if they want," Bender has said, raising a Pabst Blue Ribbon beer high into the air, "but no matter what they do, they can never take away our status as the headquarters, the *center as it were*, of the ICDC."

When Rogerson's findings became publicly known, Rugby blanched, but the good folks of Center, ND, had no choice but to step up to their new notoriety and civic responsibility. Unlike Rugby and Robinson, Center was an unassuming village, population 588, forty-one miles from Bismarck, minding its own business. Center is the county seat of Oliver County. It got its name because it is located near the center of the county. Little did the town fathers know! Once they realized that they had inadvertently won the North America prize, a group of local citizens sprang into action. Perhaps that is an exaggeration. At any rate, they convinced the local metals class at Center High School to fashion an appropriate "center of a continent" sign. The committee mowed and fenced a swath along the prairie next to highway ND 25 to enable visitors to reach the exact location that Rogerson designated. For reasons that are not exactly clear, they talked a nearby coal company into delivering a gigantic 30,000-pound glacial erratic boulder to the site. The circular sign says "The Scientific Center of North America, 47.1164° N, 101.2996° W." What they mean, of course, is that Center is the *scientifically determined* center of North America. The *scientific* center is probably somewhere else—at MIT perhaps or Johns Hopkins or Cal Tech out in Pasadena. But we know what they meant. Oliver County's extension agent Rick Schmidt says, "This is the first time it's been scientifically proven. Obviously, we feel this is more scientific than a cardboard cutout balancing on a pen that was done eighty-five years ago or so." No need to rub it in, Rick.

Because the folks from Center put their monument out where it belongs and not in the town itself or even on the edge of town, it is not clear how much local merchants will benefit from Rogerson's revelations. When I visited a few months ago and asked what the local folks think the economic impact of Center's center status will be, I got only blank stares. "Probably some gas and soda at the convenience store," one of the town representatives said. On a more recent visit I came away a little frustrated or at least bemused. No sign in town points the way to the monument. Once you get to the site, the glossy tri-fold brochure promotes Center's schools, the Square Butte Creek Golf Course, the annual Old Settlers' Days festival, the nearby lignite strip mine and its attendant coal-fired electrical power plant, and Nelson Lake, warmed to the temperature of bathwater by the effluents of the coal power plant. The only reference to the cartographical windfall is the cover of the brochure, which says, in its entirety, "The CENTER of North America, just ask the scientists!" That and nothing more.

Three flagpoles grace the site, bearing the flags of the United States, Canada, and Mexico, a generous and perhaps locally controversial gesture. The pathway to the actual monument is flanked by a traditional western three-strand wire fence (but without barbs). A wooden box has been erected with a visitors' register inside. The metal sign is showing some signs of rust. It needs a clear coat of protective emulsion.

The monument is perhaps fifty yards from the highway on a rising bench of land—not thirty feet away on the crest of the hill where you can see, well, forever—so I came away wondering why the monument hadn't been placed there instead for maximum *Sound of Music* effect. Possible answers? Punctilious geographic accuracy or a local landowner who was only willing to cede half an acre on the southern perimeter of his pasture. Even from the bench the view of the surrounding countryside is breathtaking, but it is marred a little, from a geographic monuments point of view, by the fact that you can see not one but two coal-fired power plants over to the east and southeast, and a colossal coal dragline off near the horizon stripping away the surface of North Dakota. Behind you is a large array of wind turbines. A few cars per minute chug along to break the silence. The site of the Center of the Nation northwest of Belle Fourche is as empty and forlorn as anything you will ever see. A few pickups may pass along the gravel road in the course of a day. Otherwise, you are alone with the immensity of America. At Center, ND, you look out on an industrialized landscape. It mars the effect. The logo on the back of the tri-fold brochure features an individual on a sailboard and a giant fish in heated Nelson Lake, a coal field, and the local power plant. The logo's frame, a squiggly oval in black, is actually depicted as exhaust gas coming out of the smokestack of the Minnkota Power Plant. Inside the circle are the words, IT'S BETTER AT CENTER. All you can say is that you cannot make this stuff up.

Rugby still owns the trademark and plans to continue advertising itself as the Geographical Center of North America. The cairn isn't coming down, and the signage is not being rewritten to direct people elsewhere if they want to visit the *gen-u-ine* center of the continent. Bill Bender took down the sign out on ND highway 36 in deference to Rugby's assertion of its trademark rights, but he refused to remove the framed newspaper and magazine articles on the east wall or the superb decal affixed to the floor of Hanson's Bar. If you are polite, he'll give you a bumper sticker for the ICDC to take away. Thanks to the internet, he gets a few hundred visitors per year, many of whom come to enjoy the absurdity of the whole thing.

Does it really matter?

Before the Copernican Revolution, almost everyone believed that the Earth was the center of the universe. Back then, the universe was relatively finite and, by our standards, puny. Now, four hundred years later, we know that the Earth is just one tiny planet in a minor solar system in an obscure part of one of the hundreds of billions of galaxies of the universe. Just why God took such an interest in this little cosmic crossroads and sent his only begotten son to save it 2,000 years ago is unclear, but pretty flattering. The principle of relativity teaches us that if the universe is indeed infinite in every direction, every place in it, no matter how insignificant, is from a certain perspective *the center of everything that is.* As usual, the Mandan Indians were right. It's a paradox, but it's true. Perhaps more to the point, every human being is the center of her or his world, no matter if you live in Tokyo or Tioga (ND), Mexico City or Mott (ND), New Delhi or Nekoma (ND). From a merely cartographical point of view, Rhode Island is clearly not the center of the United States or the center of North America. A moment's examination of a map of North America makes it equally clear that North Dakota was laid out precisely at the center of the continent, no thanks to Canada. Perhaps that ought to be enough. The Geographical Center of North America is in North Dakota, perhaps it IS North Dakota—a triumph for the whole state, not merely the inhabitants of Robinson, Balta, Rugby, or Center. It is clear that any model we choose to determine the precise center of North America is problematic, because if we decide that Greenland is *not* in North America, the cairn veers way off compass, just as much as it veers if we decide that the Aleutians stop at Unalaska rather than at Adak Station or Attu, or that Cuba and Martinique are or are not included in the definition of North America. The only way this game would work would be if North America were a perfect square on a flat Earth, without peninsulae, islands, promontories, or irregular coastlines. In other words, you can easily enough find the geographic center of Colorado or Wyoming, but it is far less easy to determine the center of Idaho,

Minnesota, or even Nevada. To determine the geographic center of North America requires a whole series of arbitrary decisions in the realm not of geography but politics, the result of which is to render the whole project meaningless or at least radically uncertain. Life was so much easier and more fun when USGS scientists just cut out a map of North America and balanced it on a pinhead. Now every pinhead in Dakota can make the claim.

I'm finishing up this essay on a stool at Hanson's Bar in Robinson, North Dakota. Bill Bender and I are talking about the next meeting of the board of the International Center for Determining Centers. Should Rugby be invited, or will they try to cause a distraction and tear up the decal on the floor? Can we trust this Rogerson or is he trying, as it were, to *Buffalo* us. I'm suggesting that we get some public humanities money, if possible, and have a two-day symposium in Bismarck to sort it out. We'd invite all the stakeholders—representatives of Lebanon, Balta, Robinson, Rugby, Center, and even Belle Fourche, plus Professor Rogerson, Jeffrey Stone, and others. I'd like to find two or three other Rogersons at other institutions of higher learning to undertake the challenge of determining the center of the continent using their own methods and without consulting each other. We'd open the envelopes on the morning of the second day and then assemble a panel of all of the scientists to see where they agree or disagree. Then, when the trial of the geographers is over, we'll hop on buses to make a grand field trip to Balta, to Rugby, to Center, and finally—around happy hour—to Robinson where the gracious Bender would provide a feast for everyone at Hanson's Bar, buy your own ale. All we need is a grant. The symposium would undoubtedly attract national and even international attention and put North Dakota, if not exactly any one claimant, on the map. I can see C-SPAN covering it, and the *New York Times*, CNN, and the *Wall Street Journal*.

Bender hands me another cold beer, pops it open before me, and smiles his warm, generous smile. "Why not? The ICDC will be the host. Everyone's views will be welcome. We may not figure it all out, but we'll have a great time and everyone, even Belle Fourche, will be a winner."

It is a central principle of postmodernism that things are dramatically more uncertain and indeterminate that they at first seem. The whole controversy just makes me tired and a little sad. I feel nostalgia for a sweeter past when things were simpler all around. For a time when Lebanon, Kansas, could assemble a Hub Club—don't you just feel that Mickey Rooney must have been a member?—to promote the town and circle the wagons against rival claimants. That feels like a chapter out of Sinclair Lewis' *Main Street* or *Babbitt*. There was a time on the Great Plains when town partisans raided the existing county seat or even the state or territorial capital in the middle of the night to steal the sovereignty tokens (official seals, legal documents, the mace or the gavel) and deliver them to some secret or heavily guarded place back home. County or territorial seat stealing was an important part of frontier life in the American West. We are so much more sophisticated now. Almost everything has gelled into permanence. I would hope that the partisans of Rugby would rent buses one of these days and lay siege to Robinson, tie Bill Bender to a barstool and threaten to tar and feather him if he didn't relinquish his appalling claims. Why not kidnap him and chain him to the cairn in Rugby—like Prometheus—to have his liver torn out all day by vultures, only to grow back at night? Why do Rugby terrorists not lurk near Hanson's Bar until closing and then brick up all the doors and windows overnight?

Like Thomas Jefferson, I like a little rebellion now and then, especially when it is harmless. What ever happened to community pride? I have had the chance in the past months to interview the requisite people in Rugby. They are so nice and decent (and I think resigned to the loss of their centrality) that while they acknowledge that their feelings were hurt by Bender and his mischief makers, they are, well, *"oh-kaaah"* with what he has done and even wish him well, just so long as he doesn't try to steal their trademark again. This is North Dakota nice on acid. Of course, the denizens of Rugby quietly wish Mr. Bender would desist and apologize, but even if he did, now that we know that Rugby's claim was flimsy even before the Robinson challenge, there is no turning back. Things will never be quite the same. A state that has very few things to boast about now must attach asterisks to the claims of any of the four current aspirants (Balta, Rugby, Center, and Robinson) and who knows how many Velvas and Harveys and Towners and Candos will hire some Rogerson-for-hire ("Have GPS Will Travel") and further complicate the problem? The madness of the national climate change debate proves that you can find a scientist who will sell his soul for a little publicity or filthy lucre. Peter Rogerson, I am absolutely sure, is not for sale. Is it enough to say the center of North America is almost certainly somewhere in the state of North Dakota, *depending*— depending on how you define North America, depending on how you design the scientific model, depending on what shows up under the melting ice sheets of the Arctic Ocean now that the planet is heating up. How would we respond if towns in southern Manitoba or Saskatchewan (say Estevan or Brandon) declared that *they* are the center of North America? Rugby is only forty-five miles from the Canadian border. We might have to go to war over that, sending tanks straight through the International Peace Garden that spans Manitoba and our own beloved Dakota.

Stay tuned.

CAPITALISM ON CRACK:
EMBRACING THE GIFT HORSE

My purpose in this chapter is to attempt to understand why North Dakota embraced the Bakken Oil Boom so cheerfully and with so little dissent. No event in the history of North Dakota (1804-2020) has been as disruptive to the normal rhythms of a rural farm state of modest and law-abiding citizens who have been accustomed from the beginning to earn their living the old fashioned way, by dint of hard work, perseverance, and sacrifice. The Bakken Oil Boom was more disruptive to the normal rhythms of North Dakota life than the two world wars of the twentieth century, than the militarization of the countryside during the Cold War, than the Dust Bowl and the Great Depression, than the experiment in state socialism during the apotheosis of the Nonpartisan League. The Bakken boom was the biggest story in North Dakota history. It is not over yet, of course, but the period of greatest disruption is almost certainly over. Just what the boom will have meant for North Dakota in the long term is not yet clear. It has made North Dakota a much richer state.

It has made the fortunes of many thousands of individuals, some of them landowners, some engineers, entrepreneurs, lawyers, lenders, and landlords. Some of them North Dakotans.

The state of North Dakota used the enormous windfall of the Bakken boom to raise the salaries of K–12 teachers, university staff and professors, and state employees. It set aside billions of dollars in a variety of rainy-day funds that will serve the people of North Dakota in good times and especially bad, for the rest of the state's history. It invested heavily in the future of higher education. It improved the infrastructure (roads, bridges, highways, bypasses, and water supplies) not merely in the Bakken extraction zone, but in every corner of North Dakota. It provided improvement and sustainability funds for scores of North Dakota institutions, from the ND State Fair in Minot to the International Peace Garden on the Canadian border. It freshened small towns throughout western North Dakota, some of them more than a hundred miles from the closest oil well, bringing home expats who had found it necessary to build their lives elsewhere, attracting new citizens from across the nation and even around the world, filling previously empty buildings on Main Street with commercial enterprises, and causing new housing starts in places that were seemingly locked in permanent decline just fifteen years previously. The population of the state ceased to decline. In fact, by July 2019 the population reached its highest level in the state's history at 762,062. The Bakken brought the people of North Dakota new hope, new energy, and new confidence, reversing decades of loss and uncertainty. For the first time in a quarter century, the Bakken boom gave North Dakotans something to boast about.

An oil boom is like a gold rush. If a rocket represents a controlled explosion in a single direction, a gold rush or oil boom is a kind of slow-motion riot, a pudding of pandemonium, the visualization of Brownian Motion in which molecules hurtle about in every direction in a seemingly random pattern, a frontier community on steroids or perhaps Quaaludes or Ecstasy. A formerly sleepy small town suddenly begins to dance as if every citizen were put on a twenty-four-hour-per-day espresso drip. Money changes hands so fast that in some sense almost any currency printed on paper becomes as common and cheapened as Monopoly money. Normally reasonable people lose their heads. The lure of sudden wealth distorts virtually every transaction and makes everyone, even the most modest and most conservative, lust for wealth beyond the dreams of avarice.

As the historian H. W. Brands wrote of the California Gold Rush, "From all over the planet they came. . . . They came in companies and alone, with money and without, knowing and naïve. They tore themselves from warm hearths and good homes, promising to return; they fled from cold hearts and bad debts, never to return. They were farmers and merchants and sailors and slaves and abolitionists and soldiers of fortune and ladies of the night. They jumped bail to start their journey, and jumped ship at journey's end. They were the pillars of their communities, and their communities' dregs. . . ."

Let me state my thesis and my conclusion from the start: An oil boom or a gold rush is something that happens to a place, like a tsunami, whether it likes it or not, whether it is ready or not, and whether it benefits or not. It comes hard and fast. Host communities spend almost all of their time scrambling to keep up, lighten the burdens on average citizens, maintain some semblance of order, protect the weakest of their residents, and manage uncontrolled growth. I believe that North Dakota did pretty well between 2005 and 2015 under difficult circumstances. We might have done better, but it would be unfair to expect perfection in such hectic circumstances. Under the competent leadership of Governors John Hoeven (2000-2010) and Jack Dalrymple (2010-2016), North Dakota worked extremely hard to take advantage of the boom with the least possible damage to our way of life. It would be possible for purists and romantics to wish the Bakken fracking boom had never happened, but they may as well be wishing the winter temperature never dipped below zero or that the wind never blows.

I believe without hesitation that North Dakota benefitted much more than it lost during the Bakken years, that most of the mistakes that we made represent growing pains rather than mismanagement or malfeasance. If the windfall is invested wisely, the entire future of North Dakota will be brighter, better, more stable, and more prosperous thanks to the Bakken. Just as the discovery of gold at Sutter's Mill in the California Sierra on January 24, 1848, was the making moment of California history, so the fracking boom that began around 2005 might well represent the making moment of the post-agrarian era of North Dakota history. There are things that I lament and deplore about the boom (see below), and I do honestly think that something in the soul of North Dakota was damaged in that mad economic adventure, but no responsible part of me could wish that it had never happened.

The Bakken Oil Boom was so many things. An overnight invasion of mostly young men from all over the country, from all over the world, by bus, by automobile, by train, by pickup truck, by commercial air flight. An invasion of heavy metal: pipe sections of every size piled up everywhere like elongated pyramids, containers, fracking rigs, water trucks, bulldozers, cranes, giant wrenches, winches, service vehicles, field welding units, wreckers, gravel trucks. Dust and grime. Burrito vans and coffee shacks. Gorgeous hookers flying in commercial from Vegas and LA, the most beautiful women the rest of the passengers had ever seen. Everything being paved at once everywhere, with tens of thousands of orange cones lined up along the highways, many of them smashed and scattered by indifferent truckers. Hours-long lines at McDonald's, Dairy Queen, Taco Bell, Taco Johns, Arby's, Applebee's. Spills. Little spills, big spills, secret spills, covered up spills. Oil spills, saltwater spills, oil slurry spills, fracking fluid spills, urine spills. Nothing more, said a pro-oil North Dakota talk show host, than a little drip of errant toothpaste before you get the cap on tight. Wall-to-wall hard drinking in the roadhouses, 250 lit men and just fifteen women. Fistfights in the parking lots. Wrench fights. Gang fights. Love triangles. Jealous boyfriends knifing their women. In the emergency rooms, women beaten nearly to death, a man holding four fingers in a napkin hoping they can be re-attached, burn victims, eyes blinded by chemicals. A convenience store that went from $3 million in sales one year to $35 million the next. Four men sleeping in a Coleman pop-up camper at twenty-five below zero. Walmart giving up shelving its goods and merely leaving the merchandise pallets open on the floor. Shysters, dreamers, misfits, felons, fugitives, con men, defrocked priests, mountebanks, disbarred lawyers, Texas landmen, waitresses turned hookers, hookers turned waitresses, Nigerians, Tarot readers, Asian massage therapists. Nineteen-year-old reporters on their first job. The steady stream of national media helicoptering in for two days to get the whole story. Stern lectures by hometown parents terrified for the safety of their teenage children, especially their daughters. Swaggering state politicians, anxious local ones. The coffee klatches of retired men displaced from their accustomed meeting places. Jails at capacity with drunk and disorderly. Widows who plan their errands so that they never have to try to make a left turn. The blue glow of a thousand LCD wide-screen televisions in the man camps. Billboards stacked up like dominoes along the roads offering good jobs with benefits and a pickup. Armies of consultants. Four-hour traffic jams on US 85 between Alexander and Williston. Two-liter bottles of urine ten to a mile tossed into the ditches. Strippers working poles on excursion buses. Drugs being handed out like chewing gum on street corners. Drugs to stay awake. Drugs to sleep. Drugs to get high. Drugs to numb the pain of the body. Drugs to numb the pain of existence. Drugs to get it up. Drugs to see God. Alcohol in oceans. The bang of shot glasses on the tables of bars and restaurants, boisterous laughter, harassment of the female servers, fifteen-year-old waitresses grabbed by their bottoms and their breasts. Car dealerships with 200 gleaming white new Ford pickups in a line along the road. Big trucks violating traffic laws let everyone else beware. Every tenth vehicle with a broken windshield. Oversize loads everywhere. Frightened highway patrolmen walking cautiously up to a jacked-up pickup with smoked windows on a remote stretch of highway. Vehicles in ditches everywhere. Gleaming man camps, modest man camps, chaotic man camps, camps of old RVs, trailers, mail trucks, panel trucks, VWs. Rebel flags. A hundred trucks lined up at a saltwater storage dump, the drivers standing in small clusters for the seven-hour wait. Music from pickups at maximum decibel, the bass throbbing the street itself. Money changing hands in every direction, giant tips for pretty servers, giant tips for pliable strippers, money thrown across the bar because there is no time to wait for change. Priests turned social workers. Porn everywhere. Broken-down men and women at AA meetings. Broken men in the back rows of Sunday church services. Men calling home to Louisiana in the halls of motels and pleading for a little more time, pleading to stay together, pleading for child visitation, pleading for her to come try living here, pleading for understanding, pleading to keep the house. Swaggering men in muddy boots in every bar and café, ordering the Frackers Feast and telling the waitress she had better bring the extra salsa this time. Nervous cops in cafés looking straight ahead. Private jets streaming over the city in their final approach. Miniature makeshift RV parks with hookups on every farm and ranch. Trash in the streets, trash in the borrow ditch, trash piled up next to all the dumpsters, trash spilling out of every barrel and waste basket. Filthy public restrooms. Head-ons four a week on the region's two-lane roads, because some Alpha male was sure he could pass a line of twenty trucks before the hill. The ubiquity of the F-word. The *beep beep beep* of vehicles backing up day and night in every direction. Dust and blue exhaust everywhere. Sex trafficking rings almost caught, but operating in plain sight in well-known motels. Boasting, bombast, boisterousness, bravado, bitching, barking, brawling, bitterness, bankruptcy, blowjobs. In the hallways and the elevators and behind closed doors in the motels, weeping, shouting matches, furniture breaking, domestic violence, raucous partying, slurred monologues of dreams and desperation. Everywhere a mix of excitement and exhaustion. Thousands of men and women looking for the main chance. The volunteer fire department flying to Utah for training in chemical burns. A babel of languages in the schools, where waves of new students suddenly appear, others gone overnight, security guards by the doors, mobile classrooms connected only by an extension cord. Angels and demons, 40,000 strong, and you are never quite sure which.

That's what an oil boom looks like.

From the beginning of White settlement in North Dakota (ca. 1832), the dominant paradigm has been extraction. At first beaver skins, then buffalo tongues and hides and eventually bones, then wheat and cattle and barley, then coal, then corn, then pool oil, then sunflowers and soybeans, and now shale oil and natural gas. North Dakota and North Dakotans produce raw commodities in one of the most difficult climates on earth. Those commodities are shipped elsewhere, usually at our own expense, and the value added occurs elsewhere.

Beginning in the late 1870s, transcontinental railroads and the Homestead Act brought hundreds of thousands of immigrants to the northern Great Plains. It was surprisingly easy to displace the Native Americans and occupy their homelands. By the time of statehood in 1889, American Indians were no longer an impediment to White settlement. The homesteaders—many of them immigrants from Europe—quickly learned that North Dakota has a brutal winter climate, that it is subject to periodic droughts, and that it is so isolated that it could not easily compete with states located closer to the centers of power, money, and markets. The land was essentially free for the filing, but life on the Dakota plains was so difficult that no more than a statistically minimum number of people chose to live here—i.e., approximately one farm family per quarter section, and the requisite number of businesses and social institutions in villages and towns close enough to those farms to supply their needs. North Dakota had only one true industry—family agriculture—and by 1920 the state had been filled up for that purpose. Then and now, North Dakota did not attract manufacturing or other significant forms of economic diversity. The state existed to produce wheat, oats, barley, rye, flax, cattle, hogs, and potatoes.

The population of the state grew rapidly between 1880 (36,909) and 1930, when it peaked (and stalled) at 680,845. Thereafter it began its long, slow decline until by the time of the millennium in the year 2000 there was widespread concern in North Dakota that outmigration might take the population down to something around 500,000 people, a kind of bare bones social and economic infrastructure to support fewer and ever-larger family farms. It had become clear early in the twentieth century that it was difficult to make a success of a farm of just 160 acres. The farms began to consolidate. Displaced farmers moved to the towns or entirely out of state. Fewer farms require fewer services. As good roads and reliable vehicles gave North Dakotans unprecedented mobility, farmer citizens were able to venture much longer distances to buy supplies. The state's early twentieth-century distribution of towns was suited to a maximum number of modest farms evenly distributed across the landscape, but it made little sense for there to be a town every ten miles in every direction when it was possible to drive much longer distances (and back) in a single day. As the birth rate began to drop, owing partly to the mechanization of agriculture, families with fewer children needed fewer schools. The rural school system inevitably began a series of agonizing consolidations* that eroded small town life and loyalty perhaps more than did regional shopping options. North Dakota is now chock full of hollow towns that either never flourished or flourished briefly more than a century ago and have declined ever since, until they exist now merely because they once existed, and a handful of people find reason to continue to live in them. The hardest truth for North Dakotans to accept is that many of its young people find the state insufficiently satisfying to want to live here. In the past, they stayed because that was all they (we) knew, because America did not have the connectivity and mobility it has achieved since the 1960s, because families like to stay together if possible. But when it became clear that Americans can live anywhere and keep in touch with their kin by telephone (now FaceTime), and thanks to a superb and relatively inexpensive transportation infrastructure, young North Dakotans began increasingly to seek their happiness elsewhere.

Because of our isolation, our colonial status, our marginality, and our history of dependence, North Dakota has no choice but to be a gratitude state. If the US military wants to place 300 weapons of mass destruction under our farms and ranches, and there is some money in it for us, we are going to embrace that destiny, and not wring our hands much about the moral implications. When the Bakken boom came, we had no choice but to embrace it—first, because we had

---

* It is almost impossible for anyone who comes from a more stable economy and denser demographics to understand the agony of school consolidation. For most North Dakotans, the education of our children is the most important thing we do in life. Nobody wants to put their children on a bus to be hauled twice a day to a town ten twenty or thirty miles away. A significant portion of a town's sense of itself is bound up in K–12 activities: high school sports, the eighth grade choir, cookie sales to send students to Washington, DC, and New York, the theatrical production that finds expression on the dusty old high school proscenium arch stage, baccalaureate services, the prom, homecoming, and high school graduation. To take that away from a small town is like taking the car keys away from an elderly man who has spent his life driving cars, trucks, and tractors.

no other options and second, because it was going to sweep over us whether we wanted it or not.

There is a reason that Nevada (where I lived for seventeen years) has accepted gambling (once regarded as sinful), legal prostitution, minimally-regulated grazing, and gargantuan mineral development within its borders, and why it was once a divorce mill back when divorce was difficult to obtain in most other states. Nevada did not choose that economic destiny because it was wicked. A person living in Reno or Pahrump or Elko is no different from someone living in Hazen or Devils Lake or Wahpeton, even someone who is employed as a sex worker or a poker dealer in a casino. They eat the same Big Macs, and watch the same television sitcoms, shop at the same Target and Dollar Stores, and cheer for the same professional football teams. Nevada's Faustian bargain, if you want to characterize it that way, has brought economic stability and prosperity to a godforsaken desert country. Nevada bumper stickers declare, "If you can't grow it, you have to mine it." Or dress it in a topless flamingo costume or in Fredericks of Hollywood teddies at the Bunny Ranch.

North Dakota's economic bargain is less sinful, at least in Biblical terms. Oil, natural gas, coal. The land in North Dakota is too precious to be used as a nuclear waste dump (as at Yucca Mountain in Nevada). We are fortunate in that. But it has been regarded as expendable enough to become the home of one of the largest concentrations of nuclear missiles and warheads in the world.

North Dakota has from the beginning relied on an economic model of extraction. Since there has been no significant manufacturing base in the state, raw commodities produced here—wheat, cattle, coal, oil, natural gas—have been hauled away to other states (especially Minnesota) for processing. Where the value added is, there you will find the most significant profits. North Dakotans have always known that an extraction economy is inherently exploitative and that it results in economic colonialism, but attempts to combat the exploitation, beginning with the Grange and the Populist Movements of 1886-1910, and including the breathtaking brief experiment undertaken by the Nonpartisan League of farmer socialism (1915-25), have all failed to solve the problem.

The two world wars brought high wheat prices and sufficient infusions of cash to quiet rural unrest for significant portions of the twentieth century. Under the brilliant leadership of North Dakota's most progressive governor, William L. Guy (1960-72), the state began to diversify its economy. His particular insight was that North Dakota should attempt to provide some of the value added at home, rather than simply ship raw commodities elsewhere for finishing. Accordingly, Governor Guy supported mine-mouth coal generation plants, sugar beet processing plants, and other industries that would keep more of the wealth in North Dakota and overcome the state's historic status as a commodity colony for out-of-state interests. Guy sparked North Dakota's state-owned bank back into life after a post-Depression, post-New Deal period of quiescence. The bank was able to take the lead in putting together the financial package that led to the construction of coal-fired power plants in west central North Dakota, and sugar beet plants in the Red River Valley.

More recently the state government, with the help of the State Bank of North Dakota, has attempted to promote small-scale North Dakota value-added enterprise, showcased across the state in Pride of Dakota packaging and showcase fairs. It remains true, however, that most of the wealth extracted from the North Dakota soil leaves the state.

Fortunately, for the last thirty years, America has become so prosperous that it has quieted rural discontent. There is simply so much more money awash in North Dakota in the early twenty-first century that the continuing economic colonialism has felt less oppressive to the people of the state than it did to our great-grandparents. Today's North Dakotans have prospered in spite of still being exploited—as always—by out-of-state interests. Because of this, the state's traditional culture of grievance has largely disappeared or morphed into a deep distrust of government, especially the national government. The irony of this is profound.

The point of this truncated history is that North Dakota was and is a dependency state. The hard-working people of the state have never been fully in control of their own destiny. Because the entire economy of North Dakota depends on a handful of raw commodities, the state has not had the economic options that more diverse states like Colorado, Minnesota, Oregon, and Illinois enjoy. North Dakota has to make the most of what it has, but it has never been able to set the price of wheat, potatoes, sugar beets, cattle, hogs, coal, or oil. In the last few decades, the state has worked hard to promote tourism, particularly to the badlands in the west, but the badlands are not the Grand Tetons and there is a practical limit to the number of people that can be lured to the state, which is not really on the way to more glamorous places. What we say half-jokingly is true: you have to want to go to North Dakota, or even through North Dakota. The federal government has been exceptionally generous to North Dakota since 1862, but only to the extent of making the state sustainable—not rich. From a historical perspective, the contempt of the people of North Dakota for the federal government is ironic, to put it mildly.

Twice in the twentieth century North Dakota faltered gravely enough to fear collapse. The years 1929-1941 were the darkest era in North Dakota history, a crushing combination of the Great Depression and the Dust Bowl. In fact, though the entire tier of Great Plains states suffered grievously during those years, no state, not even Oklahoma, was so adversely impacted. We survived those years partly because most North Dakota families had a farm connection of some sort, because we were closer to the pioneer period of ND history, when deprivation and extreme penny-pinching were the norm, because expectations were lower than they have subsequently become, and because of the large infusions of federal assistance that appeared under the aegis of the New Deal.

The Dust Bowl years may have been the darkest in our history and the most economically damaging, but it was the decade of the 1980s that did the most damage to the spirit of North Dakota. In my opinion, even now, more than thirty years later, we have not fully recovered. A prolonged drought, the sudden collapse of the oil boom of the late '70s, high interest rates, and an epidemic of farm and ranch foreclosures brought North Dakota to its knees. The best account we have of that terrible period can be found in former ND Governor George A. Sinner's memoir, *Turning Points: A Memoir*.

Part of the trauma was a recognition of how quickly things had fallen apart after three decades of growth and relative prosperity. The post-World War II economy had been robust on the Great Plains. The long process of rural electrification was now complete. With the advent of the Interstate Highway System, farmers had greater transportation options than ever before. The Cold War brought an infusion of national defense capital to the state: two Strategic Air Command Air Force Bases, 300 ICBM missile sites, a radar base at Dickinson, an array of Defense Early Warning (DEW line) radar installations along the northern perimeter of the state. Commodity prices were solid and steady. Then, in 1973, American grain exports expanded dramatically into increasingly open world markets. Farmers prospered as never before. You can still see the houses, barns, Quonsets, and other farm improvements that followed that extraordinary harvest. The first national energy crisis (1973-80) brought unprecedented prosperity to North Dakota. The state's coal industry attracted significant national and international attention, and the thirst for new sources of domestic oil brought greatly increased activity to the Williston Basin, until, at the peak, North Dakota was producing 150,000 barrels per day. Although there was a very serious statewide debate about responsible development—were we willing for North Dakota to become an energy-sacrifice zone for the nation?—

every development scenario, from "dig, baby, dig" at one end of the spectrum to "slow, orderly development" at the other end (led by Governor Arthur A. Link), implied a prosperous future for the state.

Then, suddenly, everything went bust. The oil boom pulled up stakes and disappeared from the landscape of North Dakota as quickly as it had come. A prolonged drought shattered the stability of the farm sector, then and now the most important economic engine in North Dakota. Outmigration started to feel like mass exodus. North Dakota lost its confidence. The old bumper sticker percolated through the hearts of North Dakotans: *Oh lord just give us one more oil boom and this time we promise not to screw it up!*

The state celebrated its centennial in 1989 in an atmosphere of anxiety and uncertainty. Scattered across the state were highway signs announcing the centennials of sparsely populated towns. Nobody living in those towns or driving by could be confident that there would ever be a *bicentennial* sign out on the highway. Farm foreclosures were so common that billboards went up all over the state announcing bankruptcy counseling services. Ministers were sent off to seminars to learn how to console farmers who were losing their land. Farm auctions filled the calendar. Suicide hotlines proliferated. The shocking spike in interest rates at the end of the Carter and beginning of the Reagan presidencies—peaking at 21 percent— threw thousands of farmers nationwide into the bankruptcy courts.

As the twenty-first century began on the northern plains, the state's confidence was low and the future did not look promising. Our children were leaving and not coming back. In fact, thousands of North Dakota parents and grandparents, high school teachers and advisers, priests and pastors, actually urged young people to leave the state and seek their happiness elsewhere. When that happens, when kin make rational arguments that it might be better to emigrate, a society is in grave trouble. There was a widespread feeling that the aging population would hang on and then die out. The population of North Dakota was in alarming decline.

I believe that the citizens of North Dakota have been suffering from Post-Traumatic Stress Disorder (PTSD) since the disastrous decade of the 1980s. I do not use the term loosely or metaphorically. That period of North Dakota life was so unsettling, so stark, so dispiriting, that it left the people of North Dakota bewildered and frightened, numb and feeling defeated.

My thesis is simple. You cannot understand the Bakken Oil Boom unless you factor in the high trauma of the 1980s. The perfect storm of rapid outmigration, the collapse of the farm economy, the oil bust, the state so broke that the legislature did what it could to support K–12 and university education and very little else—in aggregate, an existential threat to the future of the state—so upset the people of the North Dakota that they had no choice but to look upon any return of oil development as an act of grace. When it suddenly appeared, they were not about to look that gift horse in the mouth. The concerns of the discontented seemed like what Samuel Johnson once called "the petty cavils of petty minds," the stuff of elitists and malcontents who knew nothing about the real facts of life on the Great Plains. Whatever the environmental and social cost of oil development, it was a bargain that North Dakota dared not resist in any significant way.

Then came Bakken.

The oil boom of 2008 to 2016 was a godsend. It brought an unprecedented economic windfall to North Dakota. In the wake of the worst national economic downturn since the Great Depression, it gave North Dakota the lowest unemployment rate in the country. At one time the state reported that there were 30,000 open jobs waiting for qualified applicants. The possibility of American oil independence—something that had been written off as a mere chimera for thirty or more years—brought satisfaction to a heartland people who felt a deep disgust with American dependence on oil produced by nations that were alien to American values and hostile to America's interests in the world. Suddenly North Dakota was cool and important. National politicians accepted invitations to speak in North Dakota. Some sang the praises of the state in the national media. Others praised North Dakota as if it had invented or manufactured its oil or at least invented hydraulic fracturing. North Dakotans boasted that they were running budget surpluses, lowering taxes, and squirrelling away money in rainy-day funds, unlike "the people's republic of Minnesota" next door.

The Bakken Oil Boom didn't just happen. The welcoming business climate of North Dakota, fostered in the 1990s by Governor Ed Schafer, played a significant role, as well as former senator Byron Dorgan's leadership in securing US government funding of research into the technology of fracking. Even so, most of the windfall came from God—or from the ancient marine organisms that the earth compressed into oil over tens of millions of years. The truth is that it took out-of-state technology and out-of-state capital to release the oil from its shale trap and draw it to the surface. This oil boom replayed the traditional pattern of North Dakota economic development: No matter how much wealth was retained in the state in the hands of individuals and government treasuries, it is indisputable that the vast majority of the oil wealth left the state in semi-trucks, rail cars, royalties, and pipelines.

The thugs and the ne'er-do-wells who flocked to North Dakota got most of the media attention, but the great majority of the tens of thousands of men (and some women) who turned up in western North Dakota were good and decent people who needed work and were willing to leave behind all their normal comforts to obtain it. They were willing to work hard at demanding and dangerous jobs in a faraway region of America where they knew nobody, or maybe only the buddy who agreed to drive along. They came because they were desperate. They came because they wanted a better life. They came because they were intrigued by the social extravaganza they heard was unfolding in North Dakota. They came because they had heard that there was money to be made. They came because they had skills. They came because they were at loose ends and there was nothing at home for them. They came for the same reason several hundred thousand bikers descend on Sturgis, SD, every August, for the same reason tens of thousands attend the annual Burning Man Festival in the Black Rock Desert in Nevada—drink, drugs, drunk women, and danger. They came because they had heard a year of very hard work could pay off their student loans or the mortgage. They came because they wanted to spend some time in the most exciting place in North America. They came because they wanted to be where the action was.

A Brooklyn-based folksinger, actor, and playwright named Michael Patrick Smith spent ten months in the Bakken in 2013. His recent book, *The Good Hand*, has received excellent reviews in the national press. Part memoir, part exploration of the kind of loose-ends young men who are drawn to gold rushes and oil booms, *The Good Hand* posits that industrial capitalism depends on the availability of men and women with broken pasts—men with father wounds—to do the rough and physically debilitating work of handling dangerous heavy equipment outside in inhospitable climates. Smith writes, "Testosterone-fueled young men are working fourteen-hour shifts at jobs that can kill them in a town without friends or family. It only makes sense that the dangerous work of the day spills past sunset as parentless white boys roar through the night in F-250s."

The myth that oil development is somehow clean industry silenced any expression of anxiety. The leaders of North Dakota seemed inordinately eager to strew roses before the industry. At tables at the Petroleum Club of Tulsa and the corporate retreats of Houston oil moguls, there must have been toasts to the hospitality of North Dakota.

Thousands of desperate people rushed to northwestern North Dakota between 2009 and 2013 in search of good-paying jobs. Or just jobs. Many of them had lost or were in danger of losing their houses in Louisiana, Mississippi, Arkansas, and elsewhere. The men who found their way to North Dakota determined to save money—send money home, save their houses, pay off the credit cards, get a one-time leg up in life—mostly found themselves drinking away their salaries or putting them dollar by dollar into the G-strings of strippers. Or, flush with unprecedented cash, they bought expensive pickups and widescreen televisions (and guns), and several years later wound up limping back where they came from—older, physically diminished, addicted to drink, emotionally exhausted, or even broken.

The Bakken miracle gave North Dakota a much-needed economic boost. It made some fabulously rich and left thousands of migrants unsatisfied. It stopped the hemorrhaging of North Dakota's young people, at least temporarily, and perked up a lot of towns that were tottering on the brink of extinction. But it did not solve the long-term problems of North Dakota life.

Communities like Watford City, Stanley, Killdeer, and Tioga gambled that some percentage of the people who flocked to the state during the most hectic years of the boom would stay, either because they have learned to love the quality of life that North Dakota offers, or because they don't see better prospects elsewhere. Local leaders believed that a relatively small influx of new permanent residents gives those communities a critical mass of services, amenities, cash flow, and entertainments that will make it possible for them to buck the larger dynamics of rural decline and outmigration. Watford City doesn't need 20,000 people to survive and succeed. The addition of even a thousand permanent residents solves the Watford City problem for at least one more generation. These communities also believe that the dramatic investment in infrastructure—new public schools, community conference and arts centers, a new public library, improved police, fire, clinic, and even hospital services, better roads, roundabouts, rodeo arenas, baseball diamonds, tennis courts, and playgrounds—makes them more attractive as places to settle down and raise a family and enjoy the good life far from the madding crowds of Houston, Tulsa, Denver, or New Orleans.

It was said at the height of the boom that one should not expect to drive up and down US 85 much without having one's windshield shattered from gravel hurtled behind the tires of fracking and tanker vehicles. And that was the least of it. The boom brought widespread drug trafficking, including gang wars over sales turf; not just camp-follower prostitution, but serious sex trafficking in what was once the most agrarian state in the union; sheriffs, policemen, state patrolmen and other law enforcement officials wary of making even routine stops on the state's highways; sexual assault, and the covering up of sexual assault by some of its victims; gross sexual imposition; an epidemic of traffic violations, hit and run accidents, roll overs, auto theft, and vandalism; domestic violence, battery, housebreaking; groping of women of all ages who worked in the service industries; trash dumped out of pickup trucks on the sides of the roads; illegal dumping of industrial equipment and industrial waste; equipment theft and cannibalization; unreported spills of oil and fracking solution and other toxins; underreported spills.

All this was defended by a wide range of people with an interest in playing down any notion of a downside to the boom. The essential attitude of North Dakota to all of this development, including its excesses, has been that *such things happen* in an oil boom, that the problems of such industrial activity are essentially "the cost of doing business," that nobody had reason to be unduly concerned about the manifold disruptions, which were unfortunate but more or less inevitable. I've been particularly saddened to hear the excuses that have been made not just by industry and by North Dakotans who stand to profit from essentially unlimited oil development, but also by public servants whose devotion, one might think, would be to the long-term health and security of the land and the people of the state.

I have even heard all of the excesses, industrial spills, and criminal activity defended by average North Dakotans who live hundreds of miles from the impact zone. "Hey, you cannot make an omelet without breaking some eggs," or "They'll clean it up. Meanwhile, we're prospering," or "Most of this is probably exaggerated, but I know state government is looking out for us."

We've all heard the new narrative of rural western North Dakota: That the ranch could only support one family so four of the siblings went off to find work in Billings and Denver and Seattle, but now, thanks to the Bakken, there's enough revenue to support several families on the land. Dale and his wife Bonnie came back three years ago and are doing real well. And Brett and Tyler are thinking of moving back next year. With the school growing so rapidly, there might be a place for Bonnie to teach second grade beginning in the fall. Tyler is going to work in the oil fields until he can find a management position in town.

This is the new narrative. It is a much more satisfying than the old one, wherein we were told that Dale and Bonnie would give anything to make their home on the farm, but the numbers just don't add up, so Dale has decided to take that job selling cars down in Aurora, Colorado, where there is a chance he could be floor manager in a couple of years. Besides, the schools are better there, and it gives us an excuse to get away to Denver from time to time. Even Vegas is only a day's drive.

The new narrative is true, albeit largely anecdotal. Families *are* moving back to western North Dakota. Small towns *are not* drying up and blowing away. Young people are staying here more and more, not heading to more satisfying consumer possibilities elsewhere. I'm glad we have found a way to reverse the tide of rural decline, but I wish we had been considerably more skeptical of the industry, more willing to insist on respect for our traditional value system, more willing to err on the side of less (but more careful) development rather than more (with all the attendant growing pains). What else were these rural districts going to do? You can only support so many combined tanning and cappuccino shops in one town.

Former North Dakota Governor Arthur A. Link had the perfect koan: "slow, orderly development." I would like to be able to ask, "Who could actually disagree with that?" But I know that millions do disagree nationwide, and probably a solid majority of North Dakotans do now, too, a dozen years after the death of Art Link and forty-eight years after his famous "When the Landscape Is Quiet Again" speech in Mandan.

Once during the height of the boom, I attended the *Medora Musical* with my dear friend Sheila Schafer and former North Dakota State Senator John Andrist (1931-2018). We were at the pitchfork fondue sitting at a picnic table under a shelter eating baked beans. John was one of the leading citizens of Crosby, North Dakota (population 1,406), the publisher of the local weekly newspaper, the *Crosby Journal*. Because he loved his town, because people looked up to him, Mr. Andrist had served on every committee that called upon him in his lifetime, without compensation and without taking reimbursement for his expenses.

Andrist served in the North Dakota legislature (the state senate) from 1993 to 2014. He was a fiscal conservative but a social moderate. He was respected by everyone and loved by thousands of his fellow North Dakotans. He had served as the president of the North Dakota Press Association.

I was decrying something bad that had happened in the oil zone.

With his deep-fried sirloin just half-eaten, John put down his fork. "Listen," he said with some edge in his voice, maybe more sadness than anger, but some anger, too, "you don't live in a small town. For five decades I have watched my hometown decline, shrink up, lose population, watch its young people drift away, and get a little more desperate every year. I cannot tell you how many times

I've served on committees set up to help the town survive and grow back. We brainstorm, we hire one outside consultant after the next, we contract with a firm to build a new website, we try to attract a bike race or a skeet shooting festival. There is nothing we haven't tried to fight decline and outmigration. And every single time the town merchants and farmers pooled our money together to try to do one of these things, it has failed to stop the hemorrhaging. Nothing worked. Eventually it seemed as if there were no future for Crosby. When *National Geographic* did its story on the "Emptied Prairie" in 2008, the region of the state they concentrated on was my region, up in Divide County. Sure, there'd always be some people living there because it is cheap and easy, or because their family had always lived thereabouts, but that's not a town, that's not a real community. You grew up in what's urban for North Dakota and you have never had to live with unstoppable decline hanging over your head.

"And then along comes the Bakken Oil Boom around 2005. Now every shop on Main Street is occupied. People have fixed up old houses and there are even new housing starts in Crosby, North Dakota, of all places. Nobody ever expected that. We have two cafés now. Some people have moved back from where they were living far away, and some of our graduates are staying to work in the family business or start one of their own. We see young couples in the cafes and the shops.

"Do I wish the Bakken had come a little slower? Yes. Am I sorry to see traffic accidents, a rising crime rate, domestic violence, etc.? Of course, but you know some of those things were already going on pretty well before the boom came. Because of the boom, do I see something slipping away that we really prized in North Dakota? The pace of life, the peacefulness, the way everyone knew pretty well everyone else in the community and we were able to sort of look after each other? Yes, and I am sorry about that, but on balance I cannot be sorry this oil boom came. There are not a lot of community renewal options out where I live. You have to take what comes and make the best of it. And that's what we are doing. You need to understand that."

It was an amazing statement. I was deeply moved and so was John, who choked up a little at the end. "I'm kind of an emotional guy," he apologized with his broad shy smile.

If the question is put to you in such stark terms—drill and degrade but survive or protect and hasten the rural decline—I'm going to choose survival every time. Now whenever I let myself think that the oil boom has brought more trouble than it was worth, I involuntarily flash back to John Andrist on the terrace above the Burning Hills Amphitheater, home to the famous *Medora Musical*. And that sobers me up instantly.

A close friend of mine was the CEO of one of North Dakota's most successful and respected engineering firms. His company was undergoing unprecedented growth. He was, among other things, a great reader, an outdoorsman, a seeker after knowledge, someone who kept up in every way with local, state, and national current events, and a moderate conservationist who loved the North Dakota outback. He was so competent, fit, and confident that he seemed like a character out of an Ayn Rand novel. Governors, congressmen, oil executives, and newspaper publishers took his calls. His firm was building drilling pads, roads, laying pipeline. When he spoke at oil conferences and legislative committee hearings, everyone leaned forward to listen.

Over dinner one night with three of his friends, at the height of the boom, he told us of a call he had received earlier in the week. An oil executive from Houston called him to say he needed a gravel approach road to a promising new well site. Would my friend's firm be able to take on the project? Yes, of course, said my friend, but we've got a fairly long list of projects we'd have to complete first.

The oil exec said he needed the road right away. My friend said he was sorry to have to decline, but he needed to honor the clients already in the queue. The oil exec asked my friend what he thought the road project would cost. He thought about it for a few seconds and named a larger than necessary figure, hoping that would be enough to dissuade the executive. "What if I paid you double that to get it done next week?" That wouldn't be possible. It wasn't about the money. "What if I paid you quadruple?"

The deal never happened. Houston found another service provider.

ND highway 22 runs north along the eastern face of the Killdeer Mountains, then makes a broad curve toward the east. Suddenly the bottom drops out of the world and ND 22 snakes its way carefully down to the Little Missouri River. The view from the southern bench of this gorge is one of the most dramatic and beautiful in North Dakota. It's hard to imagine how the sluggish Little Missouri River cut so deep and wide a trench as it moves towards its confluence with the Missouri. It was a magical place to me when I was a child. ND 22 from Dickinson to New Town was once a much narrower and more crooked road than it has become by way of improvements brought by the 1970-'80s oil boom and more recently the Bakken Oil Rush. It was also more romantic and picturesque, though I freely admit I haven't ever had to move a forty-ton oil tanker along that once-dangerous stretch of road. ND 22 is wider now, and safer, and duller. I freely admit that this has been the result of progress and prosperity, but I miss the old road and I certainly miss Lost Bridge, which spanned the river at the bottom of the canyon until the end of the twentieth century.

The viewshed I am describing, with or without Lost Bridge, was one of the three or four most beautiful in North Dakota. It was one of the few places in the state that can rightly be called breathtaking.

If you were trying to persuade a skeptical outsider that North Dakota has places of great beauty, even sublimity, you would surely take him or her here.

During the height of the oil boom, Dunn County gave a permit to an oil service company to build a saltwater disposal plant right at the entrance road to Little Missouri State Park, and precisely on the lip of the great Little Missouri River canyon. Scores of eighteen-wheel trucks lined up each day to dump their waste liquids at the site. Most of them ran their engines while they waited. A place that was formerly synonymous with silence and reflection and spiritual renewal was now characterized by dust and noise, heavy traffic, and the odor of diesel exhaust. The disposal facility was built at the entrance to one of North Dakota's finest state parks. Everyone entering the park now had to run the gauntlet of the disposal plant and a series of clanking pump jacks across the way. Whatever you were trying to leave behind in Bismarck or Minot or Dickinson when you made the journey to Little Missouri State Park, your approach to those magical hiking and riding trails was now through the engine of the Bakken Oil Boom. Saltwater disposal facilities cannot go just anywhere, but they can go *almost* anywhere. Anyone dropping in from Jupiter (or for that matter Minnesota or Montana) to this site overlooking this magnificent gorge would conclude either that this must have been the only possible place to build the facility, or that the people who built it and indeed the people who permitted it can have no respect of any sort for western North Dakota. It's impossible for anyone who cares even modestly about zoning, aesthetics, the badlands, spirit of place, or even good sense, to see this siting as anything but obscene. It almost feels like a deliberate and provocative assault—to spoil the view, perhaps to create a slippery slope for all the heavy development that has been planned for the valley floor. Any sense of enchantment is gone now, as you approach the canyon from the south, threading your way through trucks lined up to dump their toxic swill. Even in a state that has done everything it can to accommodate oil development, this siting feels unnecessary and contemptuous. It would be like throwing up a porn shop or a Jiffy Lube in St. Peter's Square at the Vatican.

In the long run, geology will win, of course. The life of such a saltwater disposal plant is only a handful of years. When it is no longer needed, presumably the site will be partially reclaimed. Fifty years from now, perhaps it will be impossible (or at least difficult) to see the scar, but for the foreseeable future the disposal plant on the south rim of the Little Missouri River canyon must be seen to represent something soulless and indifferent in the consciousness of North Dakota. A state (or county) that really cared about its landscape would never have issued a permit for such a facility. More than any other location in the Bakken zone, this one tells us who we are, what we value and what we don't value.

How could we have done things differently between 2005 and 2016, and how can we still do things differently as we move forward into the third decade of the twenty-first century? My suggestions seem so modest that it is hard to believe that they could be regarded as radical in some quarters. If our goal is to cooperate with the carbon extraction industry to pump as much oil and natural gas from the under the surface of North Dakota as an oil-hungry world needs and the market can bear, but to do these important things without damaging the landscape of North Dakota or its social fabric any more than is absolutely necessary, then I suggest the following nine adjustments in the rules of engagement.

First, we could have slowed things down and still can. The North Dakota Industrial Commission could quite easily have capped the number of new wells it would permit per year. The rationale would have been that we did not want to let the boom overwhelm the ability of North Dakota's towns and infrastructure to absorb it without chaos. A state has the right to manage the pace and volume of its economic development. North Dakota does not permit every town to set up small-scale casinos in the manner of neighboring Montana. A city does not hand out licenses to every proposed bar, restaurant, or liquor store. We, as the host state of a mighty oil boom, have the right to set the rules of engagement for everyone who wants to do business within our borders. Those protocols should not be unduly restrictive, but they should protect the land and also the social fabric of North Dakota.

The notion that to moderate the pace of development amounts to a *taking* of private property is absurd. I had the honor of getting to know former North Dakota Governor Arthur A. Link pretty well in his last years. Just ten days before his death I was in his home in Bismarck. I asked him how he would manage the Bakken Oil Boom. In his piping voice he barked back, "That oil's not going anywhere. We don't need to be in any great hurry to bring it up." Governor Link's energy philosophy was cautious, orderly development. Slow it down a little. Keep on top of it. Ease it in while we find solutions to the inevitable problems we could not have anticipated until the boom came. Back in the 1970s, Governor Link staked his career—and his historical reputation—on the principle that the people of North Dakota value stewardship, community, the integrity of the land, and sustainability more than making money. His famous October 1973 speech, "When the Landscape is Quiet Again," argued that carbon development comes and goes, but our land ethic and our social values must survive each boom unimpaired. It was by no means certain that Governor Link would prevail in the fierce pro-development atmosphere of the early '70s, but in the end the people of North Dakota stepped back to think about it and acknowledged that he was right. They did not want what he called a "one-time harvest."

That was almost fifty years ago, when North Dakota was a more agrarian state. People were more deeply connected to the land.

Stewardship had a broader, deeper constituency then. By 2010, the idea of stewardship was less widely embraced. It is not at all clear that if Art Link had been governor in the Bakken years, he would have been able to convince the people of North Dakota to slow things down. "Cautious orderly development" was not the working philosophy of the North Dakota establishment between 2005 and 2019. Their argument, which makes little sense to me, was that it was not appropriate for the government of North Dakota to stand between mineral-owning citizens and oil and gas development. If the state limited the number of drilling permits to slow things down, it might be preventing Mineral Owner X from profiting from oil development. In a sense, the state would be in the position of picking winners and losers. Why not just accept the formula of willing buyer-willing seller, the sanctity of private property and privately owned mineral rights and get out of the way? State officials and the oil lobby also argued that a state-directed slowdown would in some cases make it impossible for oil companies to drill within the standard three-year mineral lease deadlines, and that this would leave the state of North Dakota open to lawsuits for impeding contracts. All these arguments have validity, but surely the leaders of North Dakota have commonwealth interests and duties that are greater than their commitment to pell-mell development.

There was also a larger concern at work. What if the state of North Dakota slowed development on the principle that there was no need to rush, but then the world price of oil collapsed? Everyone knows that oil, like other commodities, follows an endless roller coaster of boom-and-bust cycles, and that you had better make hay while the sun shines. No time like the present. When the price of oil is more than $100 a barrel, the urge to drill becomes an actual mania. Rational thinking could not compete with the great thirst. Nobody could predict how long the goose that was laying the golden black eggs would continue to be fertile. Cautious orderly development might mean that thousands of willing developers (and mineral owners) would miss the profit train. The unrestrained pace of the boom, for the carbon extraction industry, was a greedy perversion of Dr. Martin Luther King's "the fierce urgency of now." And in some important respects, they were right.

I understand these arguments and I respect them, but expediency, maximum profit, and hectic development are not the highest values of a community. North Dakota is a community—and the home of dozens of impacted communities—not a mere business plan, not the surface of an uninhabited planet. We are not more important than the oil, but it is essential that we harvest carbon without shattering the lives of the communities and the individuals who have given their lives to building healthy communities here. Social safety, social security, maintaining the quality of the lives of everyone in the community—these are, in the end, as important as money. North Dakotans know this. But we all got caught up in a period of mass hypnosis. That's how gold rushes work. Anyone who reads H. W. Brands' *The Age of Gold: The Californian Gold Rush and the New American Dream* (2003) will see how this hypnosis works.

Second, is it too much to ask for transparency in government? It's Civics 101; we pay these people's salaries. They work for all of the people of North Dakota, those who live in the areas affected by industrial development and also those (the great majority) who live elsewhere. Their allegiance belongs to the people of North Dakota, not to the oil industry. They are not elected or appointed to be cheerleaders for carbon extraction. They are not authorized to serve as public relations agents for oil producers. They are not authorized to play down problems in the oil zone, to cover up bad practices or illegal activities, or soften the bite of bad news. They are meant to enforce laws passed by the North Dakota legislature, keep the public accurately informed of what is happening in the oil fields, good and bad, and study the effects of carbon extraction—on our air, our water, our access to transport, and our social fabric—and present those findings raw and unmassaged to the public.

These government officials work for us. We are not children. Because we are adults, we don't need anyone in our government to sugarcoat the truth. We expect a lack of candor from industry. Nobody is so naïve as to believe that industry would tell the whole truth about anything that could damage their reputation or profitability. That's the nature of capitalism. We get it. Nor do we always accept what the environmentalist community has to say about resource development, because we know that some activists may wish the boom had never happened or would magically disappear, and that their modus operandi is to emphasize (and at times exaggerate) bad news, real or rumored. We understand that in a free society truth has to struggle to find a path between the distortions of strong-minded, often absolutist voices at both ends of the political spectrum. Our educational system teaches us to weigh evidence, pierce through rhetoric, think for ourselves, and bring generous skepticism to every pronouncement, whatever its source.

The one entity we have a right to be able to trust is our government. Thomas Jefferson said the whole art of government consisted of "a few plain duties performed by a few honest men." Government officials and employees have a duty to be neutral umpires. We need what Theodore Roosevelt called "a square deal." There are innumerable stories of a deliberate failure of transparency in North Dakota's government throughout the Bakken years. Of regulators partying late into the evening with the representatives of industry, and with industry picking up the check. Of off-the-record communications between government officials and captains of industry to circumvent North Dakota's open meeting and open records laws. From at least a dozen sources I have heard that the word came down from the highest levels of state government that elected and appointed officials were to emphasize the positive, play down the negative, assure reporters, activists, and citizens that everything was fine or soon would be, that there was nothing much to worry about, and that whatever they were hearing to the contrary was just unsubstantiated rumor. I know, too, that some media outlets—at least those who owned them and signed the checks of honest reporters—decided that it was not in their interest to emphasize bad news. It's unclear how an average citizen was expected to think about these things and to make the hard choices that are essential to the healthy functioning of a democracy—or any society for that matter—when they were not hearing the truth, the whole truth, and nothing but the truth. We all expect industry to put the best foot forward and to try to manage the bad news for least negative impact. But we have the right to expect that our state government will tell all the truth it has access to without trying to manipulate the public's response.

When I have asked mid-level bureaucrats if it was true that the word had come down that state agencies were expected to emphasize the positive and say little—nothing, if possible—about the negative impacts of the oil boom, almost all said yes, but they insisted that the word did not arrive by way of a memo or a mass meeting. It was just a tacit code. To that I say, we're adults. We can take it. You can tell us the truth. And by the way, you have a moral obligation to do so.

I particularly want transparency on questions of crime, violence, gang activity, corruption, rape, sex trafficking, drugs, spills, accidents, and black-market guns. Transparency is important at all levels of government, but it is particularly important on questions that could affect the safety of the people of North Dakota and the long-term health of the land and water of the state. You don't want to make your citizens panic, but you need to let them know that there are times and places where they may not be safe.

Third, the Extraordinary Places initiative should be renewed. During the height of the oil boom, North Dakota Attorney General Wayne Stenehjem created a task force to designate a handful of places in western North Dakota so beautiful, historically important, or beloved that they should be accorded special treatment by the oil industry. The initiative eventually collapsed thanks to landowner intransigence and industry's mantra, "We want no restrictions."

That this modest proposal—to encourage restraint (but not prohibition) in the vicinity of a handful of the most picturesque and inspiring landscapes in North Dakota—failed by a two-to-one vote in the three-member Industrial Commission was one of the lowest moments of the Bakken saga. The absolutism of the industry and a hastily formed Royalty Owners Association was a graceless indication of the spirit of ruthlessness that took possession of tens of thousands of North Dakotans, including the state's political leadership and its not-elected power structure. When the idea of designating a few places you would rather not see damaged by industrial development can be dismissed as radical environmentalism, elitism, and a Fifth Amendment taking, you have sold your soul for a mess of carbon.

My point from the beginning has been that the oil industry— consisting almost exclusively of people from elsewhere, who do not know North Dakota history, who do not live in North Dakota, and who see the Bakken oil zone as just another extraction platform—cannot be expected to show special care around sensitive sites because they have no way of knowing that those sites are special. Only the people of North Dakota can know what they most value. If we don't deliberate among ourselves and then inform the extraction corporations about what we value, we cannot expect them to figure it out for themselves. We have to teach the industry who we are, how we think about the land, what concerns we have about development, what places we treasure most, and what we would be sorry to see impaired. The land ethic, the aesthetic appreciation, the conservation ethos, has to come from the host community, not from the boardrooms of oil companies headquartered in Tulsa, Oklahoma City, or Houston.

Now that the bombastic first phase of the Bakken Oil Boom has ended, and life in North Dakota has calmed down a bit, now that we have the chance to step back and take a deep breath, to take stock of what went right and what went wrong, we should establish a new special or extraordinary places task force, bring all the stakeholders to the table, and hammer out a modest list of places we wish to protect. The fact that the power structure of North Dakota has largely allowed the oil industry to set the terms of engagement for the extraction of a natural resource of such consequence to our economy, our state character, and our future, is deeply depressing.

We have a gigantic repository of carbon. The world wants it. Industry is ready to extract it and ship it out to refineries elsewhere. We are not only entitled to set the terms of engagement. We have a moral imperative to do so.

Fourth, there should be zero tolerance for negligence. If you are lifting and exporting 1.25-1.5 million barrels of oil per day, some of it in pipelines, some by rail, some on the nation's highways, there will be spills. Spills of oil, spills of the water that comes back up out of wells, spills of fracking fluids. So many transfer-of-fluids events occur every day, every month, every year, that it would be irrational to believe there will never be accidents, some of them significant. Nobody wants spills. They are expensive. They consume time that would better be spent in oil production. They lower the profits of shareholders and investors. They bring negative publicity that damages a company's credibility. But they will happen.

The State of North Dakota's duty is to set very high standards of safety and professionalism, to insist always on best practices, to enforce such laws as are already on the books swiftly and firmly, to tighten loopholes in the law as they become apparent through experience, to study best practices throughout the rest of the United States and the rest of the world and to incorporate those that will make North Dakota oil production safer, to declare and enforce zero tolerance for repeat offenders, and to ban companies that flout the laws of the state.

If we accept that accidents will sometimes happen, our goal should be to do everything we can to prevent them, to hold companies responsible for cleanup and restitution, and to make sure that our laws require 100 percent mitigation and reclamation.

In other words, the whole cost of mitigation should be borne by the culprits, including generous compensation to farmers and ranchers whose surface operations are impaired by spills and by the disruptions of the cleanup activities. The State of North Dakota should set aside funds to pay for cleanup activities in such cases where the responsible parties have somehow disappeared from the scene, but the bonding protocols should be such as to make such evasions virtually impossible. In no instance should non-responsible individuals be expected to pay for the mitigations.

Every spill should be thoroughly and rigorously investigated by regulatory and judicial bodies with subpoena authority, using interviews in which industry executives and employees are under oath. Penalties for willful misinformation or perjury should be severe and include mandatory prison sentences. Wherever negligence is found, the companies or individuals at fault should pay for full restitution, but they should also pay punitive fines severe enough to discourage other entities from cutting corners or violating existing regulations. Companies or individuals found to be negligent should be given an ironclad warning that a second act of negligence will cause them to be banished from economic activity in the state of North Dakota for at least ten years.

When the regulatory agencies levy fines, those fines should in every case be paid in full and within the time limit set by the requisite state agency. Throughout the most hectic phase of the Bakken Oil Boom, the state's newspapers published front-page accounts of spills and negligence, often printing the amount of the fines in large, sometimes banner, headlines. But in most cases, the fines were reduced or forgiven, and oil companies expected to pay no more than a fraction of the original assessment. Thus, the people of North Dakota were led to believe that culprits were being punished for their crimes or their negligence, while the eventual settlement was relegated to the back pages and buried under bland or misleading headlines. I have friends in the industry and in government who have tried to explain to me why this approach (come down on the company like a ton of bricks at first, then find a way to just slap them on the wrist later) is good public policy, but I confess that I see only deception and propaganda in this protocol. At the very least, the initial front-page article should explain, at the beginning of the news story, that the actual fine is quite likely to be reduced to a pittance before the file on the incident is eventually closed.

We should work hard to avoid any spills, any accidents, any environmental damage in our pursuit of North Dakota's oil and natural gas. When accidents occur, our first goal should be mitigation. But we should also make it clear to the oil industry that we have a zero-tolerance negligence policy in North Dakota and we intend to be unforgiving in the face of repeated irresponsibility.

Most of the extraction companies that work in North Dakota have been law-abiding and responsible, but in any gold rush, no matter where it occurs, sloppy, fly-by-night, under-capitalized, and even criminally negligent individuals and entities find their way to the extraction landscape, too. It is impossible for any government entity to distinguish reputable companies from those with little or no regard for compliance and public safety. A rigorous bonding requirement coupled with zero tolerance for repeat offenders would largely solve the problem.

Fifth, the flaring needs to be reduced to a minimum. One of the "by-products" of oil extraction is flammable gas. Historically the gas has simply been flared (i.e., burned) at the top of the well. When oil wells are widely scattered over difficult terrain, it is easier just to burn the methane than to try to capture it. Even if you capture the gas, it has to be stored and transported. That means pipelines, storage facilities, terminals for trucks and trains, and—sometimes— field processing (separation) of the gasses. These things are expensive to implement. Because the collectable oil has come in such vast quantities, it has been the preference of industry to just burn the gas off. The argument is that the cost of collecting (and storing and selling) the gas is greater than its value. This isn't true, not even approximately true, but the regulators and the state legislature have been reluctant to force industry to stop wasting what is now a huge, potentially lucrative, quantity of carbon.

The editor of the *Bismarck Tribune*, Amy Dalrymple, has done important reporting on the flaring issue. Here's what she learned in a nutshell: North Dakota officials like to talk about how seriously they have worked to combat flaring, but the fact is that the North Dakota lags behind other oil-producing states. In fact, North Dakota promulgates misleading information about its success in requiring methane capture. Unit drilling (where four, six, a dozen, or more wells find their way underground from the same pad) and the manner in which scores, even hundreds, of wells can be lined up along the same country road make methane capture much less expensive and more efficient than ever. We are still flaring tens of millions of dollars' worth of gas annually, enough gas to heat cities like Minneapolis and Detroit.

Think of it this way: If it were the decided will of the people of North Dakota that flaring stop in all but the most remote sites, the industry would of course capture the gas. Obviously, we should allow exceptions for especially remote wells or wells with a very short production life or very limited gas volume. I don't know what percentage of all wells this would involve, but there is no point in setting arbitrary environmental standards that don't meet the criteria of a sane cost-benefit ratio. Any sensible and defensible policy would be complied with by industry, no matter how much they whine in their lobbying efforts. There is absolutely no evidence to suggest that responsible flaring laws would drive the industry out of the state.

And think of it this way, too: For most of North Dakota's history, hardworking people have scrimped and saved and sacrificed to eke a decent living out of the land and the communities that served that land. They survived and succeeded by wasting nothing, by sewing their own clothes, preserving their own food, handing down shoes from older to younger children, postponing most of the gratifications of life, repurposing everything that could be repurposed. That's who we were. My grandparents in western Minnesota were perfect exemplars of that spirit. When my mother and I cleaned out the little farmhouse in 2002, we found a kitchen drawer jammed so tight that we had a hard time getting it open. When we finally managed that, a collection of literally hundreds of plastic bags, some of them dating back thirty-five years, sprang out like a jack-in-the-box. She had saved every plastic bag she ever put her hands on. My mother said, *"uggh"* and unceremoniously dumped the entire drawer into a giant black garbage bag. It was the only time I ever wanted to slap my mother.*

Finally, think of this. If the coal fields did not exist and none of the oil under North Dakota's surface could ever be extracted, and the only carbon we had access to was the gas that is currently being flared at the well sites just to get rid of it, if that were the sum total of the carbon we had at our command, you know that we would collect every single cubic inch, like refugees from a *Mad Max* movie. Ask yourself how the volume, the BTUs, and the potential monetary value of all the gasses we have flared since the Bakken boom began would stack up against the sum total of all the oil and gas BTUs extracted *before* the Bakken (1951-2005), and you have some sense of the profligacy that now characterizes economic development in that family farm state where once we gathered buffalo chips on the prairie to heat our soup.

Sixth, the leaders of North Dakota, especially the regulators of the oil industry, must avoid being cozy with the extractors. We need to enact a strict but reasonable conflict of interest law in North Dakota. It's a small state, but the intimate relationship between the extractors and the regulators is appalling. Imagine what the oil

---

* Had I done so, she would have knocked me into next week Tuesday.

industry would say if the regulators were routinely hanging out with radical environmentalists. Imagine if calls from the directors of the Sierra Club, the Badlands Conservation Alliance, and the World Wildlife Fund were put straight through to the governor, but industry CEOs were asked to leave their name and number and perhaps the governor would be able to get back to them at some future time. No rational observer can argue that the state government of North Dakota has been a neutral referee in the resource development debate. A serious conflict of interest law would require complete transparency for campaign donations, PAC donations, sponsored fundraising dinners, research vacations, comped dinners here and elsewhere, tickets to *Hamilton*, fishing weekends on boats at Lake Sakakawea or Providence, Rhode Island, and golf trips to St. Andrew's in Scotland.

State employees should be forbidden from taking any emoluments, gifts, trips, stock tips, preferred stock or anything else from the industry and its friends and lobbyists. They should be required to report, in writing, any attempt by industry or others to buy influence by paying for things that would benefit the employee or the agency in any way.

The saddest thing about this situation is that legislators, state regulators, agency officials, and elected state office holders are so confident that they will pay no price for their indifference even to the appearance of conflict of interest, much less the substance, that they make no effort to hide their coziness with the lobbyists and captains of industry. They merely assume that nobody cares enough to hold them accountable, or that the North Dakota media is too overworked or friendly to expose the corruption.

Seventh, protect the surface owners. The minerals that lie under a ranch near Alexander, North Dakota, or anywhere else in the state, do not necessarily belong to the owners of the ranch. In a large percentage of cases, at some point the mineral rights were separated from the surface ownership of the property. The mineral owners have a legal right to extract the oil or natural gas. The surface owners are legally required to cooperate, and in almost every case, they do in a spirit of understanding and good will. But the drilling of a new oil well, particularly in the age of fracturing (fracking), is a serious disruption in the life of a farm or a ranch or a rural home. The development of a new oil well requires bulldozers, gravel trucks, new power lines, access roads, gigantic portable generators, pipe trucks, portable office facilities, the vehicles that haul the derrick itself, storage tanks, gargantuan pumps, and hundreds of water trucks. Fences are cut, cattle are spooked, and pastures ruined. The dust can create respiratory problems in livestock and—for the life of the drilling—diminish the quality of life for the surface owners. The noise can be deafening. Even when it is not, to listen to the clanking and the chugging of the drilling activity (or the pump jack) day after day and all through the night can be maddening (in both senses of the term).

The surface owners need to be better protected and better compensated. Industry inevitably regards them as a nuisance (the cost of doing business). But these are the North Dakotans we say we particularly prize, the family farmers and ranchers who represent the deepest historical tradition of the state. These are Jefferson's chosen people of God. They have given their lives to raising cattle or growing food. They were doing that important work before the coming of the Bakken Oil Boom and they will be doing their important work long after the last pump jack is removed from the state. They deserve special respect, even reverence, and we have a moral duty to do everything in our power to limit the disruption to their lives and livelihoods, to listen carefully to their concerns, to take their advice about where things should be sited on their property, and to accommodate whatever special needs they may have peculiar to their own farm or ranch. Our surface-owner-protection system should be so sensitive to the needs and opinions of North

Dakota's ranchers and farmers that industry officials find themselves saying, in their splendid restaurants at the top of the energy tower in Houston or Tulsa, "Those North Dakotans really must prize their farmers and ranchers, because when we come into the state they make it unmistakably clear that they expect us to limit the surface disruptions, especially where the minerals have been severed from the surface ownership. At first we thought this was kind of a nuisance, but you know what? I'm glad we're doing it this way."

Eighth, everything is sacred. There should be bylaws of the Industrial Commission, the Public Service Commission, and other participating agencies that before issuing any permit to engage in industrial activity in North Dakota, the question should be asked (and answered in writing), "What are the possible negative impacts on human and natural resources in the taking area? Is there anything that, if you lived there, you would want the developers to try to work around?" As long as we're at it, I think every permit should ask, "Would this well impair anything that the Mandan, Hidatsa, and Arikara Indians regard as special or sacred?" The state should create an advisory group of farmers and ranchers, representatives of the State Historical Society of North Dakota, historians, archaeologists, conservationists, and Native Americans, which would be routinely consulted by the extraction companies. Most permits would sail through without more than a quick review, but when any member of the advisory group believed something important to the life of North Dakota was at stake, the permittee would have to demonstrate the ways in which the development would mitigate negative impacts.

Finally, we should agree to spare the Little Missouri River corridor as we move forward. Given the advances in horizontal drilling, it should be possible to get at that oil from outside the protected corridor. Careful pad siting, a cooperative understanding between ranchers, recreationists, hunters, state government, and industry, efforts to camouflage storage tanks, pump jacks, and other industrial facilities, and an acknowledgement that the Little Missouri has extraordinary status in North Dakota would certainly help. I believe that the State of North Dakota, working in close cooperation with Theodore Roosevelt National Park and the Little Missouri National Grasslands, should pass a law (or establish regulations) that require any oil or natural gas structures to be invisible from the surface of the Little Missouri River. We should establish a system of concentric rings (or bands) around the three units of Theodore Roosevelt National Park, and along the entire corridor of the Little Missouri, from south of Marmarth to the bridge on ND 22. No development should be undertaken within a two-mile protection zone of the river (or the park). Development between two and five miles must be undertaken with the kind of mitigating protocols I have outlined above, and all badlands developments should be be reviewed by whatever Special Places Commission or subcommittee of one of the state's existing regulatory agencies has been established to handle development in sensitive areas.

Things feel better out there now. Nothing will ever be the same as it was in the year 2000, but things have pretty well calmed down for the moment. It's as if North Dakota took the blow and wasn't knocked to the canvas. It wasn't easy and it often wasn't pretty, but North Dakota did about as well as you can do when you get hit with something like this that nobody could have predicted and planned for. In the face of a gold rush, you do what you have to do to hold things together and maintain city-wide garbage pickup. Some things just sort of wash over you and dictate their own terms. There was a lot of illegal activity out there, and quite a bit of violence, including violence against women, but we managed to keep the lid on it and maintained something like civic order under very difficult conditions. At the time this book went to press (spring 2021), things seemed a little *too* quiet in the Dickinson, Killdeer, Belfield, Watford City, Stanley, and Williston corridor.

As I look back over the Bakken era, and try to evaluate what went right and what went wrong, what we could do better next time, how we can prepare for phase two (if it comes) of the fracking era, my only sharp criticism is for the fulsome cheerleaders. The ones I cannot abide are those who were so wedded to the industry that they could not really see straight anymore, who defended everything that happened no matter what, who played down every negative incident or accident or spill or fatality, who had an unconvincing glib answer to any possible criticism, who said sex trafficking is really just a fancy word for prostitution, who responded to the crime statistics by saying, "Welcome to the real world," who dismissed concerns about the social rupturing that the Bakken caused (forcing parents to protect their children with eternal vigilance, driving people on fixed incomes out of their homes in Williston and Watford City, Killdeer and Dickinson). The ones who publicly declared that criticism, however careful, of unlimited extraction was unpatriotic and elitist. These boosters didn't even waste time commiserating with the impacted ones. They just blathered on about "all the good things this is doing for North Dakota." They smiled through most criticism and shouted down anything that appeared to threaten their complacency.

As this book goes to press, the North Dakota oil industry is in a state of stunned bewilderment. It is not clear that oil prices will rebound sufficiently to make the Bakken shale profitable. Although the world is still hopelessly addicted to carbon—coal, oil, and natural gas—there are unignorable warning signs from around the planet that the First World is beginning to edge away from carbon toward less climate-threatening sources of electricity, locomotion, and heat. The end of oil development in North Dakota is not rapidly approaching, but it is possible to discern it on the far horizon. In the years or decades remaining to this industry, North Dakota should put every available oil dollar into permanent endowments that will ensure economic security for hundreds of years. We must begin to look upon oil tax revenues as a windfall with a limited shelf life. The worst thing we could do is just divvy up all that fabulous wealth. Such a procedure might underwrite the purchase of tens of thousands of new pickups and ease the student loan debt of North Dakota's young people, but it would do much more good if it were pooled and invested in North Dakota's future. It is very unlikely that fracking and other forms of oil development will be a major part of North Dakota economic life one hundred years from now, even fifty years from now. Even a partial drop in demand for oil on the world markets would have the effect of reducing the price per barrel, perhaps permanently, beyond the break-even point. North Dakota has been exceedingly fortunate to have gigantic quantities of extractable carbon under its farms and ranches. They have proved to be far more than a one-time harvest. It cannot be denied, however, that North Dakota must begin to face a post-carbon future, probably sooner than we think. The true leaders of the twenty-first century in North Dakota are going to be the ones who imagine that future without despair.

The Mosque, the Missile
The Methane and the
Martyr

Mosque, missile,methane flare, all tucked into a couple of square miles
in the middle of nowhere.

THE MOSQUE, THE MISSILE, THE MARTYR, THE METHANE—AND THE MASS

On September 11, 2001, a young woman named Ann Nicole Nelson died when the North Tower of the World Trade Center collapsed, 102 minutes after Islamic jihadist hijackers slammed one airplane into the North Tower (American Airlines Flight 11) and another, sixteen minutes later, into the South Tower (United Airlines Flight 175). Ann Nelson was one of 2,606 individuals who died in the World Trade Center on that brilliant early autumn day in New York City. She had been working on the 104th floor of the North Tower for less than a week. Ms. Nelson was one of the two North Dakotans killed in the 9/11 attacks. Her gravesite is here in the heartland, in a remote corner of North Dakota.

This is the story of Ross Township, located in Mountrail County in the northwest quadrant of the state. It has a population of forty-four, and is a perfect square of thirty-six sections of 640 acres each, so a total of just over 23,000 acres. In a small triangle that embraces no more than a few sections, Ross Township contains one of North

Dakota's 150 active ICBM nuclear missile sites, North Dakota's (and perhaps America's) first mosque, and an oil well that draws crude from the Bakken shale that brought a fracking boom to North Dakota between 2008 and 2015. Not far to the east in the next township, Idaho Township, you can visit the grave of Ms. Nelson.

The only one of these seemingly disparate entities that can be thought of as home-grown was Ann Nicole Nelson, born in Wisconsin on May 17, 1971, but raised in Stanley, ND. Like so many others, she left the state after high school and was probably not coming back. The Islamic mosque at Ross was quietly built by an Assyrian immigrant group in 1928-29. They were about as far out of their Mediterranean comfort zone as it would be possible to be—6,187 miles from Beirut in a state just thirty years old where, at the time, they were the first and only Muslims. Even today just 15,139 North Dakotans identify themselves as Muslim. That number must have been dramatically smaller in 1930. North Dakota was and is overwhelmingly Christian, European, and Caucasian. Today a full 77 percent of North Dakotans identify as Christian, and the majority of the remaining 23 percent say they have no particular religious affiliation. Fewer than 1 percent of North Dakotans identify themselves as Muslim, slightly more than the number of Hindus and Buddhists.

Oil was first discovered in North Dakota in 1952, at Tioga, just twenty-three miles from the fracking rig at Ross. North Dakota's two Strategic Air Command (SAC) Air Force Bases and the 150 remaining ICBM missiles were implanted here by the military industrial complex in the 1960s. No North Dakotan—not the governor, nor members of the North Dakota legislature, nor the commander of the North Dakota National Guard—had or has the slightest control over where those missiles were sited or where they are targeted, or under what circumstances they might be used. North Dakota's Tenth Amendment sovereignty does not give it authority of any sort over the weapons of mass destruction buried under our farms and ranches.

The mosque, the missiles, and the fracking rigs represent visitations from beyond the borders of North Dakota. Each of them found North Dakota for its own purposes. North Dakota's role in each of these visitations has been to accommodate, adjust, accept—and hope for profit. That could almost be regarded as the mission statement of the state. Accommodate. Adjust. Accept. Each in its way has brought a measure of prosperity to North Dakota.

In the beginning . . . was a vast unbounded grassland extending in every direction forever: On the east to the Red River of the North, now the North Dakota-Minnesota border; to the south to the Rio Grande and the Gulf of Mexico; on the west to the foothills of the Rocky Mountains; and north to the center of Saskatchewan and edging all the way up to Edmonton in Alberta. The Great Plains. One of the wonders of the natural world. Native Americans—Mandan, Hidatsa, Arikara, Cree, Ojibwe, Dakota, Lakota, Assiniboine, Crow, Cheyenne—lived on this American savannah for thousands, perhaps tens of thousands, of years without altering its character much or building anything that could be called a permanent structure. These Native Americans killed plenty of buffalo, elk, antelope, deer, and bighorn sheep, and sometimes a grizzly bear if necessary, but they did not draw down the near-infinitude of quadrupeds on the Great Plains. They did not dam the rivers, except perhaps to divert a little water to their fields in the bottomlands of the Missouri and Yellowstone Rivers. They poured no cement or concrete. They baked no bricks. They smelted no iron. They felled trees to build their shelters and feed their horses and lodge fires, but they made no measurable impact much beyond their villages, and they moved those villages when they had cropped too much grass and denuded the local timber supply. The notion that Native Americans were perfect environmentalists in buckskins is too romantic to fit all the facts (not to mention that it is a racist fantasy), but nobody doubts that American Indians lived lightly on the land and embedded a steady state sacramental restraining mechanism into the heart of their cosmology.

Then came White folks.

If Native Americans had an economy of harmony and accommodation, the newcomers, the Anglo-Europeans—the ones who took the continent—operated by the principle of extraction.

For 150 years at least, Whites have regarded North Dakota as a resource bank from which to extract grain, beef, pork, chicken, sugar beets, potatoes, sunflowers, coal, oil, natural gas, water, hydropower, and talented young humans. In most cases, these commodities are exported raw, at low price, and the value-added occurs elsewhere. Much of the 140-year White history of North Dakota has consisted of attempts to combat economic and political colonialism. We have never succeeded, but there is so much wealth floating around the Great Plains now that we forget to look at the percentages of what wealth remains in North Dakota and what gargantuan riches flow elsewhere down the pipelines.

Most of what was present on the Great Plains when the French entrepreneurial explorer Verendrye or the US Army officers Lewis and Clark arrived in the eighteenth and early nineteenth centuries, is gone now—almost all the native grass is gone, until now it is much easier to enumerate the places where native grasses still grow than where they have been stripped away, and even what looks like "native" grassland now is usually a sad mix of a few native plants trying to hold on against all the invasive species that have deliberately or inadvertently been introduced to the Great Plains, mostly from Russia and Ukraine. There are no grizzly bears in North Dakota now. If one were sighted it would immediately be killed "to protect the children," we like to say. The wolves have been extirpated partly to protect domestic livestock but also to satisfy whatever deep aversion humans have to wolves. A few mountain lions are permitted to live here, so long as they stay clear of every human community, and even then we send out attack dogs and their attendant "hunters" to kill them.

Thanks to Thomas Jefferson and the Enlightenment, the sinuous primordial game trails of the plains have been straightened into almost perfect linearity. Among other gifts, Jefferson gave us the cadastral rectangular survey grid system, which makes North Dakota (and the rest of the continent) look like a checkerboard from above, the world's largest landscape garden in the formal French style.

For Jefferson, straight lines meant order, regularity, control, and enlightened civilization. In 2008, a friend of mine, Catherine Meier, a stunning visual artist who draws epic murals of undifferentiated grasslands wherever they can still be found, spent a number of weeks in Mongolia precisely to see a piece of the world that has not been subjugated by straight-line roads. No grid. It was paradise for Ms. Meier, but she felt too a deep sense of disorientation that was not far distant from agoraphobia. Afterwards, she wrote, "I went in search of true openness—place unplaced. I found it, and with it fear and claustrophobia from an openness I did not know how to control. Open landscape is powerful and I believe the preservation of these extensive grasslands is as important to our human existence and environment as are the ocean, forest, or mountain terrains." Well, that explains a lot of North Dakota's infrastructural history.

The 1938 *WPA Guide to North Dakota* reports that "in 1902 a group of twenty Moslem families from Damascus, Syria, filed on homesteads SE of Ross, and since 1909, when the Federal Government withdrew its objection to their naturalization, many of them have become citizens." In fact, several thousand Lebanese immigrants came to western North Dakota in the first years of the twentieth century. They called themselves Syrians or Assyrians because the modern state of Lebanon had not yet been carved out of Syria. By the time they got to North Dakota during the presidency of Theodore Roosevelt, all of the best land in the country and most of the best land in the state had been claimed. Some of these Islamic newcomers homesteaded, but the immigrant community consisted mostly of shopkeepers and itinerant peddlers who schlepped manufactured goods to isolated farms in the region.

The village of Ross had been founded in 1887, two years before statehood, named either for Ross H. McEnany or Ross Davidson. One was a Great Northern Railroad employee, the other a banker in Minot. That's another colonial imposition on the northern grassland—nobody thought of naming Ross with a term borrowed from the Assiniboine Indians. Do we really care about McEnany or Davidson? Are they important enough to deserve place names? Just look at the nomenclature of North Dakota—our towns, cities, parks, lakes, and monuments. If that is not the definition of a colonial erase-and-replace project, what is? Maps can be part of ethnic cleansing.

According to North Dakota's principal ethnographer, Father William Sherman, "Even in North Dakota, a state which was (and is) a virtual patchwork of dozens of immigrant groups, the Ross settlers seemed unique. Their very names sounded strange: land records list Mohamed Rassake, Alley Ohmer, Abdullah Assel, Bo Aley Farrhat." The cemetery just east of Ross is one of the most compelling written records of that Muslim community: Kobby Nai Sowah 1975-2015; Kalled Jaha 1927-1967; Hamed George Jaha 1910-1985; Albert Abdallah 1921-1930; Toby Abdallah 1931-1953; Hayden Almer 1996-2011; Sarah Omar Shupe 1914-2004; Nazira Omar 1908-1998. These are not Johnsons, Schmidts, Halvorsons, or Bachmeiers. Many of the gravestones display the Islamic star and crescent. Some of these are metal sculpture; others are incised on the tombstones.

In 1939 a fieldworker with the Works Project Administration interviewed Mike Abdallah, one of the homesteaders whose family is buried in the cemetery. Abdallah immigrated to the US in 1909, the year Theodore Roosevelt left the presidency. In 1915 Abdallah filed for a homestead near Ross. "In this country we get improvements for our tax money and we can think and say what we want," he told the WPA interviewer, "while in the Old Country we could think what we wanted but we didn't dare say it." Here's how the Muslims of Mountrail County explained it more recently: "The local Islamic community consists mostly of immigrants from the village of Bire and Rafid (a region now in Lebanon). Many arrived here as young boys to avoid being taken into the Turkish army." That's the same motive that brought Germans from Russia to the Great Plains a little earlier, though the army they wanted to avoid was in the employ of Russian Czar Alexander II, who revoked the preferential rights and privileges that had been granted to German settlers by Catherine the Great and Alexander I.

Why did Muslims come to North Dakota as opposed to New Jersey or San Diego or Illinois? The answer seems to be twofold. First, the Great Northern Railroad could get them there. It was completed in 1893 and it passed through the heart of Mountrail County. Second, that portion of western North Dakota and eastern Montana was still available for homesteading. By the soil and rainfall standards of eastern Montana, the area around Ross and Stanley was comparatively bucolic. There was still a lingering whiff of the public relations campaign that portrayed the Great Plains as the "Garden of America." The old displays sang the (untrue) song of North Dakota, often accompanied by a fifty-pound pumpkin and some very bountiful ears of sweet corn.

Father Sherman concludes, "Of the sizable immigrant groups who came to North Dakota, one could probably say that Syrian newcomers faced the most difficult uphill battles as they sought acceptance in the Anglo-European world of North Dakota." And yet they managed it by keeping their heads down, behaving like good neighbors, and not calling much attention to the particularities of their religious and ethnic heritage. By the time Ann Nicole Nelson attended school in Stanley in the 1980s, the Assyrian community was more or less fully assimilated. They were shy, sometimes cautious, but they did not hold themselves apart. Ann had close friends among them, and their mothers traded recipes, hotdish for eggplant moussaka, rhubarb bars for kanafe. When I called Ricky Omar recently to get permission to visit the cemetery, I asked him how much traditional Islamic religious observance still exists in Mountrail County. "A little," he said, "on special occasions, but we are all more or less Lutherans now." How Theodore Roosevelt would have smiled at that.

The Muslims of Mountrail County built themselves a place of prayer and worship just before the Dust Bowl shattered North Dakota. That first house of prayer is gone now, but extant photographs indicate that it was not much to look at. In fact, a stranger coming upon it would not have had any way to know that it was a mosque. Perhaps that was intentional. The building was low slung, partly subterranean, with concrete sides and a low-pitched main room, with an awkward-looking, unpainted wooden entranceway (a lean-to, as they are known in North Dakota). It looked more like a bunker or a grain storage facility than a mosque—no minarets, no onion domes, no metalwork or filigree. It was in such poor shape by the 1970s that what was left of the Lebanese community tore it down. The WPA guide puts it this way: "In 1929 this colony built a basement mosque, and each Friday a member of the congregation conducts services. Each person carefully washes his hands and feet before entering the temple; the sexes are segregated during prayer." This was written in the 1930s. Ross did not have an imam (Muslim prayer leader). Local Muslims led the prayers, except on special occasions, when an imam might be persuaded to make the journey from Islamic communities in Saskatchewan or Manitoba.

Decades later, the folks at Ross came to call their place of worship "the oldest mosque in the United States." The debate over which American mosque was actually the first can get a little silly. The Rose of Fraternity Mosque in Cedar Rapids, Iowa, completed in 1934, claims its primacy by heaping up qualifying adjectives: oldest + still standing + purpose-built + mosque. It calls itself the Mother Mosque of America. Chicago's Al-Sadiq Mosque is older than the one in Cedar Rapids, but since it was converted to Islamic purposes from an existing building, it is disqualified in the unrefereed first-mosque competition. Cedar Rapids disbars the mosque at Ross because it was torn down in the 1970s. And so on. These razor thin distinctions wind up being both absurd and demeaning. It seems most reasonable and accurate to say that the mosque at Ross is one of the oldest in the United States. In North Dakota of all places!

Today North Dakota has no actual mosques, but Islamic prayer centers are located in Williston, Grand Forks, Fargo, and Minot. There are 1.6 billion Muslims worldwide, approximately 3.45 million in the United States. New Jersey and Illinois have the most, Montana the least. North Dakota's Islamic population is approximately 15,000.

A commemorative miniature mosque was built in the Ross cemetery in 2005 near the foundation of the original working mosque. At her request, the family of one of the community's venerable matriarchs, Sarah Allie (Omar) Shupe (1914-2004), built a mauve cinderblock structure of ninety-two square feet, with fifteen-foot walls, an aluminum dome, and four small minarets. It is a beautiful and strangely moving monument to an uncanny and beautiful North Dakota pioneer story. "They came for freedom. There is something especially lovely in a people from far away coming to America in search of freedom, rather than for economic opportunity." Allahu Akbar.

You cannot visit the little mosque without experiencing a sense of wonder. That so unlikely a colony would be established at so raw a time in so improbable a landscape. Although most of the descendants of those gritty Levantine pioneers have relinquished most of their Middle Eastern culture, their deep pride led them to celebrate their religious and ethnic roots at the turn of the millennium, at a time when their children and grandchildren have been wholly assimilated into the consumer-material-pop-cultural American world of the twenty-first century. It is perhaps still more remarkable that the replica mosque was built just four years after 9/11, which released waves of anti-Islamic feeling throughout the United States. I'm deeply proud to report that in the aftermath of the attacks, there was no aggression or intolerance aimed at the Lebanese Dakotans of Mountrail County. That's North Dakota—and America—at its best.

I had the opportunity to enter the mosque not long ago. It is mostly empty, but the sun through the skylights illuminates a beautiful prayer rug in the middle of the cement floor. In one corner is a metal star and crescent icon, in the other a small table on which rests a study-guide Koran, with English translation and plenty of footnotes. A tall, framed display features photographs of many of the Syrian pioneers. The interpretive signage is candid. "In the name of FREEDOM these men, women and children not only left behind family and friends but also their beautiful Mediterranean country with its warm waters and fruit filled trees." That seems ever so slightly bitter! Probably someone edited out *and wound up in this landlocked windswept sub-Arctic barren instead.* Okay, we get it. North Dakota is no Mediterranean. But hey, you chose us. The Ross Syrians came for freedom. They came, they faltered, and they endured. That, in a nutshell, is the story of all of North Dakota until after World War II. Imagine their surprise that first winter on the barren plains of that giant landscape north of the Missouri River. The Lebanese Riviera it ain't.

If you stand under the star and crescent cemetery gate near the mosque memorial, you can see one of the remaining one hundred fifty Intercontinental Ballistic Missile (ICBM) sites in North Dakota. It's pretty unobtrusive in that vast and open landscape, and it might be mistaken for a house or barn construction project that never quite got off the ground, or perhaps something to do with an oil or natural gas pipeline. If you pivot at that same spot you can also see at least a dozen Bakken oil installations: pump jacks, storage tanks, and, in the summer of 2019, a couple of wells being drilled within the 360° viewshed. Without question the mosque is the most beautiful thing there, one of the most beautiful things in North Dakota. It could not have been more tastefully designed. But it seems wildly out of place in such close proximity to America's stockpile of nuclear weapons, and to carbon extraction—which has, after all, distorted America's relations with the entire Middle East for the past seventy-five years and put us into bed with regimes no American should ever admire. Fifteen of the eighteen hijackers were Saudi nationals. So, we invaded Iraq.

The oil well that can be seen from the Ross cemetery, less than half a mile to the south, belongs to EOG Resources, headquartered in Houston, Texas. EOG emerged from the ashes of ENRON in 1999. The well is known as ROSS 15-28H. It has been producing prodigious amounts of oil and natural gas since 2010. ROSS 15-28H is regarded in the industry as one of the sweetest wells in the sweetest spot of the Bakken oil field. Less than two miles from a major national highway and an equal distance from the Great Northern Railroad line, ROSS 15-28H was still flaring waste gasses a full decade after it was drilled. Why? Why is this allowed? It produced 92,722 barrels of oil in its first 395 days of production and it was still producing 772 barrels per month in 2019.

The ICBM missile site that can be seen from the cemetery, Number I-7, just east of Ross, is popularly known as the "Prairie Rose missile." Nearby are I-6, the "Pronghorn," I-8, the "Shoveler," I-9 "Skunk," I-10, "Hungarian Gray Partridge," and I-11, "Lostwood." I found a number of beautiful, delicate wild prairie roses in the Muslim cemetery last summer, but nothing is permitted to grow inside the chain link fence of an ICBM missile site. I-7 is the second westernmost of the Minot missile field, second only to I-8, the "Shoveler."

At one point, North Dakota housed 300 missile silos, each equipped with an intercontinental missile capable of traveling 6,000 miles in about half an hour. During the early years of the ICBM era, with the Soviet Union and the United States inching towards, and then away from, a nuclear holocaust, each nuclear warhead was much more destructive than the warheads that followed as tensions diminished in the late 1970s and '80s. As the Cold War lost some of its paranoia, megatonnage yielded to kilotonnage. At the height of the missile madness, each of the 300 ICBMs in North Dakota carried three independently re-enterable warheads (MIRVs). Not counting the warheads stored on the two Strategic Air Command (SAC) bases, ready to be loaded onto bomber jets on short notice and, later, nuclear-tipped cruise missiles, around 1985 North Dakota's ICBMs alone could launch 900 nuclear warheads, each one at a different target in the Soviet Union, the Warsaw Pact satellite nations, or China. In other words, if you tallied up every nuclear device housed in (under) the sovereign state of North Dakota, the total would then have been around 1,000 warheads, *each one*, at the very least, twenty times more destructive than Fat Man or Little Boy, the atomic bombs that obliterated Hiroshima and Nagasaki in August 1945. Few places on the face of the earth, if any, housed as much potential genocide in so small a jurisdiction. And yet during those desperate years when we came to the brink of nuclear war over Berlin and Cuba, and nuclear preparedness (i.e., trying to survive a nuclear attack) was a serious part of the school curriculum, the people of North Dakota simply went about their business, oblivious or nearly so to the implications of strategic decisions made far away from the center of North America.

There is a Missile Launch Facility for every ten missiles in the Minot AFB squadron. The one that controls I-7 is located a few miles northeast of Stanley. From a distance it looks as fragile as any other prefabricated industrial structure in North Dakota, except for the giant antennas. At any given moment, two Nuclear and Missile Operations Officers (known as missileers) are down in the command bunker sixty feet below that drab yellow building whiling away the time—waiting for a nuclear emergency that they know will never occur. They run tests, read training updates, take readings, do make-work stuff, and who knows what else to get through their twenty-four-hour shifts. Four of every five missileers in the Air Force are men. Some study for advanced degrees during their shifts or just read paperbacks for pleasure. If the big moment ever came, they would receive orders to open a safe secured with two padlocks, each officer knowing one—but not both—of the combinations. If, but only if, the encrypted code they received from the White House matched the one in the safe, the officers would proceed to launch. To ignite the missile, they would need to turn two launch keys simultaneously, at locks placed far enough apart so no one person could ever turn both at the same time. The missileers holding those keys would not know anything about the intended target of their weapon of mass destruction, their Hiroshima-on-steroids. All they do is launch the thing. If they ever turn those keys together, they should probably next say their prayers and write out some last words of instruction, because it is almost certain that Russia or China or North Korea would be lobbing one or more of its surviving missiles back at I-7, and it is unlikely that the two US officers would survive the attack. In the 1970s each ICBM site, including launch bunkers, was hardened to survive a direct hit by a Soviet nuclear warhead, but I wouldn't bet on it. There is also an Emergency Escape Tunnel that angles up to the surface a little way from the bunker. It's unlikely to remain operational after a direct hit, but perhaps it allows missileers to convince (and comfort) themselves that they just might survive.

North Dakota is still known as the Peace Garden State in spite of the delicious irony that, until the fall of the Soviet Union, North Dakota housed more nuclear weapons than any other sub-national jurisdiction in the world. The 2,400-acre flower garden and memorial that bestrides the North Dakota-Manitoba border near Dunseith may be an International Peace Garden, but it would be hard to make that claim for the rest of North Dakota, unless you subscribe to the kind of military-industrial Orwellian ironies that called the MX Missile "The Peacekeeper" or that marvelous moment in *Dr. Strangelove* when an intense battle is being fought on a strategic command air force base with a large *Peace is Our Profession* billboard at the center of Stanley Kubrick's shot. "Gentlemen, you can't fight in here. This is the War Room!"

Unless you join the military or obtain a special clearance, the closest you are ever going to get to a nuclear weapon is through the perimeter fence at a two-acre ICBM missile site. Hug the fence and you will be no more than 250 feet from a 335-kiloton nuclear warhead. That's twenty times more powerful than Hiroshima. And there are 150 of them in North Dakota, which makes the fleet 3,000 times more deadly than Hiroshima, where 60,000 Japanese, mostly civilians, were vaporized on August 6, 1945. If for some reason one of these missiles made a direct hit on the Empire State Building (the scenario that ends the classic 1964 Cold War film *Fail Safe*), it would kill hundreds of thousands of people instantaneously, millions more as the radioactive fallout infiltrated every living thing downwind for hundreds or thousands of miles, and caused genetic mutations in plants, animals, and humans halfway around the globe. And that's just the one warhead behind the chain link fence at I-7. If you sent one hundred missiles against the hundred most populated cities in the world (from Tokyo at the top with 38 million, all the way down to Kunming, China, at 3.78 million), you'd be able to kill close to half a billion people between breakfast and lunch, about a sixteenth of the human population. All that before the fallout. The United States currently possesses just over 6,000 nuclear weapons, down from 31,255 in 1967. Only 450 of what were once 1,000 ICBMs are buried under three Great Plains states—North Dakota, Montana, and Wyoming.

It was John F. Kennedy who gave North Dakota ballistic missiles. In 1960 he campaigned on the notion—erroneous, and he knew it was erroneous—that the Soviets were well ahead of the Americans in missile production. As he learned when he was safely in the White House, there was no missile gap. The Soviets at the time had only a handful of viable nuclear-tipped ICBM missiles. The US had hundreds. In fact, the minute JFK's Secretary of Defense Robert McNamara looked into the gap, he found that it not only did not exist, but that the Soviets had only between six and ten ICBM-ready warheads at the time of Kennedy's inauguration. Nevertheless, Kennedy, who was a serious Cold Warrior, doubled Eisenhower's request for ICBMs and, by determining to locate them up on the Canadian border, transformed the northern Great Plains into a nuclear killing field.

Just twelve days after Kennedy told the world he would "pay any price, bear any burden, meet any hardship, support any friend, oppose any foe, in order to assure the survival and the success of liberty," the Minuteman missile passed its first successful test. Launched from Florida's Cape Canaveral, the unarmed warhead landed so close to its target (4,600 miles away) that it was hailed as a "near bull's eye." A few months later the Air Force broke ground at Malmstrom AFB near Great Falls, Montana. One of the first Minuteman missiles, known as Alpha 1, was regarded as America's ace in the hole during the Cuban Missile Crisis in October 1962.

North Dakota became a nuclear hot zone only after the Cuban Missile Crisis. The United States and the Soviet Union stood eyeball to eyeball between October 14 and October 28, 1962, and in spite of what Secretary of State Dean Rusk said, both sides blinked. Or rather both John F. Kennedy and the Soviet Premier Nikita Khrushchev blinked, while the military industrial hardliners on both sides berated their national leaders for being weak at a moment of existential danger and opportunity. General Curtis LeMay, who had helped win World War II, actually pounded his fist on a White House table in a meeting with JFK and told him—with open rudeness and condescension—that his refusal to launch an all-out attack on the Cuban missile sites, together with a 90,000-man invasion of the island, and possibly an all-out nuclear attack on the USSR and its Warsaw Pact allies, was tantamount to treason against the United States. That Jack—just forty-five years old with relatively thin war experience—found the confidence to stand up to a cluster of hoary and highly-decorated generals as old as his father Joseph Kennedy is indeed a profile in courage.

After Kennedy and Khrushchev had successfully pulled back from the nuclear brink, agreeing to a compromise that achieved the fundamental goal of each nation—the US got the USSR to pull the missiles, and the USSR got the US to pledge never to invade Cuba—LeMay called the deal "the greatest defeat in our history." It may be useful to note that both of these courageous national leaders were removed from power by October 1964. JFK was assassinated (by whom? and why?) on November 22, 1963, just 390 days after the Cuban Missile Crisis ended, and 165 days after his magnificent but highly controversial peace speech at American University calling for a reduction of tensions between the two countries. Khrushchev was ousted from power by his hardline rivals in October 1964, then allowed to live quietly in retirement until his death in 1971. In both cases, the militarists took control.

In the aftermath of the Cuban Missile Crisis, the Soviets undertook an economically crippling arms buildup in an attempt to achieve parity—or better—with the United States. Meanwhile, US Defense Secretary Robert McNamara got everything he wanted to beef up the US nuclear arsenal. It was then that the ICBMs of North Dakota were installed (1962-70) around the Minot and Grand Forks Air Force Bases. The first Minuteman I missiles were installed in the Minot range in December 1962, two months after the Cuban Missile Crisis. The Grand Forks AFB missile wing was the last authorized in the United States by the Department of Defense. Authorization dates to late 1962. The first Minuteman II missile was installed in the Grand Forks wing in August 1965. The entire Grand Forks missile wing was deactivated on September 30, 1998, North Dakota's small contribution to the Peace Dividend.

American's missile arsenal was located in North Dakota and other northern tier Great Plains states for four reasons—because land was inexpensive here, because this would shorten the distance to Soviet targets over the North Pole, because people of the heartland were unlikely to resist, and because we were expendable. If we fought a nuclear war with the USSR, and they aimed their nuclear weapons at all 300 North Dakota silos, the death toll would be miniscule compared to what it would be if they were located near major population centers or even in the rural Midwest. Historian Gretchen Heefner writes, "By isolating militarization in high-tech weapons and burying the weapons in out-of-the-way places, much of the country could have its massive deterrent without having to think of the consequences." Ouch. Scholar Valerie Kuletz calls the Great Plains a "geography of sacrifice." There's Eric Sevareid's "large rectangular blank spot in the nation's mind!" Since nobody thinks about North Dakota and millions of Americans are not even aware that it exists, put your weapons of mass destruction there and nobody will ever think about it. Says Heefner, "In the end, then, the missiles would be deployed to places long considered invisible: Great Falls, Rapid City, Cheyenne, Minot, and Grand Forks."

It is remarkable but not particularly surprising that 300 nuclear missiles went into the ground in North Dakota without a whiff of protest. North Dakotans were then a modest, even diffident, people of the boondocks: humble, heads-down farmers and small townsmen, blandly patriotic and unquestioning, eager to do their part, grateful in fact, for the economic benefits that housing nuclear missiles and their operational personnel would bring to a backward, marginal state that never got much when the pork barrels were rolled across the country. According to historian David Mills, "The construction of missile silos throughout the northern plains was not a traumatic event but an economic opportunity for the region. Even modest financial interests were stronger than fears of nuclear disaster." If the military-industrial Strangeloves had made a list of the states least likely to make a fuss about receiving hundreds of nuclear missiles, North Dakota would have been at the top of that list, ahead even of South Dakota and Montana. Maybe Arkansas and Alabama would have been equally acquiescent. Says Mills, "Patriotic sentiment ran deep in the region, so the local population generally cooperated with the government officials."

Landowner frustrations in the area around Ellsworth Air Force Base in South Dakota in the early 1960s were strong enough to give birth to the Missile Area Landowners Association (1961), but western South Dakota chambers of commerce walked off the pages of Sinclair Lewis' *Babbitt* (1922), and they quite easily won the public relations battle. The South Dakota landowners' concerns were that the Air Force was siting the missiles arbitrarily without making any attempt to limit the inconvenience to the farmers and ranchers; that extensive networks of electric cables were being buried under private property without compensation and often enough without notice; that fences were cut and gates left open; that helicopters came unannounced at low altitudes in a way that disturbed and sometimes stampeded cattle; that holes in the ground were left unfilled; and that the Air Force was not paying anything like fair market prices for the land it acquired. Almost none of these issues were raised by the North Dakotans who were similarly handled as the 300 ICBM missiles were implanted between 1961 and 1966. North Dakota's political leaders chose not to serve as farmer and rancher advocates during this period, largely because there was not much discontentment among farmers directly impacted by the military installations. North Dakotans, who have always been passive in the face of the US government's military presence on the Northern Plains, accepted all of this disruption—not to mention the storing of weapons of mass destruction under their farms and ranches—with hardly a murmur. What little protest there was had more to do with the underrepresentation of local contractors and construction workers in the project. Jobs, not nukes, were the issue in the Peace Garden State. One North Dakotan, Ernest Johnson of Dazey, ND (near Cooperstown), complained that the Air Force had chosen to place a missile on the land of a "very influential neighbor" rather than on his own.

The military industrial complex chose wisely in placing its missiles in North Dakota. After Vietnam displaced Berlin, Poland, Czechoslovakia, and the Warsaw Pact in the headlines, most North Dakotans either forgot about the ICBM missiles or simply assumed they would never be used, so what's the point of getting worked up about them? In his 2015 study, Mills wrote, "The northern plains, with few exceptions, have largely shrugged off the existence of the hundreds of missile silos located throughout the region. For decades the majority of plains residents drove by silos and launch facilities without thinking much about them. Now that half of them are gone, no one really misses them." Tony Ziden of Pisek, ND, agrees. "After you've walked around a barrel of dynamite for twenty years, and it doesn't hurt you, you sort of don't think about it." Mills concludes, "Citizens on the northern Great Plains often did not see the Cold War as frightening or traumatic but as a source of opportunity and transformation."

North Dakotans not only did not object to the nuclearization of their landscape, they took a certain pride in it. The old joke, known to almost every North Dakotan in the 1970s and '80s—as if it were something cooked up by the state tourism department—was that if we seceded, we would be the third largest nuclear power in the world. The claim was essentially meaningless, since command and control were in federal hands and there is no conceivable scenario by which North Dakotans could figure out how to defeat all the security systems that protect America's nuclear arsenal from rural conspiracy theories and wildass rural takeover schemes. Still, despite the technical absurdity of that claim, it gave North Dakotans a sense of our importance. We feed the world and we protect the world. Even with half of North Dakota's missiles now decommissioned, we'd still be the fifth largest nuclear power, behind China (ca. 290 warheads) but ahead of India and Pakistan.

Nobody will tell you where North Dakota's missiles are targeted. The Air Force refuses to answer even bend-over-backwards polite questions about the general criteria of targeting. The dedicated peaceniks at Nukewatch who specialize in nuclear watchdog vigilance admit that they are unable to penetrate the mystery of targeting. After the end of the Cold War (1991) we were told that the missiles were not pointed at anything anymore, that they were, for the moment at least, target blind. Maybe so. But the fall of the Berlin Wall and the implosion of the USSR did not usher in an epoch of peace after all. The rise of Islamic jihad culminating in the 9/11 attacks, the emergence of China as a serious threat to Western hegemony, the rogueries of North Korea, Iran's nuclear ambitions, and Vladimir Putin's attempts to re-assemble the Russian Empire one satellite state at a time, have undoubtedly created new target lists that were unthinkable in 1975. Nobody believes North Dakota's ICBMs are target blind today.

The best information I was able to glean from repeated conversations with former missileers, former officers at Minot Air Force Base, and peace advocates, is that the ICBMs are not likely to be aimed at sites in the Middle East (Tehran, Damascus, Mecca, Medina) because the US has aircraft carriers and battleships in the Persian Gulf that could lob cruise missiles at such sites; ICBMs, therefore, are not needed for that mission. North Korea can be attacked from naval vessels in the Sea of Japan. It would seem logical, therefore, that the remaining ICBMs of the Great Plains are pointed at Russian military installations deep in the Eurasian interior, as well as such Russian cities as Moscow, St. Petersburg, and Omsk, and missile sites and military installations in China, plus Chinese cities regarded as strategically important.

What is clear is that the missiles of our adversaries are pointed at North Dakota. Former North Dakota governor Arthur A. Link famously declared (1972-73) that North Dakota was not going to become an energy sacrifice zone. He won that battle, against considerable odds and serious political opposition, and now he is just short of universally acknowledged as one of North Dakota's greatest leaders. But as he uttered those words, North Dakota was already a nuclear sacrifice zone. Even forty-five years later, the presence of 150 missiles in west central North Dakota means that in the event of nuclear war, we are certain to be ground zero. According to the authors of *Nuclear Heartland*, "In addition to threatening Soviet targets, the Minuteman system was intended to serve, in case of hostilities, as a sponge to soak up the other side's attacking forces." Well, that's comforting. The irony is clear. "Rather than protecting the safety of those among whom it is deployed, the system actually does the opposite. It enhances their vulnerability, making them the likeliest targets of a Soviet preemptive strike if deterrence should fail." Even now, however, in a world arguably less stable than the bipolar Cold War world of 1960-90, North Dakotans mostly shrug. In fact, during my recent journeys to the towns in the Minot missile squadron's vicinity, I have met dozens of people who were not even aware that nuclear missiles continue to be located in North Dakota.

There was some nuclear protest in North Dakota, but most of it came after the Cold War had ended. On June 20, 2006, the Reverend Carl Kabat, Greg Boertje-Obed, and Michael Walli broke into site E-9 near Roseglen, ND, and poured blood over the silo. They were dressed in clown suits. They were, of course, arrested, then convicted in federal court in Bismarck on September 14, 2006. Reverend Kabat was sentenced to fifteen months in prison. Boertje-Obed got a year, and Walli eight months. All three refused to pay the $17,000 in restitution. Those prison terms seem like a pretty hefty punishment for jumping a fence and doing negligible damage with a ballpeen hammer to a missile site designed to survive a direct hit by an incoming nuclear warhead (the silo door alone weighs 110 tons). Heck, you can throw up an illegal bridge over the Little Missouri River in western North Dakota, in violation of local, state, and federal law, and get only a slap on the wrist. But pee on an invulnerable ICBM and you're going to federal prison. Reverend Kabat had a long history of nuclear protest, dating back to a 1984 Plowshares action in Missouri called "Silo Pruning Hooks." I have visited E-9 at Roseglen several times. The protesters chose well. It is perhaps the most completely isolated missile site in North Dakota. The nearest town, six miles away, is White Shield: population 212. On the other hand, they were wearing clown suits—not exactly incognito in a treeless immensity of grassland.

On April 15, 2010 James Richard Sauder of San Antonio, Texas, climbed over the fence at silo H-8 south of Parshall, North Dakota. While he waited for the air force police to arrive, Sauder called the *Minot Daily News* to explain his actions. He left a copy of the US Constitution at the site and what he described as "a one-ounce, pure silver coin that depicts Lady Liberty," and simultaneously released what he called his *Minot Manifesto*, a bizarre and rambling screed that had nothing much to do with nuclear weapons or nuclear policy, but included such sentences as, "The present United States Federal government is essentially a criminal syndicate or global mafia—it acts as a hyper-violent, militarily invasive, propaganda spewing, multi-trillion dollar money laundering machine, that seeks to unilaterally impose its will on the American people, and as much of the rest of the world as possible, by brute force and political deception. By any measure, the present USA government is a rogue regime, and now that it is a deeply corrupt empire in rapid decline, it is, perhaps, more dangerous than ever." Hard to disagree with that! Sauder was convicted (for bad prose?) in federal court in Minot, ND, on July 23, 2010. He was sentenced to time served, plus 100 days (for a total of 199 days). Sauder spent most of his prison sentence at the Heart of America Correctional and Treatment Center in Rugby, North Dakota.

Kabat, Boertje-Obed, Walli, and Sauder were outsiders who traveled to North Dakota to beat their swords into . . . well, a dented sword attack on the military industrial complex. But one longtime resident of North Dakota kept up a decade-long silent vigil in opposition to the nuclearization of the Great Plains. His name was Father Robert Branconnier.

On August 14, 1968, Father Branconnier led a group of thirteen young people to a big national test of the Minuteman II missile at a site (H-24) near Michigan, ND, 57 miles west of Grand Forks and the University of North Dakota, where he served as the chaplain of the Newman Center. The silent protesters positioned themselves five miles from the official observation site, where North Dakota's entire congressional delegation and 500 VIPs and Air Force personnel had been assembled from around the country to watch the big test. This was one of those exceedingly rare moments when the Air Force was willing to show the public that we had a potent nuclear ICBM arsenal, that the missiles actually worked (there was widespread cynicism), and that we were not afraid to prove it publicly. It was like the launch of that fateful year's Apollo space rockets (Apollo 6 on April 4, Apollo 7 on October 11, and Apollo 8 on December 21).

The dramatic Minuteman II countdown on the Dakota prairie came and went. Nothing happened. The launch was a complete and humiliating dud. Not even a puff of smoke. When—at least in this public test—the world ended not with a bang but in a whimper, Air Force General Bruce Holloway, the Strategic Air Command commander, declared, to no one's satisfaction, that he had "full confidence in the Minuteman missile and its part in the nation's defense system." North Dakota Representative Thomas Kleppe did not attempt to put lipstick on the pig. "I think the top echelon of the Department of Defense had better be ready to answer some questions." North Dakota Senator Milton R. Young, who had earned the moniker "Mr. Wheat" but who might as easily have been called "Mr. Missile," said, "obviously somebody goofed badly." Senator Young had spent some political capital to assemble those 500 dignitaries to witness the missile test in North Dakota.

Father Branconnier was better known in 1960s North Dakota for his anti-Vietnam protests than for his opposition to the Air Force's nuclear presence on the Great Plains. At the end of 1967, he challenged the US Justice Department to arrest him for encouraging young men to resist the draft. He said the Justice Department had been negligent in ignoring his work to impede conscription. At the same time, a Grafton, ND, Catholic priest urged UND students to boycott the campus Newman Center to show their opposition to Father Branconnier's anti-draft activities. Branconnier's appeal to be arrested got national attention, partly because North Dakota seemed like an unlikely venue for anti-war protests. The Justice Department did not accept his challenge.

By 1968 the Catholic hierarchy had had enough, however. When Branconnier announced his intention to invite young North Dakotans to burn their draft cards at St. Thomas Chapel in Grand Forks as part of a national Veteran's Day Draft Card Burning Project, he was instructed by Bishop Leo Ferdinand Dworschak of the Fargo Diocese to drop the plan. When Branconnier declined to desist, the bishop accepted his resignation, stressing, of course, that the resignation "in no way represents punitive action."

A year later, when President Richard M. Nixon announced that the nation's sole anti-ballistic missile facility would be located near Nekoma, North Dakota, Branconnier was still in the vicinity to protest, whereas most residents of the region were jubilant that all that economic activity would be coming to North Dakota. Father

Branconnier called the ABM system "a blunder of major proportions," but Grand Forks city attorney Robert McConn said, "With all the warheads in the ground around here now and the H-bombs on the bombers, what difference will some more make?" Swords into stock shares? Spokesmen in Great Falls, Conrad, and Shelby, Montana, were deeply disappointed that the ABM site would not be built in their vicinity. Before the decision, Shelby's mayor Harvey Nelson said, "They [the citizens] are all hoping that we'll get it here because it will build up the town." The $4-billion Stanley R. Mickelsen ABM Safeguard Complex was completed in northeastern North Dakota in 1975, then earmarked for decommissioning by the US House of Representatives one day after becoming fully operational, and deactivated on February 10, 1976, after only eighteen months of operation. Beware, said President Eisenhower, of giving inordinate power to the military industrial complex.

North Dakota was only a warmup act for Branconnier, who had served as chaplain at UND for fifteen years before he was forced to resign. In 1985, he got himself arrested for trespass along with seven others in Boston while protesting Reagan administration support for the Contras of Nicaragua. Branconnier returned to North Dakota on several occasions, including 1973, when he lobbied for a moratorium on new coal development in the state. Branconnier periodically trespassed at nuclear weapons production facilities in New England. Then in his sixties, he reported that he was no longer able to scale the perimeter fences, but still managed to slip through whatever gaps in the fencing he could find. As a serious pacifist he did not vandalize the nuclear facilities, but he occasionally performed the Mass "in a prophetic witness against the preparations for mass destruction."

Father Robert Branconnier died in Marlborough, Massachusetts, on December 26, 2016. He was ninety-two years old.

Ann Nicole Nelson was thirty years old at the time of her death on September 11, 2001. She grew up in Stanley, ND, where she was good friends with the grandchildren of the Muslim Americans who came to North Dakota in the 1920s and '30s. Those families were regarded as a little bit unusual, even exotic, in Mountrail County in the 1980s, but they suffered no discrimination, at least none evident to their White Christian fellow citizens. Ann Nelson—ambitious, gregarious, intellectually curious, exuberant, independent, and possessed of wanderlust—spent summers at the Concordia Language Villages in Bemidji, Minnesota, where she learned Norwegian. She was a double major in finance and political science at Carleton College in Northfield, Minnesota. During those years she did stints abroad in China and Cambridge University in England. In the years following her graduation she hiked around Peru alone in spite of her parents' protests. She worked in Chicago, then moved to New York, where she took a job with the Cantor Fitzgerald company as a bond trader. She had worked in the North Tower of the World Trade Center for just a handful of days before the catastrophe.

On September 11, 2001, her parents Jenette and Gary Nelson were just starting their day in a small town in northwestern North Dakota, 1,749 miles from Lower Manhattan. Gary had the television on in the bedroom. Jenette was combing her hair in the bathroom. Suddenly he cried out, "Come in here." When she saw the wounded World Trade Center smoking right in front of her on the television, Jenette first thought she was looking at a scene from a Hollywood movie. Then Gary said, "That's where Ann is working today." They made furious calls and frantically checked their email every few minutes. Everything was sheer confusion. They received an email that seemed to be from Ann announcing that she was alive. But they could not confirm it.

When American Flight 11 slammed into the 93-99th floors of the North Tower at 465 miles per hour, all ninety-two passengers on board were instantly killed. Everyone still alive on those floors and every floor above the impact zone was trapped. Cantor Fitzgerald (an American financial services firm) occupied floors 101-105 of the North Tower. A total of 658 Cantor employees died that morning, more than any other single WTC tenant. When the North Tower collapsed, Gary Nelson fell to his knees and cried out, "She's gone. She's gone."

It took several weeks, even more than a month, for the Nelsons to accept that their daughter, their youngest child, was dead. Even now, twenty years later, Jenette Nelson says, "I know she is dead, but it would still not surprise me if someone called to say that Annie is alive. She is alive to me. No day passes without my thinking about her. She is always with me."

The rescue teams in Lower Manhattan eventually identified portions of Ann Nicole's body, verified the tissue with DNA provided by her family, and over time returned her remains in more than a score of parcels to Stanley, where she was cremated. Grotesque and macabre as this sounds, Jenette Nelson takes satisfaction in the return of her daughter's physical remains to North Dakota. "I am glad she came home to North Dakota. Just weeks before her death she had been talking about her desire to come back."

Her father Gary Nelson designed a black marble tombstone to honor their child. Ann's grave is located in the southwestern corner of the cemetery on the west end of Stanley, far enough away from the other gravesites to feel a little unsettling. Ann's gravestone consists of incised images of the Brooklyn Bridge (undamaged by the 9/11 attacks) and the Twin Towers, the dates of her birth (May 17, 1971) and her death, and a four-stanza dirge written by her mother. I quote the poem in its entirety:

You never know what never means
Until you lose a child—
It means forever you must do without
That touch—that hug—that smile

You can't pick up the telephone
To call and just say hi
You must forever know that
Your child has said good-bye.
They have not gone away—to the other side
Never more to be with you
Until you've also died.

Never is a word of time—
It speaks of endless pain—
It makes the heart turn cold
As the ice does come from rain
It is beyond the human mind
To know it's full extent
It is a word of sorrow—
It can all hope prevent.

But on the other side
They say that time stands still
They do not measure life by years—
But how we do the Father's will
There they say that never is not a word at all
We will not fear it's terror—
It cannot make us fall.

For there we will not lose our children—
Or be parted from those we dearly love
There will be no need for never
When we return to God above.

Lapidary inscriptions, said Dr. Johnson. On the back side of the tombstone there is an etched photograph of Ann Nicole wearing a toothy smile.

Fifteen of the nineteen hijackers on 9/11 were citizens of Saudi Arabia. Two were from the United Arab Emirates. One was from Egypt. And one was from Lebanon, not far from where the Muslim immigrants of Mountrail County originated in the 1920s. None of the 9/11 hijackers were Iraqi. And yet, two years later, on March 20, 2003, the United States launched a full-scale invasion of Iraq, ostensibly because Saddam Hussein possessed (or nearly possessed) nuclear weapons. No nuclear materials were ever found on Iraqi soil. That was more than four trillion dollars ago. American deaths in the war numbered around 5,000, with many tens of thousands wounded, some of them grievously. Iraqi deaths in the second Gulf war have been estimated at over 400,000. The fact that most of the hijackers were Saudi, and America's response to that fact has been, well, nothing, is one of the hardest to accept truths of our long wretched war against terrorism. Oil matters so much that we responded to 9/11 by shrugging off our attackers (who were citizens of our principal oil supplier, our ostensible "ally") and invading a neighboring oil producing country instead.

The Saudi national who masterminded 9/11, Osama bin Laden, certainly never took the time to think about the life of a high-spirited young woman from the heart of the heart of America before he brought the Twin Towers down on that crisp September morning— she was a thirty-year-old single woman still exploring the trajectory of her life, a young adventurer who was following her dreams in New York City; a Christian both in church affiliation and in her basic approach to the world, a warm-hearted, loving, guileless, life-affirming young professional from the American heartland, an American patriot who had no animus for Islam, no great interest in geopolitical affairs, no particular view of Zionism, Israel, the plight of the Palestinians, or America's military presence in the Islamic Holy Land. If bin Laden had thought about Ann Nicole Nelson, he would have killed her anyway. That's how terrorism works.

Ms. Nelson did not work for the CIA. She was not a member

of the American military. She had no connection to Exxon, British Petroleum, Chevron, Shell, PetroCanada, or any other global corporation seeking to extract oil from Iraq, Iran, Kuwait, Saudi Arabia, or any other country. She had never written an op-ed piece defending Israel or condemning any Islamic cultural practice. She did not work for tech companies that might be developing software that could guide drones and cruise missiles or compromise Islamic sovereignty. She did not work in the weapons industry. She was not attempting to build McDonald's restaurants in the Islamic world, was not a proponent of Disneyland or Britney Spears in the Saudi homeland, and she was not trying to convince Middle Eastern hotels to feature adult movies in their rooms. She did not sell liquor. She was just one of 143 million American individuals who go to work in the morning assuming they will still be alive by quitting time.

If you make a list of every one of Osama bin Laden's indictments against America, from our support for the building of Israeli settlements on the West Bank to American aid to the Saudi security forces, Ann Nicole Nelson was absolutely innocent. Her only crime was being an American. If bin Laden had spent a morning with Nelson drinking coffee in Minot or Bismarck or Tioga, she would have listened to his diatribes with sincere interest and she would probably have agreed with some of his grievances.

Several years after her death, Ann's parents found one of her laptops in the basement of a family-owned building in Stanley. The computer contained a file called Top 100, which at first Jenette mistook for a music playlist. When she finally opened the file, Jenette discovered a list of experiences Ann wanted to make happen in the course of her lifetime. Many of them were the stuff of New Year's resolutions—drink water, remember birthdays, never be ashamed of who I am. Some were about the development of her mind—learn a foreign language, learn about wine, get my CFA. A large number were about adventure—visit Maine, visit Nepal, climb Kilimanjaro, scuba dive in the Great Barrier Reef, go kayaking, and—heartbreaking—helicopter ski with my father. One of Ann's dreams was to build a house in North Dakota. Because she was so widely loved, in the years after her death her friends (and complete strangers) built Annie's House at the Bottineau Winter Park up in the Turtle Mountains, dedicated to providing adaptive winter sports for handicapped individuals. Post-9/11 celebrations of her life were held at Carleton College, the Wayland Academy in Wisconsin, at Aspen, Colorado, and elsewhere. An auditorium on the campus of Minot State University is named in her honor.

We North Dakotans are so far from the corridors of power, the hotspots and flashpoints of the world, the crisis zones in the Middle East, that we have a very hard time realizing that the world is not a Rotarian fantasy land where people have cheerful nicknames for each other, where the Class B basketball game is as important as national trade policy, where everyone is decent and basically civil. If you live in New York—that polyglot cauldron of global citizens of every religion, ethnicity, and language, the home of the United Nations, a great multicultural conurbation—you cannot help but see the interconnectedness of the world. Out here in the heartland the distances are so great and ethnic homogeneity so pronounced that we don't really feel part of that faraway global bazaar. It is possible to live on the Great Plains for months and even years without experiencing the mosaic of language, nationalities, lifestyles, and gender constructions that the people of New York or London or Paris simply take for granted. People out here are so far from all the madness of the world that we forget how rich and intricate and problematic the actual fabric of twenty-first century civilization is.

When 9/11 happened, when Ann died, the most common question asked by the people of North Dakota was, "Why do they hate us? . . . What have we ever done to them?" We are insulated from the hot spots of America (and the world) by hundreds of miles of grass and grain and a big sky that seems to encompass everything. How could that not make us somewhat insular? We are so homogenous here that we fail to realize how heterogenous the rest of the world is. We're pragmatic and clunky and peaceful and good-humored and neighborly and law abiding and respectable. Utterly normal and perhaps a little dull. And we think if the rest of the world is not like us, well they should be. Bring us this bin Laden, we think, and we will teach him to love hamburger hotdish and pinochle.

For the last eight or nine years I have done some teaching and consulting for the University of Mary in Bismarck, North Dakota. This has taken me for parts of five semesters to the university's Rome campus—a priceless opportunity for students to deepen their faith while expanding their horizons in one of the world's greatest concentrations of art, architecture, music, history, and devotional activity. Here at home I take the same students to the badlands of the Little Missouri River, to Lewis and Clark sites, and to Native American sacred sites.

In August 2019, I had the pleasure of accompanying a group of forty-some University of Mary students to Winnipeg, Manitoba, to see the fabulous Canadian Museum for Human Rights, and to attend something called "Folklorama," a food and culture showcase featuring representatives of scores of nations whose emigrants have found a home in the Canadian West. At the $300 million human rights museum we viewed exhibits on the conquest of North America by Europeans, Americans, and Canadians; on the Indian boarding schools where indigenous North Americans had their hair docked, their religious traditions outlawed, use of their native languages forbidden, contact with their families and home communities severely limited, and traditional dress confiscated. At these schools, designed to "kill the Indian and save the man," the First Canadians were beaten, punished with solitary confinement, and not infrequently sexually abused. All deplorable, but the Canadians, unlike their counterparts across the forty-ninth parallel, have established reconciliation commissions (in the manner of South Africa) where victims of forced assimilation can tell their stories, confront their tormenters, enumerate their grievances, and—often enough—offer forgiveness to those who have trespassed against them.

We also explored the trajectory of women's rights in Canada. We had a haunting encounter with the Nazi holocaust. We studied the UN's 1948 Universal Declaration of Human Rights. On the high wall near the entrance these words are incised into the very fabric of the museum: "All human beings are born free and equal in dignity and rights." We learned about the Canadian civil rights movement that paralleled the events of 1952-68 in the United States. It was a spiritually fulfilling and at the same time an emotionally exhausting day.

On our return journey to the UMary campus, after learning how serious border control can be in the post-9/11 world, we stopped at a former ICBM missile site near Cooperstown, North Dakota. It is one of two former ICBM sites that were saved from demolition when several of the nation's missile field squadrons were deactivated in the aftermath of the collapse of the Soviet Union. One of them is a National Park Service site just east of Wall, South Dakota. The other is the Ronald Reagan Minuteman Missile State Historic Site in east central North Dakota, the only remaining evidence of the 150-missile squadron formerly managed by the Strategic Air Command at the Grand Forks Air Force Base. The Cooperstown missile (N-33) was deactivated on July 17, 1997. It has been a North Dakota State Historical Society facility since 2007.

Months earlier, I had suggested to Monsignor James Shea, the brilliant young president of the University of Mary, that we celebrate mass either in the Missile Launch Facility (the command bunker) at Cooperstown or—if that violated the doctrine of separation of church and state—at the N-33 missile site a few miles away, also managed by the state historical society. During my time with the university's Rome program, I had stood at the periphery of masses celebrated in St. Peter's Basilica, in the Roman catacombs, in a grotto on top of the mountain at Assisi where Saint Francis prayed, and along the ancient Roman Appian Way. Though I am not a Catholic, I felt that celebrating mass at a nuclear missile site would be a profound experience for the students of the university, and for me—as a historian of the Reformation and the Renaissance—one of the most meaningful experiences of my life. I remember seeing the Soviet artist Yevgeny Viktorovich Vuchetich's 1959 sculpture, "Let Us Beat Our Swords into Plowshares," in the north garden of the United Nations complex in New York when I was about their age, and experiencing that wandering of the soul that comes when you see a great idea embodied in an unforgettable way. A few weeks before our field trip to Winnipeg we had chosen the missile site itself for the mass, because the bunker could not safely accommodate all forty-five of us at one time.

The students, all born after the collapse of the Soviet Union, were curious and intrigued to visit the Reagan Missile complex, but it did not stir anything in them. They could appreciate the Biblical profundity of Isaiah 2:4—"swords into ploughshares"—but most of the significance of the mass came from their deep respect and even reverence for Monsignor Shea, a man, a priest, an intellectual, and now a university president who brought an irresistible mix of gravitas and gaiety to almost every homily he delivered. That President Shea had embraced the idea of *Mass at a Missile Site*, a former storage container for a weapon of mass destruction, guaranteed that they would appreciate the significance of the experience. But these earnest students had never known atomic anxiety.

It was the end of a long day on a bus. The students set up a makeshift altar on the thick concrete slab that covered the missile silo. On top they spread an altar cloth. Monsignor Shea disappeared for a few minutes and came back wearing beautiful vestments, made more beautiful by the softening evening light in the middle of harvest season in one of the most peaceful and agrarian places in America. He wore an eggshell-colored chasuble with a golden stole. His assistant placed the paten and chalice on the altar. Monsignor Shea had returned directly from a monthlong silent retreat in Israel to join us on the field trip to Manitoba. His homily, which was thoughtful, gentle, somber, and insightful, carried the reflections of a deeply religious man breaking a monthlong silence. Shea grew up on a dairy farm near Hazelton, North Dakota. Under his remarkable leadership, the University of Mary has emerged as a nationally significant conservative Catholic liberal arts college in what can only be regarded in international or even national Catholic circles as the middle of nowhere.

It was a perfect August day in North Dakota—seventy-five degrees, an agreeable breeze, a slight haze in the air from the harvest dust. There was a nearly imperceptible hint of autumn in the evening air. Because I could not participate fully in the mass, I had an excellent vantage point as an observer. The students sat on the ground, some of them on the concrete missile cap, in small clusters not far from the makeshift altar. Monsignor stood, of course. The sun was setting over his left shoulder. It was as peaceful a moment as you could possibly imagine.

It was, by the way, August 6, 2019, seventy-four years to the day after the United States vaporized the citizens of Hiroshima.

Inevitably, Monsignor Shea quoted Isaiah 2:4—"They shall beat their swords into plowshares. And their spears into pruning hooks; Nation shall not lift up sword against nation, neither shall they learn war any more." The Bible has few more beautiful passages, few more hopeful and improbable, given what we know about human nature, the iron burden of habit and history, and—if you are a true Christian—original sin.

With a John Deere combine slowly swishing its way through a wheat field nearby, the sound muted by distance, the scene, the tableau at the missile site, felt like a combination of the myth of Prometheus,

the Titan who stole fire from the gods, and Peter Bruegel's painting of
Icarus plunging silently into the sea while a nearby farmer, oblivious,
plies a field behind his horse-drawn plow. The field behind us was
surely harvested in 1962 at the time of the Cuban Missile Crisis, and
all the way back to first settlement in the last years of the nineteenth
century—and it was probably being prepared for planting on April 17,
1961, when the Kennedy administration half-supported the invasion
of Cuba by CIA-funded and -trained insurgents at the Bay of Pigs.
That same field will be growing wheat or corn or soybeans in 2065,
at the hundredth anniversary of the installation of the Minuteman
II missiles in North Dakota, though it is quite possible that all
agricultural field work will be robotic by then—or much sooner. It
is hard to imagine a future for North Dakota that is not dominated
by food production. We all felt the timelessness of the moment.
Something magical happens in North Dakota at wheat harvest.

Monsignor Shea never opens his mouth without uttering
something remarkable. He quoted in its entirety Thomas Merton's
Prayer for Peace, delivered to a joint session of Congress on April 18,
1962 at the heart of the most intense period of the Cold War, one year
after the Berlin Wall went up, one year after the Soviets detonated the
most powerful nuclear device ever built (Tsar Bomba), and just six
months before the Cuban Missile Crisis. The most pertinent stanzas
could not have been more perfectly targeted at all that megatonnage
that had once been stored beneath our feet.

Merton spoke directly to God:

From the heart of an eternal silence, you have watched the
rise of empires
and have seen the smoke of their downfall. You have
witnessed the impious
fury of ten thousand fratricidal wars, in which great powers
have torn whole
continents to shreds in the name of peace and justice.

A day of ominous decision has now dawned on this free
nation. Save us then
from our obsessions! Open our eyes, dissipate our
confusions, teach us
to understand ourselves and our adversary. Let us never
forget that sins
against the law of love are punishable by loss of faith, and
those
without faith stop at no crime to achieve their ends!

Help us to be masters of the weapons that threaten to master
us.
Help us to use our science for peace and plenty, not for war
and
destruction. Save us from the compulsion to follow our
adversaries
in all that we most hate, confirming them in their hatred and
suspicion of us. Resolve our inner contradictions, which now
grow beyond belief and beyond bearing. They are at once a
torment
and a blessing: for if you had not left us the light of
conscience,
we would not have to endure them. Teach us to wait and
trust.

It was clear that Monsignor Shea was deeply moved by the
moment, by Thomas Merton, and by the mass. The students lined
up quietly to receive the Eucharist. They solemnly ingested the host.

After the mass we climbed back into the bus and headed for
home—for the university campus three and a half hours away.
We were all uncharacteristically silent for much of the first hour.
At sunset the sky glowed for the full 360 degrees around us on the
Dwight D. Eisenhower National Defense Highway, Interstate 94,

designed in part to facilitate the rapid transit of men and materiel, including nuclear warheads and also civilian refugees, in the event of war with the USSR.

Swords into ploughshares? Gretchen Heefner in her book, *The Missile Next Door*, wonders why the United States did not move more quickly and more completely to dismantle its Cold War arsenal after the Soviet Union collapsed in 1991. "The crumbling of the Cold War called into question the necessity of this nuclear landscape," she wrote. "If the wall could fall, perhaps so too could the missile fences. In fact their dismantling seemed inevitable, written into the very logic of nuclear deterrence. Missiles had been required to stymie a Soviet attack. If there was no Soviet Union, then there was no need for deterrence—or at least not for the massive forces built up over forty years of Cold War." Historian David Mills said it perfectly: "Missiles might be necessary to preserve a free world but would never set the world free." It is not surprising that that insight might be lost on the geopolitical establishment, but it is disheartening to think that it has failed to leaven the hearts and minds of the congressional delegations of the Great Plains states. Or that the people of North Dakota have not led their political representatives in the quest for peace.

I look forward to the day when the last 150 ICBM missiles are removed from the state of North Dakota, the Peace Garden State, when all the other nuclear warheads now stored at Grand Forks AFB and Minot AFB are removed and, I hope, dismantled. Without descending into the question of whether our use of atomic bombs at Hiroshima (August 6, 1945) and Nagasaki (August 9) was justified (particularly the latter), the continuing post-Cold-War nuclearization of the American West seems impossible to defend—except economically.

One of North Dakota's greatest sons, Eric Sevareid of Velva, finished his 1946 first-phase autobiography, *Not So Wild a Dream*, with a somber reflection on the way the war in the Pacific ended with atomic detonations at Hiroshima and Nagasaki. By now Sevareid was urban, urbane, sophisticated, tempered by war, famous, and entitled. He was never coming back to a clunky village in central North Dakota. In the last pages of his superb memoir, Sevareid wrote, "The issue seemed to be scraped bare of all intervening layers, the matters with which I had been concerned and which now appeared in the cold and desperate vision as misleading superfluities. Up to the sixth of August, 1945, we had been trying to make it possible for men to live better. Now we should have to try to make it possible for men to live." Sevareid was a Norse melancholic. For most of his life so far Sevareid had thought that Velva and provincial heartland towns like it were the problem—miserly Sinclair Lewis hamlets full of hypocrisy and humbug. Now, in the face of the coming nightmare of a world threatened by nuclear weapons, and after all the barbarities he had witnessed in Europe during the war, he decided maybe Velva, and towns like it all over America, were the solution after all. "All that America truly meant, all that Americans had perished for, would be devoid of consequence or portent unless the image of society that America showed the world was that of the little Velvas I had known, remembered and cherished them." This seems like more than nostalgia for the America of one's childhood.

There is something not only paradoxical but morally negating in North Dakota's allowing itself to be the home of part of America's nuclear arsenal. The presence of weapons of mass destruction among us is the very definition of cognitive dissonance. The fact that they have never been used does not guarantee that they never will be used. The highest and best use of the 45.287 million acres of land within the rectangular boundaries of North Dakota is to grow food for ourselves and for the world. Or to turn significant chunks of it back to grass to support buffalo, pronghorn antelope, mountain lions, elk, bighorn sheep, deer, and jack rabbits. It may not even be too outlandish to contemplate a time, not yet on the horizon, when the re-indigenization of North Dakota might make it possible for communities of Native Americans to live partly off of the grass and the quadrupeds it supports.

In his insightful 1989 book, *Great Plains*, Ian Frazier tries to figure out what each ICBM missile site has cost, not just in research and development—actual materials costs, the cost of creating the silo, updates and upgrades, silo hardening, missile replacement, security, etc. The Air Force is vague about this subject, but Frazier reckons that each of North Dakota's 300 silos cost as much as $150 million over time. Not much of that money found its way into the pockets of the people of North Dakota. Nor did that vast expenditure of tax dollars give us anything to celebrate. "To the eye, it is almost nothing," Frazier wrote, "just one or two acres of ground with a concrete slab in the middle and some posts and poles sticking up behind an eight-foot-high Cyclone fence; but to the imagination, it is the end of the world."

Frazier ends his book with a severe and somewhat misleading summary of the White history of the Great Plains. It's too long to quote in full but it can be summarized as follows: extraction, conquest, poor stewardship, greed, broken dreams, depopulation. And then he writes, "And in return we condense unimaginable amounts of treasure into weapons buried beneath the land which so much treasure came from—weapons for which our best hope might be that we will someday take them apart and throw them away, and for which our next-best hope certainly is that they remain humming away under the prairie, absorbing fear and maintenance, unused forever."

I share both of his hopes. The day when the last nuclear device is hauled out of the sovereign state of North Dakota will be a day of enlightenment, a restoration of the core idea of North Dakota. We grow food. We are as life affirming as it gets. That our politicians spin their gyros making up baseless reasons to retain nuclear weapons in the state when even the military industrial establishment would remove them is a shameful misuse of power. If one connected the dots between Hiroshima (and Dresden) and the death of Ann Nicole Nelson on September 11, 2001, the flow lines would be circuitous but nevertheless discernable. "If you live by the sword . . ." Matthew 26:52. How the world sees the United States is quite distinct from how America chooses to see itself. Much of our bewilderment in the face of anti-American sentiment and behavior abroad stems from our inability to measure the ramifications of what we are and do. No matter how much evidence stacks up, we cannot not see ourselves as the shining city on the hill, the Enlightenment nation, the continental "polis" of Pericles' funeral oration. Our refrain, "Why do they hate us? Why would anyone want to harm us?" plays well enough at home, but it is pretty threadbare beyond the borders of the United States.

Ann Nicole Nelson was as innocent of the burden of the cost of America as anyone could be. Let her rest in peace out there on the broad plains of western North Dakota. That, as Eric Sevareid told us in the shadow of Hiroshima, is not so wild a dream.

THE FUTURE OF NORTH DAKOTA

North Dakota land is fertile. It will always produce food for a hungry world. The state's energy reserves are enormous, and its people are hardworking, committed to individual responsibility and self-reliance. These factors make for a solid foundation on which to build the future of North Dakota, but I believe that we are going to have to open our minds, reform some of our habits, and think outside of the box if we expect to thrive in the remainder of the twenty-first century.

For the moment, things seem to be just fine. The last time I drove around the state in a big way—on the back highways and into the seldom-visited corners—I was amazed at how well-groomed and prosperous everything looked. The barns had been painted, many of the houses were new and splendid and sited a hundred yards from an excellent ranch-style farm home built in the mid-'70s. The vehicles, especially the pickups, looked as if they had just been driven off the sales lot. The state's roads were all in good shape. The small towns were not exactly thriving, but most of them no longer looked like they were on life support. My mind kept flashing back to what Harold Macmillan told the British people in 1957: "you've never had it so good." As far as I could tell from externals, North Dakota was more prosperous in 2019 than it had ever been before. Things were humming. Life was good and getting better.

Still, the future is uncertain. We are living through the first phase of what is going to be the greatest agricultural revolution in North Dakota history. The first fully robotic farm is being built in Cass County. The governor and other tech-enamored North Dakotans look on this development with joy. I'm not so sure. I see a huge reduction coming in the number of people living on the land and in North Dakota's small towns. If your farm in Stutsman County is on autopilot, you may as well be sipping herbal tea in St. Paul or renting a winter home on Malta as spending the harshest months of the year in a windswept, sub-arctic place. I feel a double loss coming: fewer actual farmers, but more low-paid farm laborers to check on the combine and the baler as field managers now check on oil wells and oil tanks in the Bakken, and the final disappearance of the *culture* in agriculture. Who will actually live in North Dakota when its economy is fully automated? Fewer farmers means fewer small towns. People are not going to stay in those towns when there is no ag-related work to be done. Robotic agriculture will require dramatically fewer support players in town, partly because their work, too, is being automated by the Teslas of the world. We are going to have to find some other reason for rural people to stay in rural places if we care what happens to those places, which I believe we still do, though not with the passion we felt even a generation ago.

It might be possible to rejuvenate small-town life in North Dakota, but the people of those towns would have to be willing to make some significant changes. It does not do anybody any good to rebuke today's young people for wanting more than Mott or Langdon or Lidgerwood now provide. We would be sorry if they all settled for what a barely-holding-on small town in North Dakota can now deliver. We need to take North Dakota up a couple of notches to make it a cultural and social magnet that will convince our children and grandchildren to cast their lot with us, preferably in their hometowns. We need to stop talking so much about gay marriage, same-sex bathrooms, abortion, the bane of political correctness, whether the LGBTQ community has rights we must legislate to protect—and lutefisk! We North Dakotans need to stop circling the cultural wagons in a rearguard action against the forces of modernity. We need to learn not just to tolerate eccentrics but to embrace them.

We need to pass legislation that instructs the State Bank of North Dakota to create a range of grants and low-interest loans for new small-acreage farmers, plus low-interest land and operating loans to new pioneers for forty-acre family farms on which they actually reside. Not all of them will be White or Christian. We need to legalize marijuana for both medical and recreational use. We need to pass legislation requiring the North Dakota Department of Agriculture to create a series of programs designed to help small family homesteaders succeed—free agricultural advice from individuals committed to the success of the program, paid internships on existing farms and ranches, scholarships and grants, public relations and marketing help, and incentives to avoid carbon-addiction. Humanities North Dakota should provide grants to young writers, documentary filmmakers, artists, photographers, and philosophers to document the movement and increase the likelihood that new young farmers will learn from each other. Towns that are interested in this program should provide houses or home plots at well below market value, office space for the group of small farmers, reduced prices on fuels. And how about a Thai restaurant? Is that too much to ask?

Farms in North Dakota are getting larger and larger. There is no practical limit to the acreage an enterprising individual can farm with robotic equipment. I respect that form of agriculture—

besides, here it comes, like it or not—but I believe there is a great hunger, especially among young people, for a resurgence of human-scale agriculture—small plot farming, niche farming, CSA gardens, genuine organic farming, vineyards and orchards, and farm-to-table enterprises. This hunger exists not only among some of the young people of North Dakota, but in fact all over the country, all over the world. I believe that if we respect, honor, and then tap that interest, we can rebuild North Dakota rural life in a way that will astound us. The search for the authentic—especially in our food supply—is going to be one of the significant passions of this century. People want to know where and under what conditions their food was produced. They want to know what place their food supply occupies on the petrochemical spectrum. They want to know the people who grew that food. In many cases, they want to know the live animals they will subsequently ingest, and they want to ensure that animals raised for food are treated with trans-species respect. Skeptics will say that there are not enough of such producers or consumers in the state of North Dakota to make this work. That may be so (now), but there are enough nationwide who would move to North Dakota for that purpose *and no other.*

What I have in mind is a New American Homestead Act. The details are beyond the scope of this book, but I believe America is ready for that social revolution to repopulate the heartland with people who want to participate in the creation of their food supply, who want to create a true rooted agrarian community for themselves and their children, and who want to live closer to the bone of authenticity than is possible even at such purveyors as Whole Foods and Trader Joe's. I can envision a North Dakota with 5,000 to 20,000 small-scale farmers diffused all over the state, pursuing their dreams and helping us rebuild. New homesteaders, new perspectives, new ideas, new creativity, new diversity. There is nothing particularly improbable about this proposal. If we build the infrastructure—

grants, low-interest loans, training programs, internships, and a ready subdivision of a tiny fraction of the farms in every county—I very strongly believe they will come. We have nothing to lose. The scale does not have to be large. It only takes a handful of new families to revitalize a small town.

We are going to need help if we choose to reboot North Dakota. Perhaps this is a good time to make the larger argument. We North Dakotans need to get over our antagonism to the federal government. Federal assistance has made North Dakota possible, enabled it to survive the 1930s, built most of our highways, dams, and bridges, stabilized our agriculture, funded much of the best research at our universities, stepped in during floods, droughts, and other crises, given us two great economic engines called Minot Air Force Base and Grand Forks Air Force Base, and brought electricity to our widely dispersed rural homes. But the federal government is also going to need to play a deeply supportive role in the future of North Dakota, and a score of other rural states, if they are going to survive the social and economic disruptions of the Great Plains in the twenty-first century. We should not try to pretend that we built North Dakota by ourselves, or prospered as much as we have, without very significant subsidies from Uncle Sam whom we love to decry and denounce in our morning and weekend coffee gatherings. We should cheerfully call on the federal government to take an even more active role in our destiny. We should play the Jefferson card—"those who labour in the earth are the chosen people of god,"—for maximum tugging on the nation's nostalgia for its lost agrarianism. Meanwhile, we should remain center-tolerant on the social and lifestyle issues and talk about them much less.

If we want to pump new life into the small towns and villages, we have to get enough reliable rural health care in place so that families with young children have access to a general practitioner and a dentist, and so that older people from the small towns don't feel forced to move to one of the cities—Bismarck, Fargo, Grand

Forks, Minot—to get the adequate medical attention they need. My neighbor Eileen moved to Bismarck from the Sauerkraut Triangle sixteen years ago so that her ailing husband (a retired farmer) could get the medical attention he needed. When they first moved to the big city, they felt like the Beverly Hillbillies. He died fourteen years ago. She has lived in the big house across the street ever since. My sense is that he felt like a fish out of water in Bismarck. This story proliferates in every direction to an alarming degree. People may feel rooted in the land, but they find dialysis in the cities.

If we liberalize the social order a little, and at least accept a bit more diversity (you may have to bite your tongue in doing so), and create serious economic incentives for young people to take up small family farms across North Dakota, and give them the advice, help, and even training that they require to succeed, we may be able to turn back the pendulum of rural decline. We will NOT turn the pendulum if we don't. Small towns can either continue to become more inconvenient and more *basic* in a depressing way, and slowly reach the collapse point, whether it is five years from now or fifty, or they can do these things and make it quite likely that they will not only survive but revive.

The other possibility, of course, is to move to the other end of the social and political spectrum, and become a haven for the ultra-conservative, the *posse comitatus* types, the Freemen, the White supremacists, the Tenth Amendment crowd, the American Firsters and the Know Nothings. We are on our way.* That would bring in thousands, perhaps hundreds of thousands of new Dakotans, people who would like to live in an overwhelmingly White and northern European enclave, away from the White-minority America that will arrive by 2050 or 2070 at the latest. It would be an interesting experiment to cut off all their federal funding for ten years and return all federal taxes that emanate from North Dakota—and to see how well we do during that interesting experiment. And perhaps it would be time, if we reject federal stabilization of rural America, to close the two big air force bases and the nuclear missile field in North Dakota. The problem with our loudly-shouted belief—that we are a self-reliant people who built this state by ourselves—is that it is a pure myth. I do not doubt that it took great effort and perseverance among the pioneers who populated this state, and I honor them. Them more than us. How can it be that the most foreign-derived

---

*   Just as I was finishing this chapter, I had the following chance encounter at a box hardware store in Bismarck, North Dakota:

Me: Excuse me, I'm in your way.

He: No problem. Narrow aisles.

Me: Crowded here today.

He: You're telling me. Notice the plates in the parking lot?

Me: No, why?

He: Lots of plates from a lot of other states.

Me: Is that bad?

He: Well, I hope not. Lot of people coming her from other states, especially cities, where the Democrats are allowing mayhem in the streets. If they come here, I hope they don't bring their Democrat values with them?

Me: Like what?

He: Defund the police. Stand by and watch the rioting. Guaranteed income. Free cell phones for the poor and illegal immigrants.

Me: Really? That's what they want? I don't think we are in any danger. Mr. Trump won by 63% here.

He: I hope you are right. Look, there is not a racist bone in my body, but look at immigration. This Obama, he let in 45 million Muslims to this country. We have got to keep North Dakota what it has always been.

Me: Really? How do you know that? I've never heard that. 45 million?

He: You got to open your eyes, man. It's well known. You can't trust Biden and the Democrats. They want to destroy this country. Look what they are doing with mail-in voting. If they get away with it, they will win in November and that will be the end of America.

Just then his cell phone rang so we were unable to complete the conversation.

state in the United States in 1915—Germans, Germans from Russia, Norwegians, Bohemians, Finns, Ukrainians, Russians, and more— has become one of the most anti-immigrant and anti-diversity states in America? I can't think of any young person who would want to migrate to a homophobic, ethno-centric, patriarchal, America First, anti-abortion state. If they did, I would try to talk them out of it, unless they lived in Fargo and Grand Forks, and even then I would warn them that there is a pronounced narrowness here.

I know this much for sure: Rural life in North Dakota is not sustainable in the present configuration. We are conservative enough to be seen as backward, provincial, and bigoted by about two thirds of the nation, perhaps more. If they think about us at all. We have to change that. The good news is that by trying to change that, by actually getting to know people of a wide range of backgrounds, lifestyles, orientations, and ethnicities, by fighting our xenophobia, we will overcome our prejudices, which mostly turn out to be lack of contact rather than any really rooted prejudice. We have to invest in the future, spending some of the great oil windfall we have received, in taking North Dakota to a higher level of possibility, access, and culture. If we do not, we will continue to decline, and even if the general population holds steady, the great majority of North Dakotans will migrate to the cities, where the things that gave their life meaning are swallowed up in a sea of drab and nearly identical suburban houses. Nor is the industrial gigantism of our agriculture sustainable, no matter how many robotic systems you embrace. The planet cannot take this level of military-industrial-petrochemical agriculture much longer. At some point the federal government is going to get serious about the global climate crisis and change is going to be forced on farms in unprecedented ways.

We need to scour the planet for answers to our questions. We need to invite the best minds in the world to come here to tell us what may help us invent a sustainable future. We need to require each of our universities to create a Reviving North Dakota Program, looking at technology, art, infrastructure, access to the internet at its cutting edge, education, social organizations, libraries, poverty, race, gender, and religion. We created these universities to be incubators of a better future for North Dakota. From the beginning of statehood in 1889, we have essentially created a number of potential think tanks strategically located throughout the state. We need to charge them with the task of systematically modeling possible futures for North Dakota, and publicizing those models throughout the state and the country.

I'd put together ten interest groups of young people between the ages of twelve and thirty, from every corner of the state, chosen at random (not just the usual student council types), each for half a day, and ask them, "What would it take to keep you here?" And "What are the amenities that would make your life better in your town?" And "Is what you dream of doing in your life possible here, and, if not, is there something we could do to change that?" Then have somebody with writing talent produce a thirty-six-page paper summarizing and analyzing the results of these sessions. At that point, of course, we have to be willing to act, and also to invest. North Dakota has long been run by a gerontocracy. They are going to have to take their stiff bow and empower much younger people to lead us into the future. I remember once, when my wife ran a small-town grain elevator, two men in their late seventies sat at her desk for forty minutes trying to decide whether to sell their wheat or store it in hope of better prices. They just couldn't make up their minds. Finally, the older of the two said, "Well, we'd better ask Dad." He went out to the gravel parking lot and brought in his ninety-seven-year-old father to make the decision. That is a parable about North Dakota leadership.

When I step back to think about what young people seem to want most in life, after well-paying and soul-satisfying jobs, it appears to be access to the amenities that their counterparts enjoy in New York or

LA, and even in Bozeman and Missoula, but not in Harvey or Minot. It is possible to envision a future in which there is ethnic food (Greek, Ethiopian, Vietnamese) in most North Dakota towns, and it might even be possible to envision modest brew pubs in improbable places, but a town of 1,800 or 2,300 can only support so much and whatever that is is unlikely to be enough. The old paradigm of accepting a small-town life of basics—the post office, the café, the senior citizens center, the library open a couple of afternoons per week—cannot survive Instagram. It worked when there were no other options. It worked when there wasn't much mobility. It worked when the rest of the heartland looked more or less identical. It worked when people had little or no discretionary income. It worked when people didn't have social media and 750 television channels to see every day what life can be like elsewhere. Even to the extent that Amazon.com can airlift in amenities on a farm-by-farm or town-by-town basis, young people want more from life than personal access to things that used to be available only in faraway cities. They want community.

There are many hundreds of thousands of people in America and around the world who would want to live in a more vibrant and less conservative North Dakota. It's hard to know whether our inhospitable climate or isolation is the bigger problem in keeping and importing the kind of people who might leaven the economy *and* the social structure of North Dakota. From a certain point of view, climate appears to be something we cannot do anything about, but that is not quite true. The gear has become so good—clothing, boots, hats, trucks and automobiles, farm equipment, hand and foot warmers—that life is not as raw in a North Dakota January as it was in 1970. From an "insulate yourself in every possible way from the bitter cold" perspective, the climate of North Dakota feels milder because we are now better adapted and equipped than our grandparents were. Still, the teenage binge drinking rate, the opioid addiction, the alcoholism, and recreational drug abuse suggest that the problem is not finally about climate. It is about isolation with its attendant cousins: boredom, loneliness, cultural claustrophobia, the feeling of being trapped in a place that wishes it were 1952. It is, I believe, about too much homogeneity, a lack of fundamental diversity, a lack of creative freedom, a repetitiveness, a kind of humble smugness (the arrogance of humility), and about the sense that North Dakotans *settle* for less than they once dreamed of. Nobody can say that rural North Dakota is thriving. Take the Bakken shales away and the towns that are experiencing success would revert to marginality, all but a couple of them.

The most likely scenario for growth and prosperity is what might be called the Fargo model. At some point in the last thirty years Fargo reached the take-off point. It's now a vibrant small midwestern city more than a North Dakota metropolis per se. Naturally, Fargo draws off talent from all of the rest of the state of North Dakota, including Grand Forks. Nobody really disputes that it is the most exciting, creative, culturally advanced, and diverse community in the state. If you want the best meal North Dakota has to offer, you go to Fargo. If you want the best art or theater, you go to Fargo. If you want the most alive downtown, you go to Fargo. If you want the greatest concentration of innovative thinking, you go to Fargo. If you want to purchase something in a shop (rather than off the internet) that might be hard to find in North Dakota, you inevitably go to Fargo.

Fargo's spectacular success has arrested at least some of the exodus of young people from the state. Those who wish to stay can fulfill more of their dream of life in North Dakota than twenty or even ten years ago. Though North Dakotans do not like to talk about it, retention of some of the most creative, intelligent, resourceful, and ambitious of its children gives the state a better chance of flourishing down the line. In the 1980s and '90s, many of the most remarkable young North Dakotans not only fled the state to fulfill their dreams elsewhere, but were actually encouraged to leave by their parents, peers, guidance counselors, and spiritual advisers. That chorus has diminished.

Once the water supply problem is solved (often much too much, occasionally far too little), there is no reason why Fargo should not grow into a city (perhaps a city-state) of 250,000 people or more. Under the right leadership, it could be the most interesting place between Minneapolis and at least Missoula. It is possible to envision a North Dakota that is mostly outback, with second and third tier cities that are doing pretty well, and the rest mostly emptied out except for some tough regional service communities like Bowman and Stanley, Carrington and Lisbon. Fargo would remain the principal economic engine of the state as well as the cultural capital. Enterprising young people who in the past have been disposed to move to Denver or St. Paul would be as likely to move to Fargo instead.

The rest of North Dakota would have to come to terms with this dynamic in good grace. It has long been fashionable to grumble about *Imperial Cass* County and to find something to deplore in Fargo. The kind of phenomenal growth I am predicting for Fargo has the potential to make that old habit worse, because all the parts of North Dakota that are likely to be left behind would be tempted to envy and despise what they see over there in *greater Minnesota,* but cannot emulate.

From time to time, some enterprising North Dakotans want to change the name of the state to something else, either to shake things up or to seem more attractive to people from elsewhere. Established names are exceedingly tenacious, so I don't think this is something that is likely to happen now or later. The notion that the state might seem more inviting if it removed the word North from its name is amusing. I know the American people are said to be ignorant and uninformed, but surely they are not *that* stupid. If North Dakota had a lovely and evocative name—Plainsland, Grassland, Skyland, Eden, Arcadia, or

Lakota—do you think droves of tourists would suddenly start to turn up? North Dakota by any other name would smell like alfalfa and the winters would not be any shorter or less brutal. I've studied all the lists of alternative names. Only three appeal to me. One is Lakota, but the Mandan, Arikara, Hidatsa, Ojibwe, and Assiniboine would almost certainly object to that. Besides, the adoption of the name of a people we vanquished to make room for our White selves is inherently problematic. My ironic favorite is Baja Manitoba, which is also sometimes claimed for Minnesota, which already has a great name, so back off, Minnesota. I'd be very happy if we changed the name to simply Dakota. I'd be even happier if we combined the two Dakotas into just one big Great Plains state with two sets of badlands. Welcome to Dakota or Dakotah for that matter. I'm all for the name change, if we can persuade South Dakota and the government of the United States to let us do it, but I don't think that would solve any significant North Dakota problem.

Most North Dakotans know in their hearts that, short of worldwide economic collapse or political chaos at the level of the French or Russian revolutions, rational people are not going to move to North Dakota as twenty-first century pioneers. They might come for good jobs. But they are not coming for the temperate climate, the mild winters, the prairie zephyrs, the independent theater, the rainbow diversity, the cutting-edge dining culture, opera, ski resorts, mountain climbing, and poetry festivals. If you are twenty-four and moving somewhere, you are probably not going to consider North Dakota, unless there is some compelling reason for overcoming good sense: romance, an excellent job, a forbidden taste for borscht, love of ice fishing.

Windswept undifferentiated prairie and plains with brutal and seemingly endless winters are a tough sell. I have kin in western Kansas on the High Plains. Life is much the same there. But even

Kansas has one tremendous advantage over North Dakota—latitude. Winters are shorter. Blizzards sweep through and then usually it melts. Spring is longer and milder. If you had to choose between godforsaken western Kansas and godforsaken western North Dakota, I would argue all night and through the weekend, too, that North Dakota is the better choice. But eighty-five or ninety people out of one hundred, after hearing the pitch of both communities, are going to choose western Kansas, *unless* the jobs in North Dakota are more satisfying and more lucrative than what is available in western Kansas. We have oil. They don't (or not much).

There are things we just cannot do here. We cannot have a major league sports team. We cannot have the finest opera company in the world. We cannot host outdoor tennis tournaments! We cannot create our own lunar exploration missions. And so on. But there are things we can do. We could have the best K–12 education system in the United States. We'd need to invest very heavily, and revolutionize the way K–12 education is delivered, keep class sizes very low, and hire the best teachers from around the country and around the world whatever the cost, but we could accomplish this.

We all have to fall in love with North Dakota in a new way. We have been living on the fumes of our nostalgia for farms and small-towns for a long time and that's not enough social glue to hold us together or determine our identity any longer. So we have to get out onto the land again to fall in love with this stark, endless, grass savannah we have the privilege to live on. We have to drive the back roads of the state, and even the gravel county roads, and not with our smartphones navigating. We have to get ourselves onto the existing network of hiking trails and create a great number of new ones.

The national North Country Trail passes through North Dakota, but it is almost entirely unimproved by such things as signs, markers, and a recognizable trail. It would be easy enough to quintuple the state's hiking trail system, using money from the carbon bonus we have received, money already set aside for conservation and recreational purposes. We need to create new statewide recreation programs, including winter recreation programs, that don't have anything to do with the internal combustion engine. We need to provide university scholarships, perhaps free tuition, to young people, including young people from elsewhere, who pledge to spend five years in a small town in North Dakota. We need to encourage older people to stay in the state and not flee right after Halloween for Arizona. We need to provide economic incentives for farm and ranch families to play host to interns from all over the country (and world) for varying periods of time. We need to help Native Americans thrive because the more they thrive and revive an authentic indigenous culture, the more hundreds of thousands and even millions of cultural tourists will visit from Europe to see what a thriving Native American culture looks like. We need to set aside more land for state parks. We should create three or four primitive state parks that only tent campers can use, and create weekend programming at those parks, programs designed with the help of young campers. We need to create grants for photography contests, essay contests, poetry contests, dance contests, history projects, micro-farm and garden projects, so long as the subject is the northern Great Plains. We need to start advertising North Dakota for its empty landscapes, its spirit of place, its wonderful pragmatic clunkiness, and its raw character-building climate, instead of fishing derbies at Lake Sakakawea. We need a multi-year campaign to attract young people from all over to come to North Dakota and try to make a life.

We are going to have to develop a better conservation ethic. The Bakken Oil Boom revealed how thin our conservation consciousness is. The farmers and ranchers of the state have a good record of general stewardship, but responsible farming is not the same as conservation. North Dakotans have been engaged in monoculture for decades. Most of the land of North Dakota has been plowed up and harnessed for agricultural production, and that which is regarded as grassland has been heavily compromised by invasive species introduced from elsewhere. We White people have remade the state in our image. The overwhelming majority of the acreage has been turned into a semi-organic revenue-generating machine. But we still have wetlands, marshland, prairie potholes, coteaus, rolling hills, buttes, ridges, the wild country west of the Killdeer Mountains, the three units of Theodore Roosevelt National Park, four National Grasslands units (Little Missouri, Sheyenne River, Cedar River, and Grand River), sixty-three US National Wildlife Refuges, a fairly large number of state wildlife management areas, and several Native American reservations where much of the land has been only lightly transformed. There is a lot of public land to conserve, but each chunk of it needs the same kind of vigilant advocates that fight for the sanctity of Crater Lake and Glacier and Arches National Park.

The conservation ethos of other states—Colorado, Oregon, Washington, California, Minnesota—is dramatically more pronounced. The sorts of development activities that raise scarcely a murmur in North Dakota generate intense debate in these other states. The conservation community in other states, including Montana and South Dakota, is better organized, better funded, more vigilant, and dramatically more likely to cry foul than in North Dakota. The North Dakota media, except for the *Fargo Forum* and more recently the *Bismarck Tribune*, has found little to criticize in the hectic economic development of the last half century. We North Dakotans need to realize that what still exists in something like a pristine state is precious and deserving of stern protection, that wild country once lost can never be what it once was, that since 95 percent of the state is privately owned and open for business, we can afford to be protective of the tiny amount of our landscape that is publicly owned and managed, that to love one's homeland is to want to take good care of it, and that to want to conserve what is most beautiful and most fragile in North Dakota is not the same as being a "radical environmentalist," or a "leftist who wants to lock the state up for a handful of hikers," as one Billings County official put it to me a few years ago.

The best way to develop a conservation ethos is to get out onto the public lands in the state, to camp in tents (not fifth wheels), to take long hikes, to lie on the ground and listen to the grass, to lie under the stars in empty noiseless places and wait for the coyotes to sing, to venture into the back country to see Roosevelt's Elkhorn Ranch for oneself, to go to all the endangered places in the state, take photographs, post vlogs and blogs, share our impressions with our friends here and far away, and to find remote places along the Little Missouri River to take a kind of stewardship responsibility for. Most North Dakotans have never been to the Elkhorn Ranch, so they don't know why it is so important to protect it. I feel certain that if we could take every North Dakotan to the Elkhorn or to Bullion Butte or to the base of Pretty Butte north of Marmarth, in groups of fifty or fewer, the overwhelming majority of those visitors would say, "we have to do whatever it takes to protect this place."

The forces of development and extraction have been delighted that North Dakota has such a thin conservation consciousness, and they have done what they can to demonize those who speak out on behalf of the public or private lands. We have given them a near blank check to extract value from the state in the way most satisfying and efficient to themselves.

North Dakotans accepted the federal Conservation Reserve Program (CRP, begun 1986) because it was lucrative and it was temporary. The CRP paid farmers to return marginal land to native grasses and to keep it out of production for the life of the contract. Now that the program is being phased out, those marginal acreages are being plowed up again to support crops. At the same time, the shelterbelts that were planted (and carefully nurtured) during the '30s, '40s, '50s, '60s, and even '70s in North Dakota are being bulldozed into enormous piles of dead wood and burned, just to get rid of them. In the immensely fertile Red River Valley, already overwhelmingly devoted to till agriculture, the last few marsh and wetlands are being tiled to bring them under agricultural production. This has the expected destructive impact on wildlife, of course, but it also exacerbates flooding in the valley. The dominant ethos of North Dakota in our time seems to be "Grow, Baby, Grow," as well as "Drill, Baby, Drill."

North Dakota emphatically rejects one of the best tools for stabilizing family farms and ranches and easing the serious farm succession problem—conservation easements. For reasons that are embedded in a stubborn primordial obsession with the sanctity of private property, North Dakota does not permit permanent conservation easements. The longest permitted covenant period is ninety-nine years. Entities like the Nature Conservancy are usually unwilling to invest in temporary leases. Besides, even temporary conservation easements must jump through so many deliberately prohibitive hoops that North Dakotans have given up trying to pursue a strategy that has been enormously successful elsewhere, including in our neighbor Montana, where they are not discouraged by grumpy and irrational legislators. Opponents of conservation easements argue they take land off the county tax rolls, that outside environmental groups are trying to lock up the lands of North Dakota, that there is already plenty of wildlife protection in North Dakota, and so on. The great paradox—and hypocrisy—of their position is that they have an absolutist commitment to the rights of private property owners, *until* that private owner wants to do something with the property that other property owners don't like. Of the dozen or so laws in North Dakota most in need of change, the existing conservation easement protocols are at the top of the list.

In east central Montana a new entity is being formed called the American Prairie Reserve (APR). The idea is to create a 3.5-million-acre fenceless pasture on both sides of the Missouri River between Lewistown and Malta. The APR is a public-private partnership that embraces the Upper Missouri Breaks National Monument and the Charles M. Russell National Wildlife Refuge. As privately owned ranches in the district come on the market, the APR attempts to purchase them to incorporate them into what will become the largest unfenced buffalo pasture in North America. As you would expect, there is a considerable amount of local opposition to the plan, some of it fierce. I've spent a good deal of time with the Prairie Reserve board and staff and just as much time with ranchers from the region who are "1000 percent" against the idea. I have deep respect for the ranch community, and I understand their point of view, and agree with it to a considerable extent. They believe that the highest and best use of the land in question is farming and cattle ranching, that valuable land should not be taken out of production, that lands taken off the tax rolls reduce the amount of already-scarce money available in rural counties in isolated regions of Montana, and that it is wrong, perhaps morally wrong, for rich urban liberals who live hundreds or thousands of miles away to sweep in with their blank checks to buy up land that should be lived on and operated by authentic Montanans. The fact is, however, that the APR is not a predatory organization. They do not try to pry land out of the hands of the private owners. In fact, they provide marketing expertise and valuable assistance to ranchers who cooperate with their vision. The APR is quite content to see a private ranch sold to another ranch family or left to an heir. But when a ranch is sold on the open market, the Prairie Reserve calls upon the deep pockets of its wealthy supporters around the United States to attempt to purchase the property. This is, in every instance, the case of a willing buyer and a willing seller, which, if you think about it, is one of the most sacred principles of American life.

Moreover, it's not as if hundreds or even scores of young Montanans (or any other Americans) are lining up to buy ranches in eastern Montana. I cannot speak for Montana, but I know that

almost every heritage ranch in western North Dakota faces serious
succession challenges. Ranch life is not sufficiently attractive to
sustain a presumptive transfer from parent or grandparent to the
next generation of the family. Rural life in these isolated regions
is hollowing out, whether the APR exists or not. In some limited
sense, an ungulate is an ungulate, a quadruped is a quadruped. The
American Prairie Reserve visionaries believe that their plan to build a
vast buffalo refuge will actually increase the economic activity in the
region, and augment the tax rolls. They believe, and I think they are
right, that hundreds of thousands of visitors—call them eco-tourists
if you wish—will come to experience that buffalo reserve, the *only*
place in the world where you can see what the Great Plains looked
like before the great die-off occurred in the post-Civil War period
of the American West. The APR is working closely with Native
Americans at the Rocky Boy and Fort Belknap Indian Reservations
(as well as with the Crow and Fort Peck reservations) to create ways
for those prior sovereigns to play a meaningful and significant role
in the project. The historical homelands of these Native Americans
were much larger than their current reservations, of course. The
APR would make it possible for indigenous peoples to restore some
part of their traditional lifeway on a vast landscape without fences.

If buffalo come (the herd already numbers more than 800), other
plains creatures are sure to find the Prairie Reserve: elk, mule deer,
mountain lions, wolves, eagles, hawks, and probably even grizzly
bears. It is, in short, quite possible that these visionaries will find a
way to rebuild what was once the American Serengeti in a very large
miniature. The Reserve would inevitably become a World Heritage
Site. It would resurrect some of the romance of the American West.
It would attract thousands and perhaps millions of visitors with
money in their pocket and an automatically appreciative view of
"what's going on in Montana."

Some version of this would be possible for western North Dakota,
too. It is true that North Dakota is not quite so hollowed out as that

portion of Montana, and the oil boom has certainly filled the region with industrial infrastructure, but it would be possible to create some immense buffalo pastures in the Little Missouri River Valley, in Divide, Burke, Mountrail, Dunn, McKenzie, and Williams counties, and also in the empty quarter of Sheridan, Wells, Benson, McHenry, and Pierce counties. This would have to be done without even the slightest use of eminent domain. And with all the compensatory gestures, guarantees, and incentives to ease the anxiety of the host communities. You want tourists in North Dakota? This would solve that problem in perpetuity. As the world gets more domesticated, paved, mediated, and compromised by decade if not by year, there is a huge and growing hunger among peoples everywhere to see untrammeled landscapes. To see America as it once was, when it was the most compelling idea/myth in the world, would be an amazing (and realizable) achievement for North Dakota. The English philosopher and political theorist John Locke once said, "In the beginning all the world was America."

Before you condemn this idea, I ask that you sit back and contemplate it for a moment. Ask yourself how it would work, how it would be accomplished, and how it would be managed. Even better, get in your car and drive out to the American Prairie Reserve near Malta, Montana, and see for yourself. I have been there several times. It is breathtaking in all sorts of ways.

One reason I write about this with trepidation is that I remember the response to the buffalo commons idea that was described (not proposed) in 1987 by Rutgers University professors Deborah and Frank Popper. They wondered if those portions of the plains that were emptying out might not be turned into a giant native grasslands park. The figure then being bruited about was 139,000 square miles (about twice the land area of North Dakota). The people of the northern plains were both hurt and outraged by the Poppers' thesis, which had been offered by way of description and diagnosis much more than as a prescription for what the people of the Great Plains should do with themselves and their communities. Even now, just to mention the Poppers or say the words "buffalo commons" will produce angry outbursts in some quarters of North Dakota.

The idea originated more than a century before the Poppers popped up. After the painter and ethnographer George Catlin traveled through the Upper Missouri country in the early 1830s, he concluded that the highest and best use of the Great Plains was to leave them alone as a gigantic national park and refuge for buffalo and all their attendant species, and for Native Americans. His proposal is breathtaking:

> This strip of country, which extends from the province of Mexico to Lake Winnipeg on the North, is almost one entire plain of grass, which is, and ever must be, useless to cultivating man. It is here, and here chiefly, that the buffaloes dwell; and with, and hovering about them, live and flourish the tribes of Indians, whom God made for the enjoyment of that fair land and its luxuries.
>
> And what a splendid contemplation too, when one (who has traveled these realms, and can duly appreciate them) imagines them as they might in future be seen (by some great protecting policy of government) preserved in their pristine beauty and wildness, in a magnificent park, where the world could see for ages to come, the native Indian in his classic attire, galloping his wild horse, with sinewy bow, and shield and lance, amid the fleeting herds of elks and buffaloes. What a beautiful and thrilling specimen for America to preserve and hold up to the view of her refined citizens and the world, in future ages! A Nations Park, containing man and beast, in all the wild and freshness of their nature's beauty!
>
> I would ask no other monument to my memory, nor any other enrollment of my name amongst the famous dead, than the reputation of having been the founder of such an institution.

We should have done this when we had the chance. We can still do part of it. It will not degrade North Dakota to follow the lead of the American Prairie Reserve. In fact, I believe it would be the sanest and most likely to succeed of all economic development plans for the state. *Que Sais-je.*

North Dakota calls itself the Peace Garden State and we do have one—that we share with the province of Manitoba—but we have never found a way to realize its potential. For one thing, it is too remote, tucked way up there on the Canadian border. It's hard to get to (you have to want to go) under the best of circumstances and it is harder now, when borders are stronger, starker things than they once were. Ironically, given its name and purpose, since the September 11, 2001, terrorist attacks on the United States, the experience of visiting the Peace Garden has become somewhat unsatisfying. The border guards of both nations, but particularly on the US side, routinely hassle people who want to explore the Peace Garden, enjoy the beautiful gardens, read the wide variety of peace quotations in the bunker chapel, and perhaps jump back and forth across the border for photo ops.

I'm certainly not the first person who has wondered why the Peace Garden could not become a genuine global demilitarized zone where nations in conflict would come to negotiate and seek peace in a bucolic landscape garden at the heart of the North American continent. The usual answer is that the Peace Garden is just too far from everything, too hard to get to, and too low on the kind of amenities—large, secure hotels, secure meeting facilities, secure communications centers, an airstrip that could support the sorts of airplanes that most nations and stateless groups now routinely have at their disposal. These problems could certainly be overcome, though not solely with funds in the treasuries of Manitoba (population 1.4 million) and North Dakota (760,000). The United Nations could help to fund such improvements and the two sovereigns, the United States and Canada, could supply the money without breaking a sweat.

It is not so wild a dream. Why shouldn't the International Peace Garden, spanning the 5,525-mile U.S.-Canadian border—the longest peaceful border on the planet Earth—be the Geneva of the Western Hemisphere, or the Paris? If you can hammer out a peace treaty between Bosnia, Serbia, and Croatia at Dayton, Ohio, you can certainly accomplish similar things on the northern Great Plains and the Canadian prairies. The usual excuse—geographic isolation—is not very persuasive. The Great Circle Route makes Bottineau, North Dakota, easier to get to than you might think, and if you are trying to settle the decades-long dispute between India and Pakistan over Kashmir, the extra time and fuel between Camp David (or New York City) and North Dakota is essentially negligible.

You could start small. Why not have talks between Manitoba and North Dakota about the Red River take place at the Peace Garden? Why not have every U.S.-Canada issue, including every border issue, shared resource issue, trade issue, transportation issue, work itself out at the Peace Garden instead of in hotels in Toronto or Vancouver? The Peace Garden infrastructure could be improved to accommodate those gatherings, where security issues are not as pronounced, and if the location turned out to be propitious for negotiations, a much bigger leap into the future could be undertaken. Canada could take the lead in all of this since it is regarded internationally as more synonymous with peace than its more bellicose southern neighbor. Any significant improvements at the Peace Garden would bring new life to Bottineau and to Dakota College at Bottineau, formerly the ND School of Forestry. Why should we let this fabulous place be nothing more than a wedding location, the site for summer music camps, and an admittedly superb cactus collection?

Meanwhile, we should create something called the Medicine Line Foundation at Bottineau. Native Americans used the term "medicine line" for a boundary line that is invisible to the naked eye.

A natural boundary would be the Powder River or the Little Missouri or the Front Range of the Rocky Mountains, because everyone who approached it would know that it divided jurisdictions. The forty-ninth parallel is the boundary between the United States and Canada, but it pays respect to geometry rather than to the natural contours of the Earth. It would be hard for anyone from Jupiter to know just where the US-Canadian border is, except for the fences, markers, and border facilities. And yet, as anyone who has spent time in Canada knows, the "medicine line" between the two countries might just as well be 500 feet high. North Dakota and Manitoba, North Dakota and Saskatchewan share a bioregion more or less, but they organize their societies quite differently. Think of the difference between US and Canadian gun laws, health care delivery systems, penal systems, relations with indigenous peoples, educational infrastructure, resource policy, the social safety net, foreign policy, and much more.

The Medicine Line Foundation would exist to study the ways that these two British-derived nations, sharing a common continental base and largely sharing the same language, can have quite distinct social and political structures. The Foundation would engage in a wide variety of cultural exchange programs, conferences, symposia, cultural tours, farm, ranch, and industry tours, and lecture series. The Foundation would study best practices on the plains and prairies, and elsewhere in the two great nations. It is clear to any objective observer that Canada does some things better than the United States and vice versa. The Foundation would study the historic roots of these differences. At the regional level, Saskatchewan-Manitoba and North Dakota-Montana face many of the same issues—isolation, a short growing season, a largely agricultural economy, economic colonialism. So it's surprising, almost astonishing, to think of how little serious cultural exchange exists across the forty-ninth parallel. There is nothing to lose and everything to gain from a systematic enriching of the cultural exchange at the heart of the continent.

One of the greatest assets of North Dakota, and without question the most underused and underappreciated, is the Native American community. It was their land first, of course, and Anglo-Europeans took it from them, as legally as possible and as ruthlessly as necessary. We arbitrarily determined the location, size, and land use protocols of the Indian reservations we *reserved* for their use. No treaty, no covenant, no executive order, no sacred place or tradition has been permitted to stand in the way of White land lust and economic development. Attempts to fully assimilate Native Americans into the mainstream of American life—drumming out most of their *Indianness* and remaking them as ethnic cousins of Irish-Americans, German-Americans, Italian-Americans, Norwegian-Americans, and so on, with a thin cultural memory not far different from St. Patrick's Day or Cinco de Mayo—have mostly failed. There are two pronounced cultures in North Dakota—White culture (with a *Lefse* here and a *kolache* there)—and the world of Native Americans, where poverty, unemployment, substance abuse, malnutrition, and substandard housing are dramatically more prevalent than among non-Indians. The two cultures occupy the same state, use the same single area code, shop at the same Walmarts and malls, but they mostly live in parallel universes.

There are historical explanations for all of this—essentially it is what the Colorado historian Patricia Limerick calls the "legacy of conquest"—but today it represents the continuing tenacity of systemic racism and actual, overt racism. You can hear actual unguarded overt racist remarks about Native Americans on any given day all over North Dakota and particularly the closer you get to the five reservations.

It's an appalling problem. It's unsustainable. Most White people in North Dakota live their lives with the least possible interaction and regard for the Mandan, Hidatsa, Arikara, Dakota, Lakota,

Assiniboine, and Ojibwe people. The 2016-17 DAPL Pipeline controversy called attention to the usually quiet gulf between the two cultures. Every thoughtful person who lived through that crisis realized how much basic work still needs to be done to establish a healthy dialogue between Whites and Native Americans; how much sadness, anger, rage, sorrow, bitterness, distrust, and disillusionment damages the lives and hearts of thousands of American Indians in North Dakota; and how much indifference, contempt, rage, and race prejudice still percolates in the hearts and minds of tens of thousands of White Dakotans. Almost all good and decent people were shocked by what we saw when the curtain of frigid civility was lifted. We thought we were farther along.

What will the story of North Dakota's Native Americans be as the twenty-first century unfolds? Conquest (1850-1890) was followed by Bare Survival (1900-1934), followed by quiet accommodation or what Thoreau called quiet desperation (1935-1973), and then finally by the awakening of Native American determination to climb back towards intact communities, true self-government, and cultural renewal. Native Americans in North Dakota are still poor and their communities still suffer from a range of colonial and post-colonial dysfunctions. But there is perceptible, measurable improvement off and on the reservations. A modest but growing professional class of Native Americans have reached maturity. For decades Whites have shaken their heads and said, "The Indians just need to get their shit together." Now it is happening,

In my opinion, the single greatest thing the White people of North Dakota could do to thrive in the twenty-first century would be to reach out to the Native American community with respect, humility, curiosity, patience, and love, to find ways to sit down and break bread with Native Americans, to *listen listen listen listen listen,* and to do everything in our power to accommodate Native American suggestions, requests (and demands). This will not be easy and, at the beginning at least, it won't be fun. The recent bestseller *White*

Fragility by Robin DiAngelo describes how Whites tend to react to any suggestion that they are complicit in the legacy of slavery, the Black Codes, Jim Crow, separate-but-equal, lynching, the targeting of African Americans in the judicial system, voter suppression, etc., with denial ("I don't have a racist bone in my body"), dismissal, hostility, and open rage, and they resort to trotting out tired stereotypes and narratives to exonerate themselves and slam their ears shut to any suggestion of complicity. All the same dynamics exist among the White people of North Dakota when they are confronted with their attitudes towards Native Americans, whether we like to admit it or not.

If we would create reconciliation commissions in the manner of those that have worked so well in South Africa, and in Canada, if we would create a genuine, full-hearted dialogue with North Dakota's Native Americans, and do what we can to help heal the souls of Native Americans (and ourselves), we could together create one of the most interesting state cultures in the United States. If we could help Native Americans (mostly by removing our metaphoric knees from their necks) help themselves as they seek to rebuild their songs, dances, languages, crafts, agricultural practices, medical systems, oral tradition, religious rites, clan structures, and more, we would not only be doing the best thing for the aboriginal peoples of this state, but for everyone who lives in North Dakota.

Not only do Native Americans have a great deal to teach us about how to live in this windswept, sub-Arctic place (they have been at it forever, we Whites are children of yesterday), but if we find a way to help them thrive on the northern Great Plains, we will be honored and visited by millions of people worldwide. The rest of the world is much more generous, fascinated, and respectful of Native Americans than we Dakotans. They long to see Native Americans practicing authentic cultural traditions that harmonize as much as is possible with the inevitable changes that have come to Indian country in the last two centuries. They want justice for Native Americans, and they wonder why White Americans, in this case White North Dakotans, are so completely tone deaf with respect to a world of vast potential and opportunity for every citizen.

North Dakota cannot sustain eleven institutions of higher education. They were created at a time when people had far less mobility than they do now. I don't know quite how many colleges and universities we need in the state, but it is probably somewhere around half of what we now have. The cost of higher education just goes up and up, and no matter how much money the state legislature appropriates, it is never regarded as enough. The North Dakota taxpayers are not exactly fed up with higher education, but they are restive and skeptical.

Look at the situation from a purely rational perspective: The two flagship universities in North Dakota, UND and NDSU, are located right on the eastern border of the state, just seventy-five miles from each other. Why the fourth least populated state in America would place two full-service universities that close to each other is logically inexplicable. It is just something that happened, but it shows very poor geographic distribution, and it would never happen today if we were starting over. Some other low-population states combined their flagship and their land grant universities into a single institution: the University of Nebraska at Lincoln, the University of Wyoming at Laramie, the University of Minnesota in Minneapolis and St. Paul. That makes more sense.

Add to this that Mayville State University is merely forty-three miles from the University of North Dakota in Grand Forks, and provides no student services that are not available at UND or NDSU, fifty-nine miles away; and Valley City State University is merely sixty-two miles from Fargo and NDSU. This proximity also fails the test of rationality. Meanwhile, Bismarck, the state capital, and the second largest city in the state, has only a community college. From a purely geographical point of view, it would make most sense to locate North Dakota's universities in Fargo, Grand Forks, Minot, Bismarck, Dickinson, and Williston. Even that would represent plenty of universities for a low-population state.

It might make a kind of sense if each of the eleven universities had a different educational mission or specialty, or there was some formula that balanced fair geographic distribution with the least possible reduplication of programs. Perhaps we need nursing programs at all or most of the state-funded institutions, but do we need business or history majors at every one?

If we rationalized our higher education system, we could save a great deal of money for the North Dakota taxpayer. But that is not the most important reason to reform the system. The digital revolution has disrupted a great number of our assumptions about education, including higher education. For most of European and American history, the university has been the sanctuary of knowledge and professors—the priests of wisdom and information. Students were invited to come sit at their feet to learn about history, literature, philosophy, religion, economics, physics, chemistry, geography, and the law. Thanks to the digital revolution, today's average eighteen-year-old has more knowledge at her or his fingertips, literally, on the device they take for granted as one of the basic tools of living, than entire universities in the age of Thomas Jefferson or Thomas Aquinas. YouTube and other platforms offer lectures about Chaucer and the planet Jupiter and the philosophy of Hegel and quantum mechanics that are as good as or better than the lectures students can hear live at most universities in the country. There is almost nothing that an eighteen-year-old cannot know—if we are talking about data and information here—by consulting a smartphone. As higher education becomes more and more expensive, including in the state of North Dakota, and student loans now number in the hundreds of thousands of dollars per graduate, families are going to be more and more strategic (and skeptical) about how to invest their limited higher education dollars. The tendency towards workforce training and certification is becoming a major force in North Dakota life, and the liberal arts, and especially the humanities, are in rapid retreat.

The old model—of the freshman who turns up at a dorm in Fargo or Minot or Dickinson, takes a full load of classes in person, gets involved in some extracurricular clubs and programs, drinks a little, experiments perhaps with other intoxicants, seeks satisfactions that were not available at home in Cooperstown or Grafton, and spends four years attending football, basketball, and hockey games, partying on the weekends, and cramming for final exams—that model is not likely to survive the twenty-first century.

No matter how many institutions of higher learning we maintain in the state of North Dakota, we are going to have to rethink the mission of higher education. The question is, what do we want a twenty-two-year-old North Dakotan to know when she graduates from college? How best can we prepare her for the challenges of mid twenty-first century life? What skills does she need? What body of knowledge should she have assimilated? What insights about life, love, citizenship, and our place in the cosmos should she have developed in several years of study?

It is ironic that we have spent so little time thinking about these things, considering the staggering cost of higher education to both families and the taxpayers of North Dakota. If we called in consultants from Jupiter, and told them to design a purely rational higher education system for the second half of the twenty-first century— to take seventeen- and eighteen-year-olds from across the state, and transform them into complete adults with a mature consciousness and significant intellectual skills, and some useful understanding of how the world works—what would that educational system look like? Not like ours.

Because of the small size of North Dakota, and because we face serious historical challenges as we move ahead, I believe we have nothing to lose by stepping back and completely rethinking higher education. Even if the educationists and the state's establishment do not wish to take the challenge, the taxpayers of North Dakota are going to force the conversation. And however frustrating that will be to higher education professionals, that can only be good for the future of the state.

We send our children to college to learn skills. To master bodies of information. We send our children to college to be certified, to get a diploma, which is the entry license to a great number of professions. We send our children to college to provide them a safe place to experiment with the formation of their adult character and personalities. And we send our children to college to engage in the life of the mind, by which I mean to read *King Lear*, to understand existentialism, to be able to explain the Copernican Revolution, to recognize a paradigm shift, to understand how Christianity emerged as the state religion of the Roman Empire, to know why Newtonian mechanics break down as things approach infinity or the infinitesimal, to learn how White people came into possession of what is now North Dakota.

We now know that it would be possible to form a competent and reliable adult using only the tools available on the internet, without that young man or woman ever stepping foot on a college campus. We all still understand the value of the campus experience, of the late-night pizza in the hall of the dormitory when we ask questions about God and life and love and truth and death. But it is far from clear that that experience is worth $35,000 per annum or double that.

There is a reason that states provide higher education. It is an investment in the future. We have universities in North Dakota primarily to engage in the formation of new adult North Dakotans. We could just as easily send our children off to Montana or Minnesota for college. We do it here partly for geographic convenience, and partly because we believe it is the duty of a state to form and inform its own citizens. We must now ask ourselves what that process really should entail in the twenty-first century. If we were starting over today, with rational planners from Jupiter, I feel certain we would not design a traditional college campus anywhere in North Dakota and certainly not put two of them, three really, on the Minnesota border.

Twenty years ago, we thought the world was running out of carbon. Now we are awash in it, but the First World, at least Europe and the United States, has begun to try to envision what a post-carbon industrial economy would look like. In spite of appearances—that we are sitting pretty on a fabulous quantity of fossil energy—North Dakota needs to be part of that national conversation, and it needs to begin to prepare for the world after coal, oil, and natural gas.

North Dakota has an essentially infinite amount of oil and natural gas. In other words, with the continual improvements in extraction technology and efficiency, it seems likely that North Dakota could pump up several million barrels a day for 100 years, if our civilization is willing to pay the price to bring it to the surface. But it seems equally likely that the world will graduate out of its addiction to coal, oil, and natural gas long before there is any biting diminution of supply.

Nobody can really predict just where things are headed, but the existing evidence suggests that the potent cocktail of government regulation, technological ingenuity, public opinion (or mythology), and market forces will create a post-carbon America well before the twenty-second century. That does not mean there will not be an oil and natural gas industry in North Dakota: there will. But it will not dominate the economy and the landscape as it does now. Coal will be the first of the carbon industries to collapse.

I know lots of enlightened people love to hate coal, and surely there are cleaner, more efficient, more easily recovered sources of fuel on and under North Dakota, but it needs to be remembered how important coal has been to the history of the state. There is a reason that Beulah, Hazen, Washburn, and Center are more prosperous and better populated than small towns farther away from the strip mines. Coal brought some diversity and considerable stability to North Dakota and protected it from being a one-industry state. Even as we move away from coal, we should feel great gratitude for the jobs and general prosperity it brought to North Dakota. Only a hypocrite would fail to realize how much we have depended on it, not just economically, but for the inexpensive electricity that has made our lives infinitely more comfortable than those of our great-grandparents.

Even if the world graduates to much better and cleaner energy sources, a gargantuan amount of lignite will remain under the surface of North Dakota. It amounts to a permanent strategic reserve. If the world collapsed (and it might), North Dakota would have an energy-rich source of fuel near the surface of the earth, one that could, if necessary, be carted off in wheelbarrows to sod houses.

Oil and natural gas are much cleaner than coal, but they too contribute to global warming and they will almost certainly be attenuated or phased out entirely from the energy equation before the end of the century. We North Dakotans have to start thinking hard about what a post-carbon economy will look like. We may well still be heavily involved in the energy economy, but we are going to have to position ourselves to take advantage of every promising innovation that appears on the horizon. The worst thing we could do is declare, in ignorant defiance, that, "There will *always* be a carbon economy and people who think otherwise are fooling themselves." We should continue to work towards cleaner and cleaner carbon use, but we should be helping to find innovative new uses for carbon once we cease to burn it.

There will be plenty of people who will argue that we don't need to do anything differently, that things are just fine in North Dakota, that we will find a way, because we always have. They will argue that we produce things the world needs and wants—food and fuel—and that nothing needs to change, as long as commodity prices or the price of a barrel of oil don't collapse. They will want to believe that the cessation of outmigration that coincided with the Bakken Oil Boom, in fact, the growth of the population of North Dakota in the last decade, represents a permanent reversal of fortune.

Maybe they are right. But I do not think so.

Until we learn to love North Dakota in a new way, and exude a welcoming new confidence in ourselves and this place, we cannot look to a future that preserves all that is best in the North Dakota tradition.

The world is all before us. In the *Four Quartets*, T.S. Eliot explained it perfectly.

> We shall not cease from exploration
> And the end of all our exploring
> Will be to arrive where we started
> And know the place for the first time.

The future of North Dakota?
You decide.

THE LANGUAGE OF COTTONWOODS

When I was a child growing up in western North Dakota, our mother let my sister and me use her Green Stamps once a year each to buy something we chose from the local Green Stamp store. One year I got myself a little starter aquarium, another time a mess kit. But when I was about nine, I traded the stamps for a hatchet. It was actually a pretty good hatchet. In the middle of the long summer vacation, my sister and several of our friends went on a little field trip to a highway rest area on the Green River about eight miles east of Dickinson, my hometown. My mother drove us there, left us for a couple of hours, and returned to get us at the end of the afternoon. We were like kids in a Tom Sawyer novel. Towards the end of the afternoon, along the banks of Green River, I chopped down a fifteen-foot tree about four inches in diameter. It was, if I remember right, an ash tree, not a cottonwood. When my mother came back to pick us up and my sister (naturally) blurted out what I had done, Mother was livid. Not spanking mad.

Much worse: *I'm really disappointed in you* mad. She explained that North Dakota was a treeless state, that in such a place every tree matters, that to chop down a tree just for the fun of it was irresponsible, that it might even be a violation of state or federal highway law. Okay, in the end she took it too far, but you see how upset she was. I still have that Green Stamp hatchet, which has more often been used as a hammer than a chopper, but it has never again nicked a live tree.

A cottonwood tree begins its life by flying. A single mature female tree can release millions of seeds, each attached to a pillowy fiber called cotton (hence the tree's name). Germination must occur within a couple of days. The downy parachute that carries the seed can travel both on wind and water. The wind can only carry the parachute a short distance, but if the seed raft lands in a stream, it can be carried a long way before it dies or settles out on the shoreline. The embryo produces a root and a shoot, one of which burrows into the earth and the other—astonishing if you think about it—defies gravity to stretch up into the sky. If you want to be reawakened to the power of gravity, go outside and jump as high as you can ten times in a row, or hold a gallon can of paint in either hand and climb up ten flights of stairs. Everything depends on where the seed happens to take root. As Peter Wohlleben puts it in *The Hidden Life of Trees,* "once it has sprouted in the spring, the die is cast. From that point forward, the seedling is bound to this little piece of earth for the rest of its life and must take whatever life hands out."

The seed has enough onboard food storage for just a few days, during which, if things go well, the root anchors the future tree to the ground and the first two leaves, shaped like angels' wings, begin to perform photosynthesis and provide their own food supply. If the conditions are not just right—plenty of sun, moist soil, no overshadowing obstructions—the seed dies, a good thing, because if even 10 percent of the seeds produced viable cottonwood trees, they would crowd out every other living thing on earth. Nature is profligate. Most things die before they have a chance. The survival rate for cottonwoods beyond a few months is no more than one per million. Think of it this way: If the mission of cottonwoods is to reproduce themselves (survive) and perhaps take advantage of promising new habitats, an individual tree is successful if it gives birth to a handful of surviving shoots in its hundred-years-plus career of annual reproduction. Cottonwoods have been around for 55 million years. They arrived just after the dinosaurs vacated the premises. As a species they have been astonishingly successful. They will be here when we are long gone.

Because they have been adapting to the Great Plains ecosystem for millions of years, young cottonwood shoots can survive sharp spring frosts. On April 19, 1805, Meriwether Lewis reported that the cottonwoods near today's New Town, North Dakota, had begun to grow new leaves. Two weeks later the expedition experienced a sharp frost and several inches of snow. This filled the Virginian Lewis with wonder. On May 4, he wrote, "the snow has disappeared; the frost seems to have effected [sic, throughout] the vegetation much less than could have been expected the leaves of the cottonwood the grass the box alder willow and the yellow flowering pea seem to be scarcely touched; the rosebushes and honeysuckle seem to have sustaned the most considerable injury." I don't remember a North Dakota spring when it did not freeze, often several times, after the trees budded out. Plants, animals, and humans must be tough and resilient to survive on the Great Plains.

Cottonwood sex, like most sex, is a sticky business. When the light returns in the spring and the BTUs rise to a threshold level, the female exudes a sticky cluster of tapioca-colored flowers. Alerted and aroused, the male cottonwood sends out a gazillion mites of pollen and assumes the wind will do the rest. If the pollen chances on the sticky receptor, the first steps of reproduction take place without much visible fanfare. But who knows what pleasures this may bring beyond the narrow range of human observation? Do trees feel? Do trees think? Do trees have attitude? Do trees know pain and pleasure? Do trees have orgasms? We don't really know. The pairing of pollen and flower produces thousands of tiny seeds, which fill a dangling line of pods that resemble shiny green beads on a necklace. When the moment is right, the pods crack open—then suddenly a gentle cotton snowfall carpets the plains. I have driven through small towns in North Dakota in June and July when every street and sidewalk is covered with a downy cotton film a quarter-inch thick. It makes you ache with love of the Great Plains and small-town life.

The English language has no adequate term for this cotton down. The Russians call it *pookh*. The etymology is unclear, but *pookh* has a wonderful onomatopoetic sound, and it refers to the cotton produced by Moscow's 100,000 cottonwood trees. The urban legend there is that Franklin Delano Roosevelt (who had some wild notions about shelter belts) advised his wartime ally and fellow head of state Josef Stalin that cottonwoods grow fast and provide plenty of shade. Just what led to this conversation is unknown, but we do know that the sheer volume of *pookh* in Moscow has become both a nuisance and something of a public health hazard. Some call it "FDR's revenge," but as the Yalta Conference (February 4-11, 1945) showed, Roosevelt had an unjustified soft spot for Stalin and Soviet good will.

Today it is illegal to plant cotton-bearing trees in most North Dakota towns and cities.

Try to grow a cottonwood tree sometime. Go ahead and love it to death because you *will* love it to death. I've planted a couple of dozen in my suburban yards over the years, some of them already far enough along that they are unlikely to die, but most of them die anyway. Even better, try to transplant a baby cottonwood tree. They thrive where they thrive, but they are a fish out of water in some arbitrary spot you happen to choose for it. Every year I transplant one or two and almost all of them die in a single summer, at most two. Still, by now, through sheer perseverance, I have five very large cottonwood trees in my big back yard, one right next to the place where my friends and I sit to sip and talk in the cool of the evening. They give me enormous pleasure, in part because *somehow* I kept them alive or—to speak truth—managed not to kill them. But here's the rub; every summer I find two or three or five *volunteer* cottonwood shoots growing in my yard downwind from the ones that are mature. They jumped the breeze from the tree to a new site. A few find the right mix of spongy soil, moisture, and light, and they grow four feet in a single summer. Colorado nursery owner Mike Jeronimus has said they can grow "head-high in a year." Unfortunately, I have to mow these volunteers down, because they sprang up where I cannot allow them to grow, and every time I have tried to transplant one it has died in defiance.

My backyard trees languished at first, for two or three or four years, but the ones that survived eventually struck water down there and now they suck the hillside aquifer dry. One tree grew two feet in four years and then six feet in the fifth alone. I love my home-grown cottonwoods, but I have to admit that they feel a little like zoo animals, very much alive and delightful, but stripped of their deepest authenticity by being domesticated.

North Dakota has the fewest trees per square mile of any state. Less than 2 percent of North Dakota's 44 million acres can be called forested even by the most generous definition. The most recent estimate puts the entire North Dakota tree population at 346 million, which sounds like a lot of trees, until you compare ND with Virginia, which has 11.2 billion trees, or Maine at 24 billion. Even the second most treeless state, Nebraska, has nearly twice the number of trees as North Dakota. I spent a week in Virginia recently, then flew to Atlanta-Minneapolis-Bismarck in a single afternoon. From seat 18D on a small regional jet descending to the Bismarck airport I gazed out at a vast, nearly flat landscape dusted with snow as far as the eye could see in every direction. After Virginia, the appalling treelessness shot straight to my heart. *I'm home! Home, home, home, home. Home.*

Meriwether Lewis was fascinated and a little disturbed by the treelessness of the Great Plains. On April 10, 1805, just getting underway for travel season 1805, Captain Lewis wrote, "The country on both sides of the missouri [sic throughout] from the tops of the river hills, is one continued level fertile plain as far as the eye can reach, in which there is not even a solitary tree or shrub to be seen, except such as from their moist situations or the steep declivities of hills are sheltered from the ravages of the fire." Lewis died in 1809 before he could finish his projected three-volume Enlightenment report on his transcontinental journey. On March 24, 1807, he had published a prospectus of the report he intended to write. Volume one would be a connected narrative of the journey. Volume two would concentrate on geography and the ethnology of the fifty-some Native American tribes the expedition encountered. Part two (volume three) would "be confined exclusively to scientific research," with a "full dissertation" on plains phenomena, including "some strictures on the origin of Prairies," i.e., an attempt to account for the treelessness between the bottom of South Dakota and the Rocky Mountains. By May 26, 1805, near the mouth of the Judith River, Lewis was willing to pronounce, "This Countrey may with propriety I think be termed the Deserts of America, as I do not conceive any part can ever be settled, as it is deficent in water, Timber & too steep to be tilled." Lewis may well have been right. Although eastern Montana was fully settled—four farms to a section—during the Homestead Era, soon aided by such supplemental legislation such as the Timber Culture Act (1873), the Desert Land Act (1877) and the Newlands Reclamation Act (1902), it has been slowly emptying out ever since, until it is now one of the least densely populated regions of the United States. Unless there is intense profit to be made, almost nobody wants to live in this 600-mile Empty Quarter. Most of my favorite places on the northern plains languish in this semi-arid region.

In his seminal study *The Great Plains*, published in 1931, Texas historian Walter Prescott Webb argued that it would have been impossible to move Euro-America civilization out onto the plains had it not been for three inventions—barbed wire (replacing the split-rail fences of Abraham Lincoln's Midwest), windmills, and the sod house. There are only a handful of sod houses left on the Great Plains. They were once ubiquitous. Necessity is the mother of invention, of course, but sod house historians trace their roots (as it were) to the steppes of Eurasia, an equally treeless environment. The Germans from Russia who migrated to the American Great Plains beginning in the 1870s brought the idea of the sod house with them. More recently, historians have located the technology among some indigenous peoples of North America and northern Europe. Because there were no trees available in Dakota in the 1880s and it was way too soon for the manufacture of bricks, plains pioneers cut out large blocks of sod and stacked them like Legos. The first barbed wire fences were strung in Texas in 1875, just one year after Joseph F. Glidden of DeKalb, Illinois, received a patent for his design. In most locations wood was too scarce to burn for heat, so pioneers dug pit coal where it was available and burned twisted grass and buffalo manure (chips) until their supply ran out when the buffalo were hunted nearly to extinction.

Kansas pioneer Uriah Oblinger explained sod house construction in a letter to his wife Mattie. "I am building my walls 2 1/2-ft thick and have got them 3 1/2 feet high, but the weather today and tonight looks as though I would not do much at it tomorrow . . . looks as though it would freeze some before morning. . . . I suppose you would like to know the size of my house (I won't say ours till you get here) it is 14 by 16 ft. inside, is this room enough for you to spread out in, if it is not I will build larger this fall and take the present one for a stable." It would be fun to see Mattie's answer.

I drove across North Dakota east to west not long ago trying to see the state, as it were, for the first time, how others must see it who have no prior experience of North Dakota or the Great Plains. I knew the Red River Valley is almost perfectly flat. So that's everyone's first impression if they are coming into North Dakota from the Midwest. Talk about rude awakenings. You leave the idyllic lake country of Minnesota, characterized by hill and dale, barns and silos and horse sheds and lucid streams and trees everywhere, and suddenly you are inching across a landscape flat as a pancake and breathtakingly treeless. The sky opens up into an alarming boundlessness. Your car suddenly feels swallowed up. The wind becomes a factor. If you are subject to agoraphobia, you may begin to feel uneasy. All I can say is, just wait.

I wanted to see if I could spot the westernmost *beach*, the shoreline of glacial Lake Agassiz, a vast inland waterway that covered a large vee in eastern North Dakota and western Minnesota until about ten thousand years ago. But I passed without spotting it. The transition from perfectly flat to very nearly flat somewhere near Casselton is undramatic, to put it lightly. North Dakotans are more awake to the change than others because we have no choice but to cling to contour, however nuanced or muted, and we are militantly defensive about the inevitable visitor's observation, "Wow, North Dakota sure is flat." Because I have been thinking incessantly about the question, *Just what is North Dakota and what does it signify?* I was trying to see the state as someone from, say, New Jersey or Florida or Jupiter might see it. What I noticed first was that there are in fact lots of trees in North Dakota—if lots means some. But what is important to remember is that nearly every one of those trees was planted by White people, mostly to cut the wind and prevent soil erosion, in part perhaps to create a bit of domesticity, a bit of the Midwest, around the scattered family homesteads. I tried to imagine North Dakota before the Homestead period (1880-1910), and particularly before the New Deal's conservation programs, including the Soil Conservation Service (September 13, 1933).

Before the coming of the plow, North Dakota would have been a vast treeless savannah. The grass in the Red River Valley would have been waist high, and in places shoulder high. Such trees as existed in that sea of grass would have been confined to the hollows and along the watercourses. The novelist O.E. Rølvaag captured the nature of the prelapsarian prairie perfectly in *Giants in the Earth*. "The caravan seemed a miserably frail and Lilliputian thing as it crept over the boundless prairie toward the sky line. Of road or trail there lay not a trace ahead; as soon as the grass had straightened up again behind, no one could have told the direction from which it had come or whither it was bound. The whole train—Per Hansa with his wife and children, the oxen, the wagons, the cow, and all—might just as well have dropped down out of the sky. Nor was it at all impossible to imagine that they were trying to get back there again; their course was always the same—straight toward the west, straight toward the sky line." Every North Dakotan should read this book.

Such native trees as there were in Dakota were essential to the success of the Lewis and Clark Expedition. Of the cottonwood, Lewis and Clark scholar Paul Russell Cutright has written, "Of all the western trees it contributed to the success of the Expedition more than any other." Imagine how many cottonwood fires the Corps of Discovery sat around between St. Louis and Idaho. The expedition determined to send its big keelboat back downriver from Fort Mandan in the spring of 1805. It was too bulky to travel much farther up the Missouri. The captains selected a small crew to float the fifty-five-foot barge safely back to St. Louis. On board were French voyageurs (payload specialists, grunt labor) who had been hired only for the first year of travel; several enlisted men who had been discharged for bad behavior; a few Native Americans who had reluctantly agreed to make the long journey to Washington, DC, to meet the Great Father; copies of journals, reports, and charts; letters to family members; a large number of artifacts for the curious president; and a little live menagerie consisting of four magpies, a sage grouse, and a prairie dog. By the time all these things reached the White House, only the prairie dog and one magpie were still alive. Jefferson loved that prairie dog and made sure skeptical Federalists got to hear it chirp.

So the expedition needed a new fleet to replace the bulky keelboat. On February 28, 1805, the expedition's carpenter Sergeant Patrick Gass walked upriver until he found a stand of very large cottonwoods six miles up and a mile and a half east of the Missouri. This was the closest location where sufficiently large cottonwoods could be found. Gass and a crew of fifteen others felled the trees, stripped off their bark, and hollowed them out with axes and adzes. All of this was done in just three weeks. The new canoes were carried to the Missouri River on March 20 and 21, 1805. That must have been a backbreaking portage, but Gass reports it as just another expedition task undertaken, completed, and crossed off the to-do list.

When the expedition departed from Fort Mandan on April 7, 1805, to "penetrate a country at least two thousand miles in width upon which the foot of civilized man had never trodden" (as Meriwether Lewis erroneously but magniloquently put it), the flotilla now consisted of "six small canoes and two large pirogues." The Missouri River first grew those cottonwoods and then floated the expedition nearly to its source in their repurposed trunks, a distance of at least 1,100 serpentine river miles.

The zone where Patrick Gass found his canoe trees still produces giant cottonwoods. The trees at the Fort Mandan replica site near Washburn are tall, strong, magnificent. Long ago I observed one of the best thunderstorms of my life among those trees. The 120-foot trunks bent over with the wind to what I would have expected was the breaking point, like reeds or tall grass. Their flexibility and resilience were astonishing. When the storm passed, they stood back up in matronly dignity with no more damage than a couple of hundred tennis racket-sized branches strewn across the forest floor. Across the river from Fort Mandan, Cross Ranch State Park preserves far the best and perhaps the oldest cottonwood trees in all of North Dakota.

The Great Plains are so treeless that the panhandle of Texas actually commemorates the first tree that was planted there. Unfortunately, it was not a cottonwood. When Thomas and Melissa Cree took up a homestead in 1888, near the future townsite of Panhandle City in Texas, they fashioned themselves a dugout because there were no trees from which to cut out lumber. Like the femme fatale in a medieval romance, Dame Melissa then sent her mate on a quest to find a tree that could be transplanted in their yard. She wanted to plant some token that they were not after all marooned in an infinite sea of grass. The sapling Thomas Cree brought back to the ranch was an Osage-Orange. The restless Crees moved away four years later, but by then the tree had taken root. Many decades later, on October 23, 1963 (one month before. . .), Texas Governor John Connally declared that tree a Texas Historic Landmark. The Osage-Orange died in 1970. According to published reports, the First Tree did not die of old age or natural causes. Having survived droughts, blizzards, thunderstorms, and for Christ's sake the Dust Bowl, it died at the hands of the industrial petrochemical complex. It was agricultural herbicides that killed it off. Roadside signage on US highway 60 commemorates that tree. "Cree traveled 35 miles at his wife's request to find a sapling, and planted it here. He watered it from a nearby lake that he dug from a buffalo wallow. The tree never grew but lived many years."

Imagine a sign to celebrate a single tree in Virginia or Illinois. It would have required a lynching or President Washington's graffiti ("George loves Sally") to rise above ho hum there.

For many years I thought the cottonwoods along the Little Missouri River in southwestern North Dakota were defective or diseased. Almost every tree I observed supported a combination of healthy and ghost limbs. There might be leaves over 75 percent of the canopy, but in almost every case some of the branches were as bare as the whole tree in winter. The trees had a shaken and shattered feel. Often enough even the parts that had the usual number of leaves looked a little sickly and half-hearted. These fifty-year-old cottonwoods were still very much alive, but they appeared to be on the brink of an early death. Perhaps they were not getting enough water. They looked mangy. Marginal. Then I realized that they were not suffering from some variation of Dutch elm disease or the ravages of the pine beetle. This was in fact the normal look of at least half of the trees along the Little Missouri River, especially where the stand of trees was thin— half a dozen trees in a short irregular line along the riverbank, the next copse two hundred or five hundred yards up or down river. If there is no prolonged drought, they will live out their sixty-to-120-year life, but they rarely flourish like the trees closer to the river's mouth or those along the Missouri River proper. Cottonwoods guzzle water—if they can get it. A mature cottonwood can drink up to a thousand gallons a day.

The only time cottonwoods were ever really valued by White people on the Great Plains was during the Steamboat Era (1832-1880). Steamboats were a technological miracle, but they ate trees without any regard to sustainability. According to historian Donald Jackson, "A vessel the size of the *Yellow Stone* burned ten cords of wood a day during a normal daylight run. A cord is a stack of wood cut into four-foot lengths, measuring four feet high and eight feet in width. A day's supply for the *Yellow Stone* would just about have fit on a standard railway flatcar of today, and its sheer bulk must have taxed the ingenuity of the crew in finding storage space for it." In his book, *Navigating the Missouri: Steamboating on Nature's Highway 1819-1935*, Dr. William E. Lass wrote, "The timber supply was of great concern to steamboatmen, who usually needed to refuel at least once a day. With their inefficient high-pressure engines, steamboats usually consumed about 1.25 cords of wood per hour. . . . A cord of cottonwood, for example, ranged from 2,160 pounds for very dry and 4,400 pounds for green cut during the growing season." In his logbook for an 1841 voyage on the Missouri, Captain Joseph Sire wrote that in the ten years since boats had been operating on the upper river, all the easily accessible wood had vanished, "and unless one takes measures to replenish in advance I would not be surprised if in the future boats will fail . . . because of wood." Lass cites a captain who said that as early as 1841 wood was becoming rare on the stretch between the Niobrara and the Big Sioux rivers.

If the steamboats had not been suddenly retired by the completion of the transcontinental railroad, they might have denuded the Missouri Valley completely. Says Donald Jackson, "Consider the *Yellow Stone* on a voyage of seventy days to Fort Pierre, and another fifteen days to return to St. Louis helped along by the current. Disregard the fact that the boilers might require less wood going downstream, and that the wood would surely be of various kinds and quality. The amount consumed on this single voyage would have required the equivalent of 1700 oak trees that might have been growing for half a century."

"The steamboatman," says Jackson, "was always convinced that around the next bed he would find not a tree or bush." And for good reason. Jackson's conclusion is startling. "We can estimate that during her lifetime of six and a half years, the *Yellow Stone* spent about two thousand days under way. A total of forty thousand trees were consumed, then, in the sooty firebox of one steamboat." That's just one steamboat. Nobody knows just how many steamboat trips were made up and down the Missouri River during that era, but the number is in the thousands. Oak burns longer and hotter than cottonwood, so figure 2,500 cottonwoods per journey, thousands of journeys. Not all steamboats lasted six years. In fact, it is estimated that nearly one in three steamboats eventually sank into the muddy waters of the Missouri. So, if the average life of a steamboat was, say, four years, and during that time it consumed 25,000 trees, and let's say just 1,000 boats plied the river during that era, well, that's essentially all of the cottonwood trees. If technology had not changed in the 1860s and '70s, the steamboats would have been put out of commission by exhausting their fuel supply. Sound familiar?

Theodore Roosevelt ventured out to the badlands of Dakota Territory in September 1883 to kill a buffalo. He lived in three different cabins in the North Dakota badlands, one that he took over from previous inhabitants, and two built as headquarters of the two ranches he established. Those ranches were the Maltese Cross, a few miles south of the Northern Pacific Railroad tracks on the east bank of the Little Missouri River, and the Elkhorn Ranch, thirty-five miles north of the tracks on the west bank of the river. His first cabin—on the Maltese Ranch-Chimney Butte site—consisted of square pine ties that had been cut far upstream and floated down towards the construction corridor of the Northern Pacific Railroad. They had been milled for use as railroad ties, but when that project fell apart ranchers and others who lived along the river simply appropriated them for their own uses. The law had not yet come to the badlands; squatters' rights prevailed. At the Maltese Cross the pine ties stood side by side vertically. Roosevelt met Sylvane Ferris and Bill Merrifield at that cabin on September 7, 1883, on his way to what Sylvane's brother Joe, his guide, thought might be the last buffalo stand in Dakota Territory. Less than two weeks later, Roosevelt decided to go into the cattle ranch business, and he impulsively bought the grazing rights to the Maltese

Cross Ranch, such buildings as were on it, and the cattle that grazed nearby. When he handed Ferris and Merrifield a check for $14,000, they asked him if he wanted a receipt. If I didn't trust you, TR said, I would not have handed you the check. Roosevelt departed for New York at the end of September, with the shaggy head of the buffalo he killed on upper Little Cannonball Creek stowed in the baggage car. Before he left, he instructed his new ranch hands to build him a more spacious cabin of cottonwood logs. That cabin—which has traveled extensively beyond the borders of North Dakota to grace expositions and historical commemorations as far away as St. Louis and Portland—now rests permanently on the grounds of the interpretive center of Theodore Roosevelt National Park. Just how many nights TR spent in the Maltese Cross cabin is unknown, but it could not have been very many. He spent fewer than 350 nights altogether in the Dakota badlands between 1883 and 1900, most of them at his second Little Missouri headquarters, the Elkhorn ranch house.

Roosevelt built his Elkhorn Ranch house with cottonwoods. Mostly. He ordered the finishing wood from St. Paul, but the structure itself was made of stout cottonwoods, felled with axes, squared with adzes and planes, lifted with the help of neighbors, horses, and pullies. If there had been a Home Depot nearby he might have built the Elkhorn of better wood—almost anything would have been better than cottonwood—and yet it is possible that he would have disdained better lumber as not in resonance with the spirit of the place. If he had imported his lumber, people would have made snarky comments like, "Yep, this is what you would expect of the wealthy New Yorker Mr. Roosevelt, who of course would not be content with the normal wood we use out here to build our shacks, our cabins, our huts, and even our houses."

You can be certain that the French aristocrat who sought adventure in the badlands at the same time as TR, the Marquis de Mores, did not use cottonwood to build his hunting lodge up on the ridge overlooking Medora. He would have been embarrassed to build with cottonwood. He imported his building materials, because he wanted to use his badlands lodge as a place of comfort and a display of wealth and power, not take his cues from the available resource base or blend with the habits of the local folks. If his western house had been built of cottonwood logs, would we call it (as we do) the *Chateau* de Mores?

After the untimely deaths of his wife and his mother (Alice Hathaway Lee Roosevelt at age twenty-two, and Martha "Mittie" Bulloch Roosevelt at age forty-nine) in the same New York City brownstone on Valentine's Day 1884, Roosevelt determined, a little histrionically, to disappear into the Dakota badlands, perhaps forever, where he would grieve and hunt and write and ride alone along the ridgelines—and perhaps become the first governor when North Dakota became a state. But he could not do his brooding at the Maltese Cross Ranch, which was too close to civilization (just seven miles) on a well-traveled trail. In June 1884 he rode north of the bustling new village of Medora in search of genuine seclusion, in quest of some remote vale where he would establish an isolated second ranch where he could grieve alone. A man named Howard Eaton, later the creator of the West's first dude ranch, directed him to a perfect location, a benchland on the west bank of the Little Missouri River thirty-five miles north of the railroad tracks. It is still remote 140 years later. Roosevelt had inherited the name Maltese Cross (also known as the Chimney Butte Ranch), but he named his second ranch the Elkhorn, because he had seen nearby, he claimed, the interlocked antlers of two buck elk who had been doing alpha-male head butting and subsequently starved to death. This was just the sort of Darwinian signifier TR loved, especially in his grief, though recent research suggests that he may only have heard about the interlocked antlers, which were discovered about the same time out in Montana.

To operate the new ranch, Roosevelt cajoled two Maine woodsmen he had known in the north country when he was a frail teenager, William Sewall and Wilmot Dow, to relocate from Island Falls, Maine, to the Elkhorn. They were skeptical but willing, partly because they loved Roosevelt and partly because Roosevelt's financial offer guaranteed that, at worst, they would lose nothing but their time. Once he got them to the site, the restless Roosevelt instructed them to build a sixty-by-thirty-foot cabin for him in a beautiful grass pasture on the west bank of the Little Missouri. The only available trees large enough for this undertaking were cottonwoods. TR naturally wanted an *authentic* wilderness cabin so that he could play Daniel Boone, Davy Crockett, and George Rogers Clark on the western frontier. The cabin was built on site in the autumn of 1884 and the spring of 1885.

Any close examination of the extant documents indicates that the seasoned Maine woodsmen did most of the construction work. Especially the finishing work. Characteristically Roosevelt wanted in on what he regarded as the manly work. He was at the ranch long enough during this period to do some of the tree felling. Asked how the project was going, young Dow, not knowing he was within earshot of TR, reported, with wonderful affection and irony, "Well Bill cut down fifty-three, I cut forty-nine and the boss, he beavered down seventeen." Perfect diction—*beavered.* Not bad, really, because you can assume the hyperkinetic Roosevelt was swinging for the bleachers rather than employing his ax in any efficient way. Cottonwood fractures and buckles and twists and shatters, and the wood is not very hard. But it was what was available and none of the builders thought they were erecting a cabin with a long shelf life. In his 1913 *Autobiography,* Roosevelt articulated one of his core principles: "Do what you can, with what you've got, where you are." On another occasion he wrote, "If you are cast on a desert island and need to build a boat in order to get off, it would be better if you had a saw, but if you only have a screwdriver and a chisel then you have to go with the tools you have. And so it is with men." Cottonwood it was!

The Elkhorn cabin has long since disappeared. Once it became clear that TR had returned to the East more or less for good, the locals appropriated the lumber from the Elkhorn for their own purposes. Today nothing remains at the site except a handful of sandstone foundation stones marking the perimeter of what was once the 1,800-square-foot house. I know some badlands ranchers who claim they have original boards from the Elkhorn. That's a lovely claim to make, a harder one to authenticate.

Today I am sitting with my back to a cottonwood in a state park on the banks of the Missouri River north of Bismarck. It is mid-October. At least half of the leaves are still up in the trees, but one more sharp cold snap will pull almost all of them off within the next week or ten days. The breeze is gusting to fifteen miles per hour this afternoon, but it is usually just half of that. There are almost no periods of dead calm. The autumn rustle-rattle of the cottonwood tree is ecstasy to my ears. The leaves are brittle now. They are not brilliant anymore. They have the look of a banana that has sat on the counter two days too long. Some are yellow, some gold, but some tan or gray and, no matter what their color, they have lost their luster. Some are shriveling up the way old things do. Every twenty seconds or so a stray leaf helicopters down charmingly to the grass. Across the way, an older man in a beige uniform is raking up leaves (why?) with a spring-loaded rake and burning the leaf piles (why?). It cannot be good to let these trees generate so much biomass and then to remove it from the ground whose little ecosystem provided all the nutrients that made the leaves in the first place.

It's an absolutely perfect autumn day in North Dakota, the more perfect because everyone I encounter this week goes out of her or his way to declare that we are about to face winter—maybe as early as tomorrow. Ten times in the last twenty-four hours I have been somewhere where I have encountered a fellow North Dakotan.

When they mechanically ask how my day is going, I say, "This is an absolutely perfect North Dakota fall day. We get a few dozen like this. It is as perfect a day as you could ever ask." To which every single person has said something like, with a mix of weariness and sarcasm, "Well, enjoy it while it lasts because come Wednesday," or, "Yeah, just wait." This always makes me sad or grumpy. I want to say, "Hey, don't you see that what makes this day so magnificent is that we know we are living on borrowed time? If we could expect a hundred days like this in a row, we wouldn't be filled with poignant joy. And winter, by the way, is one of the best times in North Dakota. You are not really a North Dakotan if you don't love this place in all of its moods." I might be able to get away with the first two sentences, but almost everyone would turn away in disgust if I tried to make the case for the third. Nor is the word *poignant* likely to win me many friends.

The ground all around me is half-covered with leaves. More than 95 percent of them are tan-gray and decorated with black dots (age spots?) as if someone sprinkled finely ground pepper from a balloon over the trees. I'm not sure if this is a pigmentation thing, or some kind of fungus. The fallen leaves are brittle. The ones that have been here for more than a few days shatter like potato chips when you step on them or bend them even a bit.

The motion of the leaves still up in the trees is nearly magical. Your eye cannot focus on any limb or sector very long, the motion is so hypnotic. There are probably more than 250,000 leaves directly in front of me, between me and the Missouri River, which is today as blue as a river can ever be. The fall blue of a plains river just breaks your heart it is so beautiful. This whole cottonwood forest is dancing now, every single leaf doing a riff, and yet the whole sound is muted, not in any way overwhelming. Gentle in a late-season, borrowed time sort of way. The wind plays many instruments—the clank of a flag chain on the metal pole, the periodic groan and screech of a homestead windmill, the swish and swoosh of wind in the grass, the genuine howl of fierce wind, the blare on the ear when the wind is too strong for your olfactory nerve to take it in, the grit in the harsh winter wind gnawing away at the siding on your house, like nano-termites. But this surely is the wind's best music, the tintinnabulation of the cottonwoods.

I wish I could camp here tonight, sip a glass of pinot noir near sunset and gaze at the cottonwoods until it's too late to see anything more than gray-black motion against the stars.

The thousand or so cottonwoods I can see in a single glance are tall. Some are seventy-five feet tall, a few even taller than that, and they average fifty feet or more. Their trunks are thin, even wispy. Even though I am not fifty yards from an asphalt parking lot, not one hundred from the banks of the Missouri River, and a few human stragglers are wandering around the park trails, I'm in as peaceful a place as you could ever imagine. It's still seventy-five degrees but in the last ten minutes the temperature has dropped enough that I can feel a little chill in the air. This is when most people pull on a jacket or go fetch one. I have found from many years of living on the Great Plains that it is worth resisting that impulse for a while. The period in an evening when the chill is gently approaching, and you know that *at some point* you are going to need to add layers (a blanket, a sweater, a coat, a stocking cap) or just give up and go inside, is one of the finest moments of a day, a month, a year. A slight chill is actually a deeply sensuous pleasure, if you let it lave you as the last caress of the day. It heightens your senses, because you are for once aware of that mechanism in your body that checks the temperature and decides if you are doing enough to protect your body heat.

I have been lolling here alone for two hours now. The light is beginning to soften. The sun is now behind the trees, though there are still two hours before dark. Not once during this period have the leaves stopped dancing, even when the breeze seemed to have entirely ceased. Not once have the plains been silent. Even when the breeze drops close to zero, some branch of fifty or 500 or 5,000 leaves still stirs and jingles just a little. There is a purity to this sound, like the sound of a perfectly performed clarinet. Nor has there in two hours been a single moment of windblast, when the leaves dance so fast they become a cacophony, when it gets orgiastic out here, when the tree's ability to absorb the wind with dignity breaks down and the higher tree limbs begin to bend away from the force. The motion in the cottonwood limbs—more exposed than at any time since June, and yet more foliated today more than any time until next June—is slender and subtle, at times as gentle as if the gods were rocking a cradle for an easily awakened child.

The problem in lying out here leaning on one elbow worshipping cottonwood trees while living on borrowed time on a perfect fall day is that unless you are Henry David Thoreau, this cannot be your job description. You have to earn a living in some other way. In North Dakota earning a living is not necessarily easy to do, and the ways we do it here are mostly extractive. Fortunately, ever since the steamboat era ended, cottonwood trees have not been good for much, not even for the fireplace and the fire pit, so they have mostly been left alone. In the twenty-first century more cottonwood trees are lost in North Dakota to urban sprawl than to any other purpose. We cut them to get them out of the way of our pedestrian dreams. I don't know how many North Dakotans love cottonwoods. Some. I don't know how many seek them out every autumn as I do—but I have made a fetish out of it. I am sitting here today because I know three things: First, in two weeks all the leaves will be gone and it will be at least seven months before I can sit below cottonwood leaves again; second, in ten days I will be gone for three weeks and when I come home it will be winter; third, if the grim matrons of the grocery store are right, by this time tomorrow I will shake my head in wonder that I was able to sit out in my shirtsleeves today. (That turned out to be too true.) I suppose all North Dakotans, were they here, would agree that these cottonwood trees are beautiful and that what they represent is somehow quintessentially the stuff of the Great Plains, of North Dakota, of our homeland. This is not birch land, or maple land, or oak land, or magnolia land, or elm land, or (this far north) even pine land. On any given day in North Dakota you are more likely to see a Russian olive (a decidedly non-native tree, to my mind a weed tree) than a cottonwood. A farm shelter belt is more likely to harbor evergreens than cottonwoods. In fact, I know of no soil conservation service that would urge you to plant cottonwoods on the north end of the house or at the edge of the wheat field. But beyond the earnest arbors of humankind, the cottonwood is the tree you are most likely to encounter on the Great Plains. I try for a moment to think about what the Great Plains would be without the cottonwood, and I shudder.

If they would listen to me, I would bless these cottonwood trees before I venture back to my car. I wish I believed that I could talk to them or that they would appreciate it if I hugged them. Still, though they may not have ears to hear, I say to these cottonwoods, "You have brought so much joy to my life. You are one of the most important satisfactions in living here. If you were not here, I would decidedly not be living here. You ask nothing of us except to be left alone, and for us to flush up the Missouri now and then so your succession will be guaranteed. We take you for granted, but Great Plains life would be so diminished without you."

I'm glad I saved this chapter for the end of the book—the man who talks to trees.

The great dams that plugged the Missouri River in the 1950s and '60s affirm the law of unintended consequences, plus some really appalling intended consequences. First, the intended. They were built with complete contempt for the sovereignty, the dignity, the sacred places, and the lives of Native Americans. They domesticated the Missouri River, confined it within human-determined channels, and transformed one of the world's great rivers into a series of slackwater lakes. They redefined the Missouri River as a water resource rather than as a force, perhaps even a being, of nature.

The great dam builders wanted to tame the Missouri River once and for all. They succeeded, or nearly so. They did not spend any time wondering how the dams would impact the pallid sturgeon (an ancient fish). Or the piping plover (a bird). Or the cottonwoods that line the banks of the stretches of the river between the dams. Compared to the catastrophic floods of 1943 and 1952, such trivialities were dismissed as of no consequence. So far as the documentary evidence indicates, such consequences were not even considered. The dams were built by the construction arm of the US Army, the Corps of Engineers. They were begun when America was at war with Hitler's Germany and Hirohito's Japan. The chief engineer was Lieutenant General Lewis A. Pick, who had just finished building the Burma Road on some of the most inhospitable landscape in the world. He approached Garrison Dam with the same military single-mindedness, at the high water mark of the industrial assault on the North American continent. He seems to have regarded the Natives of the Dakotas with no more sympathy than he accorded the Natives of Burma (today's Myanmar). Whatever appreciation he had for the Missouri River was measured in anger rather than a sense of wonder. The designers were not seeking subtle solutions to the problem of the Missouri, which was that it flooded farms, towns, and roads. Pick and his fellow engineers did not regard the Missouri as a living river. They had no bioregional consciousness. They knew or cared nothing about ecosystems. For them, the Missouri River was a thing that flooded, nothing more or less. To solve that problem they threw concrete and millions of tons of rolled earth athwart the current, and they did not care much what they had to inundate, particularly if it was occupied by a bunch of powerless Indians.

Among the unintended consequences, the cyclopean Missouri dams prevent the spring and early summer surge floods that brought silt and nutrients to riverside cottonwoods. The old trees are in most cases still alive, but they are reaching the end of their lives, and they are not being adequately replaced. Well more than half of the cottonwood stands along the Missouri River are more than fifty years old. Only about 15 percent of the stands are younger than twenty-five years old. Even the Bureau of Land Management (no collection of men and women in Birkenstocks) "has warned that in a few decades, river floaters might have to start packing their own shade with them because there won't be enough trees left to cool their campsites." Is it really a question of the comfort of recreationists? I regard the cottonwoods as a barometer species that informs us how intelligently we are living on the Great Plains. Heck, even the US Army Corps of Engineers acknowledges the problem. A 2010 study conducted for the Corps concluded, "In a sense, the large cottonwood forests remaining across much of the floodplain are a legacy of the past and could be thought of as 'the living dead,' currently helping support a high diversity of plants and animals but unlikely to be replaced by regeneration in the future." Stark, but at least honest for a change.

In the past twenty years, the Corps and its sister agencies have been persuaded to undertake cottonwood replanting initiatives on selected stretches between Fort Benton, Montana, and Kansas City. The results have been mixed and inconclusive. Even if the replanting regimen worked, it would cost an enormous amount of money to restore cottonwood health along the full 2,341 miles of the Missouri River. The American public has not expressed a sense of urgency about the great river's cottonwood stands. Besides, such mitigations are only permitted to work around the edges, never to challenge the continuing legitimacy of all the dams, irrigation diversions, barge traffic, hydropower plants, flood plain housing projects, shopping malls, and McMansions that have sprung up in the shadow of the colossal dams. The best we can do, at great expense, is save a fraction of the trees. We should do so.

Do trees have souls? Well, of course they do. Only a civilization that has disenchanted itself—and severed the magical arteries of the universe in order to reduce everything, including other human beings, to the status of commodity—could deny souls to other animals, other living beings, like grass and trees, and to things that seem inanimate, like rocks and clouds and rivers. All *primitive* humans have what is known as participatory consciousness, and most *civilized* people have lost it. Native Americans had it in spades. Just read John Neihardt's *Black Elk Speaks* if you have any doubts, or John Lame Deer's *Lame Deer: Seeker of Visions*. Peoples who have not been denatured by a scientific revolution, by the Baconian-Newtonian paradigm shift, see being and purpose and intention and consciousness in everything around them, and they find ways to communicate with all that is numinous—and everything turns out to be numinous. As one scholar of Lakota religion puts it, "For the Indians . . . the world of nature itself was their temple, and within this sanctuary they showed great respect to every form, function, and power. That the Indians held as sacred all the natural forms surrounding them is not unique. . . . But what is almost unique in the Indians' attitude is that their reverence for nature and for life is central to their religion: each form in the world around them bears such a host of precise values and meanings that taken all together they constitute what one would call their 'doctrine.'"

We Euro-Americans cut ourselves off from participatory consciousness 400 years ago. That eventually gave us the Empire State Building, the end of smallpox, and the moon shot, but it also gave us Auschwitz, DDT, and Hiroshima. It would be great if we could enjoy the best of the scientific paradigm without the dark side, but since we bring human nature to each of our technological discoveries, we just get better at destroying things, including—possibly—the planet itself, or at least the version that supports human life. I doubt that humans can destroy the planet, but as Woody Allen might put it, if you make it impossible for our species to survive, where do you get a steak on a Saturday night?

If cottonwoods have no souls, why do the females shed their seeds at different times in different places to take advantage of the spring freshets? Why do cottonwoods respect each other's boundaries, growing to the near proximity of the next tree but not overlapping it? This is known as "crown shyness," a perfectly beautiful phrase. How do the root structures of cottonwoods pause when they meet a rock or unhealthy soils, and then figure out a workaround? Why do cottonwoods sacrifice the branches and leaves farthest from their water and nutrition source in times of drought to ensure the survival of the tree? How and why do they cooperate?

Sometimes in the fall I go out to the badlands to loaf under a copse of cottonwood trees. I usually take a book. There are a handful of places in western North Dakota where, on a late September or early October morning, you can be sure of having a little grove of cottonwoods entirely to yourself. A few of them must have been young when Theodore Roosevelt was young. He died. They live on.

About a mile and a half northwest of the Elkhorn Ranch headquarters, there is a crescent of ancient cottonwoods that were left to themselves in a sea of grass when the river shifted, dozens or scores of years ago, over towards the cliffs on the west. They grew up on the banks of the Little Missouri, but for much of their life they have been marooned in a huge grass pasture by the shifting whims of the river. It's hard to know exactly, but I'm guessing a few of these trees are 150 years old. That means they were there when Roosevelt lived and ranched in Dakota Territory. He would have seen them, of course, in his hectic horseback rides up and down the river in search of adventure, strayed cattle, and something worth shooting, but he probably never noticed them the way I do, because they were young then, venerable now.

Every one of these ancient cottonwoods has seen better days. Whole sections of them have sheared off, either struck by lightning or blown down in some fierce windstorm. In some cases, a huge limb has collapsed, bent over like a safety pin, but somehow it is still connected by some tenuous fluid dynamics to the root structure. In some cases, the tree has continued to produce leaves in a section of itself that is barely hanging on, its plumbing somehow still operating in reduced fashion, large garish leaves extruding out of something that looks like it should already be dead. The life force is astonishing. As Jeff Goldblum (Dr. Ian Malcolm) says in *Jurassic Park*, "Life finds a way."

Whenever I go to this grove of superannuated cottonwoods, I find an old bleached log to sit on for a while, or sit with my back to, if the ants are not too pesky. I doze and daydream and study the trees. Whenever a trunk or huge limb falls and loses all its linkage to the mother tree, the rest of nature immediately moves in to harvest it. At first the thick gray-black bark has the knobs, ridges, troughs, and protrusions of giant tractor tires, sometimes two or even three inches deep. Their parallel ridges stay close together all the way up the limb. Soon little sections of the bark begin to slough off. They are the size of dinner plates or platters. If you set up a time-lapse camera for fifteen or twenty years you could watch almost every slice of bark drop to the ground as whatever juices held it onto the tree dry up and disintegrate.

The death of a cottonwood is as impressive as its life. It's fascinating to observe.

For a very long time the bare limbs or trunk remain adamantine hard. If you thump them with your knuckles they yield no more than would a two-by-eight piece of milled lumber. But over time the fallen trunks hollow out, for water weakens the fiber and what is chewable inside gets eaten by all sorts of insects. Thumping the dead limb produces a greater drumbeat every year. If you get down on your knees and study the now-smooth ghost-white limb or trunk, you can see hundreds, even thousands of little wormholes. Some live thing is burrowing into the wood, eating as it descends. I'm guessing a range of insects and some birds find dead cottonwood a suitable feast, and there is plenty for everything that lives on that scale. Eventually the wood gets spongy and loose, like shredded wheat. It is losing its integrity. Its dead fibers are breaking down. Creatures are finding enough nutrition in it to devour it. Billions of fungi now begin to play their role.

If you sat there long enough, if you kept a time-lapse camera at the site for fifty or one hundred years, you would reach the day when the tree was simply gone—eaten, absorbed, dis-integrated, disappeared. Except for a few hard knots and a slice of kindling, every bit of a once magnificent cottonwood tree would have been repurposed and reabsorbed by Nature until there was nothing left. The life of this one tree is the life of all trees, those at least not hauled away to build a cabin, frame a house, or burn in a fire circle. If you think about it long enough, you realize that the life of this one tree is the life of everything. Everything has its birth, its childhood and adolescence—if it survives the infant mortality rate—and the mortality rate in Nature is staggering. Then for a period of time—ten hours, ten days, ten years, 150 years—it thrives, flourishes, and seeks to reproduce itself. Now a long gradual decline, a slow decay, one by one the loss of limbs, perhaps even part of the trunk, and finally death, usually brought on by a harsh winter, an appalling windstorm, a bolt of lightning, a drought. The seven ages of man and the seven ages of a lone cottonwood tree are not dissimilar. At first "the infant, mewling and puking in its nurse's arms," and all the stages that follow, but before you know it the once virile tree becomes "the lean and slippered pantaloon with spectacles on nose and pouch on side." And finally, "second childishness and mere oblivion." It's the same with everything in life. Ashes to ashes and dust to dust are the story of "this strange eventful history."

As I sit with my back to a tree that has not lost its skeletal strength, not yet, I think of my own mortality and hope, against all the odds, that I can die and be reabsorbed so beautifully and gracefully. My civilization would rather keep me alive after my trunk sought to subside into the grass, would rather stick tubes in my nose and down my throat, drip nutrition into me from a hanging bag, affix electronic sensors to my body, thump it and probe it and insert things into all my moist crevices, dull my soul with opioids and eventually morphine, and—when all my systems finally collapse—send me across town to an industrial plant where I'll be soaked with preservatives, injected with formaldehyde, tucked into my best clothes, subjected to facial makeup for the first time, displayed like Madame Tussaud's North Dakotan in a room with cheap wallpaper, prayed over pro forma, and then locked first in a wooden chest inside a concrete casement (like Russian nesting dolls), and finally sealed under six feet of prairie sod, forever side by side with other mummies. In other words, those parts of me that analogize with the elements of this cottonwood tree will be denied the honor of giving back to the grass and the dung beetles and the badgers and the crows. At some point a nurse is going to come into the room with a practiced grimace and begin pulling the electrodes and the feeding tubes from my body. And then my beloved daughter will be subjected to the Dickensian mortician rubbing his hands together and bending into conversation like Uriah Heep.

I am as much a part of North Dakota, as much a part of this diminished American Serengeti, as the cottonwood I am contemplating, no more and no less. It's not that I could have lived anywhere, but had I chosen to I could have lived anywhere in America, from Bozeman, MT, to Boulder, CO, from Portland, ME, to Portland, OR, from Santa Fe to San Francisco to San Jose to San Juan. Against the better judgment of my professional friends, I choose to live in North Dakota. Some people claim the American Museum of Natural History as their project, their adoptive stepchild, their focus of philanthropy. Some choose the Statue of Liberty or a cemetery in Wadena, Minnesota, or a veterans' memorial in Broken Bow, Nebraska, or the Bismarck-Mandan Symphony or National

Public Radio or Baptist missionaries in Borrioboola Gha. They give time and money to what they especially love. I was born in North Dakota and I intend to die in North Dakota. If possible, I would like to die in the badlands, within sight of the Little Missouri River, under a golden autumn cottonwood dancing in the breeze. That is almost certainly not going to happen, not without a conspiracy of help, and probably not then. Besides, my principal co-conspirator, the mayor of Marmarth, Patti Perry, is dead. She was afraid of nothing. In the best of all possible worlds, I would be left alone there in the badlands, stripped to my boxers and a discreet t-shirt so that I could not easily be identified, and left to the sacred rites of reabsorption. If a badger finds my tired and shriveled heart a delicacy, with a liver and kidney chaser, what better end to all that restless aching heartthrob that has been my life? And if a coyote rips the tendons off of my Achilles heel, how could I rightly complain, when I have worshipped coyotes all of my life and tried to call them in close to my fire again and again and again, only a few times with even modest success? That humans think so highly of themselves that they deny their organics to bugs, fungi, ravens, and badgers is why we are jeopardizing the planet. When we convinced ourselves that we have transcended nature, that we are not really like dolphins or bighorn sheep, not like ponderosa pines and cottonwoods, not even like gorillas and orangutans and chimpanzees, we indeed liberated energies and creativity unprecedented in the history of humankind, unprecedented in the history of the planet and the solar system. This gave us Hoover Dam and St. Paul's Cathedral, Milton's *Paradise Lost* and Michelangelo's David, the jet airplane and the dune buggy, the computer and the internet and smart cars. But it so alienated us from all the rest of creation that we lost our access to the most important laws of life. And so we are now stark mad. I am.

Let me die in the badlands and not be found until I'm nothing more than scattered and bleached bones with a few tufts of skin and hair on the ones that even the coyotes rejected. And whatever little quantum of nutrients my pocky corpse contains, let them be the difference in the survival of a cottonwood tree that grows a hundred feet tall and lives 150 years, unknown, unmolested, unvisited.

Bury my heart on the Little Missouri.

APPENDIX:
RETHINKING OUR RELATIONS WITH
NATIVE NORTH DAKOTANS

After long observation and study of this question, I wish to offer the best advice I have to the White people of North Dakota and the Great Plains. If you follow this advice, the future will be so much healthier for everyone.

We are going to have to get over our idea that the bad habits of some Native Americans today (alcohol, domestic violence, unsteadiness) tell us who they are. We have to realize that the legacy of conquest is the creation of a broken culture doing everything it can to work its way back. We broke that culture or very nearly did, on purpose. We have to understand that the worst sorts of behaviors we observe among Native Americans now are not inherent to their cultures, but products of our occupation, wars, ethnic cleansing, and cultural genocide.

We are going to have to do some real reading. Start with Ralph K. Andrist's *The Long Death* and John Neihardt's *Black Elk Speaks*, and then read Evan S. Connell's *Son of the Morning Star*. Every one of us needs to learn the history of White-Indian relations, but also the story of the tribes in question. I'm happy to recommend fifty books to anyone who wishes to have the list. Every North Dakotan should read Paul VanDevelder's *Coyote Warrior*, the story of the damming of the Missouri River and its appalling impact on the Mandan, Hidatsa, and Arikara.

We need to realize that hereafter, federal law more often than not is going to be on their side. Because of the conquest and the near destruction of Native American cultures, the tribes have had more important things to do (i.e., survive) between 1920 and 1990, but now they are sending some of their children to medical school, law school, and other professional programs. There is more money for litigation. The tribes know their rights better than White people do, and they are poised to assert those rights, demand recognition of those treaties still legally binding, sue for return of confiscated lands, etc. We White people are going to lose some "battles" in the next hundred years. This will be hard, but we have to remember that the justice really is mostly on their side.

When things matter to Native Americans, they really matter. They don't mess much with the routine politics of the non-Indian world, and much of what White people fret about is not of great interest to them. But when something really touches the deepest values in their tradition, they feel very strongly and they need to be taken seriously.

Native Americans live in two cultures. We live in only one. It is very hard to live in two cultures, especially when Natives' basic ways of seeing are quite distinct. They do not wish to fully assimilate. They wish to be distinct subcultures in the broader civilization of America. They do not want to do what Irish Americans did, and Polish Americans, and Mexican Americans—to assimilate noiselessly as fast as possible. They want to hold on to parts of their culture that are hard for White people to respect, or even understand. But it is not our choice. They were here first, and each one of us now lives on land that was once sovereign to a tribal nation. You should be able to name the tribe on whose lands you now dwell.

When Native Americans say something is cultural appropriation, it is. It's that simple. We have no right to use Native American iconography, language, dress, or music without their permission. If they feel that we are being culturally insensitive, we are. It's obvious. If we were culturally sensitive, we would sense that something we are doing makes Native Americans uncomfortable. The fact that we "just can't see it" means that we are, in fact, insensitive. This includes names. If the Nez Perce want to be called the Nimiipuu, it is not for non-Indians to cling to a previous term (in this case French, and inaccurate at that).

Our basic system of cultural suppositions has worked well for us, stupendously well in some respects. On our playing field, Native Americans have done less well, not only because they don't yet have particular aptitude for those things, but also because some of those things actually thwart Native American cultural norms. The Native American worldview does not survive intact, and most American Indians want to enjoy conveniences of both worlds, but the parts that are at the core—that everything has being, that we must use resources in a sacramental way, that we do not really own anything, that family is more important by far than contract, that humans are not the lords of creation at the top of the Enlightenment's Chain of Being—are in some important respects either superior to our systems and values, or at least a very useful check against some of the unquestioned assumptions of the dominant culture's way.

The reverse of our attitude is true. We have more to learn from Native Americans than they do from us. This is very hard to swallow, but it is the beginning of the reconciliation.

ACKNOWLEDGMENTS

t's this simple. If Mike Jacobs had not taught me how to be a naturalized rather than an accidental North Dakotan, I would not have written this book. The whole trajectory of my life would have been different. I feel certain I would have left North Dakota in my twenties and almost never returned, except to spend holidays with my family. I owe him an incalculable debt of love and gratitude. I love him.

It takes a village to write a book. This one would not have been possible without the help, direct and indirect, recently and over decades, of a large number of people, some of whom could not know they were contributing to my understanding of our beloved homeland North Dakota.

Thanks to my friend Russ Eagle of Carolina, who let me process the writing of this book in letters to him over the last two years. He's writing a book now, too, poor bastard, and I hope I can be of as much use to him as he has been to me these last couple of years. My friend and colleague Sharon Kilzer read the manuscript with her usual discernment. Our conversations about the future of North Dakota have been invaluable to me. Our friendship is central to my happiness. Thanks to my young friend Levi Bachmeier for his belief that this book will matter to the ongoing conversation about the meaning of North Dakota. He's the future of our leadership.

Melanie Choukas-Bradley helped me think about cottonwood trees. Joe Lovell of Amarillo, Texas, and Quentin Hope of Garden City, Kansas, both children of the plains, helped me understand the significance of the first tree ever planted in the Texas Panhandle. Joe read this book in manuscript and told me, to my endless joy, that this book is as much about the panhandle of Texas as it is about Dakota du Nord.

Thanks to Jim Fuglie and Lillian Crook who gave me confidence that I understand what is at stake in the Little Missouri River Valley. Jim has been my friend for fifty years. He never holds back, but he has no enemies. I love him. Thanks to Darrell Dorgan, Troy Coons, Keith Trego, and Gary Peterson. Thanks to David Swenson, the semi-permanent guest host of the *Thomas Jefferson Hour.*

Rich Hartlaub of Monument, Colorado, provided useful information on the history of America's ICBM missile system.

Loren Kopseng has taken me flying over much of the state. He'll circle back half a dozen times so I can get exactly the photograph I need and land the plane where no man has gone before.

I owe a particular debt of gratitude to Sara and Troy Vollmer of Wing, North Dakota. They represent all that is admirable in rural life. They are the true North Dakotans. They have read portions of this book and served as a reality check when I try to explore the character of this strange fascinating place. Sometimes they just roll their eyes. Thanks to them, I have ridden a horse named Doc on four sections of the Maah Daah Hey Trail, usually upright. Sara accomplishes more before breakfast than I accomplish in a week.

My friend Beth Kaylor has been an indispensable part of the workflow of my life for several years now and she has wandered with me in search of the true geographical center of North America. She tells me which of the plates I am spinning are wobbling in time for me to keep them aloft.

Thanks to Peter Rogerson of the University of Buffalo (NY) for his insights about whimsical geographic quests, and to that rascal Bill Bender of Robinson (ND) for pointing the whimsical way to rural regeneration.

Thanks to Dennis McKenna, Melanie Carvell, Beverly Everett, Doug Ellison, Ed Sahlstrom, Lauren Donovan, Kevin Carvell, Patti and Gary Perry, Robert Hanson, John and Jennifer Hanson, Lance Loken, Linda Clark, Jenette Nelson, Laura Schmidt-Dockter, and Tracy Potter.

Thanks to my finest comrade in the Republic of Letters, David Nicandri of Tumwater (WA), the only writer I know who can use the words "aver," "dispositive," "perplex," "ineluctably," and "typology," and make you glad he did. I cannot imagine writing books without him metaphorically at my side. We have laughed and argued agreeably at Lochsa Lodge, Dismal Nitch, and the tailgate parties of the Nicandrithals.

Thanks to my editor at Koehler Books, Joe Coccaro, and my publisher friend John Koehler. Our meeting at an event in Norfolk, Virginia, has altered the trajectory of my life. With their help I am now able to call myself a writer without blushing.

My gratitude to the North Dakota artist Katrina Case is enormous. Her painting of the Little Missouri River Valley graces the cover of this book. It is just one of a series of paintings she has undertaken to help me understand this fabulous and subtly beautiful place. I can describe a landscape to her and she can paint what I can barely articulate. Her painting of the Little Missouri River with that little industrial irritant perfectly captures the meaning of this book.

The late Everett C. Albers taught me that humor is the lubricant of ideas, that in the end all you can do about the enigmas and catacysms of life is laugh. I miss him every single day.

Joanna Walitalo produced the maps for The Language of Cottonwoods. I noticed her work in a Lewis and Clark context and recruited her to draw whimsical maps and illustrations for this book. I am so grateful.

For the last quarter-century I have done nothing without holding my daughter Catherine at the center of my mind and the core of my heart. If she returns to North Dakota, she will help lead us into a better future. I love her more than life. She knows the Great Plains in all of its magnificence, but she feels its burden, too.

They are both dead, but I want to acknowledge my parents. Even thirty years later, I do nothing without thinking about that brilliant accidental North Dakotan, my father Charles E. Jenkinson, the wittiest and most elegant man I ever knew. My mother, who lived some of my adventures in the Little Missouri River Valley, would have loved this book. We talked about all of these themes over "remarkable stew" west of the Killdeer Mountains. And how I miss Patti Perry of Marmarth, who would have lovingly derided 90 percent of what I have written here. She would have laughed her 7,000-cigarette laugh and said, "You make me craaaazy."

Clay Jenkinson
Bismarck, North Dakota
December 18, 2020

CLAY JENKINSON is a North Dakotan, a plainsman who has spent his life exploring the northern Great Plains. He is a frequent "talking head" in Ken Burns' documentary films, one of the creators of the Theodore Roosevelt Center at Dickinson State University, and the host of the nationally syndicated radio program and podcast *The Thomas Jefferson Hour*. He studied at the University of Minnesota and Oxford University, where he was a Rhodes Scholar. This is his fourteenth book.

CPSIA information can be obtained
at www.ICGtesting.com
Printed in the USA
LVHW041726030822
725111LV00002B/77

9 781646 630998